THE ARCHAEOLOGY OF POWER

ENGLAND AND NORTHERN EUROPE AD 800 - 1600

John M. Steane

TEMPUS

First published 2001

PUBLISHED IN THE UNITED KINGDOM BY:

Tempus Publishing Ltd
The Mill, Brimscombe Port
Stroud, Gloucestershire GL5 2QG
www.tempus-publishing.com

PUBLISHED IN THE UNITED STATES OF AMERICA BY:

Tempus Publishing Inc.
2 Cumberland Street
Charleston, SC 29401
1-888-313-2665
www.arcadiapublishing.com

Tempus books are available in France and Germany
from the following addresses:

Tempus Publishing Group   Tempus Publishing Group
21 Avenue de la République   Gustav-Adolf-Straße 3
37300 Joué-lès-Tours   99084 Erfurt
FRANCE   GERMANY

British Library Cataloguing in Publication Data.
A catalogue record for this book is available from the British Library.

ISBN 0 7524 1933 1

Typesetting and origination by Tempus Publishing.
PRINTED AND BOUND IN GREAT BRITAIN

Contents

List of illustrations

Front cover Château of Saumur, built by Louis II of Anjou, in the background of 'September' from *Les très riches heures du Duc de Berry* (fol 9v), Musée Condé, Chantilly

Back cover King of England. Sculptured effigy by Thomas Canon. South end of Westminster Hall, London, *c*.1385

Text figures

Colour plates

Preface

The genesis of this book arose out of an event in my life which proved a turning point. For 23 years from 1953-76 I had taught in a succession of schools, all boys', and all selective entry. I was wedded to the idea of the grammar school. Academic excellence was to me a preferable goal to social engineering. I saw the schools I taught in as channels whereby boys from disparate backgrounds could better themselves, and thereby serve society. For me the emergence of a meritocracy was wholly desirable. I was engaged on a straightforward and worthy task which Robert Lowe defined in a remark attributed to him after the winning of the vote by the urban working class in 1867, "Now we must educate our masters".

The event occurred within the period of my teaching. I was appointed in 1964, at the (then) early age of 34 to be headmaster of a grammar school and thus acquired power! Referring to his own period as Prime Minister Macmillan stressed "Power? It is like a Dead Sea fruit! When you achieve it, there is nothing there really." I disagree profoundly. As headmaster of 750 boys from a broad swathe of Northamptonshire including the town of Kettering (40,000 then), the small towns of Rothwell and Desborough and the farmland between them, I had plenty of talent, a wonderful mixture of social class and life experience to work on. The school was respected in the community. It had existed in one form or another since 1555 so it linked the area firmly with memories of the past. In the 12 years I spent at Kettering Grammar School I was able to carry on the academic tradition of my predecessors (the school had produced, among other major figures, the novelist H.E. Bates and the eminent social scientist and Fellow of Nuffield College Professor Halsey), but also to promote four key ideas which had shaped my own life:

1. Interest in the natural environment.
2. Political consciousness. The European idea. World citizenship.
3. An awareness of the continuum between the past and the present.
4. The idea of research. Schools were not just places where knowledge was transmitted but could be exciting places at the cutting edge.

To these ends:

1. I founded with R.S. Jeffery a field study centre at Govilon, near Abergavenny, Gwent, where boys and girls from the Grammar and High schools could experience in week-long courses a totally different environment from that of the Northamptonshire Uplands with its boot and shoe towns, and (somewhat) nar-

row expectations of what life had to offer. Instead they spent a week away from their mothers, climbed mountains, dabbled their feet in mountain streams, collected specimens, did research, explored, and met the Welsh.

2. I encouraged the teaching of Modern Languages including Russian and did not take kindly to the demise of classical languages (forced on me eventually by the staff-student ratio imposed by Northamptonshire County Council). Boys were sent abroad on Voluntary Service overseas, they reported back at meetings of the Council for Education in World Citizenship. We held conferences to which we invited the sixth forms of neighbouring schools. I set an example myself by being the founding Secretary of the Kettering Civic Society. I told the boys about its exploits at morning assembly.

3. The awareness of the past was promoted by the foundation of a small society to study the archaeology and history of the area. This achieved some fame to set beside, or against, the glory of the school's satellite tracking group which I privately thought contained a strong dash of self promotion. The success in worldly terms was the generation of seven archaeologists: R. Walker, S. Dunmore, R. Carr, B. Dix, R. Croft, P. Stamper and P. Crane. Perhaps the most remarkable was the last. Professor Crane FRS, formerly boy secretary of the local History and Archaeological Society is now Director of the Royal Botanical Gardens, Kew.

4. Schoolboys can be harnessed to the research idea. I wanted to involve them in projects which lasted beyond the short time (at the most seven years) of their secondary schooling. Aided by brilliant teachers such as T.C. Simmons, D. Slater, G.F. Perry and T.E. Watson the school became noted for its involvement in research projects involving Biology, Physics and Meteorology. The story of all this has been told in considerable detail by its participants in a volume entitled *Cytringanian Farewell Kettering Grammar/Boys School (1577-1993)* Old Cytringanians Kettering, 1995. The school was comprehensively reorganised in the period 1974-6. Thereafter it suffered a slow decline in numbers which necessitated its closure in 1994. Some said it was judicially murdered. Its achievements had certainly been far brighter than those of many schools in the county.

So it was possible to exercise considerable power in shaping the community. There was my *experience of power*. With it went the *trappings of power*. I had a large room with a big desk. It overlooked the senior yard where I could watch potential roughs playing football. It also oversaw the bike sheds, the equivalent of stabling in the medieval palace! I wore a distinctively authoritative set of garments, namely well cut suits and a long black MA gown with a crimson hood for speech days, hung conspicuously from a peg on the door. I was literally (in those days) the head master; who still taught a third of a timetable himself to keep his hand in, maintain credibility among his colleagues, and frankly, because he enjoyed it. I wore tweed suits and shoes with steel tips which echoed in the corridors. I deliberately fostered the idea of the all-

1   *Plan of part of ground floor of Kettering Grammar School 1964-76*

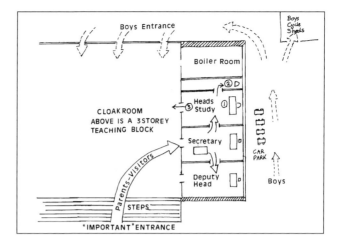

seeing eye of the head. The NCC had kindly helped me in this by providing each classroom door with a glass panel so I could pause in my peregrinations, see what was going on, without the necessity (debilitating for weak teachers) of directly intervening. The County architect in addition had shown some skill in designing a building in which my (benevolent!) power could be exercised.

The seat of power, the head's study, was particularly cunningly designed. The headmaster sat in a specially comfortable chair chosen by himself with his back to the large glass window. This meant that the light was behind him; parents, staff, boys when admitted, stood, or were seated in ordinary chairs — or special guests (such as Chairman of Governors) occupied the only other cushioned chair in the room. Access to the head was carefully controlled. The tradition was that you knocked on the door of the outer office to be admitted to the school secretary. She (it was always a woman) phoned through to the head announcing the presence, and the business of the visitor. The head had four options made available by the architecture of the school. He could refer the visitor to the deputy head, whose room opened out of the school office on the other side. He could retreat into his inner sanctum, the private WC or privy as it would be called in a medieval castle/palace context, and thus disappear. He could issue out into the school through his front door and vanish (on school business, what else?) or he could sit there and ask the visitor to be admitted. Now, I only gradually became aware of all this as I used it over 12 years but it struck me that among the vital things in exercising power are (1) Distancing oneself from the petitioner — in a word making oneself 'hard to get'. This aids prioritising. (2) Having a siphoning process to exclude the unwanted, the trivial, the dangerous. (3) A perpetual need to display oneself, to remind everyone within the institution who is in charge. These were the days, remember, when heads led from the front, before they were relegated (by the huge size of comprehensive schools) to becoming the chairman of various committees within the school. (4) The importance of face-to-face contact in one's relations with staff, parents, boys. Ruling the world, like Philip II of Spain, by means of pieces of paper, just didn't work. In fact it produced resentment and harboured opposition, as I knew from bitter experience in previous schools. I could see how the late medieval monarchs of Europe were forced into an enervating round of (nevertheless) meaningful rituals, to progress perpetually through their dominions while their budding civil servants took on the administrative functions formerly performed in person by their early medieval predecessors. (5) The school secretary was in the position of the chancellors of medieval kingdoms — at the hub of power-dealing with the more mundane but essential matters such as feeding the court (school dinners), financing the institution (school fund and budget — the county insisted on strict accounting) and chasing those reluctant to appear in court (i.e. the absentees) nowadays fashionably called truants. (6) The policing of the court (school) was done by the deputy head: he dealt with all but the most serious offenders. Also transport (the school buses and the minibus) was his area of command. He combined the functions of marshal, usher in the hall and watchman. He was elevated into the position of head (but did not occupy the seat of power!) if the head (rarely) was away. He acted as an essential liaison between head and staff, not the creature of the head but an *eminence grise*.

These thoughts matured over a long period of time. In the meantime the boys and I studied in person and by visits all aspects of the medieval landscape in that part of Midland England. Even the RCHM acknowledged the value of our work in tracking down deserted medieval settlements in the Lyveden valley between Brigstock and Oundle (RCHM Northants, 1975, xxxix and 72-4, Taylor, 1974, 24-5). In the main our excavations led onto experimental archaeology; the replication of pottery kilns and iron smelting furnaces, dug the previous summer, in time for parental open days.

It was with a sense of *déjà vu* that I read seminal articles on the functional analysis of medieval buildings. First Faulkner, then Emery and thirdly Fairclough appeared to have stumbled on the truth that the layout of medieval buildings contained the clue as to their use. Fairclough's article in *Antiquity*, 1992, entitled 'Meaningful Constructions — spatial and functional analysis of medieval buildings' struck me as particularly relevant to what now became my leading theme: the archaeology of élite groups within medieval society, the subject of this book. Other authors went on writing books which though useful *compendia*, did not take this fully on board. I felt halls divorced from their courtly contexts were an abstraction. Bishops' houses (why not abbots' houses? or for that matter why not the houses of the aristocracy?) again seemed only part of the story. The essential piece of the jigsaw missing in these books was an understanding of the demands made upon builders and patrons by contemporary society. Bishops, abbots and nobles had multiple roles thrust upon them. They were military leaders, top civil servants, royal ministers, ambassadors, as well as having to run congeries of estates and perform dozens of daily ritual acts. Their buildings developed, evolved, dropped away and disappeared to suit the changing requirements or historical accidents of their position in society. Archaeology, the technique of closely studying the material remains of past societies whether structural or artefactual, unmoving buildings or mobile objects, was an ideal tool. The interface between the material assemblages and the (profuse at times) documentary record was an attractive area of enquiry to an historian turned archaeologist in mid-life. The result was this book.

Acknowledgements

This book is dedicated to the memory of Professor Karl Leyser, Fellow of Magdalen College and (ultimately) Chichele Professor of Medieval History in the University of Oxford, a great teacher, a consummate historian of the early medieval political scene, and a steadfast and hospitable friend over the years. Parts have been enriched by being read and commented on by Gerald Harriss, Christopher Dyer, John Blair, Julian Munby and Paul Brand.

It has benefited by weekly discussions with Brian Durham, Dan Miles, Malcolm Airs, John Ashdown, Edith Gollnast, Roger Ainslie and Martin Henig (the last in particular has been very encouraging). Julian Munby has provided a steady stream of ideas, books, articles (from his capacious library) and ever curious mind. Tom James I owe a special debt to in shared visits ('jaunts') to medieval towns. Peter Salway has unlocked the secrets of All Souls College for me. Richard Sharpe, Sandy Heslop, Robert Peberdy and Paul Brand have illuminated aspects of medieval law and government. James Ayres has cast a watchful eye on my excesses and has plumbed his own library for me in search of material relevant to my theme. John Blair has provided an academic benchmark to aim for. His books are in my view among the liveliest and most provocative statements to appear in medieval archaeology in recent years. Former pupils of Kettering Grammar School 1964-76, adult students at the University of Oxford Department for Continuing Education, and the archaeological in-service trainees of 1976-90 have all contributed. Ideas were tested out and refined. Those currently or formerly involved in the field like Edward Impey, Graham Keevil, Rick Tyler, Tim Allen, Tom Hassall, Brian Durham and Dave Wilkinson have all generously made available their published and unpublished works. Among archivists who have helped me Caroline Dalton, Stephen Bailey, Robin Darwall-Smith and Janey Cottis are pre-eminent. Erhardt Dornberg, Mary Anne Steane, Emma Steane (by translations) unveiled the German palaces for me. Christopher, my brother, has loaned me books from his library and I have discussed parts of this book with him. My daughter Anna (and grandson Bruno) have lured me to the south of France over a number of years so I have seen the important palaces of Perpignan, Narbonne and Avignon. Kate, her sister, has similarly attracted me to Lincoln, the seat of the largest medieval diocese in England. Discussions with Alan Vince at Lincoln have been particularly valuable. I have received help with ceramics from Maureen Mellor and David Gaimster. My colleagues, John Cherry, British Museum, and Arthur MacGregor, Ashmolean Museum, have made their collections available for study. A visit to Poland was prompted by Andrew Lack of Oxford. I was guided round the Hungarian Palaces by Joseph Laszlovszky and Gabor Viragos. I thank Charles Coulson for providing me with offprints and stimulating discussion, John Watts and Marion Campbell for letting me see papers in advance of publication and Peter Addyman, Kate Giles and Sarah Rees Jones for illuminating the archaeology of York for me. I am grateful to the Dean of Chapter of Norwich Cathedral, Brian Ayers, the President and Fellows of Magdalen College, Oxford, the Warden and Fellows of New College Oxford, the headmaster and archivist of Winchester College and the archivist of Windsor Castle for making their buildings and treasures available for study. This book could not be written without the courteous and efficient service provided by the staffs of the Ashmolean, Bodleian, History Faculty and Department for Continuing Education libraries of the University of Oxford. I also owe a debt to the incomparable riches of the library of the Society of Antiquaries London. It has benefited from the photographic flair of Ian Cartwright and Vernon Brooke. The provision of a text for the publisher has been due to the patience and computer skills of Melanie Fyson. David Brown has proved a never failing source of new books — he is one of the great archaeological catalysts of our time. I should like to thank Peter Kemmis Betty for commissioning me to write this book and for his unfailing encouragement during its writing. Finally I have been supported during the last decade by the dear memory of my first wife, Nina, and by the presence of my second wife, Elaine. Without Elaine's remarkable services as travel agent and fellow walker I would never have reached the farther parts of Europe; and probably would not have survived into the twenty-first century.

John Steane
Oxford
September 2001

1 The ideology of power 800-1600

Certain key ideas dominated thinking in Europe between AD 800-1600. They included, in no particular order:

1. *Romanitas*. The continuing influence of the idea of a Roman Empire despite its long decline, fall and subsequent fossilisation in Byzantium. This idea was deliberately fostered during the eighth and ninth centuries by the Frankish rulers of the parts of the Roman Empire formerly known as Gaul, Italy and Germania (the part of modern day Germany east of the Rhine). Charlemagne, the greatest of their rulers and the type monarch of the whole of the Middle Ages, crowned himself emperor in Rome on Christmas Day AD 800. He thus claimed in a sense to be the successor of the Roman Emperors of the past. His power base however had transferred from the Mediterranean to the interface between Frankish and Teutonic worlds; his capital, if that is the right term for it, was Aachen, not Ravenna, nor Rome. He kept in touch with his co-emperor the ruler of Byzantium. Together they reminded their subjects of the time when all Europe round the Mediterranean and west of the Rhine was subject to the rule of one ruler, one administrative structure and owed obedience to one law.

2. The concept of Europe. Following on from this the '*Pax Romana*' was still an aspiration if hard to realise in a world increasingly threatened (as was the older Roman Empire before it) by external attack. The incursions of the Vikings from the North, the Magyars from the east and the Moslems from the south positively brought into existence the idea of a Europe united by a common code of knightly values and based on the possession of land — which was labelled feudalism by nineteenth-century historians.

3. Feudalism. A reaction to external threats to the revived Roman Empire. The heirs of Charlemagne split his empire into two parts, Austrasia and Neustria. As the central power of the emperor declined under this threat the Germanic concept of a band of warriors united in kinship and blood brotherhood to their lord began its rise. Rulers like Henry the Lion in Germany, William Duke of Normandy (and subsequently king of England) used novel concepts such as earthen and timber castles and heavily armoured cavalry to further their political ambitions. To bind their supporters to their feudal masters land was distributed strictly on the understanding that the *quid pro quo* was military service. The economy of Feudal Europe was largely based on agriculture not commercial towns.

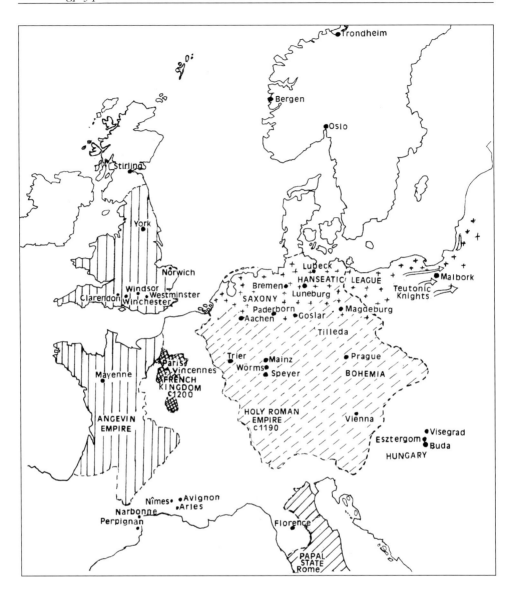

2   Map of Europe, showing some of the chief seats of power

4. A largely agrarian economy. Whereas the Roman Empire had been an urban and commercial economy bound by a network of roads and seaways round the Mediterranean, Europe AD 800 onwards was primarily based on land, not totally landlocked but certainly agriculturally orientated. Peasants ploughed, clerks sang and wrote, knights fought — all on behalf of an hierarchically organised society. The countryside, farm, hamlet, village, fields, forests and wastes were the whole world of most men and women in medieval Europe.

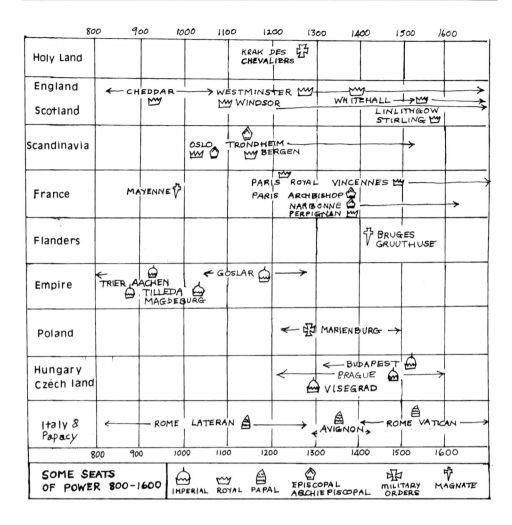

3   Seats of power

5. A sense of hierarchy ran through all aspects of European Society 800-1600. Emperors, popes, kings were at the apex. Barons, nobles, abbots, bishops on the next rung down. Below them knights, squires, burghers and merchants and so on down to the sweating peasant, at the bottom of the pecking order but still with a valid niche or place in the system. The church encouraged this. It reflected the hierarchical ideology mirrored in God ruling the heavenly kingdom, buttressed by choirs of angels, supported by seraphim, cherubim, elders, prophets and kings.

6. The centralising power of the Roman Catholic church. During the first 300 years of the period 800-1200 popes based, for the most part, in Rome, attempted to rival emperors as successors of the powers of the Roman Empire. During the Investiture Contest which was a power struggle between pope and emperor for the control of the appointment of bishops and abbots, the papacy somewhat overreached itself in the time of Hildebrand (Gregory VII 1073-85) but emerged triumphant for a time during the rule of Pope Innocent III (1198-1216). The popes consolidated their power during this period by building up the college of cardinals and a formidable bureaucratic machine, the most advanced governmental organisation in Europe. Respect for their power waned as they increasingly involved themselves in power politics attempting to depose emperors and creating for themselves a central and centralised papal state which managed to put back the cause of Italian unification some 400 years.

7. Unfortunately the Imperial and Papal ideas began to be rivalled in men's loyalties by the rise of **Nation States** in the later Middle Ages. First *England* (under effective Norman, Angevin and Plantagenet kings) then *France* (particularly the Capetian Philip Augustus and the Valois line) were united and national consciousness was born. Edward I played a leading part in this for *England* by doughtily defeating the Welsh and by taking on (at the same time) Scotland and France. Under the blows of '*Malleus Scottorum*' the English nation was forged. Its armies were used with devastating effect for France in the fourteenth century by Edward III and the Black Prince to expand little England into France and thus to claim some sort of political eminence on a par with the Holy Roman Emperors in Germany. For a brief and glorious episode (the reign of the Angevin Charles IV) *Bohemia* attracted to itself a glittering court and might have wrested the imperial crown from the Hapsburgs permanently if the Hussite Reformation had not destroyed its hopes. The *Hungarian* state, too, had a brief period of glory but was largely overwhelmed in the fifteenth century by the Ottoman Turks.

13. A further characteristic idea of Europe 800-1600 was the **growth of towns** in the west and the spread of the urban phenomenon from Flanders and North Italy into the rest of Europe. Cities enriched on trade and defended by walls were able to act independently of kings and emperors, form alliances, wage wars, trade and create banks and other commercial mechanisms. The merchant aristocracies characteristically formed themselves into guilds and associations such as the Hanseatic League. With the emergence of urban élites and industrial proletariats within the framework of towns, society tended to polarise into the rulers and the ruled, even in towns where the air was supposed to make men free.

9. Outside towns in the European countryside the *baronage* first developed into the *nobility* and then into an *aristocracy*. The late medieval aristocracy was international, its members intermarrying across frontiers. The greatest families — Hapsburgs, Plantagenets, Burgundians, Capetians, Valois — monopolised the positions of crowned heads by building up dynasties based on primogeniture (the automatic descent of an estate to the eldest legitimate son). Only the position of the emperor remained elective. This was a positive disadvantage in the struggle to rule Germany effectively. The Prince electors gave their support to a candidate conditionally, with the result that it required exceptional qualities of character for an elected emperor to act as managing director rather than as chairman of the board! The complexities of governing Germany were compounded by the traditional imperial interventions in Italian affairs.

10. Two further ideas dominated Medieval Europe: **crusade and pilgrimage.** The crusades channelled the energies of an aggressive and land hungry baronage into winning estates in the Levant, the Iberian peninsula, and Poland, at the expense of the Moors, the Arabs and the Slavs respectively. Knightly codes of conduct provided the ideological stiffener in a series of wars waged ostensibly to win the Holy Land and Jerusalem back to Christendom from the infidel, but actually resulted in setting up a number of Frankish Feudal kingdoms in the Near East based on the forcible subjection of their Muslim subjects. Similarly the battles in Spain (producing folk heroes like El Cid and Roland) led to the creation of a united Christian kingdom. German farmers following Teutonic knights expanded eastwards to set up a network of towns in Poland. Hitler's search for *lebensraum* has a long pedigree going back to the thirteenth century.

11. Pilgrimage was an idea which accorded with medieval Europeans' need to express their religious and spiritual yearnings in a practical fashion. A penitential trip to Canterbury, Compostella or Jerusalem not only raised the spirits, but cultivated a sense of solidarity and even propagated literary masterpieces like Chaucer's *Canterbury Tales*. Pilgrimage was serviced by those typically medieval institutions, the monastery and the hospital/almshouse. Medieval men and women were perpetually on the move.

12. Another important idea radiating through medieval European society was **monasticism**, which aimed at providing some sort of stability and intellectual lead in a society teetering on the edge of chaos. It originated in the violence of the 'Dark Ages' following the collapse of the Roman Empire. Again it appealed (to begin with) to the penitential side. Monks took vows of poverty, celibacy and obedience. They joined the innumerable houses of international orders founded by barons, notables and kings desirous of purchasing divine favour and a shortened period in purgatory. The monastic ideal was soon overtaken by more mundane practices. The monasteries like the bishoprics became congeries of vast estates, battening on the body politic and their principal offices taken over by the emerging aristocracies who used them as a useful dumping ground for younger landless sons and unmarried daughters.

13. Heresies, Cathars, Hussites, eventually Protestant Reformation. Finally the medieval church, as it matured and gradually became set in its ways, bred reform movements which blossomed into doctrinal heresies. The Papacy triumphed over the Cathar heresy of the thirteenth century largely through the invention of the Inquisition. It took a broadside amidships from the Hussites of the fifteenth century and was finally forced to reform itself in a major way when faced with politico-religious revolution of the Lutherans and Calvinists in the sixteenth. All this intellectual turmoil left an ineffaceable mark on the archaeological record from Cathar Castles to Hussite destruction of images, and wholesale demolition of monasteries throughout Northern Europe.

This book will be tracing the interactions of these main ideological threads and will draw unblushingly and equally from documentary sources and the material evidence, the fragmentary structures and objects. It is to be hoped that it will help to act as a corrective to the spate of excessively academic theoretical and jargon ridden books and articles continuing to pour out of universities such as Cambridge and certain American institutions, which, to my mind do a disservice to the ordinary man's understanding of his past. Ethnography is a better guide to less sophisticated past societies. The Masai have more to teach us than the proponents of theoretical archaeology.

2 The palace: purpose and location

Roman origins

Before tracing the evolution of the palace in north-western Europe between AD 800-1300 it is helpful to try to define the meaning of the term which changed greatly over this long period to fit evolving concepts of power. The word *'palatium'* originated in a nexus of grand town houses set in gardens covering the Palatine hill in Rome which became the main and typical imperial residence from Augustus' time onwards (Millar, 1992, 19). There was no formal layout to begin with; here Augustus lived in ostentatious modesty. Temples, *auditoria* (reception rooms for ambassadors and petitioners), dining rooms, grew up. It was Domitian who provided a more regular architectural expression to the imperial pretensions of power. He gave an impressive façade to the exteriors of his new buildings on the site. He also made the entire imperial complex off-limits to the unwelcome (Darwell Smith, 1996, 214). In the later empire *palatia* were established in other places than Rome throughout the Empire. Often sites formerly occupied by kings (now conquered by the Romans) were chosen. Such 'chains of buildings' (Millar's phrase) were distinct from mere *mansiones*. They accommodated the emperor's friends and men from every city who came either as public ambassadors or private petitioners. They included temples for the emperor, either regarded as a God, or descended from Gods, who was expected to pursue a ritually rich *régime*. One exceptionally influential building, the Constantinian *auditorium* at Trier, survived intact into the early Middle Ages to inspire Carolingian emperors renovating the Roman past (Wightman, 1970, 103-10).

Byzantine palaces and palace ritual

Constantine's relocation of the capital of the fourth-century Empire from Rome to Constantinople was dictated by a desire to celebrate a victory over his rival, rather than part of a grand strategic design! He plucked up a population and resettled it in the easily defensible peninsula on the established route from the Danube to the Euphrates. A substantial diversion of tribute-corn was necessary to feed this 'unstable populace' and Constantine thus recreated the 'bread and circuses' syndrome that had characterised the ancient political centre (Millar, 1992, 54-5). Literary sources, often long after the event, describe the vast area of buildings which were added to and altered over the next few hundred years. They have never been sys-

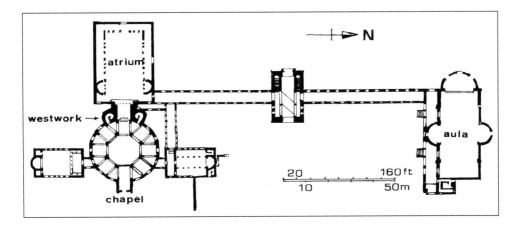

4   *Aachen, Carolingian Palace. Reconstruction as it might have appeared 792-805.*
    After Conant, 1978

tematically investigated owing to the dense reuse of this central area. What is clear from books of ceremonies is that there were processional thoroughfares, large open squares, an enormous church (Santa Sophia), as well as sufficient accommodation (Cameron, 1987, fig. 18, 106-36). Most of the complex rituals which characterised the Byzantine court took place inside the palace. They involved the governing class of the empire and demonstrated publicly the relative positions of the officials in the pecking order of the court, as well as providing an impressive backdrop to the processions of the emperors and the imperial family from one part of the city or one church to another. The Byzantine court throve on splendid ritual. Its influence radiated out westwards into the Carolingian world.

Royal and imperial palaces in the west

Charlemagne's empire was a fusion of the Frankish and the Roman worlds; 'the *palatium regis*, the *sacrum palatium* was a part or rather the very centre of the *totum regnum*, the entire royal government' (Zotz, 1993, 74). It was, in fact, the building(s) within which the ruler carried on the business of government. The rituals of the court, the materials from which the palace was constructed, the central planning all resonated with references to Rome and Byzantium. In addition Charlemagne and his successors used numerous *palatia*, scattered across the empire, on their peregrinations. Such buildings, associated with the charisma of the emperors, represented the *persona* of the monarch when he was absent, a continual reminder of imperial power.

The central palace of Charlemagne's empire had been, since 795, at Aachen. It was known from 966 as *precipia cis Alpes regia sedes* 'the pre-eminent seat of royal power this side of the Alps'. Here Charlemagne deliberately sought to

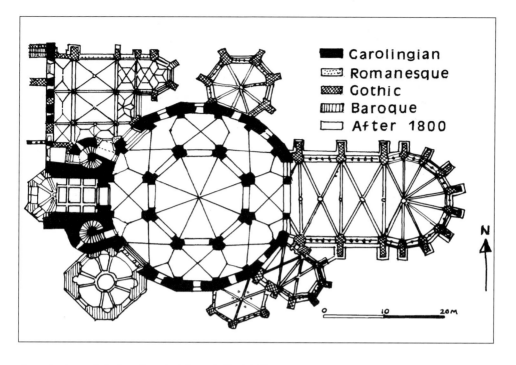

Carolingian
Romanesque
Gothic
Baroque
After 1800

5   Aachen. Palatine chapel. After Gall, 1963

attach his regime to the Christian Roman Empire. His decision was connected with the fact that he was attracted to its springs because he suffered from rheumatoid arthritis. There was a genuine Roman town underneath but the plan of his building complex completely disregarded the orientation of this. The rigid Romanesque layout involved two main complexes of buildings joined by a galleried wing. The great hall or *auditorium* was modelled on the basilica at Trier (**36**), the Constantinian building which has miraculously survived to the present day. The Aachen hall still has a good deal of Carolingian masonry; in its apses' ends were placed thrones and here crown wearings took place (**colour plate 2**). Charlemagne's palace at Aachen is arranged along a north–south axis with apartments and galleries providing quarters for officials, clerics and servitors (Conant 1978, 47-8). The ample imperial quarters included a bath and an audience chamber. The group was meant to remind visitors of the Lateran Palace, Rome. The palace was decorated with mosaics and Ravenna was plundered to produce a huge equestrian statue of Theodoric and a large bronze pinecone, likely to have been connected to a water feature, was placed in the atrium of the palace chapel. Ravenna was stripped of mosaics and marble in a conscious transfer of power to Aachen (Greenhalgh 1989, 105).

The design of the chapel at the southern end of the complex at Aachen was in every sense a building of power. It reminded men of contemporary Byzantine imperial practice. It had an aura which made some literary men compare it with the Temple of Solomon, a prefiguration of the Temple of Jerusalem. To the west of the church was an entrance way which led into an atrium with two stages of galleries in turn dominated by the tall west-work façade of the church. This atrium was reminiscent of the planning of old St Peter's Rome (Conant 1978, 39). It accommodated about 7000 people who could then be addressed by the emperor appearing at the tribune in the west-work of the church. A similar communications system operated in the fourteenth-century palace of the Popes at Avignon, whereby the Pope could address a courtyard full of pilgrims from an arcaded gallery at first-floor level. These are foreshadowings of Hitler's public address system at Nuremberg. The pope and the dictator appear in raised places to brainwash their followers.

Within the Carolingian minster the theme of imperial power was pursued. It was planned around a central octagonal space surrounded by an ambulatory connected by heavy, plain, semi-circular arches. Above these is an annular gallery divided from the central space by screens of columns and bronze parapets, *spolia* brought from Italy. The actual incorporation of building material from the Roman past was a constant reminder of the claims of the emperors to be involved in the renewal of the empire. The throne which dates from the reign of Otto I rams this point home (Hugot, 1993, 29). It is composed almost entirely of reused classical materials. The five steps are cut from Roman quarter columns. The seat itself is made of slabs of Porian marble held together with bronze clips. Behind is a tabernacle with recesses for relics. Between 935 and the sixteenth century the throne was ascended by 29 German kings after they had been consecrated and crowned at the altar of Mary. The Emperor seated on this throne could gaze down on the high altar. Everyone below had to gaze back up at him.

Mayenne: an early tenth-century 'castle'?

As the administrative structure of Charlemagne's empire slipped into confusion during the ninth century, the pressures of external enemies such as Northmen, Magyars and Moslems forced men in north-western Europe to take measures for their own personal safety. The origins of the castle may be sought in these circumstances. Most early fortifications in both west and east Frankish dominions were of earth and wood. It is generally reckoned that castle ringworks, moated sites and fortified manor sites were widespread in France from the time of Charles the Bald's capitulary of Pistes in AD 864 onwards (Higham and Barker, 1992, 95-111). An important excavation at Mayenne in the 1990s has, however, shown that the situation was more complicated. Here a timber structure of uncertain form and function was succeeded *c*.900 by a stone building with a great room at first-floor level. Attached to the south-west corner was a masonry tower and a stair turret (conceivably to house latrines if access to the floors of the '*grande salle*' was by ladder). These structures were surrounded by a wall enclosing a small courtyard. All these elements remind one of the way castles developed in the eleventh and twelfth centuries in France, England and Germany. An

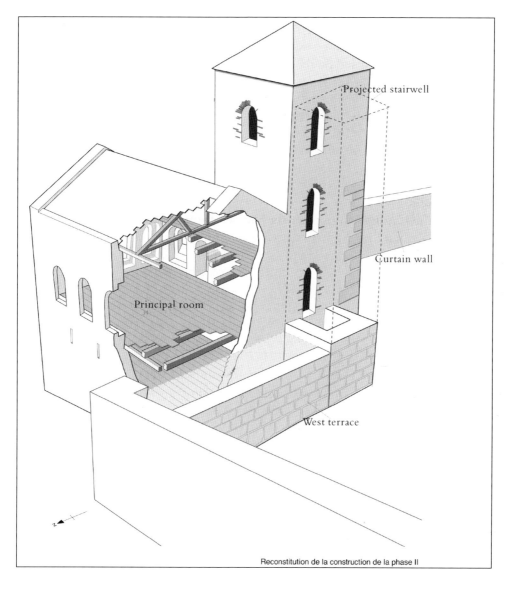

Reconstitution de la construction de la phase II

6 *Mayenne Castle, France. Stone 'proto-castle' with great room at first floor level, masonry tower and wall enclosing small courtyard. Note use of granite blocks and bricks in window heads (both second hand from Roman buildings) c.AD 900.* Illustration: Oxford Archaeological Unit

additional touch is supplied by the building materials and the style of the fenestration. Both were imbued with *Romanitas*: the granite blocks and the tiles used in turning the window heads were brought from a major fortified Roman site at Jublains of the third century, 12km to the south-east. The large round headed window openings at first-floor level in effect were a reinvention of those of the Roman building six centuries earlier. The replication of Roman features, it is tempting to suppose, was a symbolic reference to Roman order and Roman power. This was badly needed in tenth-century France descending rapidly into disorder from which Feudalism only partly rescued her (Early, 1999, 15-36).

The questions arise: who built the proto 'castle' at Mayenne and what purpose did it serve? Documents are sparse and ambiguous. A 'villa' was apparently restored here to the bishops of Le Mans by Charlemagne. Four suggestions are made by the excavator; it was residential (but unheated), defensive, ecclesiastical (but no apse), symbolic. Here Mayenne was located at a strong point on the frontier with Brittany: it dominated an important river boundary. Perhaps Charles the Bald ordered it to be built as a defiant gesture to raiding Vikings or Bretons; maybe it was a statement of Frankish imperial power (Tyler, 1998, 36).

Itinerant kingship

Over a reign of 46 years Charlemagne had succeeded in holding his diverse kingdoms together and expanding his empire into Italy, Saxony and Spain by being prepared to move his court and palace perpetually around Europe. His Frankish successors in the ninth century similarly had to keep moving from place to place to assert their authority, put down revolts, launch campaigns, and hold councils promulgating capitularies of imperial policy. When we turn to Germany in the tenth to twelfth centuries a similar problem generated a similar solution.

How did the Ottoman, Salian and Hohenstaufen dynasties hold together a territory which stretched from the Rhine to the Elbe, from the North Sea to the Alps, and indeed to parts of Italy? The answer is itinerant kingship. This refers to a system in which the king carries out the functions of government by periodically or constantly moving through the areas of his dominions. On his accession the king was crowned, usually at Charlemagne's palace chapel at Aachen; he secured assent to his election from assemblies of nobles who did him homage. Election was supported by anointing. The king assumed sacral status which raised him above his subjects; he was seen to be *rex et sacerdos*, king and priest. In this, liturgy played a dramatic part; art in the form of numerous pictorial representations of the Ottoman and Salian kings, elevated them into God-like figures on a plane with Christ and his Saints (Mayr-Harting, 1999, 128). No sooner crowned than the king took to the road, rarely spending more than a few days or weeks in any one place; in fact keeping on the move for perhaps half the total time of the reign.

The purpose of this constant life-on-the-move was complex. It demonstrated that the king had the ability to undertake a journey without hindrance throughout the realm. Frequent gatherings together of the nobility and frequent crown wearings enhanced the status of kings. They laid claim to the scattered royal properties and exercised royal prerogatives in the areas visited. Gifts and honours were conferred, charters issued, justice was pronounced. Enemies such as Hungarians

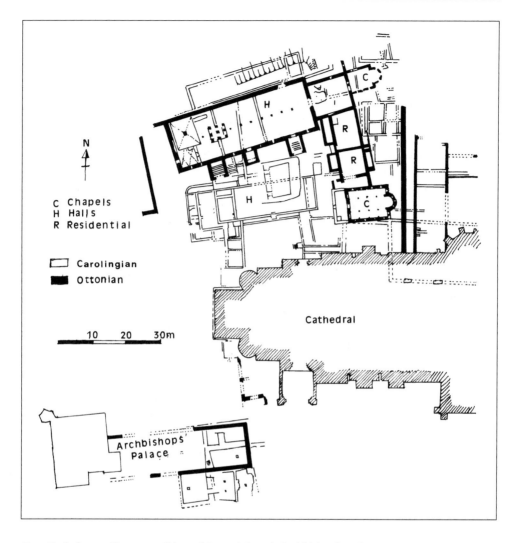

7   *Paderborn, Germany. Plan of Imperial and Archbishop's palaces.*
     After Fehring 1991

and Slavs were fought, rebels punished. The 'royal itinerary dramatised in concrete terms the fact that the king was ruling' (Bernhardt, 1993, 47).

Clearly such journeys were only possible with a great deal of forward planning
and careful administration. The numbers of the royal entourage are thought to
have varied from 50 to about 1600 persons and horses. At times they reached the
scale of an army on the move. They travelled along royal roads, controlled and
maintained by royal vassals. Accommodation was supplied at royal palaces or
manors, in episcopal cities or royal monasteries. Much research has been devoted
to tracing the itineraries of these early German medieval kings and the picture has
become increasingly sharply focused around three types of geo-political regions

8   *Paderborn, Germany. The Ottonian and Carolingian palaces. In the foreground the
     excavated (and consolidated) foundations of the Carolingian palace. The first floor hall
     of the Ottonian palace, heavily restored in the upper parts and roof level, is ranged
     alongside but on a slightly different alignment. See plan.* Photo by author

or zones. The core and central regions (*Kernlandschaften*), the remote regions
(*Fernzonen*) and the transit zones (*Durchzugsgebiete*). The core regions were in
east/south Saxony and North Thuringia where there was a large conglomeration
of Liudolfing family lands. Here the king tended to spend the greatest blocks of
time; there were rich episcopal and monastic properties owing him *servitia*; he
could return to this base of operations each year at the end of his cyclical journey
round the realm and enjoy a sense of security. In addition to the Saxon heartland
the Ottonians and their successors could call upon the resources of the middle
Rhineland around Frankfurt, Mainz and Worms and the lower Rhineland round
Aachen and Cologne. Here there was a dense concentration of royal palaces, fiscal properties and royal churches. The more remote regions such as Bavaria,
Swabia, Upper Lotharingia and the northernmost parts of Saxony were those
where royal power was more rarely exercised and royal resources were limited.

    The *transit* zones linked the central heartlands of the Reich as well as accom-
modating the roads linking Saxony to Italy via Bavaria. Movement was largely
confined to two main routes; roads led from the Harz region through Western
Saxony and Westphalia to the lower Rhine. A more southerly group of roads led

through Thuringia, Hesse and Eastern Franconia to the middle Rhine-Main area and leading east to Bavaria. These roads were studded with royal monasteries and bishoprics from which kings could expect, and indeed demand, major political and economic support. Such were Essen, Werden, Corvey, Soest and Paderborn along the *Hellweg* or Westphalian transit zone. Along the more southerly routes were Corvey, Helmarschausen, Hilwartshausen, Kaufungen, Hersfeld, Fulda, Mainz and Bamburg.

Routes had to be mapped out; messengers sent with warnings that the royal party was on its way. The size of the court meant that staggering amounts of food and fodder had to be collected together. It has been calculated that Otto I's court required on a daily basis a thousand pigs and sheep, ten wagon loads of wine; as much beer and a thousand measures of grain, eight heads of cattle as well as chickens, pigs, fish, eggs, vegetables. Altogether to feed the court cost the equivalent of 30lbs silver daily. To provide these quantities would have been ruinous if the royal monasteries had not been endowed on a princely scale. In addition their abbots had to act as ambassadors and negotiators, their writing schools produced books on royal commission; their smiths even manufacturing armour and weapons. Their responsibilities included the upkeep of roads and bridges in the vicinity. All this on top of praying for the king and his family, a central function of a royal foundation.

German royal and imperial palaces *c*.AD 900-1300

Much systematic research has been undertaken on the subject of the king's palaces of early medieval Germany (Konigspfalzen). Three massive volumes containing numerous articles have appeared from the Max-Planck-Institut für Geschichte in Gottingen entitled *Deutsche Konigspfalzen*. Large-scale excavations, particularly in the middle of towns, have yielded much information about the internal planning of such sites.

An interesting evolution of German palatine policy has been recently suggested (Zotz, 1993). With the election of the Saxon Duke Henry as King of the East Frankish empire in 919 he carried on using traditional Carolingian locations such as Worms (in 925 and 926), Salz (927 and 931) and Frankfurt (930-3). Soon however he tended to focus his government in the areas in which his family, the Liudolfings, were powerful. He shifted the centre of gravity of the kingdom; it moved east. Henry's son Otto's victory in Lechfeld in 955 over the Hungarians led to his choice of a palace at Merseburg where a painting was commissioned to celebrate his triumph (Zotz, 1993, 80). As he gained confidence he supplemented traditional Carolingian locations by using as centres of government more and more places eastward in Saxony such as Werla, Pöhlde and Quedlinburg.

The Saxon successors of Henry I also made a point of referring back to the locations of their imperial past. Otto I had himself crowned in Aachen; the archbishop, Hildibert of Mainz who officiated, was Frankish; the Saxon had himself arrayed in Frankish robes. This was in part a desire to share in the charisma of

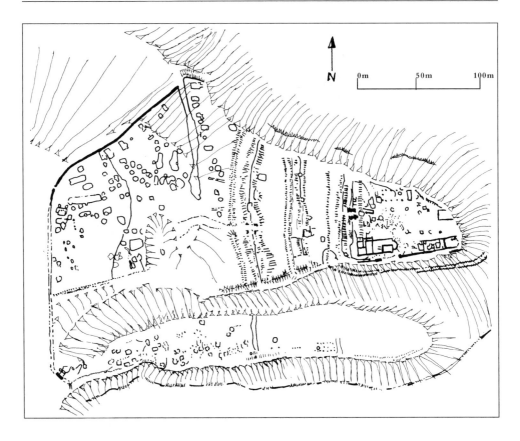

9   *Tilleda Palace. Plan of Ottonian palace mentioned in texts between 972 and 1194.*
     After Grimm 1976

Charlemagne but Otto I was also making a political point, that the East Frank's claim to Lotharingia was being displayed to the West Franks. Otto I continued to visit Aachen on eight occasions, and Frankfurt on thirteen, but what is particularly striking is that he also continued the general movement eastward that his father had done.

The palaces of the Ottonians can be divided into two main types. A number developed out of fortified enclosures; necessary in view of the constant wars with the Slavs and Magyars. In the second type a conscious attempt was made to refer back to a Roman past via Charlemagne's buildings at Aachen. At the same time the dynasty added something of its own.

Among the most thoroughly investigated of the first type are Werla and Tilleda. At Tilleda the Pfingstberg, a spur on the north side of the Kyffhaüser hills, there was a fortified Frankish farmstead which became the nucleus of an important defended palace site in the second half of the tenth century (Fehring 1991, 133-4). The main upper enclosure was defended by massive ditches and a gatehouse; it contained palace chapel, hall and residential quarters for the king. Guards and ser-

10 *Magdeburg,
    Germany.
    Equestrian statue of
    Otto I, thirteenth
    century*

11 *Magdeburg Cathedral,
    Germany. Thirteenth-
    century sculpture of
    Emperor Otto I and
    his English wife
    Empress Editha. Their
    tombs are in the choir
    of the Dom.*
    Photo by author

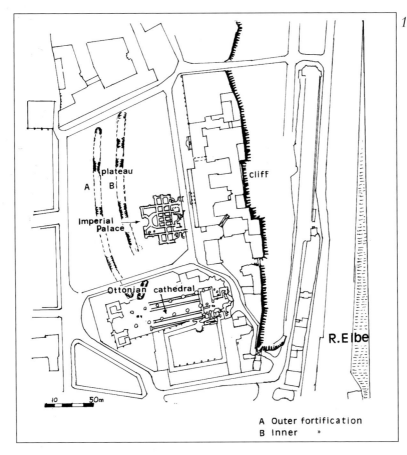

12   Magdeburg. Plan of excavations showing (A/B) lines of fortifications, imperial Ottonian Palace, Cathedral. After Zotz, 1993

vants were accommodated in *Grubenhaüser*, sunken floored buildings randomly scattered over the site. The lower enclosure had more than 190 *Grubenhaüser* with considerable evidence of manufacturing cloth, and working of ivory, horn and bone, the production of copper, bronze and lead objects, iron working and pottery making. It was not difficult to see how an early urban settlement might develop out of such a palace complex.

On the windswept square in front of the baroque Rathaus at Magdeburg there is a figure of a king on horseback under a canopy, accompanied by two female attendants. Known as '*Die Reiter*', this thirteenth-century representation of the tenth-century emperor Otto I, is perhaps the earliest equestrian sculpture in medieval European art. The place is significant. Magdeburg in the reign of Otto I was a heavily defended frontier town at the furthest eastern limit of the Reich. Its position on the west bank of the river Elbe was important strategically in the incessant wars against the Slavs. It was a favourite place of Otto I who visited Magdeburg 22 times and seems to have regarded it as 'nothing less than the Ottonian counterpart of the Carolingian Aachen' (Zotz, 1993, 89).

Architectural expression of the importance of Magdeburg was provided by the construction of an imposing *palatium* above the west bank of the Elbe and

13 *Magdeburg, Germany.*
    Foundations of palace of Otto I
    — see plan. Tenth century.
    Photo by author; museum
    display

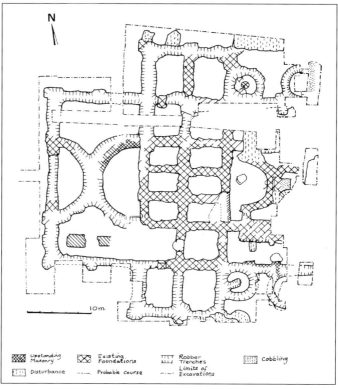

14 *Magdeburg. Plan*
    of excavations of
    Ottonian Palace

	Upstanding Masonry		Existing Foundations		Robber Trenches		Cobbling
	Disturbance		Probable course		Limits of Excavations		

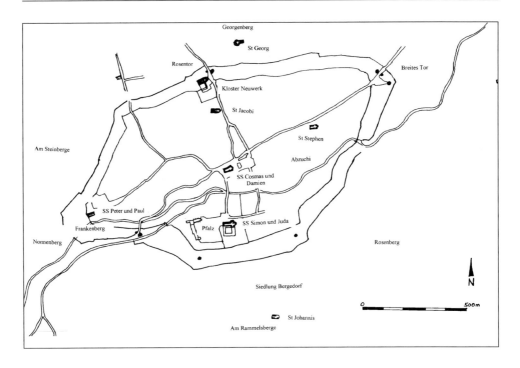

15 Goslar, Germany. Plan of town showing medieval monuments

encircled by ditches and ramparts. The site is now devoid of buildings but it lay under the immense space to the north of the Dom. Its foundations were uncovered in the 1960s. It is thought to have been built between 955, the year of Otto I's decisive victory over the Hungarians at Lechfeld, and 965. A comparison between the topography and the ground plans of the imperial palaces of Magdeburg and Aachen is instructive. There is similarity in that the secular and ecclesiastical elements lie parallel with each other in an east-west direction in both sites. Aachen, however, is laid out on a grander scale with a space 130m long lying between the two as compared with 50m at Magdeburg. The great hall at Magdeburg runs north-south and is of a different shape: it had apses placed opposite one another as in the architecture of late Antique *thermae*. Aachen, on the other hand, has a hall with apses derived from the Constantinian *aula* at Trier. There was in both places the same close relationship between secular and ecclesiastical. The palace at Magdeburg lies near the church of St Mauritius. The foundations of the major Ottonian church lie under. It was selected as the seat of an archbishopric in 968; it was designed to be the missionary centre from which the pagan Slavs were to be converted to Christianity. It also served as the mausoleum for Otto I himself. His tomb and that of his Anglo-Saxon wife Edith lie under the present gothic Dom. To sum up, Otto I took care to refer back to the imperial traditions of Aachen, but also to make his own personal dynastic statement.

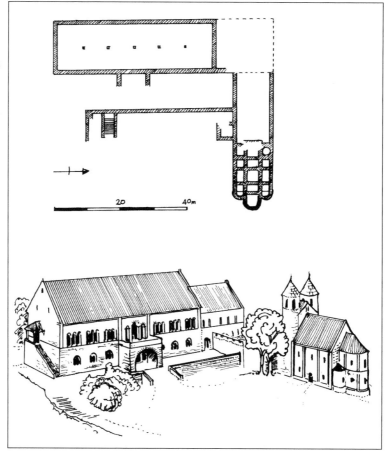

16 Goslar, Germany. Plan and reconstruction of palace in eleventh century (after Schulze 1991)

The later Ottonians, Otto II, Otto III and Henry II, continued to visit Aachen and Magdeburg on a roughly similar number of occasions. Otto II and Otto III stayed in both places five times, Henry II ten times (Zotz, 1993, 94). It is significant however that certain changes were taking place in the palatine policies of the latter. Merseburg was visited 22 times by Henry II: he also founded a new palace at Goslar that was to be of great importance in the next century.

Goslar was one of the Salian kings' most favoured stopping places: Henry II visited seven times, Conrad II six times, Henry III 21 times and Henry IV 32 times. Its location at the foot of the wooded Hartz mountains meant that there was plenty of hunting to be had in the surrounding royal forests. The nearby silver mines at Rammelsburg supplied the mints with ready bullion and the monarchy with huge profits. The town which grew up became the most important market place in Saxony.

The Palace at Goslar became an embodiment of imperial status. Henry III built an *Aula Regis* in *c.*1050 which collapsed in part in 1132 and was replaced. The site is impressive. It is placed transversely at the top of a long slope. The populace gathered on this slope on official occasions and followed the proceedings through open-

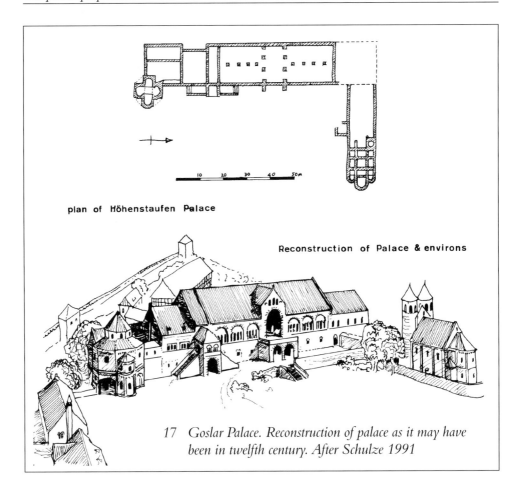

plan of Höhenstaufen Palace

Reconstruction of Palace & environs

17   *Goslar Palace. Reconstruction of palace as it may have been in twelfth century. After Schulze 1991*

ings in the façade of the hall. The ground floor is enclosed but could be heated on occasion (here it was similar to the Constantinian basilica at Trier). The main hall on the upper level is on a tremendous scale, longer than Charlemagne's hall at Aachen, with twin naves and wooden roof. There is a central throne room marked off by parallel arcades and communicating with a balcony. The throne room and the rest of the hall open onto the outdoor assembly place through rows of double and triple arches, now glazed. The whole building was over-restored in 1873 and the interior covered with bombastic frescoes telling us more about Prussian nineteenth-century aspirations than about the German imperial past (Conant 1978, 418-19).

As at Aachen the palace of Goslar is buttressed by ecclesiastical power. Henry III surrounded it with a number of churches: these included two houses of canons, the Palatine foundation of St Simon and St Jude and, east of the town, the church of St Peter. The palace itself was connected to a church of St Mary at one end which projected at right angles from the '*Kaiserhaus*'. At the other end Frederick Barbarossa built a two-staged chapel dedicated to St Ulrich. The plan is interesting, circular below and octagonal above, resembling, in fact, an imperial crown in stone. Below is buried the heart of the Emperor Henry III. The upper part was reserved for the royal family: again there are resonances from Aachen. The double layered chapel is found frequently in the later Middle Ages at Perpignan, the Sainte Chapelle in Paris, St Stephen's chapel Westminster.

A strange feature about Goslar is that it has lost its cathedral, demolished in the early nineteenth century. At the foot of the slope below the palace only the western narthex is left, housing a number of outsize statues. Within is a very significant object, a splendid piece of cast bronze openwork — the upper part of a throne. The back and sides are decorated with intertwined foliage, as if from the page of a medieval manuscript. The throne is enclosed on three sides with a low wall with panels of sculpture including a serpent and a lion (Das Reich der Salier, 1992, 254-6). This is the so-called *Kaiserstuhl*; it dates to the eleventh century, was used by the Salian and Hohenstaufen kings and, seated on this, Kaiser Wilhelm I announced the Reichstag of 1871, a seat of power over nine centuries!

Centres of power in Anglo-Saxon England: minsters and *villae regiae*

Like much else in the history of England of the sixth to ninth centuries AD the way in which the Anglo-Saxons ruled themselves, or were ruled, remains bafflingly obscure. Their monarchical tradition ran deep; its ancient foundations were recorded in King-lists, royal genealogies and origin myths. The earliest lists only take us back to *c*.AD 800 but they refer to kings in the dim and distant Germanic past, heroic figures with names like Hengist and Horsa in Kent and Cerdic and Cynric in Wessex. The search for venerable ancestors went beyond legend into myth; Anglo-Saxon kings traced their progenitors to heathen gods especially (and predictably for warrior kings) to Woden the God of War. All this represented a desire within emerging communities for order, stability and antiquity. Kings, like Alfred, were zealous to add a further layer to royal authority in assuming the role of protector of the Christian church, by inspiring educational, moral and religious reform (Cannon and Griffiths, 1988, 78-81).

Parallel, and contemporary with this, the period saw the rise of a network of ecclesiastical centres, minsters and cathedrals in which religious life was concentrated. Kings and aristocrats in early Anglo-Saxon Society vied with one another in endowing richly with huge tracts of land communities of priests who settled in and around minsters. These were stable institutions, their enclosures often strategically situated on confluences of rivers or road functions. Clergy encouraged communities of craftsmen to stay, and minsters, settled and ordered houses in an unstable and shifting world, became nascent centres of commerce.

In contrast the kings of the period of the Heptarchy were peripatetic, moving round their kingdoms with their followers, living off food renders and housed, often as not, in tents and occasionally in more permanent quarters. They used the hospitality offered by the minsters, abused it, and ultimately, if Blair can be believed, absorbed most of the economic wealth of the minsters. He has proposed, in a recent reinterpretation of the scattered and slender evidence, that the rich and powerful minsters were gradually taken over by the eighth- and ninth-century kings and, following their example, by the aristocrats of Anglo-Saxon society (Blair, forthcoming, 2001). In fact, in his view, the minsters were already seriously weakened before the age of the Viking invasions. Previously historians had seen the Northmen as villains of the piece, attacking monasteries for their wealth, raping nuns and gravely undermining the Christian basis of Anglo-Saxon society. Now they are regarded as wounding, in some cases giving the *coup de grâce* to already weakened institutions.

This model has certain attractions but it also poses further conundra. The royal centres, *villae regiae* or *vici regales*, as they are called, are places where kings and their courts assembled, consumed their food renders, attested charters, and even began the festal crown wearings which begin to be regularly recorded in the eleventh century. Their locations are ill known. Of 27 places (excluding Roman sites and hill forts) described as royal vills before AD 750, 13 are, as yet, unidentified. Some of those whose position is known failed to make it into the medieval period. During 750-820, 26 occur for the first time but again the location of the majority (14) are unknown. By AD 800, however, certain names and places attached to them are starting to emerge from the mists. Tamworth is recognised as a major Mercian royal centre with King Coenwulf beginning to hold a regular, almost Carolingian, cycle of courts at Christmas, Easter, and Pentecost there. Blair also draws attention to a very small number of other major and stable centres of royal power — in Canterbury, London, Dorchester (Dorset), Benson (Oxfordshire) and Bath; maybe the centres of the Kentish subdivisions called lathes, can be added. For the rest he sees the kings of Wessex and Mercia as meeting on open-ground sites chosen for their proximity to road and water transport. He thinks the use of the concept 'palace' is largely inappropriate to a time when residence, food-render collection and formal assembly did not need to occur in the same place. Minsters, on the other hand, were stable, well endowed, had permanent build-ings, their sites providing sanctuary and immunity from taxes were so well cho-sen that many became fortified burhs, and a majority ultimately attracted towns and survived into the medieval period. They were helped by being modelled on an urban and bureaucratic Mediterranean world. For these reasons they were seen as highly desirable prey to be exploited, first by the kings of eighth- and ninth-century England, and only secondly by the Viking raiders.

The problems which this interpretation poses are as follows. Who endowed the minsters in the first place? Was it a case of the kings giving with one hand in the sixth and seventh centuries and taking it back with the other hand in the eighth/ninth? Further, while kings had a clear need for a source of high quality artefacts to redistribute among their followers, make ambassadorial gifts to foreign powers and so on, it is hard to see where these came from. While there is a total absence (despite the considerable areas excavated) of industrial debris at the royal 'palace' site of Yeavering (Northumberland) it is perhaps stretching the evidence to suppose that the minsters supplied the need. To extrapolate from the Irish experience and to imagine that English minster sites rang with the noise from smiths' hammers or were ankle deep in horn and bone debris is attractive but as yet archaeologically unproven. Precious little is known about *villae regiae* in the archaeological record. Tamworth has produced a technologically highly compe- tent mill. Cheddar has shown a succession of royal halls, but there is a temporary air about it, a feeling that this was merely a lodge occupied from time to time by kings attracted by the hunting potential of the area. The 'palace' at Northampton has been reinterpreted as a religious building, one of a string of linked clusters across the site (Blair, 1996). Blair's hypothesis certainly makes sense of sites such as Westminster and Cookham. In the former the late Anglo-Saxon palace was squeezed onto the Thames side of Thorney Island already occupied by a rich and famous minster. Nevertheless the royal cuckoo in the Westminster nest hardly succeeded in pushing out the monks as happened at Cookham (Berkshire). Here a flourishing minster was gobbled up by a royal vill so that by 1086, the church had diminished and the royal manor ruled supreme. It is also true to say that in a great many places cited the royal manor came to occupy minster sites; in turn minster sites provided the nuclei for royal fortifications (called burhs) and subse- quently these 'proto towns' as they are labelled, prospered commercially and became urban places in the eleventh and twelfth centuries.

English and French palaces

The historical background
The Norman and Plantagenet kings of England created a strong monarchy and governmental institutions ruling over a unified state, the earliest in western Europe. It was the result of an accident, three powerful rulers in a row, William I, William Rufus and Henry I each outstanding military leaders, dominant person- alities and efficient administrators. Despite baronial revolts their combined will prevailed and England emerged in the twelfth century ready to challenge the infant kingdom of France for dominance in western Europe. The Angevin Empire of Henry II straddled the channel and included more than half of Capetian France. The domains of the Capetian monarchy were still landlocked, ruling a kingdom between Paris and Orleans, hemmed in by an obstreperous nobility. During the twelfth century the balance began to alter in favour of the French. A series of determined kings culminating in the reign of Philip Augustus saw the taming of the great lords and the patient construction of administrative systems which were to last throughout the Middle Ages. A change of dynasty put the Valois back on the throne in the fourteenth century. They had to withstand the repeated invasions and raids of the English during the first part of the Hundred Years War. The English won the battles, but unwittingly strengthened the French state. Each gained something, incipient warlike spirit hardened into national feel- ing in both. England profited by war gains in land, ransoms, treasure. In France centripetal tendencies in government and politics eventually began to prevail over

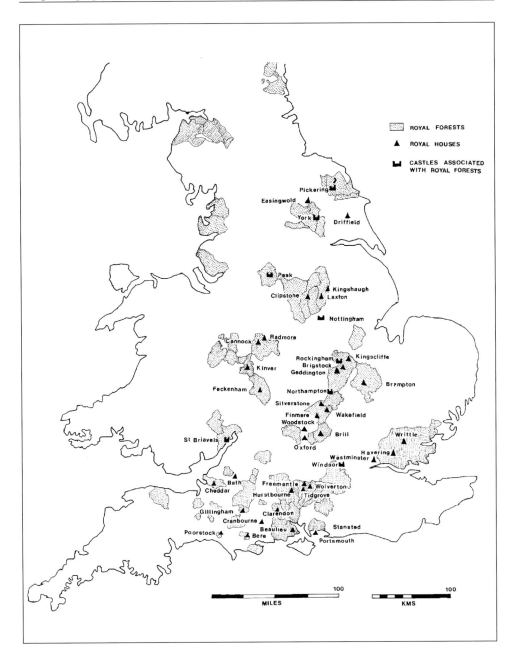

18   *The King's houses, 1154-1216. The predilection of the Angevin kings for hunting is demonstrated in this map. The area shown is only the northern segment of Angevin dominions, stretching from the Cheviots to the Pyrenees.*
After Brown, Colvin and Taylor, 1963

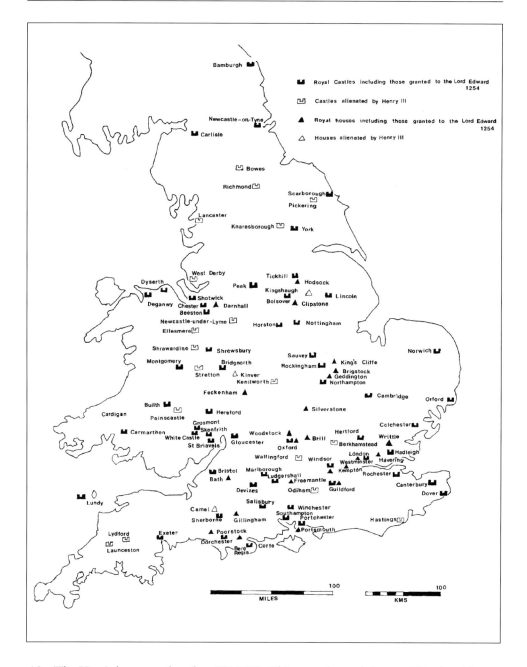

19   *The King's houses and castles, 1216-72. This map shows their astonishingly wide distribution, with a total of more than 60 royal castles and houses during the long reign of Henry III. After Brown, Colvin and Taylor, 1963*

41

centrifugal under the hammer of war. The country emerged, war torn, but larger and stronger and by the end of the fifteenth century ready to challenge England and the Empire for hegemony in Western Europe.

Palaces in Medieval England and France

Because of their political dominance the Plantagenet kings of England did not need strongly fortified palaces. In general the king's 'houses' in the thirteenth and four-teenth century lacked frowning walls and crenellated gates. They were not sited on easily defended hilltops but were frequently found in good hunting country. Clarendon admittedly is on the ridge of downland overlooking the new town (in the thirteenth century) of Salisbury but it is there because of the view, and the hunting not because of the military potential of the site. The numerous royal hunt-ing lodges like Writtle (Essex), Kings Cliffe (Northamptonshire) and Clipstone (Nottinghamshire) were surrounded by ditches but these were aimed at excluding burglars and interlopers while the royal masters were away. The physical layout of Plantagenet 'houses', which was a term more frequently used than 'palaces' fol-lowed the general piecemeal lines of domestic manorial residences (Wood, 1968). A gatehouse, a courtyard or two, round which were to be found separate units each providing a separate service, loosely linked by pentices or grouped round cloisters. There were stables and workshops. Round the hall (the largest component with an imposingly lofty roofline) were grouped kitchens. Royal suites of rooms were added to in a haphazard way; they tended to be two-storey and to consist of com-plexes of halls and chambers and chapel linked by roofed walkways. As will be seen these last three elements could be richly decorated by wall paintings, coloured glass and wall hangings. Furniture was sparse and spartan. Many textiles, some furnish-ings and all plate would have been packed up and carted round since the court would be involved on continuous journeying, like the German kings, the Plantagenets in the thirteenth century were always on the move. We can recon-struct their itineraries without too much difficulty (Hindle, 1978, 170-8). It has been calculated that King John moved on average 12 times a month through his 17-year reign. Henry III was slightly more sedentary making 80 moves a year. Edward I, frequently on campaign, undertook no less than 107 moves a year. This meant that the 60 or so royal houses were frequently empty. Their maintenance was a headache. Clearing up and repairing after a visit by the court must have been a chore. Unblocking drains and flushing garderobes would have been necessary. Plastering, glazing, tiling in preparation for a royal visit must have stretched the patience and the pockets of the sheriffs to whom the peremptory writs informing them of the imminent arrival of the court were addressed.

As the fourteenth century progressed the number of English royal residences in regular use began to fall. There were a number of reasons for this. The monarchy grew less peregrinatory, preferring to spend longer periods in fewer but certain favoured places. The machinery of government, increasingly departmentalised, centred on London. Kings found it more and more difficult to raise taxation with-out making political concessions from parliaments. This meant that less ready cash was washing around the kingdom but the standards of luxurious living of the international aristocracy and the costs of providing them, were continually rising. Consequently more resources were invested in fewer buildings. Most of the king's residences in the later Middle Ages are found in the south-east of England. Their number began steeply to decline in this century. Edward III possessed about 25 early in his reign. As he became older and more tired he seems rarely to have moved outside the Thames valley but we must remember that much time was spent organising and running campaigns in France. During the fifteenth century again the number dropped to about 10 during the reign of Edward IV. At the same time the size of the English court was tending to expand from about 120 people during Henry I's reign to as many as 800 in Henry VI's. Fewer but more grandiose royal residences were the result. Of course not all kings at all times occupied their own houses. Edward I spent many weeks at Lanercost Priory in the last few weeks of his life. Henry VI spent much of the last four years of his reign 1456-60 living in monasteries and taking part in interminable services (Wolff, 1983, 305). The Tudors favoured riverside palaces such as Sheen, Richmond and Hampton Court but Henry VIII showed an avaricious propensity for acquiring other men's houses only matched by Plantagenet John. These were again centred mainly in the Thames valley and Southern England.

The design of royal palaces in England, and even more in Scotland, during the later Middle Ages was strongly influenced by what contemporary rulers were building in continental Europe. We shall notice later on in this book that Henry III, that most perceptive royal architectural patron, was impressed by what Louis IX was building in France. The French king had already provided his fortress overlooking the Seine at St Germain-en-Laye with a charming pocket chapel in the 1230s; his much greater work in the royal palace in the centre of Paris, the Sainte Chapelle, was being built in the 1240s concurrently with Henry III's works at Westminster. Rheims and Paris were certainly centres of inspiration for the English. Edward III's transformation of Windsor into a glittering fortress palace outshone for a time the French who responded by bringing the Palais Royal up to date, equipping it with the latest ideas in openwork staircases and by building in the woods outside Paris an answer to Windsor, the castle/palace of Vincennes. Edward IV during his enforced exile experienced the palatial splendours of Burgundy and applied some of the ideas learned when he was restored to the throne. For example he was billeted upon Louis, Lord of Gruuthuse in Flanders and visited his house in Bruges which survives today. Both king and lord constructed virtually identical oratories in the St George's chapel Windsor and in the church of Notre Dame Bruges (Thurley, 1993, 15-21). Edward IV, in addition, invested heavily in Netherlandish wall hangings. His court festivals were also probably influenced by Burgundian fashions. Henry VII's reconstruction of Greenwich Palace shows innovative features including a five storey donjon which can be closely compared with Princenhof and Ghent. Greenwich is unfortified like the other Tudor houses; it bears the marks of being inspired by the urban houses of the Burgundian nobility despite its rural setting. Henry VIII emulated

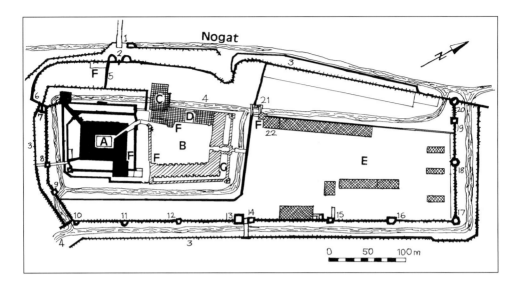

20 Marienburg (Malbork). Plan of fortress/palace of Teutonic knights. A: high castle; B:
    middle castle; C: palace of grand masters; D: refectory; E: outer ward. After Haftka
    and Mierzwinski 1992

his contemporary, Francis I of France in dazzling people with his temporary structures in the field of the Cloth of Gold. He also employed continental painters and
decorators in building Nonsuch, one of the first palaces to be constructed all of
one piece, on a fresh site (apart from a demolished church) and planned symmetrically to fit the increasingly hierarchical demands of the Tudor court. Nonsuch
was admired for its elaborate and expensive decoration but it is the plan-form
which was of greater long-term significance. Instead of the rambling and incon-
sequential layouts of earlier medieval palaces there is a rigidity of layout in which
all functions are integrated into buildings round the two great courts. This would
influence strongly the buildings of the powerful as the Renaissance deepened its
hold over their minds in the second part of the sixteenth century.

The palace/castle of the Teutonic Knights at Marienburg
(colour plate 1)

The crusading movement of Christian Europe generated three major military-reli-
gious orders: the Templars, the Hospitallers and the Teutonic Knights. Their *raison
d'être* was to protect pilgrims to the Holy Land, to live a communal and ascetic life
and to fight the infidel; thus combining monasticism with chivalry. The third group,
the Teutonic Knights, whose ranks were mainly drawn from the upper *echelons* of
society within the Holy Roman Empire, withdrew from the Holy Land and sought
a new outlet for their energies. They had already responded in the 1220s to an appeal

from Duke Conrad of Mazonia for protection against the pagan Lithuanians, Jacuringians and Prussians. In 1271 after the loss of their last base in Palestine they pulled out and proceeded to the Baltic region. Here, fired by missionary zeal, and hungry for land, they used their formidable fighting qualities to annihilate the Prussian Slavonic population, opening the way for German colonists to found towns and villages in their place and on their land. Politically their aim was territorial conquest; economically they had ambitions to control the Hanseatic towns in what they considered was their sphere of influence; religiously, enforced conversion of their Slav enemies was a less preferred option than genocide. They pursued their ferocious aims by setting up a theocratic political order. They looked around for a Baltic base for their headquarters and moved from Venice to Marienburg, 'the fortress of Mary' (modern Polish Malbork) in 1309. A huge statue of Mary was housed in a niche in the eastern wall of their chapel looking menacingly eastwards.

Marienburg is one of the most powerful fortress cities of medieval Europe. Despite the damage inflicted by the Swedes in the seventeenth century and by the Russians in the closing stages of Second World War its much patched lofty rings of brick walls, multiple towers, drawbridges and machicolations still impress the visitor. It was a triple structured building comprising monastery, castle and palace, extending over a 20ha (50 acre) site. This was at the northern edge of a narrow, long and at the same time high peninsula. It was protected from the west and north by the Nogat river and from the east by a wide marshy valley. From the south access was easier and fortification needed; wood and earth were succeeded by brick walls. The elongated site determined the long narrow shape of the town tacked on to the west end of the castle. It had a single broad market street instead of the more spacious market square typical of German colonial towns. Here stood the parish church of St John and the town hall.

The building history of Marienburg castle is complex and has been well analysed by Hafta M. and Mierzwinski 1992 (English translation). Two parts particularly call for attention. The monumental knight's hall, with a spacious vault supported by a central row of pillars and lit by 14 large Gothic windows provided a venue for the great refectory feasts. Here knights, including guests from western Europe, were entertained royally and signed up for the 'crusade'. Here aristocrats from England, scions of the Lancastrian (Bolingbroke), Beauchamp and Bohun families, knights, socially out of the top drawer of society, gathered. They had to prove their nobility to join the order, taking vows as monks. Like the Cistercians they had a numerous body of lay brothers to service them. The knights undertook a punishing programme of carefully organised raids (*Reisen*) into Lithuanian territory, taking advantage of the climate and the terrain. They attacked when the waterways were frozen (in February) and in the summer season after the marshes had dried out and the Lithuanian peasantry was otherwise engaged in getting in the harvest. Gradually as less emphasis was placed on monkish vows, the warrior ethos came to prevail. Eventually the largely foreign and imported aristocracy comprising the knights fell out with the urban and rural peasant colonists who had established themselves in the sandy and wooded plains of Prussia. By the middle of the fifteenth century the order proved unable to resist the combined opposition of the Poles and Lithuanians.

21   Marienburg (Malbork), Poland. Palace of the Teutonic knights. The main range of the quarters of the Grand Masters. Brick, begun in 1382. Heavily restored after the Second World War. Photo: Courtauld

The early sixteenth century saw them converting to Protestantism and withdrawing to a new capital Konigsberg. Marienburg was integrated into the Polish kingdom.

In the meantime Marienburg was built up as the capital of the Teutonic state. The building occupied by the commanders is particularly relevant to our theme. What had been a typical commander's castle of the thirteenth century was transformed in the next 100 years into the main administrative centre of the missionary-invaders. The architecture was adapted to meet the requirements of the Grand Master, the highest dignitary of the order and his court. As early as *c*.1330-40 the first modest residence was raised in the south-west corner of the old castle. In 1382 the Grand Master Conrad Zöllner von Rotenstein began to construct a palace which could compete in magnificence with the finest residences of magnates in Western Europe, and this at a time when Edward III's huge palace at Windsor Castle and Charles V's Vincennes were rising.

A great western projection jutted out towards the river; a four-storey residential tower, its corners, crowned with machicolated and crenellated turrets, housed two magnificent rooms at first-floor level, the so-called summer and winter refectories, roofed with late Gothic radial vaults supported on one centrally placed pillar.

This main floor of the palace contained the private space devoted to the housing of the Grand Master; here he had his dressing room, bedroom, privy, bathroom. Here was his private chapel (St Catherine's) whose chancel projected into the courtyard of the Middle Castle. Most of these rooms were richly painted; the vaults were covered with lush grapevines or acanthus. The walls had painted imitations of hanging curtains, ornamental and heraldic figures. On the ground floor which had a separate entrance, there were the order's archives and chancellery run by clerks. As in the Papal palace at Avignon the administrative hub of the organisation was sited right next to but under the quarters of the top man, in this case the Grand Master. Marienburg and Avignon can be usefully compared as major seats of government, the one aiming at dominating large chunks of the Baltic states, the other a more centralised capital than Rome of the so-called universal church in Europe.

Hungarian Royal Palaces of the later Middle Ages

The Magyars

The Magyars were a people who came out of Asia in AD 895-6. Their plundering raids and campaigns took them to the heart of Germany, eastern France and even central Italy. They also invaded the Byzantine territory as far as South Greece. Here they were bought off by Greek patriarchs and next were defeated in battle by the armoured cavalry of the German Dukes. The battle of Lechfeld near Angsburg was decisive and they were pushed back into Hungary. They became Christian and organised themselves into the form of a state. Their conversion deprived the Christian rulers of central Europe from the excuse to attack them as heathen. It also qualified the Hungarian ruling dynasty for intermarriage with the other royal houses of Europe.

In the year AD 1000 King Stephen formally ordered the conversion of all Hungary. The kingdom of Hungary thereafter remained attached to the Roman Church and politically was independent of the German kingdoms.

The Hungarian crown (colour plate 23)

Geza I (1074-7) received the Byzantine crown which forms the lower half of the Hungarian royal crown. On the peak of this crown is an enamel of the Redeemer the Byzantine Pantocrator, shown sitting in state. Below him to the left are the Archangel Michael, St George and St Cosmas; on the right the Archangel Gabriel St Demetrius and St Damian depicted in enamel. At the back of the crown on the same level as pictures of the redeemer is an enamel portrait of a Byzantine emperor identified by a Greek inscription in red letters as Michael VII Ducas (1071-8). Under him to the left is another imperial figure inscribed in red letters 'Constantine'. This must be Michael Ducas' son or brother and co-emperor, and to the right another male figure with a Greek inscription in blue letters reading Geza the faithful King of Turkia (Hungary) i.e. Geza I.

The inscriptions show that according to Byzantine ideas the King of Hungary was inferior to the Emperor of Byzantium in rank and dignity. Hungary stood behind the emperor in the hierarchy of states. But Hungary was not in a position of political subjection to Byzantium. Indeed the Emperor recognised Geza as King of Turkia (Hungary) and this was a guarantee of the independence of the kingdom.

The double cross of the Hungarian coat of arms was introduced by Bela III (buried in 1196). Up to his time the royal emblem of the Hungarian kings was the single Apostolic cross. The double cross appears for the first time on Bela III's coinage *c*.1190 when he took it over from Byzantium where it was the imperial emblem from the ninth to the thirteenth centuries. It was used by Charles Robert of the Angevin dynasty in the fourteenth century who attached it, together with his coat of arms, to the orb which becomes part of the coronation regalia.

Bela's purpose in adopting the double cross was to represent the dignity of the kingdom of Hungary as similar to that of the Byzantine Empire. Charles Robert's motive was doubtless to refer to the symbol of the Arpoid dynasty thereby emphasising his right to inherit the throne. The *corona latina* is not a truly independent crown, it is an arch shaped like a cross, made up of bands, and it received its name from the Latin captions on the enamel plates that they decorate. There are enamel plaques showing Christ seated with eight apostles: it is clear that it has been used for another function and has been cut down. The form of the crown was created at the end of the twelfth century possibly by Bela III and thus created the crown which Hungarian tradition credits to St Stephen. When the old Byzantine circle was welded together with the western upper crown the resultant Hungarian royal crown became similar to the imperial emblem worn by the Comneni.

To illustrate the importance of the crown, King Matthias Corvinus (king of Hungary from 1458) needed it. It had been taken to the court of the German

Emperor Frederick III, and when Matthias, who did not have royal blood, was elected to the throne in 1458 he declared that the recovery of the crown was of national importance. Frederick III made him pay heavily for it: to begin with he offered it for 40,000 gold guilders but then subsequently relinquished it only after 80,000 gold guilders had been paid for it. It returned to Hungary in 1463 (Zsuzsa, 1986).

Likewise considered essential by the Hungarian kings was the maintenance of a magnificent court both to overawe their own subjects and to impress foreign visitors. The model court of course was the Byzantine one at Constantinople, the subject of an 800-page treatise. It outdid all others in its addiction to elaborate and expensive ceremonial. The Hungarian royal capital of Esztergom with its monumental cathedral and expensively furnished palace caused wonder among western knights en route to the crusades. Early in his reign Bela IV attempted to introduce Byzantine magnificence at court by making himself personally inaccessible, receiving requests by writing and adopting Byzantine rituals.

The royal palaces

The coronation city of the kings was at Székesfehervar located in the centre of the ruling dynasty's private domains on the pilgrimage route to Jerusalem. In 1323 King Charles Robert established his capital at Visegrad nine miles north of Buda on a steep cliff overlooking the Danube. The site was well defended with a fortress on the site of a Roman military station, a great tower and a walled city. Buda across the Danube from Pest was often used for ceremonial purposes during the fourteenth century but its full establishment as a capital was delayed until Sigismund built a palace there in the fifteenth century. Visegrad was refurbished by Matthias Corvinus as was Buda and both places acquired many of the comforts and distinctive architecture of Italian Renaissance palaces. Hence the capital city established early in Hungary's history was moved about the country, usually to conform to a change in the state's political centre of gravity.

In fact the sovereign frequently went on tour. As in other kingdoms of western Europe; the monarchy was itinerant. The government was located where the ruler happened to be. Such royal peregrinations were the best possible means of keeping in touch with the leading men of the realm. The personal ties created in this fashion played an important part in keeping the state together. Royal processions also permitted ordinary people to view the monarch in the flesh, magnificently attired and accompanied by a splendid retinue. They promoted loyalty by exposing to the public the reality of the monarchy's presence. The year round maintenance of the royal court, including hundreds of people and horses would have been an undue burden on any one district. It was easier to move the court to its supplies than the supplies to the court. The characteristics shared by these three palaces are that they were all on the Danube. They were all in highly defensive positions — Esztergom is on a rocky hill, wedge-shaped with a cliff on the Danube side overlooking a bridge crossing into Slovakia. Visegrad is topped by a great fortress, a donjon called Solomon's tower and a wall. It sits at the foot, terraced into a cliff. Buda is on a hill overlooking the Danube.

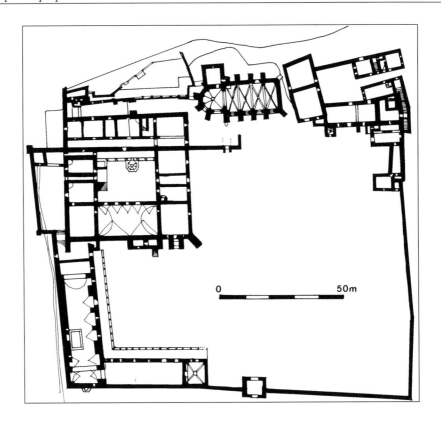

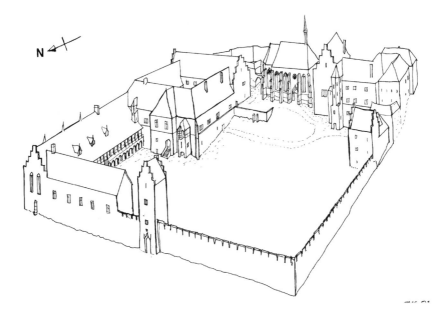

22   *Visegrad Palace, Hungary. Plan as it was in the fifteenth century and reconstruction.*
    After Laszlovszky 1995

They remind us that one of the chief functions of Hungarian kings, in fact medieval European kings in general, was to act as war leaders. The Hungarian kings had to establish themselves as Christian monarchs over a heathen lawless people; they had to withstand the attacks of the Mongols, Asiatic horseman who swept into Poland and Hungary in the thirteenth century. Aided by speed, surprise and swift means of communication they won every battle they fought. Eventually they were diverted by their ambitions to conquer and rule China. Hungary in the fourteenth century became the most powerful state in East Central Europe. King Charles Robert (1310-42) directed his ambitions towards the southern frontier and asserted rule over Croatia, Dalmatia and Bosnia and sought conquests in Serbia and Bulgaria. His son Lewis the Great (1342-82) conducted a similarly energetic foreign policy against the Serbs, the Venetians and Bulgaria but inadvertently weakened the resistance of the minor Christian powers to Ottoman encroachments.

The Palace of Visegrad

In 1323 the King of Hungary Charles Robert Angevin moved his court to Visegrad. He owned several houses in the new capital the most significant of which was found near the site where the palace was later situated. A chapel consecrated to St George was joined to this building. In 1366 King Lewis the Great added a palace chapel consecrated to the Virgin Mary. The building was finished by King Sigismund of Luxembourg. The chapel was finished and also a new homogeneously designed palace complex was built. The gatehouse of the complex 123m x 123m was raised in the middle of the façade near the Danube. The gate opened to a huge reception courtyard with a great hall on the north side. Between the great hall and the gatehouse several impressive rooms were situated. Facing the gate on a terrace was a chapel which was joined to two residential palaces with inner courtyards on the north and south sides. The main ornaments of the palace complex were the wells decorating the courtyards and the niche with a canopy on the façade of the great hall. King Sigismund founded a Franciscan monastery beside the old abandoned St George chapel before 1425 and after 1425 he added a new cloister to it and built a new church consecrated to the Virgin Mary.

Between 1405-8 Buda became the palace of royal residence. So when Matthias Corvinus began to restore the palace at Visegrad *c.*1479 this royal residence was of less significance than during its building in the fourteenth century. Archaeological work has revealed that these works were undertaken.

The old window and door frames were replaced with late Gothic ones. The halls were vaulted and a two level loggia, Gothic below and Renaissance above, was built in the courtyard of the north-east palace in 1484. In front of the palace wing of the lower reception courtyard a Gothic columned loggia was raised: the terraces of the palace were enlarged and wide ornamental stairs were built in front of them. The fourteenth-century wells were replaced by late Gothic and Renaissance marble fountains and wall fountains. The monumental façade of the palace was enriched with a large Gothic niche which was decorated with coats of arms and other ornamentation. Some parts of the roof were covered with coloured glazed tiles (Laszlovsky, 1995).

The palace of Buda

Meanwhile Sigismund had made major additions to the palace at Buda. Here on the top of the rock overlooking the Danube was a royal suite of rooms, a small council hall and a great hall or knights hall in which festive ceremonies and conferences were held. The hall was about 70m long and 18.5m wide. It comprised two naves and was divided into nine bays by eight pillars. It had plenty of galleries and balconies to enable spectators to enjoy spectacles in the courtyard below from as many angles as possible. Here pageants, tournaments and festivities took place. In the same area King Matthias Corvinus fought in the tournament staged at the festivities of his wedding. It was the chief scene of chariot races, lion hunts and acrobatic performances. Sigismund also equipped the palace of Buda with a series of glazed tile stoves. These went with the aqueduct which caused water to be pumped up from the Danube to the palace. He also refortified the Buda palace to adapt it to resist artillery. Essentially these walls packed with earth survived the wars with the Turks and the period of Turkish occupation and remains still exist (Gerevich, 1971, 83 et seq).

In 1974 the archaeologist Laszlo Zolnay discovered a number of sculptured fragments which had been used to help fill the bailey. The carving of the majority had been completed. Some had been coloured although in some instances the surfaces were unfinished. Drilled holes designed for the attachment of various items by means of pegs e.g. head dress, crowns, mitres, objects placed in the hand such as sceptres, metal fittings for belts had been made and not used. We can deduce from this that the statues were never finished and never erected in their final place of destination. There is no sign of weather erosion; they are carved of soft stone and were probably designed for inner rooms. The figures are almost life-sized and represent armoured knights, kings, women and bishops; attendant figures wear court dress and form pairs. Smaller figures are shield-bearing pages. Two fragments of coats of arms are the arms of Hungary with the apostolic cross; the others bear the crest of the Bohemian kings. These refer to King Sigismund of Luxembourg (1387-1437) and to the period after his election to the throne of Bohemia (1419) so they are a bit of a mystery, probably prepared to decorate a building which was never finished (*Royal Palace and Gothic Statues of Medieval Buda*).

Matthias Corvinus

Hungary became an important centre of Renaissance culture in the fifteenth century. The decisive figure in the development of Italian humanism in Hungary was Matthias Corvinus who reigned 1458-90. He was elected to the throne by the nobles at the age of 14, an age too young for him to have made any enemies. He was also profiting from the military reputation of his father John Hunyadi who had waged a series of largely successful wars against the Ottoman Turks who were now greedily ravening against Hungary's southern frontier. A third advantage the young Matthew had was the large wealth he administered from the family for-tunes. On the debit side he lacked the legitimacy of royal ancestry as the son of a renowned general. Consequently he had to fight hard to be accepted by his fellow monarchs. He was highly educated and embodied in his own person the new idea that talent should prevail over royal lineage.

His interest in the Renaissance was certainly motivated partly by the cultural pres-tige which glorified himself and his ancestors. He commissioned historical chroni-cles written in the humanistic style. In 1486 he engaged the Italian humanist Antonio Bonfini to write an exhaustive history of Hungary; the result was the immense *Rerum Ungaricorum Decades*, a compilation of native and foreign sources beginning with the Magyar settlement of Central Europe and ending in the year 1496.

King Matthius also patronised another remarkable Renaissance scholar, Regiomontanus, a great astronomer and inventor of modern trigonometry. His book *Ephamenides*, a nautical almanac enabling sailors to calculate their position according to the observations of the stars, was used by Christopher Columbus. He was put in charge of the famous Corvina library: Matthew spent 30,000 gold florins on this and filled its shelves with fine vellum manuscripts adorned with painted miniatures. He sent agents far and wide to procure beautiful and expen-sive specimens. He also patronised the new art of printing by setting up a press at Buda which in 1473 brought out a Latin chronicle of Hungarian history as its first publication. Started in the early 1400s the library grew rapidly and the king had to put in charge of his acquisitions Taddeo Ugolino. His buyers, copyists and illus-trators were busy working in many Italian towns and also in Vienna. The work-shop in Buda employed 30 men on copying and illustrating. After Matthias' death the splendid library was promptly dispersed and many distinguished scholars bor-rowed its volumes and never returned them. This pilfering proved beneficial: if the library had remained intact the Turkish occupation would have destroyed it. As it is some 170 volumes have been preserved and we know the titles of more than 300. The diaspora of the library served European humanism: early editions of Pliny, Ptolemy, Heliodorus and Latin translations of great historians are often based on MSS once in the Corvina.

He also married an Italian, Beatrice of Naples, who vied with her husband in patronising Italian Renaissance scholars.

Corvinus and the Palace of Buda
But it is in his reconstruction of Buda palace that he made the most remarkable tangible contribution to the Italian Renaissance's influence in Hungary. After the coronation of 1458 we hear that he proceeded to Buda with some of the lords and peers and spent the summer quietly there. Day after day they enjoyed the sight of various spectacles. Horse races and chariot races, lion hunts and gladiators' fights were not missing. He himself took part in the jousts, staged daily in the hippo-drome and pitted his axe against that of the strongest adversaries. Chariot races were common occurrences.

Unfortunately the upstanding work of the fifteenth-century palace has almost entirely disappeared. We only have the foundations and Bonfini's descriptions and an illustration known as the Hartman-Schedel engraving. But we do have large quantities of architectural fragments and these have been collected together and form an impressive architectural museum in the vaults of the present palace which has been rebuilt after extensive damage in the concluding days of the Second World War (Gerevich, 1971, 101 et seq).

The library occupied the first storey of the eastern wing of the courtyard. This was the scientific one. The chronicles, annuals and archives were kept in the western wing of the internal courtyard built by the Angevins. Bonfini stated 'He has erected palaces, whose magnificence does not differ from those of the Romans. Huge dining rooms and splendid living rooms follow one another. Their gilt ceilings are distinguished by different signs.' These have not survived but the description appears to fit the coffered ceilings of the quattrocento to be found all over Italy. Benedetto da Maiano was probably the maker of these coffered ceilings as well as the furniture. The above description refers to the arcading of the inner courtyard loggias. In the state rooms would have been festoons, emblems, badges, coats of arms and allegories of victory — as are on the triumphal arch representing the victory of the house of Aragon on the Castello Nuovo at Naples. Numerous red marble fragments of icons and windows have cornices decorated with trophies and with the allegory of the Danube. Doubtless the wing had been built after victories.

Another description: 'proceeding you will see suites of rooms for winter and summer, with high vaults, balconies, gilt rooms, deep recesses, silver bedsteads and chairs'. This probably refers to the southern, Angevin block of the palace. High vaulting and frescoes, their gold background being typical of the fourteenth century. The red marble fragments of windows and balusters came from a big courtyard with galleries reconstructed by Matthias; 'on the inside there is a corridor of fine red marble with high columns' says Gerlach's description. There were coved and intersecting vaults, pilasters and wall piers with richly decorated fields provided the vertical articulation of wall surfaces. The red marble covering of the walls disclosed the peerless costliness and pomp of the palace. The external façade was enlivened with simple, plain cross windows (fenêtre à croisée) and twin or triple windows with pilasters, with string courses and cornices in the height of the upper floor and under the roof. This horizontal proportioning is the most important feature both of the external and of the interior wall surface. In later phases the huge pilasters carry the upper storey as well as the roof. The same structural features are found in the contemporary Ducal Palace of Urbino.

Bonfini also describes 'The multi-coloured squares covering the floor are mostly burned glazed tiles.' Hundreds of coloured tiles with lead glaze and tin glazed titles with figural or ornamental decoration were excavated. Each small square tile is surrounded by four oblong hexagonal ones. The dark majolican tiles with their backgrounds densely decorated represent the emblems of Matthias and the House of Aragon. They probably covered the throne room floor. A number of

Italian workshops from which masters had come to the royal workshop of Buda are seen here: some appear to be influenced by the Bertini workshop in Faenza; some majolica tiles appear to be Neapolitan. They were probably made in Buda; some are wasters. Also fragments of stoves, with tin and lead glazes, Bonfini again: 'In many places cold and warm baths can be found. The stoves in the dining rooms are covered with breast shaped tiles abounding not only in beautiful colours but excelling in a variety of creatures called into life by fantasy.' There are scenes from Hungarian history, saints with emblems, kings, first of all Matthias, enthroned and in allegory as David against Goliath, also representations of pornographic material, a person raising his shirt, a woman showing her backside. The realism of figures is remarkable, as is the representation of portraits.

Matthias had been elected on the strength of his father's wealth and military reputation. He was faced with a major threat from the Ottomans but in fact paid little attention to the dangers on his south-east frontier. He turned his gaze towards Italy and Western Europe. His lack of royal ancestors meant that he needed recognition from the traditional powers of Europe. He spent most of his remarkable military talents and the power of his so-called 'Black Army' with impressing himself on the powers to the north and west of Hungary. He took Moravia, crushed the Hussites, thus demonstrating that he was a good and faithful son of the church and became king of Bohemia. He regarded the Emperor Frederick III as his enemy; he captured Vienna in 1485 and at the time of his death ruled Silesia, Moravia and Lower Austria. In effect Hungary became a bone of contention between the Habsburg and Ottoman power blocs each of which wished to use it as a buffer against the other. All possibility evaporated of a successful combined defence against the Ottoman Empire. Matthias was so successful with setting up a powerful kingship that his nobles deliberately engineered the election of a weak successor. His victories were short lived. Hungary fell apart. At Mohacs 1526 the Ottomans achieved a decisive victory and were able to rule half Hungary for 150 years (Sinor, 1959).

Bishops' houses in town and country

Up to this point we have been concerned with the residential requirements of emperors and kings in northern and western Europe from AD 800-1500. It is time to turn to the housing of archbishops, bishops and abbots. The first thing that strikes one is the similarity of needs between lay and ecclesiastical leaders. The functions of medieval bishops and abbots were inextricably intertwined with those of secular rulers. Bishops by AD 1200 had very full lives. They had pastoral duties, being responsible for the choice, ordination, and subsequent support of priests selected to work within the diocese. They had duties of inspection of monasteries and nunneries — the right of visitation. They had responsibilities arising out of their position as landowners and feudal lords. They were bound to contribute to the maintenance of the feudal army by providing knight service —

or the financial equivalent. They were judges and magistrates holding courts to pursue their rights and to uphold canon law; appointing deputies to preside over courts. They were expected to attend the royal court, and act as the king's counsellor and member of the royal council, the forerunner of infant parliaments. They were sent by the king to foreign powers to act as ambassadors, to negotiate marriages, to arrange truces, and broker treaties. There would seem to be not much time left over for scholarship. And yet men like Robert Grosseteste, bishop of Lincoln, Archbishops Stephen Langton, Robert Kilwardby, John Pecham and Robert Winchelsey, all managed to write books; Grosseteste, in particular, was a scholar of European significance, an outstanding intellect as well as a spiritual force to be reckoned with in thirteenth-century England (Moorman, 1945).

An example will help to drive home the fact that bishops had to perform a multiplicity of roles. Take Hugh Northwold, bishop of Ely 1229-54; he was known as a builder, as Grosseteste's friend and Matthew Paris's ideal of the good monk — a bishop, but his high calling nevertheless enmeshed him in worldly affairs on a daily basis. He was present with the king in Wales; he acted on behalf of the Papacy as delegate against the disturbers of the peace of the realm necessitating a journey to Worcester. He was chosen as ambassador of Henry III to the Emperor, and brought the king's bride, Eleanor of Provence, over the channel to Dover in 1236. Nor were the demands made on him lessened in old age. He is found acting as 'executor' of the crusading tithe granted to the king in 1252 (Miller, 1951, 77-8). To accomplish this punishing programme Northwold doubtless would have taken to heart Bishop Grosseteste's advice to the Countess of Lincoln: 'Every year, at Michaelmas . . . arrange your sojourn for the whole of the year, and for how many weeks in each place, according to the seasons of the year . . . and do not in anywise burden by debt or long residence the places where you sojourn, but so arrange your sojourns that the place of your departure shall not remain in debt . . .' (Lamond, 1890, 145).

We have highlighted the itinerant life imposed on Anglo-Saxon kings and German emperors. Bishops, too, were compelled to live as nomads. A roll recording the household expenses of Bishop Swinfield of Hereford for the years 1289-90 shows him moving his household no less than 81 times during the 296 days covered by the document. A bishop, in fact, moved round his diocese followed by a large retinue. Swinfield in his tours was accompanied by between 30-40 horsemen whose animals needed to be stabled each night. At the chief feasts of the Christian year this number rose still further; 55 horses required to be stabled at Christmas, 70 at Easter (Moorman, 1945, 177). All this needs to be kept in mind when understanding the excavated remains of medieval bishop's houses.

Those in England have been the subject of a recent comprehensive survey (Thompson, 1998) so I shall therefore limit my discussion to three examples from this country, a rural 'palace', an urban residence (both belonging to the Bishops of Winchester), and the see palace of the archbishops at Canterbury next to the cathedral in Kent. I propose then to cross the channel and look at urban fortress-palaces of the archbishops of Narbonne and of the Papacy in Avignon. Finally, a contrast, we shall move to northern Europe to Norway, a country that was Christianised as late as the tenth century, and study the palace of the archbishops of Trondheim. In each case archaeology, either by excavating below-ground structures, or by dissecting and analysing standing buildings, has contributed in a major way to unravelling their evolution, and thus shedding light on the activities of these ecclesiastics. Inevitably these chopped and changed over the years, according to the comparative wealth, ages, ambitions, abilities and proclivities of the holders of the office.

A rural episcopal 'palace'

The bishops of Winchester were the wealthiest English ecclesiastical potentates in their day. In 1291 according to an assessment of clerical revenue called the *Taxatio Nicholai IV* the see was valued at £2988 15s $\frac{1}{2}$d and the bishop's estates consisted of 50 manors. This compares with Durham, Canterbury and Ely, all with over £2000 (Moorman, 1945, 135, 169). Winchester was granted virtually all the land in four Oxfordshire parishes centring on Witney by Queen Emma in 1044. At some time early in the twelfth century the bishops invested in building a manorial centre here from which to run this estate. Witney was 60 miles to the northwest of Winchester; clearly the bishops needed to stamp their personality on the landscape if they were to exploit the economic potential of their estate to the full.

A series of excavations has uncovered considerable parts of a stone manor house at Witney. While there is no documentary evidence for the first stone building, decorated architectural features suggest a date soon after 1140; a sumptuous chapel was added soon after in the period *c*.1150-80. Although we cannot be certain it seems likely that Henry de Blois, brother of the king and a great castle builder, was responsible for some of this. Further buildings brought the accommodation up to date in the thirteenth century. The site does not seem to have been defended in the first place; there was no primary curtain wall but only a minor ditch defining the inner court. This reveals the self confidence so characteristic of Norman manorial lords, whether lay or ecclesiastical, in the third generation after the Conquest. Within this inner court sits the 'solar tower'. Although ostensibly keep-like, the comparative slightness of the wall thickness (2.5-3m) unsupported by clasping pilasters, the penetration of the ground floor by four heavily splayed windows, and ready access through a doorway at ground level from the adjoining wing, all suggest that defence was secondary in the minds of the builders. It was, on the other hand, a building of power, reflecting the high status of its lords. Sited next to the church on a slight prominence above a crossing of the river Windrush, the tower was multi-storey, doubtless with chambers, wardrobes, garderobes and, likely, a chapel. Excavation showed that it was primary, together with the adjoining wing, which contained a narrow hall. It acquired a fine chamber at first floor with a pillared stone vault supported on a masonry block inserted at ground level. All this was built of limestone rubble with plentiful use of ashlar masonry quarried at Taynton 10 miles to the west. The walls were rendered externally and internally. Elaborate garderobes, perhaps two chutes per

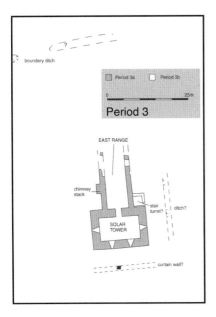

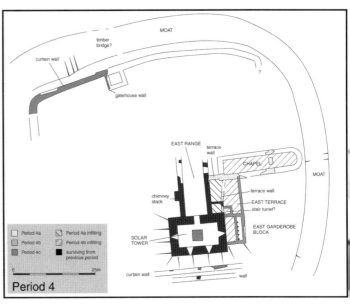

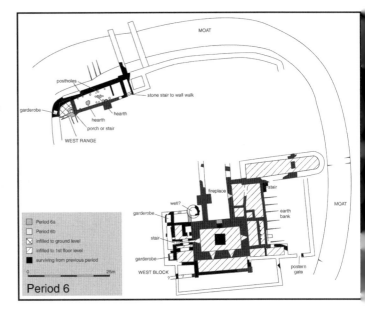

23 *(this page and opposite)*
Witney, Mount House,
Oxfordshire. Phased plans
from twelfth-thirteenth
centuries of excavations of
Bishop's 'palace'. Courtesy of
Allen T. *et al.* 2001, Oxford
Archaeological Unit

storey, with four arched culverts leading to the moat, were added onto the east side. They would have been flushed by pouring water from ceramic pots from above. Some of the pots were dropped in the process! Whereas a small chapel may have been incorporated in the tower from the start a larger two-storey one, decorated with a chamfered plinth and external pilasters with roll mouldings, was added a little later, probably during the episcopacy of that ambitious prelate-builder, Bishop Henry de Blois. This was linked to the bishop's quarters within

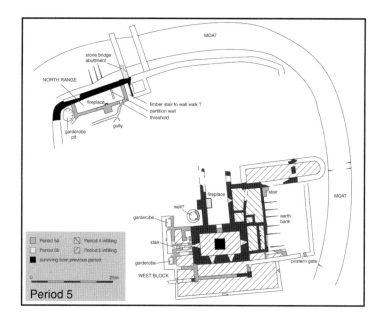

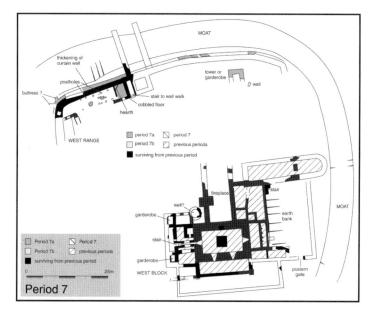

the tower by a terraced walkway. Here the bishop and his social equals prayed; the servants performed their devotions below. The tower, early on in its life, was adapted by filling in the ground floor (the fill incorporates coins of King Stephen thought by the report writer to have come from neighbouring middens) and then building up terraced terraces on the east and south sides. This blocked the windows. Tempting though it is to associate this with making the tower more defensive, it is now interpreted as 'a conscious integration of the structure and the landscape', a characteristic noticed in other high-status buildings of the period. Biddle has recognised it at Wolvesey, Winchester. Similar terraces are known at the bishop's palace of Beauvais, and in the comital palace of Henry de Blois' family at Troyes (Biddle, 1986, 30). Less is known of the adjoining wing to the north, which, judging from other contemporary examples, is likely to have held a narrow hall. An external chimney base indicates that it was two-storey. There was a simple gatehouse, but no curtain wall in the first phase.

Effort was expended in making Witney Bishop's 'Palace' apparently more formidable in the thirteenth century: by then the planned town was coming into existence to the north and maybe the bishops needed to make an architectural/political statement to impress the burgesses whom they were attracting into their new town. A rock-hewn ditch was dug on the north side of the inner court with a one-arched gatehouse. A long, two-storey residential building heated by a ground floor lateral fireplace with a grand chimney hood was added on to the curtain wall which was now built round the inner court. It was probably occupied by the bailiff — who would be increasingly left in charge of the manor in the long periods when the bishop and his retinue were elsewhere. Why was this impressive manor house built at Witney at all? It was convenient for the bishop to reside in when the king and his court were only eight miles away at Woodstock. King John came to stay, attracted, no doubt, by the good hunting available in the bishop's park and Wychwood Forest. Otherwise it was not on the regular itinerary of the bishops. The lack of high status finds emphasised that it was little used by the episcopal court. Its main function was to act as a centre from which the bailiff ran the estates for the bishop in this far-flung corner of his domains. We know from the Pipe Rolls of the bishops of Winchester that there were other agrarian buildings, dovecote, barns and yards. These have not been found. One suspects they are to the east between Mount House (as it is now called) and the river Windrush (Allen *et al.*, forthcoming).

An episcopal town house
Bishops of Winchester, as indeed the other members of the episcopacy, were national figures. They needed to have ready access to their patron, their employer and their lord, the king. Their presence was required increasingly at meetings of parliaments held in Westminster. To carry out their responsibilities effectively they needed a town house, a foothold in the capital. Henry of Blois, perhaps the most powerful bishop of Winchester in the twelfth century, put it well. He describes:

> the many inconveniences and losses [that] I and my predecessors have sustained through the lack of a house of our own to use when called to London on royal or other business . . . and therefore, moved by such concerns, I . . . have purchased the house and land that were of Orgar the Rich, and many other lands lying around them, of the soke of the church and monks of Bermondsey. (Quoted by Carlin, 1985, 34.)

Winchester House, the palace of the Bishops of Winchester, was on the Southwark side of the river Thames, between Bank End on the west and St Mary Overy's ditch on the east. Its convenience for water transport is significant. As well as functioning as a town house, it was a prestigious setting for royal guests, an administrative centre and an entrepôt for the bishop's estates and it housed a prison, the so-called Clink. Henry of Blois was not alone in seeing the advantages of a London-based home. By 1300 46 bishops and abbots had invested in London inns (as these aristocratic town houses were called) either in London or its extra mural suburbs of Westminster and Southwark (Barron, 1995, 4).

Much is now known about the Southwark house from excavation; much can be reconstructed from plentiful documents, particularly the annual financial accounts known as the Bishopric of Winchester Pipe Rolls to be found in the Hampshire Record Office.

It seems that the twelfth-century house was on the north-eastern corner of the 40-acre site near the river but the buildings were on a different alignment to their replacements in the thirteenth century. The excavator considered that they remained in use as the new hall arose in the early thirteenth century a little to the north. The chapel, on a skewed alignment, may have continued in use (a suggestion made by Yule, 1989, 39).

The new, huge stone hall, in existence by 1220-1, was one of the largest secular buildings in medieval London. Considerable remains can still be seen, although it is now dwarfed by warehouses and insurance offices. Its walls were $3\frac{1}{2}$ ft (1.1m) thick, internal breadth 28ft 7in (8.7m), internal length 134ft (40.9m). These walls were massive enough to support the first-floor level hall on a vaulted cellar, probably used for the storage of wine. Entrance was by an external porch on the south western corner. At the east end the bishop had a chamber, partitioned off for privacy. This became known as the Great Chamber when a further, and more exclusive *camera privata* was built on a north-south alignment by Bishop William Edington in 1356/7. This suite of rooms, reconstructed from the documents and pictured by Hollar, was in a two-storey block, connected by a passage to the old chapel, and supplied with a new oratory; below was a parlour, a latrine and the bishop's study. Above was the chamber with glazed windows and a fireplace. Entrance and exit was by means of the bishop's postern next to his chambers, a stone's throw from the dock, the chamber block overlooked a privy garden (Carlin, 1985, 41).

If we go back to the hall for a moment; it was serviced from the west end by a ground-floor kitchen in series originally detached (for fire protection) and linked by a staircase (as at Bishop William of Wykeham's foundation of New College, Oxford). Three great buttresses formerly supported the west wall. These were necessary to strengthen it because three extant doorways were cut in it leading to the buttery, pantry and kitchen (a classic feature found in dozens of élite houses in medieval England). Above, a 'rose' or wheel window was pierced in the western gable sometime in the fourteenth century. Although made of soft clunch it is still there, a remarkable survival of this luxurious mansion. The buttressed gable end of the hall was enveloped in building when the kitchen was joined to the hall sometime between 1540 and 1640.

The London house of the bishops of Winchester is interesting in the light it sheds on other aspects of the aristocratic episcopal way of life. The excavators found traces of long north-south ranges in the inner courtyard which were occupied by the knights, clerks (on the side nearer to the bishop's own accommodation) and by the valets and squires (on the side nearer to the service end of the hall). The congery of buildings was arranged round two courtyards. The outer was entered through a prestigious gateway, rebuilt in 1319/20 in timber, stone and marble. A stairway led to two solars over the gate. Around the courtyard was stabling for the very considerable numbers of horses required by such a magnificent household. Following the death of bishop John de Sandale in 1319 the normal stable complement of 50-60 horses was increased to 102 horses on the day of his death and to 157 on the day of his funeral (Carlin, 1985, 46). We have mentions of the 'long' or 'great' stable, the stable of the bishop's pal-

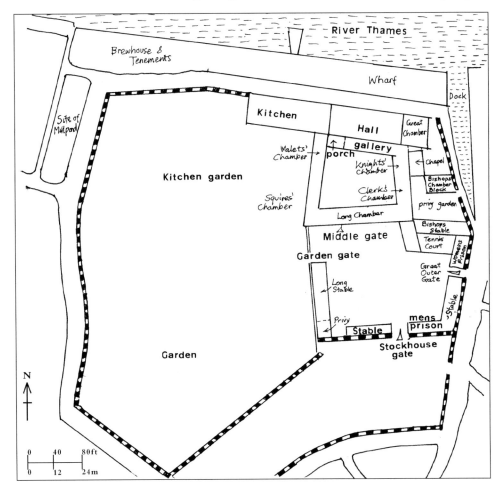

24 *Southwark, London, Winchester Palace.* Left-hand plan after Carlin; opposite plan after Rule 1989

freys, the stable for the draught animals, the stable of the clerks and squires of
the manor and the *hakeney* stable. Horses in fact were valuable. They could not
be left tethered to posts. They needed special arrangements, akin to our modern
requirements for car parking.

This reminds us that Winchester House was not just an impressive town
house; it was the economic base from which much material produce was stored
and distributed to satisfy the hungry food requirements of nearby London. Barns
and cellars provided the necessary storage space. During the later Middle Ages,
however, this aspect of the bishop's business declined. Winchester House changed
from being a manorial centre to being solely a high-ranking residence.

Surrounding the outer courtyard were other indications of episcopal power
— prisons to punish the transgressors of canon and common law, in particular

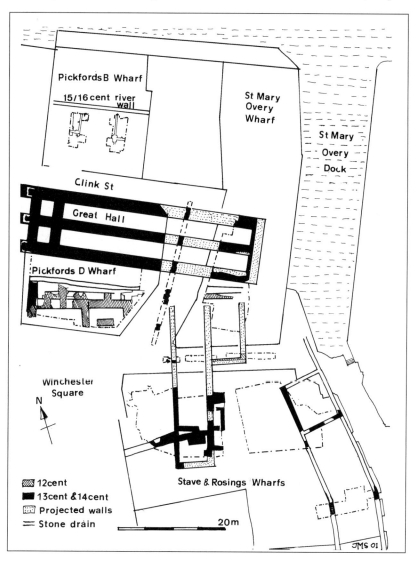

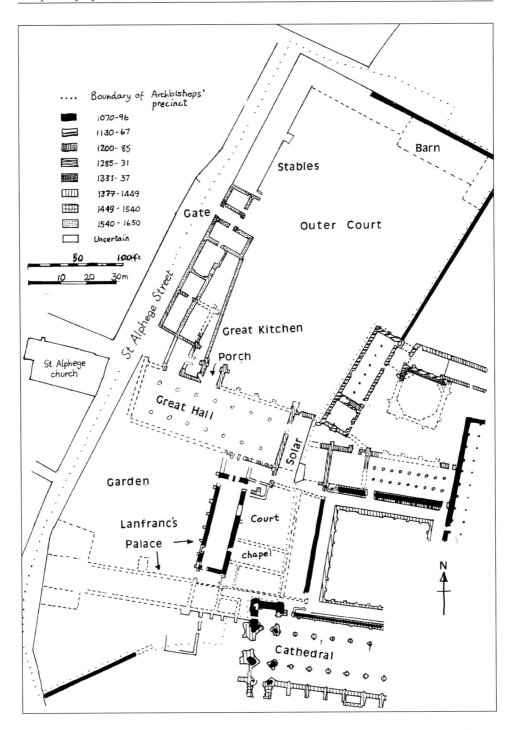

25   *Canterbury, Kent. Plan of Palace of Archbishops of Canterbury.* After Bowen in Tatton Brown 1991

clerks, falling foul of the bishop's jurisdiction. There were separate buildings to house male and female prisoners. The pipe rolls mention frequent repairs and replacements to the wooden buildings; fetters, iron bars, inadequate sanitary arrangements all speak of foul conditions of incarceration. It seems that later in the Middle Ages, clerks from the London side of the diocese were tried at Southwark, and, if convicted, were transported to serve their sentences in the episcopal prisons at Farnham, and at Wolvesey (Winchester). The notorious Clink Prison (the word entered the English language as a slang term for a gaol) amalgamated these three types of prisoners: laymen, women and clerks were from the fifteenth century housed hugger mugger. Things in fact got worse than in the Middle Ages.

A more pleasantly scented part of the palace complex was the gardens. These were approached through the west wall of the outer yard. A gate led into the kitchen and the pleasure gardens. The northern or kitchen garden was conveniently next to the kitchen and offices (salsary, bakehouse, brewhouse, coal house, woodyard, butchery, poultry house). It grew, in the thirteenth century, saffron, garlic, hemp, grapes; in the fourteenth leeks, beans, pears and apples are mentioned. A gardener was paid in 1210/12 the very substantial sum of 45s a year for his livery and 5s for his stipend. The pleasure gardens included a great deal of grass, five lawns are mentioned. A tiled latrine and a summer house were horticultural amenities provided respectively in 1356/7 and 1415/16.

The archbishop's palace at Canterbury

The third example is taken from Canterbury, the seat of the archbishops of the southern province since the Roman mission of St Augustine in 597. There had been an Anglo-Saxon monastery here and when Stigand, the last old English archbishop was deposed, the monk Lanfranc, abbot of Bec was appointed in his place. Lanfranc, perhaps the greatest reforming archbishop in the whole history of the church in England, decided to divide both the monastic buildings and all the monastic landed endowment between the monks and the archbishop. He caused a wall to be built between the reconstructed Norman cathedral with its main monastic adjuncts to the north and the site of the new archbishop's palace. Two ranges of buildings were put up, immediately north-west of the north-west tower of the cathedral. The core of the range, that running north-south, has been found in archaeological work; attached to it and forming a T-shaped plan was another range, running east-west. This has now disappeared but is known from the Commonwealth Survey. In plan Lanfranc's palace was similar to the earliest version of Wolvesey Palace, Winchester, and is comparable to the so-called *palatium tau* plans found on the continent (Tatton Brown, 1991, 5). So far Canterbury palace is of interest in that it illustrates the ambition of the Norman episcopate. The ranges are considerable in scale, east-west 46-61m (150-200ft) long and 10.75m wide (35ft) while the north-south is *c*.34m long (110ft) and *c*.10.75m wide (35ft). It also indicates the determination of the archbishop to keep his entourage separate from the community of the monks in Christchurch. A third feature is that there was no intention to make the precinct defensive. Archbishops, as yet, had no fear of urban mobs, the knight-killers of Thomas à Becket had little difficulty in forcing an entry.

The next important stage in the development of the archbishop's palace was taken 30 years after Becket's murder. This was the building of a new hall. Its start date is attributed to Hubert Walter, archbishop from 1193 to 1205. The construction of this enormous hall (it was, according to the Parliamentary survey of 1647, 168ft long, 64ft wide and 40ft high) requires some explanation. It was, after all, second only in size in the kingdom to Westminster Hall. The clue is to be found in the position occupied by the medieval archbishop of Canterbury. Election to the metropolitan made him one of the wealthiest landowners in England; his demesnes, mostly of fertile arable land, much of it in east Kent, brought in an annual income of £1345 in 1200 rising to £3178 by the Reformation. His household or '*familia*' moved round with him. By archbishop Winchelsey's time it consisted of three grades 'knightly figures' and 'literate laymen' who served as steward, 'our special valet', cook and marshal, tailor, usher, almoner, barber, scullion, janitor, pantler, baker and other, unnamed 'men of office' (Carpenter, 1988, 78). The archbishop was, in addition, a military figure, with castles to keep and garrison; he ruled over lands vulnerable to French attack. He was, of course, a spiritual leader, liaising with the Pope and his legates but also leading his suffragan bishops and at times resisting both royal and papal pressures to control the church through patronage to high office. Loyalty, however, was demanded by the king who had appointed him and we find archbishops frequently acting as the power broker between king and barons, between crown, bishops and papacy. The archbishop's position was, to say the least, ambiguous. All this meant that he mingled with the royal family and highest nobility on equal terms. He needed to dispense hospitality on a grand scale in great halls.

Hence Hubert Walter, who spent most of the 12 years of his archbishopric immersed in secular affairs, initiated important building projects in his London palace at Lambeth and at Canterbury. He was justiciar in Richard I's reign, and chancellor from 1199-1205, the year of his death. His successor, Stephen Langton, was a papal nominee, imposed by the imperious Innocent III on the England of King John. He spent the years of the Interdict in exile and emerged in 1213 as a statesman, a baronial leader and a shaper of Magna Carta. Hubert and Stephen together built the great hall at Canterbury whose completion was speeded up to coincide with the celebrations of the translation of the body of St Thomas to the newly added Trinity Chapel.

Its architecture has been brilliantly reconstructed from early engravings and watercolours, exiguous building fragments and the Parliamentary Survey already alluded to (Rady, Tatton-Brown and Bowen, 1991). A mighty porch seen in an eighteenth-century print had survived, showing that the 'important' side of the hall was on the north. Visitors approached through a gate in the present St Alphege Street. It was well lit; the fenestration could be reconstructed from the two and a half bays in the south wall showing the internal arrangements. Moreover on the north side of the Great Hall in the bay to the west of the porch is a fine lofty window with double pairs of lancets and quatrefoil plate tracery. This is similar in design but even larger than the windows in the contemporary royal hall at Winchester Castle. Further the two arcades were supported by clustered columns of Purbeck marble, an expensive material also used for the central mullions, transoms, internal nook shafts and seats. A stone dais provided a raised platform for the seats of the great and the good at the east end. Such a building was clearly designed to rival, if not to outface the king's hall at Winchester. The hall was levelled with the fall of Charles I. Its materials were built into the fabric of early modern Canterbury: some, like the marble columns ended up stacked 'like billets on a wood-stack' as a garden rockery (Rady, Tatton-Brown and Bowen, 1991, 24-6).

The question arises: Why was the power centre of the archbishops of the southern province of England sited at Canterbury in the first place? Canterbury was not a vigorous community of Romano-Britons by the end of the sixth century, it was not even a recognisable Roman town. The Roman provincial administration had collapsed irretrievably (Brooks, 1995, 1-2). It pre-eminence in the history of the English Church arose out of an historical anomaly. Pope Gregory, when planning the conversion of the pagan English sent Augustine to Kent. He was supposed to move on to London, the former capital of the Roman province. He never did. He was greeted hospitably by Ethelbert who was married to a Christian Frankish princess, Bertha, and the missionaries began their work in Kent, the nearest port to the Frankish dominions and most prone to continental influence. Ethelbert's overlordship of the other petty kings of Anglo-Saxon England was another attraction to the Roman monks. Unfortunately it was short-lived. For a time the conversion faltered. Canterbury, from being a temporary centre for proselytising endeavour hardened into the ecclesiastical centre of the renewed religion. Rome had provided the model and the personnel; it could not provide the administrative framework within which Augustine and his monks worked because this had long gone.

Palace of the archbishops of Narbonne

It was otherwise in continental Europe. In the south of France the Roman presence was much more deep seated and long lived than in Britain. Many towns in the Midi preserved traces of their Roman municipal administration into the early Middle Ages. In Arles, for instance, the thirteenth-century town hall still preserves the stone bench from which the consuls of the 'republic' of Arles dispensed justice (see **64-5**). In Narbonne, similarly the twelfth-century councillors took the titles of '*nobiles viri*' or '*probi homines*', and they subsequently adopted the name of the consuls. The archbishops also took advantage of the prestige emanating from '*Romanitas*'. They chose as a site for their cathedral the Roman forum: the towered wall of the Roman city partly encircled their palace in Narbonne. In 1096 the archbishop Dalmatius claimed the title of primate of all the Gauls. In 1212 the

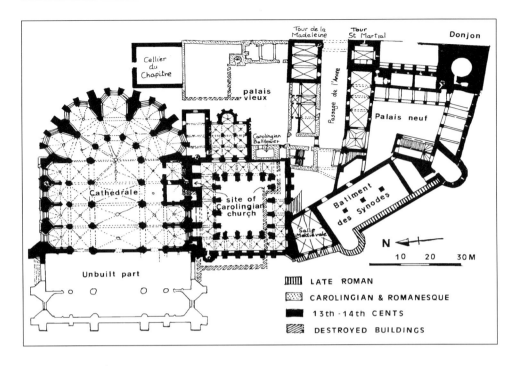

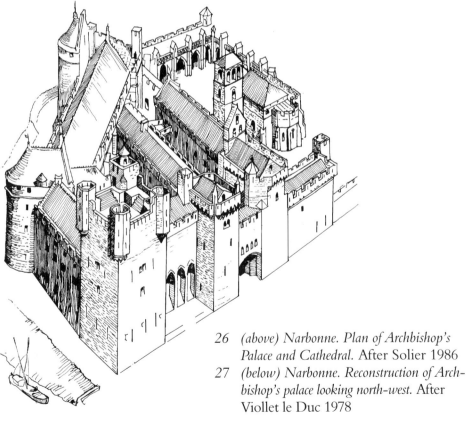

26 (above) Narbonne. Plan of Archbishop's
   Palace and Cathedral. After Solier 1986
27 (below) Narbonne. Reconstruction of Archbishop's palace looking north-west. After
   Viollet le Duc 1978

archbishop and papal legate Armand Amalric declared himself Duke. They felt themselves the successors of Rome; they also had high aspirations of their own. Their palace in Narbonne reflected these ambitions in its complex ensemble of civil, religious and military architecture.

The most noteworthy element is a great square tower, 40m high, not far from a Carolingian tower built grandiosely of great blocks. This tower of the archbishops dominates its part of the city and faced down the tower of the vicomtes (the archbishops' main political rivals) across the market place. It is only a matter of 10m away from a navigable river with its adjoining quays and bridge crossing. It was built by Gilles Ascelin in 1290 (Solier 1986, 125). The circular room at ground level served as a prison and was connected by a trap door to the vaulted room above. This was octagonal in shape and was probably the archive room of the archbishop. Above were guard rooms and a path round the crenellated battlements which were flanked in the angles by a watch tower and three octagonal bartizans.

One penetrates into the palace by a fortified alleyway — known as the passage of the anchor. This refers to the anchor suspended at the entrance which symbolised the economic rights of the archbishop in the past. It divides the two groups of medieval buildings, to the right the old palace and to the left the new.

Each group is organised round a courtyard. The old palace is overlooked by the bell tower of the Carolingian cathedral, already mentioned, and by two residential ranges set square. These are two-storey buildings with five carved doorways and windows dating from the eleventh and twelfth centuries. At the junction of the two wings is the gothic donjon of the Madeleine, the work of Pierre de Montbrun which contains the first-floor private chapel of the archbishops dedicated to St Mary Magdalen. It is richly decorated with frescoes and is accessed by an external staircase.

Entrance into the new palace is through a porch with a grand chamber on the left communicating with the ground floor of the tower of St Martial. The buildings round this courtyard were begun in 1290 while the construction of the gothic cathedral was in full swing. The tower, as we have seen, was in the first stage of the building. This was followed by other campaigns between 1346 and 1375 led by the Cardinal de la Sugie which created luxurious surroundings befitting the office of the archbishop. This resulted in the synodal building and its annexe known as 'the medieval room' (*Salle médiéval*). The latter is roofed by four original vaults springing from a central pillar. The synodal building includes two vast rooms, one on the ground floor opening onto the interior court; on the first floor, accessed by a magnificent balustraded staircase built in 1628, is the room of the Synod which hosted many sessions of the estates of Languedoc. It was lit by high windows under a gallery providing a fighting platform: it was heated by a huge chimney of which traces are visible outside.

It is clear that several features of the archbishop's palace at Narbonne are found in other episcopal palaces elsewhere; the emphasis on defence is closely paralleled at Avignon; the provision of two great halls; a first floor chapel is seen at Avignon and at Reims. Another feature common to a number is the cloister at Narbonne connecting the northern of the two courts to the cathedral; on the roof of the cloister is a terrace from which one can view this congery of buildings providing a picturesque silhouette surmounted in one corner by the great donjon and on the other by the colossal bulk of the cathedral.

The Palace of the Popes at Avignon

Petrarch was expressing an extreme view when he described the Avignon of the Popes in the fourteenth century:

> Unholy Babylon, thou Hell on earth, thou sink of iniquity, thou cess-pool of the world. There is neither faith, nor charity, nor religion, nor fear of God, no shame, no truth, no holiness, albeit the residence within its walls of the supreme pontiff should have made of it a shrine and the very stronghold of religion . . . of all cities that I know its stench is the worst . . . what dishonour to see it suddenly become the capital of the world, when it should be but the least of all cities.

The decision on the part of the Papacy to move the centre of their operations to Avignon from Rome at the beginning of the fourteenth century is not so extraordinary in the light of the political circumstances. Between 1198-1305 Popes had spent less than 40 years in Rome; the struggles between Guelphs and Ghibellines in Italy and Germany meant that Rome was frequently too hot to hold them. Occasionally popes had requested help from the kings of France who liked to pose as 'the most Christian kings'. They had an interest in the territories of South France, and owned the lands of the Comtat de Venaissin. Avignon was in fact a more centrally sited place than Rome from which to run the Catholic church in the west. Despite what might have been thought the Avignonese popes were not creatures of the French kings. In the main they were men of Provence, more akin to Spanish and Italian cultures and remained aloof from the French court.

The Palace of the Popes at Avignon was exceptional in a number of ways. It performed three main functions: it was the palace of a temporal sovereign whose resources enabled him to build impressively; it was the seat of the leader of Christianity, a bureaucratic centre from which the Pope ruled the universal church; it was a powerful fortress built to resist force which might well be applied in an attempt to topple the papacy in these unstable times.

This remarkable building was the product of a programme which was rapidly put into execution by a succession of energetic and ambitious builder Popes. John XXII (1316-34) installed the Papacy in the episcopal palace of the town where formerly he had been bishop. He reserved the Dominican convent and the episcopal chateau to which he added the sites of several neighbouring buildings. For 18 years he enlarged, embellished and fortified the site. Most of the old palace disappeared. The new palace centred round two courtyards, one enclosed and one open on a north-south axis. The enclosed one was trapezi-um-shaped, determined by the steep rocky site. The court was enclosed by a two-level galleried cloister, one indication that Avignon was strongly influenced by monastic predecessors (**28-9**).

Benedict XII (1334-42), a simple Cistercian monk of austere tastes, carried on the building with the help of his architects, Pierre Poisson from Mirepois, and Jean de Louvres. Together they constructed a palace 'of marvellous beauty and extraordinary power, with its walls and towers'. Four wings surrounded the cloister, each with two or three stories. At the corners were towers of four or five levels (**colour plae 3**). Work began with the *Tour de Pape* — now known as the *Tour des Anges*. Each floor fulfilled a different function. At the bottom was a dungeon; then the Treasury room; halfway up was the Pope's room. His chamber was a room 33ft square with a polished floor, timber ceiling and large windows facing east and south across an enclosed and terraced garden. It was heated by an enormous fireplace. Above this was the chamberlain's room. He was the head of the papal curia; at the top was a library. With walls 3m thick the seat of Papal power was strongly fortified.

Around this tower private apartments were constructed allowing the Pope access to other parts of the palace and aiming to siphon off visitors of various grades. In 1336 two large antechambers were added above the Treasury. The Pope's private dining room (known as *Le Petit Tinel*), a kitchen, a secret chapel and a wardrobe were all added to the north side of the papal chamber. On the south, overlooking the garden a small tower providing a study was added. In 1337 the old reception rooms of the former palace were demolished and replaced by a large new room the *Aula Nova*, known today as the *Salle du Conclave*. At right angles to this and lining the north-south range of the cloister was another wing, 50m long housing the public consistory on the ground floor and the *Grand Tinel* (banquet hall) on the first floor.

The Popes at Avignon certainly spared no expense on entertainment as we can see from the accounts of food served on 22 November 1324 at the dinner given by John XXII to celebrate the marriage of his great niece, Jeanne de Trian, with the young Guichard de Poitiers. On this occasion they ate 4012 loaves of bread, 8 3/4 oxen, 55 1/4 sheep, 8 pigs, 4 boars, a large selection of different kinds of fish, 200 capons, 690 chickens, 580 partridges, 270 rabbits, 40 plovers, 37 ducks, 50 pigeons, 4 cranes, 2 pheasants, 2 peacocks, 292 small birds, 3cwt 2lb of cheese, 3000 eggs, 2000 apples, pears and other fruits and they drank 11 barrels of wine. If the food was on a gargantuan scale, the plate was princely; it included trays, drinking vessels, goblets with lids, ewers, sauce-boats, bowls, jugs for wine and water, basins, silver gilt flagons, knives and forks with handles of ivory or jasper. The plate of Clement I weighed 700 marks or about 159kg: that of Clement II in about 1348 about 862 marks or nearly 196kg (Mollat, 1963, 310-11).

The *aile de familiers* where the Papal relations lived was added on the west side of the cloister. To the north-east was a great chapel and at the end of this was the Tower of Trouillas and the tower of latrines. The cloister was reconstructed with a double row of arcades and a wide stone stairway provided an official entrance to the Grande Chapelle. A finishing touch was given by a crenellated rampart including a fortified door, the *Porte Majeure*, added in 1341.

The architecture of the palace was severe with a minimum amount of decoration. The rooms as seen today, stripped of their finery, are plain and forbidding. Even in their heyday they showed 'a mixture of sumptuousness and simplicity' (Mollat 1963, 310). The floors, stone paved, were covered with matting made of straw and rushes. Glass was rather sparingly used, except for the chapel and the consistory, windows were covered with waxed linen. The main public rooms were covered with carpets, the simple furniture was hidden under rich materials. There was much fresco painting and where the walls were not covered with paintings they were hung with tapestries from Spain or Flanders or with hangings of silk, taffeta, or green or red serge. The floors on the ground floor were covered with glazed terracotta tiles.

The palace was more or less doubled in size following the accession of Pope Clement VI (1342-52), a great patron of the arts, free with his money and refined in his tastes. He decided to wall round the outer court of the old palace with new buildings. A jumble of decrepit structures was cleared away. In their place was a magnificent six bay double-aisled and vaulted *Salle D'Audience*. On

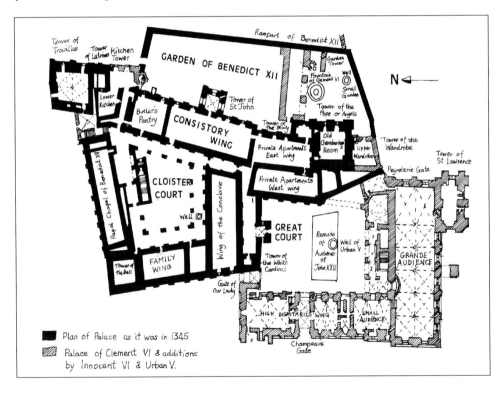

28 Avignon, France. Ground plan of the Palace of the Popes at the end of the pontificate of Urban V 1370. The black lines indicate the structure as it existed in 1345. After Contamine 1988

top of this was a great chapel designed by Jean de Louvre with a grand staircase leading up to it. The Papal civil servants were housed in another wing at right angles to the *Salle D'Audience* known as the New Treasury Building or the *Aile des Grand Dignitaires*.

The Papal chambers themselves were enriched with painting and added to. The walls of the Pope's room were painted with vine and oak foliage with large gilded volutes in them in which animals and birds sit. Near the windows are painted bird cages. The *Chambre du Cerf* was added as the study of Clement VI on the south side of the Pope's room. The paintings, probably though not certainly by Matteo Giovanetti, are virtually intact; their subject matter is entirely secular and they are set in an imaginary dark forest, within which are scenes of hunting, hawking and fishing. Among these an aristocratic falconer is about to fly his hawk, his hounds snuffle at his feet. There is a bathing scene and a ferret pursuing and rabbit watched by a richly-dressed hunter. A perspective rendered fishpond attracts the attention of a fisherman armed with a bow and arrow. In other scenes there are boys bird-nesting and a man luring game (Barber 1986, 55-6).

Clement VI was accustomed to the latest developments in French gothic architecture owing to his long experience as bishop at Arras, Sens and Rouen. He there-

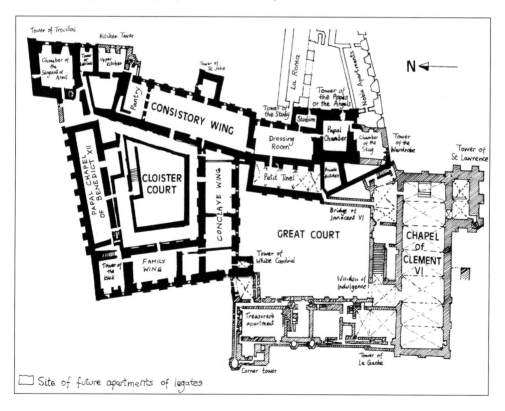

29 *Avignon, France. Plan of first floor at the end of the pontificate of Urban V, 1370.*
After Contamine 1988

fore encouraged the use of groined vaults everywhere: spiral staircases connected the rooms and led up to the roofs. Sculpture and paintings were lavishly used to decorate the palace. Less emphasis was placed on grim fortification. Two elegant turrets that overhung the Porte Champeaux give the impression of being more decorative than defensive. The *Cour d'Honneur* is pierced by many windows, uninterrupted by buttresses, in particular by the so-called window of Indulgence from which the Pope could address the assembled crowds below (Blanc 1992, 42).

The layout of the papal palace at Avignon during Clement VI's time has recently been subjected to a space analysis centring on how the building was meant to be used, how it fulfilled the needs of reception, representation and control. These, Crossley has pointed out, were manipulated 'through a complex series of spaces, ranging from public ostentation to private withdrawal'. He envisages the visitor entering at the main, Champeaux gate, turning sharp right across the Great Court (*Platea Platii*) and so *via* the high vaulted porch into the hall of the *Grande Audience*. The specially privileged would then ascend the staircase to the landing on the first floor. Here the Pope was accustomed to stand at the Indulgence window looking out on the crowds in the courtyard beneath. Turning round the visitor would have entered the ostentatious portal of the papal chapel and via a small entrance into a guardroom. This covered the upper part of the stair and led into the Pope's private apartments (Crossley, 2000, 155).

Ecclesiastical palaces in Norway at Trondheim and Oslo

The Scandinavian countries of Denmark, Norway and Sweden, on the northern periphery of the German Empire, were engaged in the difficult process of state formation in the tenth century. Ambitious Norwegian warrior-kings like Olaf Tryggvason (995-1000) and Olaf Haraldson (1015-30) adopted Christianity themselves, and imposed it, at times brutally, on their subjects. Their role, as leaders in these barbaric northern regions, was of greater importance than that of the foreign missionaries from England and Hamburg/Bremen in persuading their peoples to adopt Christianity. Whereas they were softened up by gifts and flattering messages from the leaders of the Christianised south, the truth of it was they realised that these religious commitments could lend coherence and a sense of unity to their peoples dispersed over hundreds of miles of fjord, valley and mountain. Kings worked hand in glove with bishops in the first few generations of the conversion of Norway. The church by canonising these early Norwegian rulers added the cult of saints, a further buttress to their powers. In return the prelates were richly endowed with land and were soon able to afford to replace their primitive timber churches with stone ones. Such buildings, uprearing with their white limestone and red brick walls and roofs had tremendous significance in a largely wooded and untamed landscape, among a non-literate people and a kingdom 'depending on the deployment of oral, visual and cultic media' (Nelson in Reuter, 1999, 97). This co-operation between king and bishops soon foundered. The twelfth century in Norway, as elsewhere in Europe (the Investiture Contest between the Papacy and the Empire) saw tension grow between the two. Archbishops took on the role of leaders of the opposition.

Recent excavations in Trondheim and Oslo have produced material evidence for the power struggle between royal and ecclesiastical establishments. Trondheim, on the west side of the deeply indented Norwegian coast, was linked by difficult but possible overland routes to Sweden and Russia, south to Oslo and by North Sea routes to Britain and Ireland. Geographical reasons apart, the key reason for establishing the main residence and centre of the archbishop here was that it was the cult centre of St Olav, the canonised king, Olav Haraldson. St Olav's shrine was the pilgrimage focus of the cathedral church. The archbishop's palace was placed on the highest point of the Nidaros peninsula (Nidaros, the old name for Trondheim), a dominating position signifying his authority. Wooden buildings were erected to the south of the cathedral, dated by dendrochronology to the 1160s. These were rapidly replaced by stone buildings including a kitchen, the archbishop's residence and a stone hall, all along the north front of the enclosed courtyard. Much of this late twelfth-century range still remains but the chapel at the north-east corner has gone (Nordeide, 1997, 209-13). By the end of the thirteenth century further ranges of stone buildings appeared along the inside of the precinct wall. Such a complex could be compared to the contemporary palace buildings of the bishops of Lincoln on the southern slope below the cathedral. It is thought that English masons were employed in the design and construction of Trondheim cathedral, whose west front, *c*.1180-1200, in particular shows stylistic affinities to Lincoln (Zarnecki, 1988, 99).

A dramatic revolution took place in the organisation of space in the archbishop's palace *c*.1450-1500. It reflected the changing role of the archbishop in the kingdom. Norway by then had become part of the 'Kalmar union' together with Denmark and Sweden and had no king of its own. It was administered by a Council of State of which the archbishop was the chairman. He was now, in addition to his priestly powers, a secular ruler, collecting taxes, responsible for the administration of the law and his position resembled that of the Prince Bishops of Germany and the Low Countries (also of the Prince Bishops of Durham, England). Further he took on military roles. This is seen in two developments. One, discovered by the excavations during the 1960s on the eastern side of the Trondheim palace, shows that by 1500 it had become a centre for the manufacture of coin, armour, weapons and shoes, all essential for the equipping of mercenary troops. Like Julius II, his papal contemporary in central Italy, the archbishop of Trondheim had become a war lord. He had erected timber structures which housed mints for coining, foundries and workshops among the palace buildings. In addition the numerous lead bale seals found show that the archbishop was importing large quantities of textiles with which to supply (and probably pay) his soldiers.

The last archbishop before the Lutheran Reformation, Olav Engelbrektsson, took this military role still more seriously, in 1525 when he was appointed and sought his pallium (the papal authorisation and approval of his election) in Rome. He evidently discussed military technology and the application of artillery with papal advisers on the *curia* (Leonardo Da Vinci had advised the pope on these matters 10-20 years before). He came back to Norway and at once built a new castle at Steinvikholmen on an island in the fjord some miles north of Trondheim. This still stands by the sea, a Renaissance castle, its towers adapted for cannon; protecting the roadstead. The archbishop was now an international figure with shipping interests, financing this expensive maritime palace/fortress with taxation from butter, fish and furs.

In the second half of the eleventh century another focus of royal and ecclesiastical power developed in the south-western part of Norway. Oslo was a naval base founded by Harold Haardrade who came to the throne in 1046. He needed this to counter the threatening attitude of the Danes. Oslo's position on a promontory at the northern end of a deep, narrow fjord was bounded by the sea shore on one side and by a river bank on the other. The king's palace was sited at the end of the promontory, side by side with St Mary's Church (the earliest cathedral in East Norway by a century). The proximity of palace and church symbolised the same close alliance between church and state in the primary missionary phase, we have noticed at Trondheim. Once established, relations deteriorated in the twelfth century as Norway was sucked into the vortex of civil war. The king abandoned the promontory and moved across the fjord constructing a castle on a cliff-top. The bishop moved his headquarters and his cathedral 400m to the north-east constructing a Romanesque cathedral dedicated to a local saint, the blessed Hallvard, and linked to a fortified courtyard palace by a bridge. Considerable remains of all these buildings can be seen as foundations or walls but the promontory and the site of the medieval town has been badly cut up by modern railways, roads and blocks of flats. In its heyday, the thirteenth century, the tall towers and steeples of the medieval royal palace, the cathedral, the churches and the palace of the bishops of Oslo would have been an impressive sight rising out of seething mass and the smoke of the tightly packed timber town (Christie, 1966, 45-59). Further evidence for the dual nature of political/religious power at Oslo has come from the discovery of timber caissons supporting the king's and bishop's quays built out into the waters of the fjord on the west side of the promontory.

The Palace of the Kings of Majorca at Perpignan

Overtopping the town of Perpignan in the far south of France near the Spanish border is the palace of the kings of Majorca. The first sight of it are huge brown brick walls, the remnants of the sixteenth-/seventeenth-century concentric and bastioned fortifications added when the French acquired the town. Through an archway, up a ramped entrance and several turns to the right and left to confuse a would-be attacker with firing from above on to the unprotected sword arm, one emerges into a great gardened square in front of the medieval palace. This has miraculously survived with few additions since the fourteenth century. The accretions have been busily removed by the French Department of Antiquities. It was surrounded by a rock-strewn ditch, formerly the exercise and display ground of a menagerie of lions; the goats living on pasturage surrounding Perpignan provided the meat diet for the lions. The presence of lions was an interesting parallel to those of Edward I in the moat of the Tower of London (Parnell 1993, 54). Crossing the moat is a barbican with brick crenellations. One enters the palace under the *Tour de l'Hommage*. This overlooks a huge *cour d'honneur*, the public part of the palace (Conseil General des Pyrenees Orientales, 1985).

The palace is laid out symmetrically. On either side is a great staircase leading up to an arcaded gallery, one on the Queen's side, one on the king's side. In the centre, dividing the two parts is a double-stage chapel. The upper part also served as a donjon and watch tower being easily the highest building on the site. The differentiation between the social strata was symbolised by the division between the two chapels (Mesqui 1993, 117). It was designed to protect the privacy of the princely family at its devotions (cf Sainte Chapelle Paris and St Stephens Westminster). Each chapel was magnificently vaulted with carved bosses and corbels. Both showed signs of sophisticated wall painting largely geometrical rather than historiated, possibly a sign of Moorish influence.

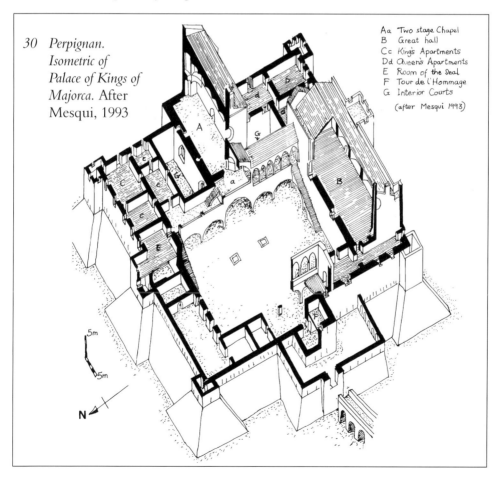

30 Perpignan. Isometric of Palace of Kings of Majorca. After Mesqui, 1993

Aa Two stage Chapel
B   Great hall
Cc Kings Apartments
Dd Queen's Apartments
E   Room of the Seal
F   Tour de l'Hommage
G   Interior Courts

(after Mesqui 1993)

5m

5m

N

The suites of rooms of the king and queen are separately organised round two small courtyards linked by the arcaded gallery. The king's rooms, which in the thirteenth century were situated in the south-west corner of the palace, were moved in the fourteenth century to the north of the chapel. They consist of a ground room, a *salle des timbres* (a chancery for sealing documents) and three rooms of different sizes, interconnecting, presumably audience and privy chambers. The Queen's rooms included a spacious and well-lit dining room with two light windows with window seats, a bedroom and a third room. There were no fireplaces so presumably heating was by brazier. The Queen's apartments were linked by a painted gallery to the great hall, *la grande salle*, occupying the whole south side of the courtyard. It had an undercroft and was well heated by three fireplaces all at the west end. Light was provided by great windows opening into the east and a small one on the other side. This contributed to security and to display on the inner side facing the *cour d'honneur* (**30**).

A remarkable feature of the Palace at Perpignan was the differential use of building materials. They varied in quality and variety to indicate the more important parts of the palace. The arch over the arcading in front of the tower of the chapel was in white marble. Inside and flanking the Romanesque portal were bands of pink and white marble. The two towers, that of the upper chapel and the tower of the *Hommages*, were in good quality limestone ashlar. The less important parts of the palace were built of bands of pebbles alternating with bands of brick.

To people this palace one has to turn to an illuminated manuscript in the Bibliothéque de Prince Albert, Bruxelles. Here are a series of brilliant scenes of life at the court of King James III of Mallorca. The king is shown with his judges, seated on a throne, preparing to feast, engaged with the *procurateur royal au timbres*, sealing documents and so on. Life in the court was conducted against a background of gardens, now swallowed up in later fortifications. There were orchards on the Queen's side where figs, olives and saffron were grown. Rabbits and peacocks were kept in the gardens. Beyond were royal forests and hunting grounds extending in a vast tract of country stretching from Rousillon to Elbe.

This chapter has attempted to cover the theme of 'Buildings of Power' in space and time. Geographically in search of material it has traversed much of northern and central Europe, from Constantinople in the east to Hungary and Poland in the centre and from Avignon to Trondheim as well as looking for examples in the countries of Western Europe, Germany, Northern France and England.

These ranged chronologically from the end of the Roman Empire, through the Middle Ages, to the Renaissance. The next chapter approaches the subject thematically, looking at the buildings of the powerful in medieval Europe, anatomising them bit by bit. It starts with looking at gates; proceeds then to halls and kitchens. There follows a discussion of lordly residences themselves then a discourse on steps and staircases and finally considers the chapel. At all stages the method used relies heavily on what the buildings (and the artefacts) tell us about their powerful patron and users.

3 The anatomy of lordly residence

Gates, gate towers, gate halls

Any visitor to the countryside when passing a farm will form an immediate impression of its comparative prosperity and the efficiency of the farmer by looking at the condition of the gates. The 'Irish' gates leading into the stony fields of the Aran islands and County Galway were simply bundles of thorns laid across the passage into the fields removable at will to allow cattle in and out. It seems likely that this technique had been used in Western Europe since at least the Iron Age and beyond. It illustrates the regulatory function of gates as important in a farm as in a walled city. There is a desire or need to control the entry and exit of people, animals and vehicles. The thorns remind one of the defensive function of gates. They were meant to provide for the security of the inmates, whether cattle, townsmen, monks, nobility or farmers. Turning from gates to gatehouses, sometimes these provided, in addition to regulation and security, accommodation for the porters or gatekeepers, whose job it was to open the gates and keep watch on entrants. A fourth function, and one particularly relevant to the theme of this book, is that they were symbolic, a statement in architectural terms of political power and will.

This last aspect provided a compelling reason for continuity in gate building in North-Western Europe from classical times into the Middle Ages and Renaissance. In the ancient east the gateway had been a symbol of heavenly authority, the entrance to the domain of the city, 'a dwelling of both godlike kings and king-like gods' (Baldwin Smith, 1956, 10). The cities of the Hellenistic and Roman East were accustomed to welcome their ruler at the gateway on his arrival (*adventus*) as a resplendent sun god. The Romans went one further by inventing the triumphal arch (**colour plates 4 & 6**), a free-standing structure, unconnected to walls, through which generals and emperors proceeded after a victorious campaign. The arch was decorated with sculptures, inscriptions and trophies. Towards the end of the Empire the two were welded together. The town or palace gateway while preserving its fortified aspects, its flanking towers, fighting galleries, gates and portcullises, was often decorated with sculptures glorifying the city or the imperial house. A number of gateways and triumphal arches were so solidly built (and respected) that they survived into the early Middle Ages. The *Porta Augusta* of Nîmes is one such, built on the instructions of Augustus in 16 BC. It has four entrances, two for pedestrians and two for animals and vehicles: it is surmounted by an inscription and by carved kneeling bulls. Above was a gallery and there were flanking towers now destroyed (Bromwich, 1993, 98). A more celebrated example is the *Porta Nigra* of Trier (**colour plate 8**), preserved during the Middle Ages because it became a church, first occupied by a holy man Simeon who made his cell in it during the eleventh century. The *Porta* was partly fortification (it had a windowless ground floor) but, more emphatically, a showpiece of Roman metropolitan might. The sheer height of the arcaded walls at first- and second-floor level were meant to impress the German barbarians whose threat to this part of the Roman Empire was imminent in the late third century (Wightman, 1970, 92-9). In Rome itself, probably visited more that any other city in the west of Europe during the Middle Ages, the antique walls, towers and gate houses were a constant visual reminder of the greatness of the past and an inspiration to would-be builders of fortifications in the future (Richmond, 1930, passim). Triumphal arches, too, those of Septimius Severus, Titus and Constantine (**colour plates 4, 6 & 7**), were saved from being used as building material because they were converted into fortresses in the turbulent twelfth century (Greenhalgh, 1989, 116-17).

Constantine's arch (**colour plate 4**) was additionally revered because it was regarded as a Christian monument, built by the first Christian emperor. It was imitated in the Torhalle at Lorsch (Conant, 1978, 54) and triumphal arches may well have influenced the design of Romanesque façades of places like St Trophime at Arles and the west front of Lincoln Cathedral (**colour plate 5**). Here at Lincoln, the yawning triple arches of the façade framing doorways into the cathedral with a band of sculptured historiated figures expanding right across the front eerily echo the design of Constantine's arch built 650 years earlier and 900 miles to the south. Similar arches, similar sculptured frieze. That the Normans in England (or their Anglo-Saxon embroiders) were inspired by antique art is most forcefully demonstrated by the similarities in design between the eleventh-century Bayeux tapestry and the frieze of sculptures on Trajan's Column. The prominence given to Duke William in the tapestry is paralleled by that of Trajan in the column. Harold takes the place of Decebalus. The wood-cutting and ship-building operations appear in both: the battle scenes with cavalry charging and infantry, their shields overlapping, resisting are strongly similar. Even the same conventions in representing trees are followed (Lepper and Frere, 1988, passim). Survival was followed by revival.

Gatehouses of power in the Middle Ages

A characteristic of the monastic churches which Charlemagne and his successors built, contributed to, patronised and resided in is the towered gatehouse or 'Westwork' (Conaut, 1978, 46). The monastic gatehouse (**54**) developed along lines quite separate from the gatehouses of castles. In early twelfth-century stone-built castles the entrance to begin with is often a simple arch in the wall, perhaps set in a projecting rectangular tower. This is strengthened in the late twelfth century by adding flanking towers: these are brought up-to-date in the thirteenth century by rendering them semi-circular with machicolations, portcullises and drawbridges.

Monastic gatehouses were often late additions to the complex, and served multiple functions; they marked the boundary between the secular and religious worlds; they acted as reception halls for visitors; from their doors alms were distributed to the poor. Above their vaulted gatehalls, there were offices and suites of rooms. The largest, such as at St Albans and Ely, housed prisons. Ely in fact has a court room. Whereas their thin walls and largely decorative arrow slits seldom offered formidable defence their towered might gave would-be rioters cause to pause. In sum they were statements of authority and influence.

This is borne out by a number of monastic gatehouses retained after the Dissolution because of their potential for profitable conversion to spacious houses. Such are those of Kirkham (Yorkshire) and Butley (Suffolk). Kirkham is enriched with a display of heraldry and figure sculpture including figures of St Philip and St Bartholomew. Between the gables are shields of arms of De Clare, England, De Roos (the founder) and Vaux. It would seem that founders, donors and supporters are being advertised. A much more dazzling display is evidenced on the gatehouse at Butley Priory, Suffolk, erected between 1320-5 during the rule of Prior William Geytone (Emery, 2000, 53). Its unusual planning with two welcoming wings, now truncated but formerly towered, lead the visitor in through two gateways. The materials, flint flushwork and fine quality ashlar from the valley of the Yonne in France (brought by sea and shipped up river to Butley to a wharf and canal), are lavish enough but the extraordinary evocation of power is provided by the heraldic display above. The use of heraldry, a secular motif, in an ecclesiastical context had already been employed on a large scale in Westminster Abbey (Steane, 1993, 172) but the front at Butley goes much further; it seems like a blazoned roll of 35 arms in stone. There is a nice sense of hierarchy with a European dimension. At the top are the arms of the main Christian powers: the Holy Roman Empire, France, England, Leon and Castile. Next, in descending order, those of the principal officers of state of England in the 1320s (De Vere, Chamberlain, Bohun, Constable and Brotherton, Marshal). Below these are the arms of the great East Anglian baronial families, and finally those of the Suffolk families, among whom there were at least five who were donors and benefactors of the house. Today prestigious fund-seeking institutions list their patrons starting with the royal family and so down the English class hierarchy. In similar ways but using visual imagery medieval monasteries, and, as we shall see, colleges, advertised and displayed their patrons and political supporters.

Collegiate gatehouses

Turning to those seats of intellectual power and learning, the colleges of Oxford and Cambridge, Pevsner commented that their towered gatehouses 'derived from the medieval castle' (Pevsner, 1970, 23). It seems to me that they owe more to their monastic predecessors just as collegiate plans and layout mirror monastic models. College gate towers are usually sited centrally or just off-centre on the

31 New College, Oxford. West gatehouse to principal quadrangle of William of Wkyeham's college. Late fourteenth century. Note Warden's lodging over entrance gate, statues of Virgin Mary with kneeling sculptured figures of the founder and an annunciate angel. Photo by author

streetward side of the principal quadrangle or court. Take New College, Oxford, as an example. Its plan was very influential though more so in Oxford than in Cambridge. Here in the late 1380s Bishop William of Wykeham laid out a quadrangle with a central gate tower. The principal entrance was on the ground floor; above it was the warden's lodging, sited strategically so he could see who went in and out. The decoration of the tower was spiritual in content and restrained in style. It was limited to a sculptured standing figure of the Virgin Mary in the centre flanked by side niches with kneeling figures of the founder and St Gabriel. Forty-five years later the gatehouse of All Souls Oxford was positioned in the centre of the first quadrangle on the High Street front. Images of the joint founders, King Henry VI and Archbishop Henry Chichele, guard the entrance to the college. Over the gateway is a sculptured Christ in Judgement looking down on all souls rising from their graves. The keynote of this somewhat unimaginative façade is honour to the founder and respect to the monarch. A less mechanistic and therefore more interesting scheme was added as the finishing touches to the

32 *All Souls' College, Oxford. Gatehouse facing onto High Street. Images of joint founders, King Henry VI on left, Archbishop Henry Chichele on right. Above Christ in Judgement with All Souls resurrecting beneath. c.1440.*
Photo by author

gate tower at Merton College. Here Warden Severy paid for its completion in 1465 and the iconographic scheme appears to have been the result of much thought by the Fellows. An image of the Trinity is orthodox enough (it was removed by Civil War zealots). Below and now immediately over the gateway is a carved stone panel full of complicated religious imagery, symbolically referring to the major events in Christ's life, as well as recalling the person of St John the Baptist. This saint was the dedicatee of the parish church, on whose site the college chapel was built. In this way the college referred to its past and to the study of theology which was one of its main *raisons d'être*. Its future aspirations were subtly referred to in the subjects of the bosses on the vault of the gatehall. As well as three Yorkist subjects there is a discreet allusion (in the form of the head of a goat) to the marriage between Edward IV and Elizabeth Woodville, which so infuriated his courtly nobility (Bott and Highfield, 1994, 233-40). When Magdalen College

33 *Merton College, Oxford. Gate tower completed by Warden Sever c.1465. Sculptured panel over gate arch with St John Baptist and theological symbols of Christ's life fitted into facade (higher up) in 1464.* Photo by author

was built in the late 1480s it was still wise for a college founder like that great survivor Bishop William of Waynflete to hedge his bets. There are statues of Edward IV, the founder, St Mary Magdalene and St John the Baptist. It seems a loyal display of Yorkist support. There are however Lancastrian roses among the Waynflete lilies. Waynflete had been chancellor to Henry VI. Until Bosworth and the marriage of Henry VII and Elizabeth of York, the future might well have gone the other way.

In general, religious imagery in gatehouse decoration diminished in the later Middle Ages although there was no suggestion as yet of an iconoclastic reaction. Power, display, emulation, in the form of heraldry is found more and more. If we look at the towered gatehouses of Cambridge colleges in chronological sequence this pattern seems to emerge. Within Trinity College is a relic of the former King's

34 Cambridge. Christ's College. Gatehouse. Photo by author

Hall, a tower known as King Edward's tower, dating from 1430. It was the first instance in Cambridge of an entrance which presented an elaborate architectural show to the street. The pomp in this case is probably connected with the fact that it was a royal foundation. The great four-storey brick tower of Queens' College followed in 1448. The bosses at the intersections of the gatehall vault are carved with St Mary and St Bernard (the college patron saints). Dignity, impressive scale, saintly intercession but as yet no serious secular takeover. Jesus College, founded *c.*1500 on the site of a nunnery by Bishop Alcock of Ely, recalls its patron in shields of arms and rebus carved round the gatehouse entrance. In addition (the Tudors have been enthroned for 15 years) there is a central display of the royal arms. Christ's College had a royal benefactor and foundress, Lady Margaret Beaufort, the king's mother. The gateway is surmounted by an enormous heraldic display of shield of arms supported by large yales (mythical beasts like horned goats) on a field strewn with daisy plants, germander and red rose — Lancastrian badges. Flanking the yales are further badges of three ostrich feathers and coroneted portcullis. The whole lot is crowned by a niche containing — the Virgin Mary? —

not a bit of it: Lady Margaret (a modern image) stands there (RCHM Cambridge, 1988, 27). The same foundress was involved with St Johns. She was now in her tomb but the glittering façade of the gateway of her college built 1511-16 has many of the same heraldic motifs as Christs' College — animal supporters, coats of arms, ostrich feathers, roses, coroneted portcullises and so on. Once again the insecurity felt by the new Tudor dynasty is hinted on. A similar rash of blatant Tudor display is seen at Kings' College (Steane, 1993, 205-6). Trinity College gateway is the culmination of the Cambridge heraldic series. It was a long time in building 1518-1614 (Willis and Clarke, 1886, 11, 484-5). The shields of arms of Edward III and his sons, together with a statue of Henry VIII (now complete with chair leg as sceptre!) were only finally added in James I's reign. At the rear are further statues, of James I, Anne of Denmark, the ill-fated Charles. Over 150 years the world had turned. Saints on gatehouses had been replaced by shields of arms of the secular nobility. The Trinity and Virgin Mary had been supplanted by images of would-be absolute kingship. High up in the Tower of the five orders of the Bodleian Library, Oxford, James I sits in an apotheosis of glory! Once again the tower was used as an ideal setting for a demonstration of power (or sycophantism).

Halls

Roman forbears to Carolingian halls

Although there is no clear progression in the building of palaces from the ancient to the medieval world it does seem that already in late Roman times the hall had made its appearance in north-western Europe. The so-called 'Basilika' which still dominates the city of Trier is the outstanding surviving example (**36**). Built in the reign of Constantine it impresses by its sheer size: 67m in length, 27.5m in width and 30m in height. The interior increases a sense of awe because of the absence of supporting columns; clever architectural design creates the illusion that the apse is deeper and more distant. The windows are smaller and the upper ones placed slightly lower. Marble veneers, rich mosaics, niches containing statues decorated the interior wall and floor surfaces. There was a sophisticated heating system whereby the apse or either half of the building could be heated separately. Channels took heating up the walls and out at gallery level. The materials used, concrete, tile, and stucco, makes it likely that an architect from the eastern provinces of the empire was used. The function of the 'basilika' is that of an imperial reception chamber. Rectangular halls terminating in apses are well known as architectural forms associated with reception or audience rooms in Imperial palaces dating to the Flavian period in Rome (Darwall Smith 1996, 183-90). Ausonius describes the awe and veneration he felt when he stood within such a building: it 'seems intended to exalt the person holding court there into something more than human' (Wightman, 1970, 108).

The 'basilika' at Trier continued to be used by Frankish and Carolingian princes and later by the archbishops. It is likely to have influenced the building of Charlemagne's palaces at Aachen, Ingelheim and Nyjmegen (**4, 37**). The emulation of surviving Roman ruins has been suggested by many art historians as one the inspirations behind these Carolingian buildings. Carolingian halls, however, could be basilican or three aisled, or two aisled or unaisled (Samson, 1994, 125). Only Aachen seems to be a spectacular imitation of the late Roman *auditorium* at Trier and it differs in that it has a tower and two extra protruding semi-circular transepts (**4**). Entrance into these royal halls might be in some cases through the gable end and in some through the centre of the long hall. Presumably the king sat enthroned in the apse. At Paderborn (**7**) a feature interpreted as an outdoor throne was sited directly outside the great hall and its throne recess. It is suggested that the great men met the king in the great hall, carried on dialogue, made decisions and that these may have been communicated to lesser men also gathered outside to listen to proclamations (Samson, 1994, 118).

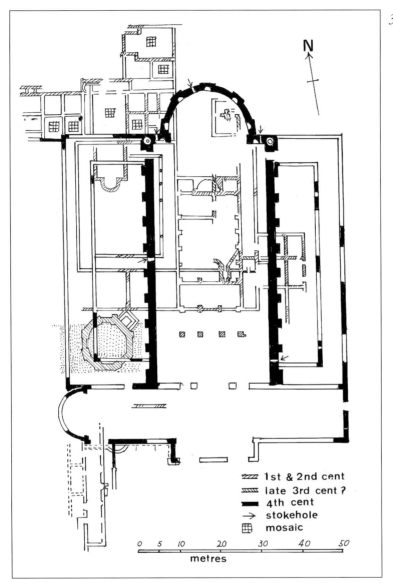

36 Trier, Germany. Plan of auditorium of Constantinian Palace. After Wightman, 1970

N

zzz 1st & 2nd cent
sss late 3rd cent ?
■ 4th cent
→ stokehole
⊞ mosaic

0   5   10   20   30   40   50

metres

Germanic ancestors: Anglian and Saxon halls

In addition to this Roman inspiration another source influenced the building of these early medieval great halls. This can broadly be distinguished as the Germanic. Ninth-century literary reference is found in the late Anglo-Saxon poem *Beowulf*. Here action centres around the great hall, called *Heorot*, where functions are referred to as mead hall, wine hall and ring hall, places where feasts are held and presents distributed. The hall in the Germanic tradition is seen as freestanding, of timber, high raftered, with a door at one end, a central fireplace, with posts and aisled; '. . . it was handsomely structured, a sturdy frame braced with the best of blacksmiths work inside and out' (Heaney, 1999, 25)

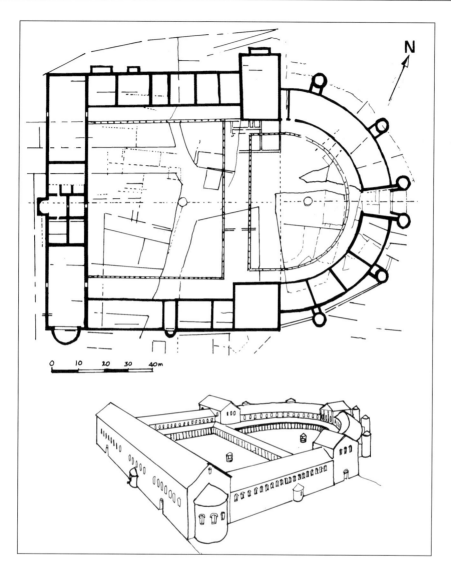

37   Ingelheim Palace, Germany. Above, hypothetical ideal plan. Below, reconstruction by H.J. Jacobi. After Fehring, 1991

Furnishings were few; the benches on which the warriors sat could be pushed back. They slept on the floor. Archaeology confirms some of these features but suggests others. The series of seventh-century halls from the royal Anglian site at Yeavering shows that here were combinations of three aisled double-square plan buildings, divided by opposed doors in the long walls (with additional opposed doors in the end walls) and made of squared, vertical timbers set in deep foundation trenches with diagonal bracing (Hope Taylor, 1977, 213). Such a hall with opposed doorways in the side walls is described by Bede when he compares the life of man to that of the swift flight of a sparrow 'through the room wherein you sit at supper in winter, with your commanders and ministers and a good fire in the midst . . . the sparrow . . . flying in at one door and immediately out at another' (Bede, 1944, 91).

The halls are the dominant architectural element of the royal residence of the kings of Wessex at Cheddar excavated in 1960-2 (Rahtz, 1979, 49-67). Here there was a succession of halls dating from *c*.AD 800 to the early thirteenth century. The oldest, the long hall was of post-in-trench construction and measured 24m by 6m; it was wider in the middle than at the ends suggesting a connection with ship-building. It was superseded in the tenth century by three consecutive west halls built of major earth-fast posts with entrances possibly at both ends. These measured 9m by 19m. In the later eleventh to twelfth centuries a much larger aisled hall was built — the so-called east hall. This had an arcade of ten bays with an entrance at the west end. Nothing is known of the roof structure nor of the fenestration. The return from open halls to halls with aisle posts has roused speculation. It is suggested that the aisle posts may have been imitating ecclesiastical piers and arches but perhaps it is more likely that the bays provided divided spaces for sleeping as in old monastic infirmary halls (Thompson, 1995, 26-7).

Westminster Hall (**9, 38**)

The greatest hall in medieval England was that at Westminster built by William Rufus and completed in 1099. It was 240ft long and 67ft 6in wide (77m x 24m). Careful observations by Sidney Smirke established its Romanesque appearance (1836, 406 et seq). It was originally an aisled building divided into twelve bays with a wall gallery and pilaster buttresses on the outside. It is uncertain whether there were two arcades or a spinal arcade running down the middle in the same way as the great royal hall in Paris was built. The windows were large semi-circular headed alternating with smaller ones. The size struck contemporaries. Henry of Huntingdon tells the story that when the king was inspecting the new hall with his attendants some remarked that it was big enough, if not too big. The king replied that 'it was not half large enough'. According to another the king's reply was that it was 'too big for a chamber and not big enough for a hall' (quoted by Allen Brown, Colvin and Taylor, 1963, 45).

Westminster Hall began life by being used for domestic, largely residential purposes but it soon acquired other functions connected with being a seat of government. In his summary of William the Conqueror's reign the author of the Anglo-Saxon chronicle wrote that the king had great dignity and wore his crown three times a year when he was in England. At Easter he wore it at Winchester, at Whitsun at Westminster and at Christmas at Gloucester and on those occasions all the great men of the whole of England were with him, abbots and earls, thegns and knights. It is uncertain whether the crown wearings took place in the abbey or the hall but it is well known that the hall was the scene of coronation festivals after the abbey ceremony. Also great banquets were given in honour of special visits by foreign emissaries, such as the reception given to two ambassadors from the Emperor Frederick II who came to ask for the hand of Henry III's sister for their master.

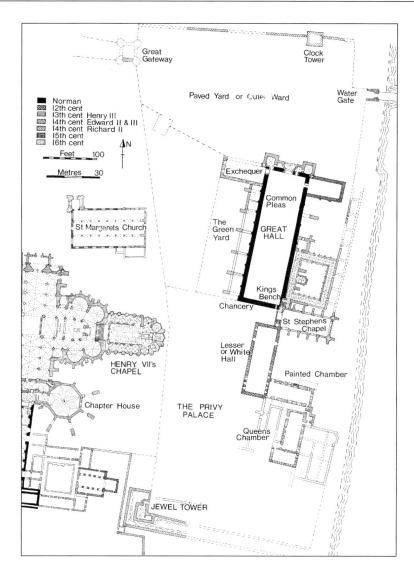

38 *Plan of Royal Palace of Westminster. Note the way the palace is crammed into a narrow site between Westminster Abbey and the River Thames.* After Colvin 1963

Social service and court use

An age which was characterised by conspicuous consumption of this kind also approved of the renunciation of wealth in pursuit of apostolic poverty. Thus Henry III invited the poor into his own homes. The *Liberate Rolls* show that Westminster Palace was the most frequent location for large-scale royal almsgiving. Between 2000 and 3000 poor were fed in a day at Westminster Great Hall and thrice in the regnal year of 1243-4 the Palace welcomed up to 10,000 poor in a single day. The numbers meant that several buildings were involved, the old and sick

91

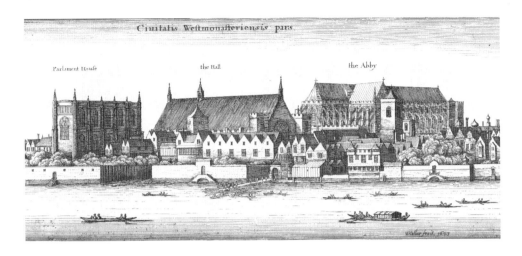

39 *View of Westminster Palace. St Stephen's chapel (Parliament House as it had become) on left. In centre, hall with houses of vicars in front. To right, Westminster Abbey with Edward III's clock tower in centre. Note succession of landing stages, two of them with prestigious staircases.* Engraving by W. Hollar (1607-77)

were sent to the greater and lesser halls, the children in the Queen's Chamber and the remainder in the Painted Chamber. This royal alms giving was taken a step further in that it was linked with the commemoration of the royal dead. When Henry III heard of the death of one of his *familia* he issued writs for commemorative masses and almsgiving (Dixon-Smith 1999, 90). The power of food and eating as a means of bonding people, whether alive or dead, runs through the use of the great hall in the Middle Ages. Almsgiving, therefore, was as much a part of the demonstration of royal power as glittering display or coronations.

Almsgiving was doubtless done with the last judgement in mind. Judgement in this world was also associated from early on with Westminster Hall. From 1178 Henry II ordered certain men to be always ready to hear complaints from his people; they sat in the hall. A central court evolved, hiving off from the Exchequer; it was called the Court of Common Pleas, or the Bench and it heard civil cases of all kinds. After 1234, when it became permanent, it sat in the hall on the right hand at the north entry to the hall. It was followed by the King's Bench and Chancery. As Stow says, 'at the upper end of the hall, on the right hand, or south east corner, the Kings Bench where please of the Crowne have their hearing; and on the left hand or south west corner sitteth the lord Chancellor, accompanied by the Master of the Rolls, and other men learned for the most part in the Civil Lawe'. It might be thought that with all this going on the hall was fully occupied, but in fact there were in addition shops and booths of petty retailers and perambulating chapmen, 'the capital seat of the king's justice presented a scene which most closely resembled not a solemn tribunal, but a bazaar' (Rosser, 1989, 164-5).

40 *Westminster Palace. The great hall is on the left with its perpendicular style facade and
flanking towers. In the background Westminster Abbey. In front the paved yard or
outer ward with fountain, Edward III's bell tower and great gateway in background.*
Engraving by W. Hollar (1607-77)

French and German great halls

So far the halls considered have been ground-floor buildings but on the continent
there was another tradition, that of the storied upper hall. In French vernacular
literature of the twelfth and thirteenth centuries heroes and other characters
approaching the royal court invariably dismount from their horses and ascend
steps to enter the hall (known as *la sale*). Such '*sales*' were distinguished from contemporary English halls by having no lower end, no screens passage, no central
fireplace (the chimney was early adopted). They included halls right at the apex of
society such as that built by Philippe IV (1284-1314) for the Palais Royal in Paris.
This was even larger than William Rufus' hall at Westminster, measuring 70.5m x
27.5m. It can best be imagined in the reconstruction drawings of Viollet Le Duc
which in turn are based on engravings by J.A. du Cerceau and the illuminations
in *Les Très Riches Heures du Duc de Berry* (Girouard, 1989, plate 42 and Pognon, no
date, 26-7) (also **43** in this book).

From these it can be seen that it was built with an undercroft with four vaulted aisles and above the great hall was double-gabled with its roof supported on a
central dividing arcade. The roof itself was a series of king-posts. In between the
windows in the main halls was a row of royal images and the end of the hall had
pairs of windows with geometrical tracery and rose windows above (Viollet Le
Duc, 1978, 600-4). Viollet Le Duc also cites another Parisian example, this time
the late twelfth-century palace of the Archbishops of Paris which survived into the
nineteenth century. Here the two-storey hall built by Bishop Maurice de Sully
*c.*1160 was wedged between an apsidal ended chapel, a tower, and a two-storey
lodging (Viollet Le Duc, 1978, 605).

41 Goslar, Germany. The main range with a first floor hall of the palace of German Emperors. The central throne room is behind the buttresses. Note the twelfth-century ceremonial staircase heavily restored in the nineteenth century. Photo by author

The tradition of building first-floor halls in the higher status palaces is also found in Germany. Despite its extensive (and imaginative) restoration in the late nineteenth century to provide a suitable setting for the apotheosis of the Prussian monarchy, Goslar provides a notable example. Its great hall measuring 57m x 17m is on the upper floor approached by external staircases: below an undercroft had columns supporting a vault. During the winter, court ceremonials were held here; the room was heated by a hypocaust under the floor. Above, on the first floor, there is a transept in the middle, with a central entrance perhaps harking back to wooden halls (Binding, 1996, 223-34). Other great German imperial halls show similar characteristics with rooms accessed from corridors which run along one side of the building, lit by rows of similarly designed windows. Such are at Wartburg, Gelnhausen and Wimpfen (Binding, 1996, 201, 275, 350).

Characteristics of medieval English halls

The main features of medieval halls in England varied very little over five hundred years of development but certain changes in society are reflected in the fabric of the buildings (Thompson, 1995).

1. *The entrance.* In English secular halls this was almost invariably in the lateral walls at the lower end of the hall. Frequently porches were added. Henry III

94

added a porch to his hall at Clarendon and this was only one of a series added at Havering (1240), Woodstock (1244), Oxford (1244), Ludgershall (1248), Guildford (1248) and Gillingham (1260) (Allen, Brown, Colvin, Taylor, 1963, 121). Monastic refectory halls which might be sited at right angles to the cloister would of course be entered from a door in the gable end.

2. Entrance was into the passage crossing the hall at the lower end. Doorways led into the buttery and pantry and into a passage leading to the kitchen (frequently detached). An excellent example is the arrangement of the three doorways at the lower end of the thirteenth-century hall of the bishop's palace at Lincoln but a small manorial hall of the fourteenth century at Fifield Oxfordshire has the same features. The passage was screened on the hall side. The screen was made of wood, it might be simply framed with uprights and rails, plank and muntin as at Chalgrove (Oxfordshire) or it 'might be panelled into compartments, enriched with carvings, or emblazoned with shields and armorial bearings'. It was an important feature separating the public area of the hall from the smells, noise and smoke of the kitchens and other offices which serviced it. It was, in addition, more a ceremonial barrier than an actual obstruction. If you passed it and entered the hall you would become an initiate, a member of the household, to be distinguished from menials or strangers. Most medieval screens have gone but often there are signs of their former existence; sockets where timbers were joined to the wall. At Shaw House, Newbury, the setting outlines for the screen can be traced on the plaster of this *c.*1580 Elizabethan hall. Screens went on being supplied, in ever increasing richness of carved decoration, classical triumphal arches, crowned by obelisks and enriched by strapwork into the Jacobean period. Oxford college halls, such as at Exeter, Jesus and Wadham carried on the tradition (RCHM, (E) Oxford plates 114, 115, 189).

3. The most obvious element facing the visitor entering the hall was the *open hearth*. This, in the case of ground-floor halls, was paved with end-set stones or tiles and might be furnished with firedogs and shovels. In the case of first-floor halls there would be a stone pillar supporting it in the undercroft beneath. The hearth was likely to be nearer the dais at the 'high end' of the wall than strictly central so that it gave more heat to the lord and his guests. Smoke would rise to the open timbers of the roof and would disperse through a specially constructed wooden vent, the *louvre*; signs of the wooden framework supporting this are frequently visible even though the *louvre* itself may have been removed. Opportunity was taken to cover the *louvre* with a lead capping and weathervanes so that it added to the decoration of the roof line. Although chimneys sited in lateral walls are known from the twelfth century (e.g. in the hall attached to the curtain wall at Framlingham Castle) they did not become usual until later on in the Middle Ages. John of Gaunt had two such fireplaces venting through chimneys in the lateral walls of his first-floor hall in Kenilworth Castle. One cannot help thinking that such an archaic feature as the central open fire retained its popularity long after

more efficient and less smoky means of heating large spaces had developed. It acted as a constraint on the size of halls. A great royal hall like that in Stirling Castle had five wall fireplaces: one behind the dais would have kept the king comfortably warm, perhaps too warm; the rest of the hall was heated by two each in the sidewalls (Fawcett, 1995, 40). Occasionally there was a second fireplace, as well as a central one; in the oriel at Kenilworth Castle hall, a second fireplace and chimney was built. It seems that the oriel was used by John of Gaunt and his successors for more private meals.

4. *The high end of the hall: the dais.* Just as steps were introduced in churches to raise the chancel and thus to demonstrate an area of greater veneration so a stone step or wooden platform was built at the upper (high) end of the great hall on which the table used by the lord and his guests was raised above the rest. The remains of a stone dais can be seen at the west end of Winchester Castle Hall where Henry III and his wife sat on seats with painted canopies (Biddle and Clayre, 1983, 28). The dais or high end of the hall was also distinguished by being lit with larger windows or with an oriel.

5. *Canopies and high tables.* Elaborate canopies were constructed above the hall high table from the fourteenth to the sixteenth centuries. They had a practical object in excluding draughts and a symbolic function as covers of honour. Even if the lord was not present, his honour was acknowledged by the existence of the canopy of estate. It was analogous to the cellure over the high altar of a church (Wood, 1968, 134). Such constructions were not afterthoughts. They appear in building contracts for baronial and municipal halls in the fifteenth and sixteenth centuries (Salzman, 1992, 457, 511, 582). An alternative seen in medieval manuscript pictures of feasts was a tapestry or hanging suspended from hooks fixed to the wall behind the high table. The general shape of the tables was rectangular; they were covered with white tablecloths. The fall of the cloth was carefully arranged. Henry III ordered 500 ells of linen for the tablecloths in preparation for the Christmas feast at Winchester. The ends of such cloths were meant to fall over the board. It has been suggested that such cloths were laid on the table double so that when one side was soiled the other could be turned up (Turner, 1851, 178).

The functions of medieval halls

To understand the place that halls had in medieval society it is necessary to grasp the nature of the noble household. This has been defined as a group of servants, friends, family and retainers, all of whom were dependent upon a noble and living together under the same roof as a single community 'for the purpose of creating the mode of life desired by the noble master and providing suitably for his needs' (Mertes, 1988). Such noble households were undoubtedly growing in size during the period covered by this book. Take the royal household. Kings Eadred and Alfred are thought to have had a household of about 20 persons; Henry I had about 120 and Henry VI as many as 800. Dukes and earls maintained between 40 and 166 people; bishops and wealthy abbots from 40 to 80. Baronial households might be as small as 20 and rich knights had as many as 30 (Dyer, 1989, 50-1).

The hall was *par excellence* the architectural expression of the household. Within it *esprit de corps*, a sense of solidarity and loyalty to the lord, was created. Contemporaries were aware of this. Bishop Grosseteste, who did not waste time on trivialities, wrote some detailed advice to the Countess of Lincoln 'to guard and govern her lands and hostel'. He was particularly insistent that good order shall be kept in the hall, that alms 'be faithfully gathered' (in the hall) 'and freely, discreetly and orderly without dispute or strife be divided among the poor, sick and beggars'. He also advised that 'you yourself always be seated at the middle of the high table, that your presence as lord or lady may appear openly to all'. Again 'as far as possible for sickness and fatigue, constrain yourself to eat in the hall before your people for this shall bring great benefit and honour to you'. All this required the appointment of a servant to keep order, 'command that your marshal be careful to be present over the household, and especially in the hall to keep the household within doors, and without respectable, without dispute or noise, or bad words' (Lamond, 1890, 135-41).

A century later William Langland makes the same point: 'consider how you may provide most generously for as large a household as possible'. He warns against eating 'in other mens houses while despising your own. For when the lord and lady eat elsewhere every day of the week, their hall is a sorry, deserted place. And the rich nowadays have a habit of eating by themselves in private parlors — for the sake of the poor I suppose or in a special chamber with a fireplace of its own. So they abandon the main hall, which was made for men to eat their meals in . . .' (Goodridge, 1959, 153).

The hall provided a backdrop against which the rulers of medieval England, kings, aristocracy, or knights could be seen with their distinctive lifestyle and a self-conscious adherence to a code of courtly and chivalric values. These values were underlined by the physical arrangements in the hall. The lord presided from a central seat placed behind a table which ran at right angles on the dais at the upper end of the hall. Above him was a canopy of estate indicating lordship. His most honoured guests sat to the left and right. The office of the Marshal of the hall was 'to summon those inside and outside in order of their rank and to seat them becomingly and with discrimination and to eject those unworthy' (Richardson and Sayles, 1955, 127). The rest of the tables were arranged lengthwise down the hall and the diners sat on benches. All were seated in strict hierarchical order. This might take some time. 'The meat will be halfe cold ere the Guests can agree on their places' (Halliwell-Phillips, 1857, 15).

The secular feast began with a procession of food to the high table. Within the hall the rules and customs of serving became steadily more elaborate as time passed. At coronation banquets great magnates jockeyed for position to serve the king, to carve, to bear dishes, to hold the towel and so forth. Guests were provided with knives (or brought their own) and spoons but not forks so that it was necessary for them to use their fingers and to wash their hands before, during and after the meal. Aquamaniles in bronze and ceramic provided water, basins or ewers were carried round with towels for the lord and his guests (**110-11**). The carvers required real skill as well as a knowledge of the different procedures laid down for the disposal of the flesh of each animal, bird and fish. The carver was expected to know how to 'splat a pike', 'spoil a hen', 'imbrace a mallard', 'fin a chub', 'untache a curlew', 'barb a lobster', 'border a pasty' and so on. He 'must know the carving and fair handling of a knife' and he should put only two fingers and a thumb on his knife. Household service was regarded as prestigious; ambitious parents encouraged their sons to be brought up in the service of some great lord. Chaucer, we recollect, said of the squire

> Courteous he was, lowly and serviceable
> And carved to serve his father at the table (Coghill, 1977, 23)

The food or drink consumed at the high table was of a better quality than that on offer on the lower tables in the hall. Dyer cites two examples. At Beaulieu Abbey wine was served when abbots, priors and dignitaries, together with some parsons were present, the rest had to content themselves with ale. Similarly in the manorial hall of Thomas Bozoun in Northamptonshire, fresh meat was served when the master was at home; otherwise the family had hard 'stock' (Dyer, 1989, 62, 65). Women were noticeably absent in the hall, and, for that matter, in the kitchen. As long as household service was regarded as a job of some prestige, it was a man-dominated world (Mertes, 1988, 57).

Halls had other uses. The furniture could be easily moved, trestle tables stacked against the wall and benches similarly dragged aside. This created a space in which dancing could take place. Minstrels sang and made merry in halls. Towards the end of the Middle Ages galleries were frequently made above the service passage to accommodate musicians or choristers. Halls could be quickly adapted by the introduction of a few wooden benches and perhaps a bar to serve as courts. The halls of the inns of court in London and those of the colleges were used for the production of plays. The halls of Christchurch, Oxford, the chapel of King's College, Cambridge, the Middle Temple Hall in London, the Banqueting House in Whitehall all functioned from time to time as theatres (Wilson, 1995, 133-5).

Kitchens

Cooking in the early Middle Ages was often done out of doors as indeed had been the custom among the Gallic and German tribes during the later Roman Empire. A vivid example, admittedly portraying events during a campaign, is shown in the Bayeux tapestry (Stenton, 1956, Figs 48,49 plate IX). Here a fire burning outside on a brandreth (an iron frame) heats a cauldron suspended over two uprights. A portable field oven with bakemeats is nearby and a succession of servitors are bringing birds roasted and spitted and handing them over like kebabs to the picnicking hungry Normans, who are using their kite-shaped shields as tables. Archaeology confirms that an element of open-air cooking persisted with even well founded manorial establishments. At Writtle, Essex, the royal hunting lodge had external ovens and hearths (Rahtz, 1969). Similarly at the fourteenth-century manor house at Northolt, Middlesex, hearths were built in yards up against walls, under lean-top roofs (Hurst, 1961).

When proper buildings were raised for culinary purposes they were almost always detached but located near the hall in palace or manorial layouts or near the refectory in monasteries. The surviving kitchen at the Bishop's Palace, Lincoln (**colour plates 10 & 11**), built *c.*1224 is reached from the low end of the hall by a passage between butteries, then across an arched bridge and finally it sits above a vaulted undercroft. The bridge and the undercroft are necessary because of the steep slope of the site. The kitchen was detached in this way from the main complex of buildings for a number of reasons. It was probably the most inflammable unit; frequent fires led to frequent rebuilding. It was desirable to separate the smells, heat, steam and smoke from the hall. In castles kitchens were always in the bailey. At Windsor (**13**) the great kitchen was situated in one side of a court to the east of the main hall. How were the raw materials, the foodstuffs and fuel brought to the lordly house? A study of the ground plan usually helps to answer this question. The foodstuffs were carted in through the outer gate in the Base Court. Cereals, peas, beans were stored in the barn which was likely to be situated along one range facing the court. The bakehouse and brewhouse were separate structures or 'houses' and were also likely to be found lining the basement or perhaps a separate kitchen court (as at Shute House, Axminster, Devon *c.*1460). Shute has a ground-floor kitchen with three chambers for cooks above (this began in *c.*1460 as a single chamber, but was subdivided) (Cooper, 1999, 57).

During the later Middle Ages great houses were designed with the aesthetics of symmetry in mind so prestige and sophisticated ways of living began to supersede the earlier medieval ideas of communal and commodious living. Society was moving away from the practice of servants eating alongside their social betters in the great hall. Kitchens were no longer detached. They were now incorporated within the body of the house and sited in basements or semi-basements. A good example is in the Bishop of Hereford's Palace at Prestbury, Gloucestershire. Here there was a detached kitchen serving the hall across a yard in the fourteenth century. Two-hundred years later the kitchen was incorporated in the house and immediately adjacent and joined to the hall. Cooked food no longer was carried in procession from the detached kitchen to the hall. It was now delivered to the individual chambers: the hall was rarely used for eating except at times of feasts such as Christmas gatherings. Servants, especially cooks and scullions, were tucked away, inferior beings, best not seen, heard or smelt. A good example is found in the compactly planned house at Chastleton Oxfordshire built 1604-10 by Walter Jones, a successful lawyer and coming from a family of Midland clothiers. Here the kitchen is sited in the basement, connected by a hatch to a short passage, and thence by back stairs to the Oak chamber which had replaced the great hall as the family dining area. It takes 45 seconds to carry a dish from the kitchen hatch to the dais end of the great hall so Jones and his friends need not have eaten cold fare! (Steane, 1996, 46).

The construction and design of kitchens naturally went through a series of developments during this long period of 800 years. There were two traditions. In England kitchens were invariably built of wood to begin with and were therefore square or rectangular in shape and required frequent rebuilding as they rotted or caught fire. The kitchen in the thirteenth-century castle at Weoley (Oswald, 1962-3, 109-34) was built with walls of vertical and horizontal weatherboarding. The roof was upheld on two arcades of earth-fast posts: whether in the form of an aisled hall with the internal posts higher than the wall posts, or whether the internal posts supported overhanging tie beams and king posts is open to speculation (Smith, 1965, 82-93). This reliance on wood is borne out by numerous references in the royal records. In July 1244 the sheriff of Nottingham received orders from Henry III to build at Clipstone (the royal hunting lodge) a kitchen in wood. In 1285 a kitchen with a hall made of plastered wood was ordered to be built at Woolmer in Hampshire for King Edward I. Such buildings were flimsy; one was blown down in a gale at Oxford in 1232 (quoted by M. Wood, 1965, 247-8).

In France there was an important series of stone kitchens attached to or rather detached from monasteries and castles. These were circular in design in the twelfth/thirteenth centuries (as at St Trinité de Vendôme) or octagonal (as at Fontevrault). In the latter the building was in elevation like an inverted wine glass with a beautifully designed central vault within which was a conical chimney and subsidiary semi-domed vaults providing chimneys for five fireplaces. A forest of little chimneys is restored in Viollet le Duc's drawing (Bernage, 1978, 384-396). During the later Middle Ages stone-built kitchens tended to be square in shape both in England and France. The famous Abbot's kitchen at Glastonbury and the monastic kitchen at Durham are cases in point, both with cunningly contrived fireplaces, chimneys and vaults. Those in France were particularly ingenious, being designed to keep the air circulating within a confined space and thus avoid asphyxiating the cooks! Again Viollet le Duc draws and reconstructs square stone kitchens at the castle of Montreuil-Bellay near Saumur set against the curtain wall; it has ovens inserted into the walls and two chimneys in facing lateral walls. The kitchen in the palace of the Dukes of Burgundy at Dijon is a perfect square in plan with a central vault carried on eight columns. Around the walls are furnaces with cooking places, an oven, a well and a channel bringing water into the kitchen to fill the boiler and the great cauldrons. The vault is supported in groined arches which lead up to a central vent and so to a chimney. A similar fifteenth-century kitchen, albeit on a smaller scale, survives at Stanton Harcourt Oxfordshire.

Having discussed the location and development of the design of the kitchen we now turn to the question how does one recognise a kitchen? How does it differ from the other buildings within the palace, manor or monastery? The first thing that strikes one when excavating a kitchen area is the multiplicity of heat sources.

Early kitchens had large hearths. They were sited centrally or at least well away from the wooden walls. That in the thirteenth-century timber kitchen at Weoley covered an eighth of the total area. At Northolt, Middlesex, there were two hearths within the fourteenth-century kitchen but an oven and no less than nine hearths were found outside. The large long hearth was 18ft long by 4ft wide and was built of roofing tiles set on edge. Tiles were also used as firebacks. Having been burnt in the kiln themselves they were proved to be fire resistant. Limestone or sandstone surrounds are found and, heavily calcined pink, formed the stone slabbing at the base of ovens. These could be free standing, circular, and domed in brick or stone or even plaster and wood, but as building techniques improved and more money was invested in kitchens they were built into the walls and corners of kitchens. We know from pictorial sources that they were operated from waist level. Brushwood was inserted through a small iron gate and fired. It was then raked out and the loaves of bread put in using a long wooden spade or peel. After the bread was baked it was removed and pastry was cooked as the oven slowly cooled.

The food was prepared on long tables. These were likely to be of stone within monastic or palatial kitchens. Chopping boards were made of wood. I remember visiting the kitchen at Magdalen College in 1982 after the Health and Safety officer had condemned the massive beech-block chopping board which had been used over the last 300 years. The chef was deeply saddened; beech, he explained, provided a natural disinfectant. The block, painted brown, has been relegated to a position outside the new kitchen. The Magdalen College kitchens are an interesting example of how kitchens were moved about and altered within a limited area over a long period. In the 1470s the east range of the medieval hospital of St John the Baptist was made into a kitchen, a functional and structural extension of the new great hall of the college founded by Bishop William of Waynflete. In *c.*1635 the site was moved bodily northwards and two massive eliptical-shaped fireplaces with chimneys were inserted at ground level. Much of the smoke, heat and steam must have escaped through the blackened roof timbers and through louvres in the apex of the roof. Finally in the 1990s the kitchen leapfrogged south and the seventeenth-century kitchen was converted into a bar and recreational area. The food during the first two phases had to be carried up the stairs (or in a lift) to the first-floor great hall (Durham, 1991, 17-75).

Where the kitchen was detached the problem arose of how to present the food hot and steaming when the hall was a walk across an open yard away. Part of the answer was the pentice, a covered way, single storey, with dwarf walls and a timber-framed upper structure and long roof; an alternative might be a single wall with a lean-to roof. The traces of pentices have been found at ground level at the royal palace of Clarendon, Wiltshire and at the bishop's manor house at Prestbury (which leads from the kitchen across a yard to the hall door). One has survived intact at Gurney Street Manor, Cannington, Somerset. A single storey pentice here leads from the kitchen door and hatch across a yard to the rear door of the screens passage (Cooper, 1999, plate 54a,b). At Clarendon there were two kitchens in the thirteenth century. The north kitchen which would seem to have been for the servants and courtiers and the west kitchen was where food was prepared for the king's mouth only. They were connected by pentices around a small cloister area and then up staircases past butteries and larders and so into the great hall (James and Robinson, 1988, 83). This separation of the cooking arrangements for the king, abbot, or great lord, is found increasingly in the later Middle Ages. With regard to monasteries it made sense for the abbot, who mingled with the great and frequently entertained them, to have a separate kitchen. We shall find the same phenomenon in the provision of double chapels.

Another convenient feature was the hatch, a kind of half-door pierced in one wall, which enabled food cooked and prepared in dishes to be passed out of the kitchen on its way with due ceremony to the hall or the chamber. This hatch system accessed by a cross passage has survived in many of the medieval college halls in Oxford and Cambridge. It is also seen in operation in the Royal Palace of Hampton Court where there is a spirited reconstruction complete with viandes, ready for the feast (**colour plate 12**). A particularly ingeniously designed pair of doorways with one opening out for exiting servants carrying food, and one opening for those bearing used dishes, is seen at the Bishop's Palace at St Davids.

Kitchen equipment is readily recognisable in the artefactual record. Ceramic pots were first supplemented by and then, in the later Middle Ages, replaced by metal cauldrons, posset pots, spigots and frying pans (these latter might be of iron) (**112-13**). The bubbling meaty contents were fished out from stewpots by means of iron meat hooks mounted on wooden handles. Fat was removed by skimmers, perforated circular bronze plates again provided with long handles. Spits appear in manuscript illuminations but I do not remember one being found in a recognisable condition. Knives and choppers are commonplace, spoons much rarer. Much medieval cooking involved pounding meat and vegetables into what we would regard as an unrecognisable mush (although I suppose our blenders do the same job). Pieces of mortars and mills are often picked up from within or around kitchen areas. There were fragments of seven stone mortars found at Northolt, four of them made of Purbeck marble (Hurst, 1961, figs 74-5). The Luttrell Psalter shows an enormous one with the cook pounding the contents with a pestle as long as himself. A method of keeping food warm at the table and warming water for washing hands was the chafing dish, frequently found in later medieval contexts. They were bowl-shaped dishes in which glowing charcoal embers were placed to heat a second platter resting on the rim projections. They were made of bronze for the tables of the wealthy but their form was closely imitated in glazed pottery. One was found with an oak leaf design and escutcheons bearing a schematic version of Bishop Despencer's arms at North Elmham (McCarthy, 1988, 121, Rigold 1962-3, fig 37).

Finally, in our consideration of kitchens for the upper echelons of society, we might look at roofs. Kitchens, in general, were tall buildings without intervening ceilings or rooms above. This was necessary as we have seen to ensure a ready circulation of air to remove the heat, steam and to enable the fires to draw properly within their chimneys. Where kitchens were rectangular, as in New College,

Brasenose College, Lincoln College Oxford, roofs with principal rafters, butt purlins and curved windbraces are found, heavily soot and grease blackened. Where they were circular, stone vaults were more usual, as seen in the French and English monastic examples already cited. One feature common to all was the louvre to provide a suitable up-draught and ventilation. Complex shutters to regulate these are still working in the manorial kitchen at Stanton Harcourt, Oxfordshire. A wooden louvre needed to be replaced frequently so it often figures among building repairs.

Lordly residence

From the earliest part of the period under discussion in this book rulers and lords and their families lived in separate accommodation from their followers and servants. They obviously shared some facilities like halls, kitchen and chapels but others for sleeping and leisure time activities were apart. The basic distinction between 'hall' (public) and 'chamber' (private) is found in Anglo-Saxon England and throughout contemporary northern Europe. As threats to security increased these distinctions were carried into the planning and building of castles. The broad generalisation that the lord and his family occupied the keep and the rest of his entourage took up their residence in the bailey is a truism. As enquiry into how castles and palaces actually functioned, what went on in the multifarious spaces within and around them, is beginning to take precedence over other aspects of the study of medieval buildings. Emery in his pioneer study of Dartington Hall, and Faulkner in his work on Bolton Castle showed the way. Access analysis was given a boost in 1993 by an important article written by Fairclough. Most influential, however, was an analysis of the social logic of space (Hillier and Hanson, 1984). Younger scholars like Richardson have taken up these ideas and applied them to Queen's apartments, a rather neglected category of monument (Richardson, 1997). There are serious difficulties. For one we, the archaeologists, have to deal with the building as it reached its final phase. Medieval palaces went on being added to in a higgeldy-piggeldy fashion. Clarendon (Wiltshire) for example is a series on buildings strung together over a period of 2-300 years with no apparent rhyme or reason. One feels the occupants, kings and all must have made up the rules for their use as time went on; constantly changing them as the size of the court fluctuated; as the season dictated; as the degree of maintenance warranted. It was not simply a matter of deciding at any one point of time who was allowed into which area. There is also a difficulty about the proposal that the further the enclosed area is from the point of access the more private. Lords often provided themselves with posterns, private doors of entry and exit, rather as film stars wishing to avoid the attention of fans slip into the side doors in theatres. These short circuit the normal routes of access. There is however evidence for royal movement by procession within palace precincts. Henry VIII, for instance, dealt with petitioners while en route from his chambers to chapel. A more profitable way to study room function in palaces seems to me to be to soak oneself in the documentation, profuse in the thirteenth century, but tailing away somewhat in the later Middle Ages. Texts about theories of kingship, household books, royal itineraries all have much to tell us about how palaces were used, how court etiquette was acted out, how frequently kings and their families were actually present in their houses. There is nothing wrong, however, with trying to argue from the positioning of doorways and the number of paces from point A to point B how spaces within palaces and castles were used in default of other evidence. Let us look at an example.

A well-known royal palace building, namely the White Tower within the Tower of London, has recently been subjected to a fresh analysis following important archaeological discoveries in the standing structure (Keevil, 2000, 92-4). It has long been assumed that the ground floor or basement of the Tower was used for storage; it is neither heated nor lit adequately. A new model has been proposed for the entrance floor above which is divided into three spaces, a long western hall and a shorter eastern chamber accessed through the former, and the chapel of St John accessed through the eastern chamber. Both rooms are heated. The western is now seen as a guard chamber and a place for assembly of those who will be allowed into the eastern which is seen as an audience chamber. A central recess is interpreted as a position for a throne. The upper floors are gained by means of a broad newel staircase in the north-east corner. Here there is a second hall and chamber with private entrance to the upper part of the chapel of St John. These large rooms were not nearly so lofty in their original built form. Recent archaeology has shown that they were roofed by two ranges of high pitched roofs whose eaves (and corresponding drainage shoots) came down further than had been realised. The result is that the rooms on the first floor were not so forbiddingly high. The galleries in the upper part served the wall tops, not the upper part of the rooms of state. All this assumes that the principal occupants were the king and his family but in fact we know little of the living habits of the Norman kings. The Tower, to be sure, was used for all sorts of other functions later on in its life from the keeping of the royal ordnance to the safe deposit of royal records.

A more reliable approach to the functioning of royal residence is that applied by Thurley to those parts of the Tower which were the subject of additions, alterations, and restructuring by Henry III and Edward I. He has linked various bursts of building activity which took place at the Tower with various political crises during the reign. Massive refortification, for instance, took place after the regime had experienced the shock of the premier fortresses of the country passing into the hands of the invading Dauphin. This resulted in Henry III's strengthening of the inner curtain with towers. Edward I, having suffered at the hands of the Londoners during the latter part of his father's reign, was determined 'Never again' and put in to action complex building operations which turned the Tower into an impregnable concentric fortress perfectly capable of dominating London and supplied by river. In this way political events acted as the trigger for structural programmes.

An intensive examination of the surviving buildings together with archaeological excavation at crucial points has established that the centrepiece of Henry III's Tower of London was the Great Hall and that the kings and queen's chambers were scarcely less important (Keevil, 2000, 96-7). The king's accommodation seems to have been in or near the surviving Wakefield Tower. Here, on what was the water's edge, the remains of a landing stage were found and the lower elements of a privy watergate. The landing inside gave entrance to the two-storey Wakefield Tower or to a spiral staircase leading up to a further Great Chamber. The upper chamber in the Wakefield Tower was supported on an ingeniously carpentered floor and certainly had room for a canopied throne, a hooded fireplace, and an alcoved chapel which was oriented east and looked down river. This private entrance was rendered obsolete when Edward I's masons built his outer curtain wall further into the Thames. On the made up ground they built a two-storey chamber block called St Thomas' Tower, with a wide water gate (called later 'Traitor's Gate'). The Royal Palaces agency has restored these rooms but the result is an uneasy mix of archaeology (exposed wall surfaces) and reconstructed 'medieval furnishings', presided over by staff in costume acting out roles. Much of the Tower has been turned into a kind of Levantine bazaar with shopping areas diverting the multitudes of visitors from the forbidding but fascinating buildings.

St Thomas' Tower was linked to the complex of royal apartments by a flying bridge (known as an *alura*, and mentioned in documents of 1324-5). So the king and his family, when resident in the Tower, lived on the upper floors, whether of the White Tower (in the eleventh/twelfth century) or of the Wakefield and St Thomas' Tower (in the thirteenth century). This penchant for the 'upper' class spending much of their time at first-floor level is found in other fortresses and palaces. At Middleham Castle, Yorkshire, for instance, there is a keep not dissimilar in scale to the Tower and split similarly by a spine wall into halls and chambers on both the ground and the first floors. There was a tiny chapel accessed in the twelfth century from the first-floor hall. The great chamber lying alongside was linked by a bridge in the later Middle Ages (the sockets for the timbers can be seen in masonry walls) to the tower of latrines attached to the adjoining curtain wall. So it was not necessary for the Neville family who held the castle from the 1280s to descend to the yard to relieve themselves. Moreover access to the thirteenth-century chapel was from the hall in the keep via a lobby into the chapel which was built protruding from the keep on the other side. Again it was unnecessary for the family or guests to descend to the ground for their devotions. 'Upper' classes they were literally and metaphorically!

Since Henry III possessed upwards of 60 houses scattered over his realm of England he had a serious maintenance problem on his hands. The royal records are peppered with his detailed instructions to carry out repairs and to prepare accommodation 'against the coming of the King (or Queen)'. He was particularly solicitous of the comfort of Queen Eleanor of Provence whom he married in 1236. He seems to have involved her in the decisions about the furnishing and fittings of her own apartments (Howell, 1998, 72-4). Various 'Antioch' chambers were created soon after the queen is known to have borrowed a book of romances involving tales about crusading. The beautiful tiled floors of the Antioch chamber or the chapel above it are among the most impressive achievements of Henry III's craftsmen although the tiles as artefacts cannot compare in quality with those made for his chapter house at Westminster or those coming from the tilery at Chertsey Abbey. We know that Eleanor's apartments at Havering were lit by 20 glass windows decorated with 40 heraldic shields 'as more fully enjoined by her' (Howell, 1998, 72). The Queen's suite of rooms at Clarendon comprised a two-storey block which grew to include a hall, a chapel, three chambers and a wardrobe. A pentice went out from the north-west corner to a tower of garderobes. Admittedly the excavations carried out by Borenius and Charlton in the 1930s found little evidence of the brilliant decoration mentioned in the documents. The flint wall bases had been robbed of their ashlar skins but in places both external and internal plaster remained. The great fireplace with double marble columns on each side and an overmantel carved with a series of the labours of the 12 months of the year was perhaps the most remarkable feature (James and Robinson, 1988, 18-19). Stothard recorded painted stones of a similar series which he found being used to block windows in the Painted Chamber at Westminster (Binski, 1986, 128-9). The windows of both the King's and Queen's apartments at Clarendon were glazed with *grisaille* glass (delicate silver gray in colour) with quatrefoil, cinquefoil, hatched and foliated patterns. The floor of one of the ground-floor chambers of the Queen's apartment was particularly impressively tiled, panels of patterned and inlaid figured tiles, in gold, gray and pink.

A significant aspect about the royal apartments at Clarendon is that the King's and Queen's suites are separate. No such division was noted in the eleventh-century arrangements in the Tower of London but a similar division occurred in the thirteenth century. Here the Queen's apartments were to the east of the Great Hall and are known only from references in the royal records and from sixteenth-century engravings. The 'Queen's Tower' was the smaller tower on the same site as the present Lanthorn Tower. It had a vaulted basement, above which were two fine chambers, placed one on top of the other. It is mentioned as having a chimney and chamber was panelled and whitewashed before being decorated with painted roses (Thurley, 1995, 39). The King's lodgings were to the west of the Great Hall and were meant to be a larger and more impressive version of the Queen's. Thurley believes that the King's great chamber, as has been seen, was on the first floor of the Wakefield Tower, but that the tower, lacking a stone vault, was never completed to its full height. He sees in Henry III's lodgings at the tower an exceptional 'coherence and symmetry which anticipates the development of king's and queen's sides in the fifteenth and sixteenth centuries' (Thurley, op cit 43). Certainly they exhibit an attempt at rationalising the planning of the royal 'houses' which is lacking in the *ad hoc* layout at Clarendon.

A further noteworthy feature about the Queen's apartments at Clarendon is that they were sited within view of gardens. There is ample evidence that gardens were a part of palace planning from the twelfth century onwards. Recent excavations at Beaumont Palace, the King's house outside the north gate of Oxford, have revealed rows of tree holes which have been interpreted as belonging to an orchard adjoining the twelfth-century 'palace', the birthplace of Richard I and John (Poore and Wilkinson 2001). The gardens at Everswell near Woodstock Palace were noteworthy because they included in Henry II's reign water features which Colvin suggested were paralleled by Moorish gardens experienced by the Normans in Sicily. Eleanor of Provence loved gardens and must have yearned for their heady scent from her Provencal birthplace. Round her chapel and chambers, beneath windows, in the angles of buildings at Winchester, Kempton and Windsor her husband provided gardens. There were walled gardens, herb gardens in which to walk, plantations of pear trees, fish ponds. They were not all small; that at Kempton is thought to have covered two or three acres. It is no great step from garden to landscaping. There is increasing evidence that castles and palaces in the later Middle Ages were set in contrived landscapes. A survey of the landscape round the royal castle at Ludgershall in Wiltshire shows that the surrounding parks were shaped deliberately to provide vistas from the upper windows of the towers (Ellis, 2000). The mid-fourteenth-century castle at Bodiam Sussex has been proved similarly to have an artificial setting composed of dams, earthworks and watercourses which impose on the visitor a series of impressive vistas. The widening of the moat by Edward I at the Tower of London which accompanied his strengthening of the approaches must have produced an incomparable vista, a reflection of embattled strength lowering over the eastern approaches to London.

The French connection

The international connections of the Plantagenet and Valois dynasties, chiefly by marriage but also by diplomatic and ecclesiastical contacts, made successive monarchs highly aware of what was going on across the channel in both directions. Architectural aspiration was driven by emulation. We have already seen that Philip Le Bel's great hall in the Palais Royal at Paris was built on an even larger scale than William Rufus' at Westminster. He added suites of chambers at first-floor level, designed by Enguerrand de Marigny. These were characterised by stone hooded fireplaces, stone window seats, glazed windows, conveniently placed garderobes ensuring a standard of comfort, wholly exceptional in medieval society outside monasteries. Within these, various ceremonial functions took place. The king held '*lits de justice*'; various rooms were known as the '*chambre de dais*' and the '*chambre du parement*' referring to certain key items of furniture. All these features mirrored the interiors of Henry III's palaces and Edward I's quarters in St Thomas' Tower, the Tower of London, and in the upper ward of Conwy Castle, Wales (Steane, 1999, 115, fig 70).

The two countries diverged in the matter of palatial planning in the fourteenth century. As France was the battleground for the Hundred Years War with the English, French palaces tended to be highly fortified. After the baronial revolts of the middle of Henry III's reign which had resulted in the refortification of the

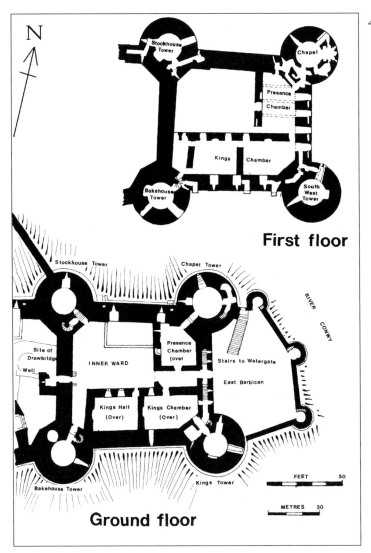

42 *Conwy Castle, inner ward. Note the access by water. Also the series of chambers at two levels; the concentration of functions (bakehouse, storage, chapel) within a very small space. After RCHM, 1956, Caernarvonshire*

Tower of London, the Plantagenet monarchy was not seriously threatened for some 40 years or so. An exception of course, is the royal apartments in Conwy Castle. Also apart from a brief period of turmoil in Edward II's reign, the monarchy could afford to live in largely undefended houses and palaces during the fourteenth century. Not so the French. Here palaces like the Louvre and Vincennes were strongly defended. Chambers were stacked on top of one another in towers. Keeps remained characteristic longer after they had been superseded by castles which relied on curtain walls or concentric lines of fortification in England. The sequence of chambers of increasing quality found horizontally in palaces such as Edward III's restructured Windsor Castle could also have a vertical application as in Charles V's donjon at Vincennes in a wooded park near Paris. Here the monarch and his family were accommodated in a great tower while princes of the blood royal and other aristocrats occupied suites of rooms in other towers studding the surrounding rectangular curtain wall. The amazing silhouette of the tops of these towers can be seen protruding above the wood in the December hunting scene of *Les Très Riches Heures du Duc de Berry* (Pognon, 1983, 38-9). Mary Whiteley in a series of articles has shown how these great freestanding and mural towers were used to play out the increasingly complex ceremonies of court life (Whiteley, 1996).

As the courts became steadily more fixed and less itinerant more money could reasonably (or unreasonably) be invested in furnishing and fittings. Only fragments remain but the wills, and *Inquisitions Post Mortem* of the top aristocracy demonstrate that ceremony was played out against a rich background of painted arras and woven tapestry. Stone furnishings include fragments of a marble table used by the kings of England when seated for coronation banquets in Westminster Hall. A circular oak table dated to the thirteenth or fourteenth century, 1.5m in diameter, with chamfered plinth and rail, shafted uprights and framework with cusped ogre headed arches, formerly painted and gilded, is kept at present in Salisbury cathedral (Brown, 1999, 76.7). It gives some impression of the stateliness of the (to modern eyes) rather sparse furnishing of medieval interiors. Colour and warmth was provided by textiles. In earlier palaces walls had been decorated with whitewash, masonry patterns in red, and more rarely with painted historiated or single figures (Binski, 1986). Increasingly in the fifteenth century the lower parts of walls of palaces were hung with painted arras, or, much more expensively, with tapestries imported from Flanders. Some buildings like Edward IV's great hall at Eltham were designed to accommodate tapestries, the windows were placed high up so there were spaces for the hanging of tapestries below them. This may be the explanation of the windows high up in the walls of the hall of the Lovell family at Minster Lovell, Oxfordshire and in the first-floor hall of the Scropes at Bolton Castle.

Political conditions changed towards the end of the fourteenth century. Great magnates in England, France and Flanders built themselves fortress palaces which while not designed to last out serious sieges yet provided powerful status symbols emphasising their political and social dominance. Again England and France influenced one another. The most expensive project in Western Europe was the restructuring by Edward III of the castle/palace at Windsor, partly paid for by the profits of war, particularly the ransom of the captured French King John. The fire of 1992 exposed enough of the medieval stonework to show that it was on a magnificent scale and was richly decorated. The 18 bays of the vaulted undercroft under the chapel and St George's Hall are now seen in all their glory, stripped of seventeenth-century and later partitions. The principal apartments were interconnected and at first-floor level. How the food was brought from the ground-floor kitchen to the great hall has not so far been satisfactorily explained. The position of the connecting staircases is uncertain. The design of placing the hall backing up against the chapel and both between two impressive towers, each with subsidiary corner turrets and gateways is more regular and symmetrical than anything built before in English royal palaces. The construction programme was driven by the royal Clerk of Works, William of Wykeham, who later used many of the ideas carried out at Windsor Castle in his design of New College Oxford (Nicolson, 1997, Brindle and Kerr, 1997).

The magnates of the north of England commanded estates and revenues sufficient to embark on building projects which provided them with commensurate standards of comfort. The Nevilles brought Middleham Castle up to date in the early fifteenth century by surrounding the courtyard within which the twelfth-century keep sits with a series of two-storey chamber blocks which would have provided good quality accommodation for family members and high status guests. Each is provided with fireplaces, garderobes and windows commanding extensive views. The Scropes, a neighbouring family higher up the dale built Bolton Castle from scratch, the high point of integrated planning in late medieval England. Here all the storage and service rooms were either on the ground floor or in sub-basements. The brewhouse, bakehouse, armoury and stables were around three sides of the courtyard. Access to the upper parts of this four-storey fortress/palace was through five gateways in the courtyard each defended by a portcullis. The hall was on one side, the chapel on the other; linking them were a series of chambers on two floors including a living room with two bedrooms in towers leading off. This provision of separate chambers for different purposes within the same household was characteristic of late medieval palace planning. So was the increasing emphasis on comfort. Everyone at Bolton seems to have enjoyed the facility of garderobes. The ruling family occupied rooms with windows opening high up in the embattled walls giving splendid views towards the west and the south. The other feature of importance in the future was the integration of the service rooms with the rest of the building. Again there is an emphasis on symmetry in design, combined with ingenuity and forethought in the provision of facilities which puts Bolton Castle in the forefront of palace design in the last years of the fourteenth century.

Steps and staircases

There was a predilection in Roman civic architecture for building flights of steps and stairways. These were used in a number of ways. To link parts of the city, to provide a setting for important buildings, to enable ceremonies such as processions to progress easily from one part of the city to another. Roman town planners enjoyed making large, neatly edged and levelled spaces. They cut into hillsides and built up slopes to create series of plazas. These they linked with staircases. The attraction of stairs arose from the fact that they were evenly and solidly layered and shed sharply delineated shadows, all of which suggested permanence and reliability. In addition 'they reinforced the sense of arriving or departing, of gaining a goal, or leaving it behind for another phase of activity' (Macdonald, 1986, 71). Examples are legion in Rome itself. The forum and markets of Trajan are characteristic (Claridge, 1998, 146-73, 230-1). Temples and civic buildings were given an air of monumentality by siting them at the top of a flight of stairs. They satisfied a need for elevation. Height in building had always suggested importance. Temples on eminences were nearer the gods.

Staircases can be considered simply as a means of communicating from one floor of a building to another. They tended to be confined in the early Middle Ages to houses of the *élite*. Poorer people had to be content with ladders and trap-doors. The king occasionally had a trapdoor and presumably a ladder that went with it. The Liberate Roll of 28 Henry III speaks of 'The descending trap (*trapa decendens*) in the king's chapel is to be removed and a staircase made in the north angle' (Turner, 1851, 203). Most of these early staircases were attached to the external walls of buildings. They were likely to be made of wood and protected by a penthouse roof. The king ordered the keeper of the manor of Feckenham 'to repair the porch before the door of the king's chamber there, and to make a certain pent house over the stair descending from that porch' (Turner, 1851, 226).

Although still attached to the outside of the building with the major rooms to be accessed staircases could be covered in and become a permanent structure. At this point they became more than a means of mounting from one level to another, they became stairways of honour. A number of Norman keeps have elaborate staircases. At Castle Rising the entrance to the keep is through a doorway in the forebuilding on the south front. There is a view straight up the two flights of the staircase through the middle doorway to the doorway of the vestibule above. This was 'the grandest and most evocative (view) of the whole castle' (Allen Brown, 1988, 42). The steps themselves are on a majestic scale. The first flight is of 15 steps, 8ft (2.4m) inside, which lead up to a middle doorway and a landing 5ft (1.5m) deep behind. Beyond the landing a second flight of 19 steps climbs to a doorway leading into an entrance vestibule. Having passed these three doors which must inevitably have had a siphoning effect of excluding unwanted visitors, the new arrival gained access to an entrance vestibule where no doubt he would be asked to wait. Feeling small and slightly out of breath he would at length be admitted into the state apartments of the lords of Castle Rising. A similar arrangement was designed *c*.1100 at Norwich Castle. Here a massive stone stairway, enclosed in an elaborately decorated forebuilding abutted the east façade. Here the flights of steps led to a drawbridge at the upper end before entrance was gained to the seat of power, in this case that of the king's representative within the city (Heslop, 1994, 29-33). Similar stairs with forebuildings to serve a second-floor entrance and intermediate late defensive gates are part of the design of Maurice the Engineer's towers at Newcastle (1171-5) and Dover (1180-6). They once existed at Hedingham (*c*.1130), Scarborough (1158-64) and Middleham (*c*.1170) (Wood, 1968, 329).

A second type of staircase which was also introduced by the Normans was the newel or spiral. Another common term was the vice (from the French *vis* (screw) and from the latin *vitis* (vine)). They seldom opened from outside and their chief use was to communicate between floors. They had a number of advantages. They could be included in the structure and indeed were very frequently embedded in the angle turrets, they took little space, they permitted the opening of doors on all their points of circumference and at all heights; they were easily lit, either with slit windows in the enclosing walls or by lanterns in niches at intervals; they were of simple construction involving a large number of units of the same dimensions; they could be blocked and easily defended (Viollet Le Duc, 1978, 479-80). In the twelfth century they were normally designed to be mounted clockwise; this allowed a defender greater room for his sword arm, the newel column and diminishing end of the step being on his left (Wood, 1968, 333). To begin with the newel staircase was made by laying the steps on a spiral vault round a newel constructed of a series of circular stones. The spiral barrel vault is supported on the central newel and on the circular facing interior of the shaft. A more speedy method was to cut the whole wedge-shaped step and slice out of one piece of stone, each one forming the support to the next. The disadvantage of this method was that the size of the stone determined the width of the staircase so it tended to remain narrow.

More elaborate designs for both kinds of staircase, the ramped and the newel, developed in France during the thirteenth and fourteenth centuries. At Montargis the hall had an external staircase accessed from three directions through a cruciform-shaped structure at ground level. The staircase leading to the Chambre des Comptes and the Sainte Chapelle in Paris had a vaulted porch leading to a long flight covered by an arched *loggia* (Viollet Le Duc, 1978, 477-8).

At Perpignan in the palace of the kings of Majorca (which is incidentally on the top of the hill overlooking the city), two ramped staircases of honour rose from within the main inner courtyard, one on either side, leading to an open loggia at first-floor level from which the king's and queen's apartments could be accessed. Such staircases were an important part of the scenery in the complex rituals that permeated the theatre of court life (see **30**).

Two examples of staircases in royal palaces in Paris show how this ritual determined their development in the late Middle Ages. The Palais de la Cité was the most ancient and extensive royal residence in the capital but it was also the centre of administration in the kingdom. Its principal courtyard, the *Cour de Mai*, was a public space open to all Parisians. Within it a great staircase was built by Philip the Fair to connect the courtyard with the *Galerie Mercière*. At the foot of the staircase was the *Perron de marbre*, a stone of justice built on an elevated stone platform. Here the usher of the parliament announced decrees and declarations of peace; here the dead and the living were exposed to public humiliation. The monumental staircase had a central flight which flared out and was supported by wedge-shaped sections. Such a design was a symbol of monarchical prestige. We know from Froissart's descriptions of the reception of illustrious visitors to the palace that groups of lords met the guests at the great gateway accompanied them across the *Cour de Mai*, and then climbed '*les grands degrès*' with them through a portal lined with sculptured figures of the king and his chamberlain and so into the palace. The great staircase was used in 1378 when Charles V, the Emperor Charles IV and the king of the Romans climbed up side-by-side after the official recep-

43   Paris, Royal Palace. Reconstruction drawing by Viollet le Duc. A: Sainte Chapelle; B: Galleries; C: Great Hall; D: Kitchens; E: Porticoes; F: Donjon (Tour de Montgomery)

tion. The steps were the culmination of numerous royal entrances, such as that of the king and queen after their coronation at Reims (Whiteley, 1989, 133-54).

The newel staircase also was enhanced in design to suit the demands of the court ceremonial. Charles V, at first regent, then king of France from 1364, moved the official centre of the court from the Palais de la Cité to the Louvre. Here Raymond du Temple converted the grim fortress of Philip Augustus into the splendid palace seen in the *Très Riches Heures of the Ducs de Berry* (Pognon,

1983, 34-5). In the west wing the rooms of Philip Augustus were retained but in the north they were rebuilt. Access to the new royal apartments was by means of the celebrated '*grande viz neuve*'. Viollet Le Duc produced a sensational design for this, based on the descriptions of Sauval and his own fertile imagination. Whiteley, in a more sober approach, has produced an alternative reconstruction based on archaeological excavation, and the published accounts. Both agree that the staircase was tucked into an angle between the great donjon and the new north wing. Whiteley thinks it was square in design, with access to the court on the ground floor. Within this square autonomous tower was a newel staircase with stone seats at the angles rising to the queen's (first-floor) and the king's (second-floor) apartments. It appears to have had four windows on each stage and sculptured figures in niches on the outside. When the king was in residence, the great vice played an important part in the daily ritual of the court. Charles V must have descended each day to take part in mass in the chapel. The Duke of Brittany when visiting Charles VI was met by 40 French lords who accompanied him up the stairway to the king (Whiteley, 1989, 142-150).

Such a staircase was the architectural progenitor of the famous spiral staircase of Francis I at the Chateau de Blois, with its open work tower and twisting stair similar to a spiral shell which may have been designed by Leonardo da Vinci. The letter F and the heraldic emblem of the Salamander both referring to Francis I are to be found among the balusters and the bosses. The pierced nature of the stonework of these late medieval staircases enabled those mounting to be seen, admired or envied by those in the courtyard below. An even more extraordinary staircase is in the centre of the Chateau de Chambord where the double spiral design is built in a cage of stone by which people can ascend and descend simultaneously (Banister-Fletcher, 1946, 697-8).

The ramped staircase reached its *apogee* in the dazzlingly brilliant design Bernini accomplished for Pope Alexander VII in the Vatican. Its purpose was to connect the colonnaded piazza di San Pedro (also by Bernini) and the basilica of St Peter's with the Vatican palace. It also served as the main ceremonial entrance to the palace. Its long tunnel-like axis continued the line of one of the main streets which led down to the Borgo and the (papal) Castle of Saint Angelo. Axiality was recognised as enhancing stateliness. The design of the staircase itself ingeniously augmented the impression of overwhelming power, convenient for the papacy which was suffering a succession of diplomatic affronts after the Peace of Westphalia. Converging paths of columns within the narrowing pairs of walls, rising flights of steps through landings accompanied by the gradual reduction of the radius of the barrel vault all exaggerated the perspective and gave an illusion of greater depth and height. It recalled the notion of a staircase to heaven, a veritable *Scala Santa* or Jacob's ladder. It was also a ritual processional path. The pope was carried down in his chair on his way to mass in St Peter's; after death his corpse would be solemnly borne down its sloping gallery. 'Along this path: the staircase was a great divider of realms; so that a guest greeted there by a host had been done a great honour' (Marder, 1997, 250). Books of etiquette emphasised that a visitor might be met at the top, but the host, if he wished to defer to his guest, could meet him halfway or, in extreme cases, at the bottom.

Chapels

Life for the élite in the Middle Ages was governed by religion to a degree unimaginable in the twenty-first century. As one travels in once largely Catholic countries like France, Belgium, Southern Germany, North Italy, one is struck by the many churches, the wayside crosses, the cemeteries, the monastic ruins (and the surviving convents) and the soaring cathedrals. But they are largely silent, often empty, the architectural shells left by a receding tide of religion. *Au contraire* the period 800-1600 saw the life of the upper and governing classes regulated by the church day in day out, Sundays, Feast Days, Holy Days, indeed for much of the time. It took three main forms, the foundation of churches, the performance of religious rituals, the engagement in pilgrimage and in the militant extension of pilgrimage, the crusades.

Kings and the higher nobility in church and state were great founders of churches. To take a few well-known examples from the English and French monarchies, Edward the Confessor spent much time and treasure in the last few years of his life, rebuilding and re-endowing the obscure monastery at Westminster into one of the greatest abbeys in the land to serve as his burial place (Barlow, 1989, 282-3). William the Conqueror's wish after Hastings, was to erect as powerful new abbey on the site of his victory, partly to exculpate himself and his followers for shedding so much blood but partly to act as a memorial for a splendid triumph. In any case it was a religious act. Henry I, on his death in Normandy, was brought back to rest in the monastery he had founded and richly endowed at Reading. Henry II, to do penance for his part in Becket's murder, rebuilt Waltham Abbey on a vastly increased scale and refounded the Carthusian priory of Witham and Amesbury nunnery (Farmer, 1985, 18-19). In the thirteenth century the much maligned John founded Beaulieu Abbey and endowed it with lands in Hampshire, Wiltshire, Berkshire and Oxfordshire (Horn and Born, 1965, 62-3). Henry III was one of the greatest builders of the Middle Ages, taking a personal delight in ordering the furnishings, fittings, decoration and structure in his 60 or so houses. The chapels in particular came in for renewal. Westminster Abbey was reconstructed as a great coronation church and Edward I turned it into a Plantagenet mausoleum. Much of the motivation for Henry III's efforts came from emulating his saintly contemporary, Louis IX of France (St Louis). De Joinville describes him ringing round Paris, the centre of his land-locked kingdom, with monasteries, hospitals and erecting the architectural masterpiece, the Ste Chapelle in his palace (De Joinville, 1938, 211). Even Edward II, not otherwise famed for his interest in building, supported the establishment of Friars Preachers at the royal palace at Langley. Here, with great solemnity, the body of the king's favourite, Piers Gaveston, judicially murdered, was laid in 1315 (Allen Brown, Colvin, Taylor 1963, 258).

These were great churches in which masses were said or sung by chantry or collegiate priests throughout the year and prayers offered up for royal and noble founders and benefactors particularly on anniversaries. We are more concerned here with the smaller chapels, the structural manifestation of this obsession with religion within the residencies of the upper echelons of society. Chapels were fitted in Norman keeps in ingenious ways that recall the intricate and compact planning of modern submarines. They are located above the forebuilding, or planned into the corners of keeps as at Middleham, North Yorkshire, so that they can be lit from two directions. They are sometimes found in pairs, one above the other, presumably to be used by the lord and his family in one, and by the rest of the household in the other (Wood, 1965, 227-9). In palaces of the thirteenth century they were built freestanding and often more than one served the same institution. Henry III maintained 'at least fifty chapels for the exclusive use of himself and his household' (Allen Brown, Colvin and Taylor, 1963, 124). These included an imposing new one which he had constructed in the lower ward of Windsor Castle. Only the west end remains incorporated in the east wall of the later St George's chapel but its quality can be judged by a door with magnificently intricate ironwork which survives (Geddes, 1999, 156-7); also a fragment of wall painting showing a king's head. This chapel would have been under construction at the same time as Louis IX was building the Sainte Chapelle. At Winchester Castle there were no less than four chapels. Henry III introduced furniture and religious imagery (statues, wall paintings and glass) into 'the king's chapel' of St Thomas. He also adapted the chapel of St Judoc by heightening the walls to produce two chapels, one above the other; the upper one was for the queen and the one beneath for her household. In addition there were the chapel of St Katherine at the top of the keep and 'a little chapel by the king's bed'.

Chapels varied greatly in scale from the huge and impressive such as St Stephen's, Westminster (**colour plate 15**), St George's, Windsor: the chapels of the Henry VI's collegiate foundations of Kings, Cambridge and Eton which are at the top end of buildings of the Middle Ages. At the bottom end there were the private oratories which opened off apartments, such as Henry III's praying place in the Wakefield Tower of the Tower of London. There was also a 'little chapel next to the king's bed' in his painted chamber at Westminster. The king could see the altar from his bed because there was a small quatrefoil opening about 4ft above the floor. For a king who went to mass three times a day (this was regarded as excessive by the saintly St Louis) it was necessary to surround oneself with chapels. The bulk of the 50 chapels that included 18 which Henry III had built *de novo* were in the medium range. Colvin has recorded that those at Clarendon and King's Cliffe (the hunting lodge in Rockingham Forest, Northamptonshire) measured 50ft by 20ft. The Queen's chapels at Kempton and Havering were about 30ft long and were 12-14ft wide (Allen Brown, Colvin, Taylor, 1963, 125). A particularly interesting feature in our search for the resonances of power is the fact that a number were ordered to be made in two stages. We have already noticed that the Queen's chapel of St Judoc's in Winchester Castle was built in this way to separate the

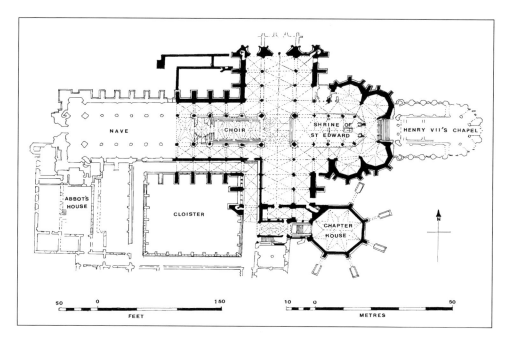

NAVE

CHOIR

SHRINE OF
ST EDWARD

HENRY VII'S CHAPEL

ABBOT'S
HOUSE

CLOISTER

CHAPTER
HOUSE

50   0   1 50

FEET

10   0   50

METRES

44   Westminster Abbey. Black indicates parts rebuilt during the reign of Henry III.
   After Colvin HM 1971, *Building Accounts of Henry III*, Oxford

queen in her devotions from the household. At Kennington the king ordered in 1237 'a chapel with a staircase of plaster which shall be 30ft long and 12ft wide, in such a manner that in the upper part there shall be made a chapel for the use of our Queen, so that she may enter the chapel from her own chamber and in the lower part let there be a chapel for the use of our *familia*' (household) (quoted by M. Wood 1968, 231-2). The Sainte Chapelle in Paris was perhaps the prototype of double-staged royal chapels built on a lavish scale. This cost the crown 40,000 livres and was built rapidly, 1242-8. The lower chapel was for servants and while darker and lower is nevertheless as richly decorated; the upper chapel was built to house the relics of Christ's Passion bought from the hard-up and hard-pressed Emperor Baudouin of Constantinople. It was used by the kings and queens of France who are traditionally said to have sat on the stone bench which 'stands back from the arcading on both sides of the third arch forming a recess' (Dillange, 1985, 150). It was certainly rivalled, if not outclassed, by the double chapel built by Edward I and completed by Edward III at St Stephen's Westminster (**colour plate 15**) nearly 100 years later.

   Where the king led the aristocracy followed. The tiny chapel in the huge Norman keep at Middleham Castle, North Yorkshire was fitted into a corner. This was deemed insufficient by the Nevilles, new owners in the 1270s. A new chapel was added by Ralph, first Lord Nevill of Raby, which projected from the side of the keep as far as the east curtain wall. This was in the upper part of a three-storey building and accessed from a lobby at the top of the stairs to the keep. It is likely that the priests serving this aristocratic chapel lived in the room beneath it. A second example a few miles to the west, but nearly 100 years later, was the chapel built into the second floor of the palace/fortress of the Scrope family at Bolton Castle. It was first mentioned in 1378/9 and was dedicated to St Anne, mother of the Virgin Mary, perhaps in honour of Richard II's first wife, Anne of Bohemia. At the rear to the west is the family's private pew, or raised gallery, entered via a narrow stairway from the Solar. A similar arrangement was adopted by the first Lord Hastings between 1464 and 1483 at Ashby de la Zouche, another palace/fortress of the later Middle Ages. At both Bolton and Ashby priests were accommodated nearby, in the former in single cells fashioned in the thickness of the walls of the castle, and in the latter in a special two-storey range attached at right angles to the south of the chapel (Weaver, 2000 and Jones, 2001).

The provision of separate service buildings solely for the use of the ruler is symptomatic of a society in which the distance between the royal person and the subject was increasing. It is allied to the emergence of an international aristocratic caste structure in the later Middle Ages. Kings were being set apart by their anointing in the coronation ceremony. All sorts of legends were given credence to support the reverence due to the monarch. The French claimed their kings were anointed with oil brought down from Heaven above to Clovis' coronation; the Plantagenets, not to be outdone, stated their flask of holy oil came from the Virgin Mary via St Thomas à Becket. Both dynasties claimed to be able to heal the scrofula (an unpleasant tubercular disease of the neck glands) by touch (Bloch, 1973). Each sallied into battle carrying sacred objects which had a supernatural origin such as the oriflamme (a resplendent banner) and a shield with fleurs de lys (French) while Edward I relied on a fragment of the true cross and felt he had won a great trophy by seizing the Stone of Scone from the Scots. Each was helped in the Hundred Years War by the cults of patron saints St Denis (France and then St Louis) and St George (England).

Emerging nationalism crystallised round these cults. The chapel dedicated to St George at Windsor provided a focus point for Edward III's foundation of the Order of the Garter. This, however, is no longer seen as of major importance harnessing the idealism of chivalry to the king's cause. It is now recognised that the order included obscure knights as well as the earls of Lancaster and Warwick, in fact it was a band of brothers united by the common experience of fighting at Crécy. It had so few members and indeed was so small in scale that it is arguable that its chief significance is that the chapel was a powerhouse for prayer for the souls of the defunct knights and the almshouse that accompanied it looked after impoverished soldiers in their old age (Prestwich, 1996, 228-9).

What is indisputable is that the cult of St George flourished in late medieval England (**colour plate 16**). Over 160 ancient churches are dedicated to him. His legendary form, either on horseback in the vision under the walls of Antioch, or dressed in a surcoat with red cross on a white ground, striking down the dragon appears on the walls of churches, in stained glass, and painted on chests. In 1415 archbishop Chichele had George's feast in the church's year raised to first rank; this after the battle of Agincourt where Henry V's famous speech invoked St George as England's patron saint. When Henry V wished to honour the Emperor Sigismund on his state visit in 1416 he made him a knight of the Garter. The Emperor attempted to match this by presenting Henry with the heart of St George (Allmand, 1997, 106).

The provision of double chapels percolated down in society. Bishops were provided with them. Robert Losinga, who came down from Lorraine built for himself in the 1070s a handsome two-storey double chapel at Hereford which was based on Charlemagne's design at Aachen. Two of the original arches of this chapel were incorporated into the wall of the cathedral cloister. The arched entrance apparently had 10 receded mouldings, sprung from as many columns on each side (Shoesmith 2000, 295). It was 44 x 40ft and eighteenth-century drawings show that it was square in shape and with two vaulted bays in the upper chapel and square piers in the lower. The upper chapel was for the use of the bishop. Other similar *Doppel-Kapellen* are found in the castles of the Rhine and North-Eastern France. Examples are in the episcopal palaces of Laon and Mainz (Wood, 1988, 227). The two-storey chapel of St Ulrich attached to the imperial palace of Goslar shows that the idea appealed to the Hohenstaufen emperors. A further refinement was developed in the late Middle Ages. Little oratories were built behind screens and accessed directly by passages or even bridges so that the ruler could follow the ritual of the mass without being involved physically, without, in fact, being seen. A small enclosed shrine was attached to the south side of Sainte Chapelle Paris in the reign of Louis XI from which the kings could watch the service through a window cut sideways in the wall (Dillange, 1985, 15). At Thornbury, Gloucestershire, there are traces of a bridge connecting the neighbouring parish church with the fortified manor house of the Dukes of Buckingham which would have provided a similar amenity to its ducal owners. A stone screen in the north wall of the Conventual church of St Helen's, Bishopsgate, London would have allowed the cloistered nuns a sight of the altar without being seen themselves.

Chapels in palaces were often richly decorated. Those in the royal palaces in London and Paris were superb repositories of the finest examples of the international gothic style. Sainte Chapelle was a large reliquary chapel; in addition to the crown of thorns there were fragments of the lance, the sponge, Christ's mantle and shroud; the precious blood, the milk and hair of the Virgin Mary, part of the skull of St John the Baptist and the Rod of Moses made up the astonishing list. It was crowned by the presentation in 1306 of the head of St Louis, canonised in 1299. De Joinville describes how he went to the King's chapel 'and found the king who had mounted on the gallery of the relics, and had caused them to take down the True Cross' (De Joinville, 1938, 222). He undertook the crusade with disastrous consequences. The chapel has lost much of the statuary which decorated the lower parts but most of the glass is intact. Nineteenth-century artists restored the rich painted decoration. Henry III provides a vivid commentary on the decoration, furnishing and fitting out of his chapels in the *liberate Rolls*. A fragment of plaster painted with green drapery was found in the ruins of the Queen's chapel at Westminster. Lead stars and crescents with traces of gilding were found at Clarendon of the same type as those running across fourteenth-century paintings in St Stephen's Chapel at Westminster. A star or sun and a crescent is present on the second seal of Richard I *c*.1197-9. It was apparently a favourite Plantagenet emblem. Perhaps the most remarkable piece of interior decoration of Henry III's palaces, which has survived, is the great circular pavement which his tilers laid out for him in the first-floor chapel at Clarendon. A segment has been re-assembled in the British Museum. It is composed of a series of ever widening circular bands of tiles, narrow green ones alternating with brown tiles with complex floriated and geometrical inlaid patterns in yellow. The outermost band contains an inscription. It is likely that the tiles were made in a kiln recovered in the ruins of the palace. This, too, has been lifted bodily and displayed in the British Museum (Eames, 1985, 48-50). Henry III could appreciate and find inspiration in his fellow monarch's achievement. He so admired the Sainte Chapelle which he saw in 1245 that, as a poet put it, he would like to have put it into a cart and taken it away with him!

The inter-monarchical rivalry continued into the next century and indeed intensified once Edward III claimed the throne of France. His completion of the upper stage of St Stephen's chapel together with its rich decoration in painting, glass, tiles and metal was an artistic challenge to the French monarchy, reeling under successive defeats at the hands of the English at Crécy and Poitiers. The smoking shell was all that remained after the fire in the Houses of Parliament in 1834 but fortunately antiquaries had been busy 30 years before taking careful measurement and making beautiful watercolour drawings. This together with the full documentary record enables us to visualise the chapel in its full glory (Steane, 1999, 177-81). (see **39-40**)

The last aspect of these aristocratic chapels to be reviewed is how they were served. Chapels require chaplains. Edward I, a man in Prestwich's phrase of 'unsophisticated piety', took care to attend mass regularly: although a generous alms giver, he made additional grants when he failed to attend chapel. These grants noticeably increased in 1305-6 as he aged and found it difficult to get out. In the meantime the chaplains who accompanied the king on his campaigns (packing the royal sacred plate and loading it onto the backs of horses) carried on reciting the daily offices. Henry V, who had gone through a moral and spiritual conversion at his accession, took part throughout his reign, campaigns and all, in a daily routine of chapel service; he was accompanied on campaign by the two clerks of his chapel, the dean (Edmund Lacy who would one day become the Bishop of Exeter) and 30 members of his spiritual staff (Allemand, 1997, 215, 350). Henry VI showed even more devotion but in a rather unpleasant ostentatious manner. It seems his principal interest in the last resort when founding his college of Eton was not educational; it was spiritual. He was prepared to dispense with the school provided that the services continued. To ensure the continuation of a daily round of prayers and masses communities of canons were established by

45   Goslar, Germany. Early twelfth-century chapel of St Ulrich attached to imperial
     palace. Lower part is a Greek cross in plan, upper chapel is octagonal. Whole building
     suggests shape of imperial crown. The heart of Emperor Henry III is buried here.
     Photo by author

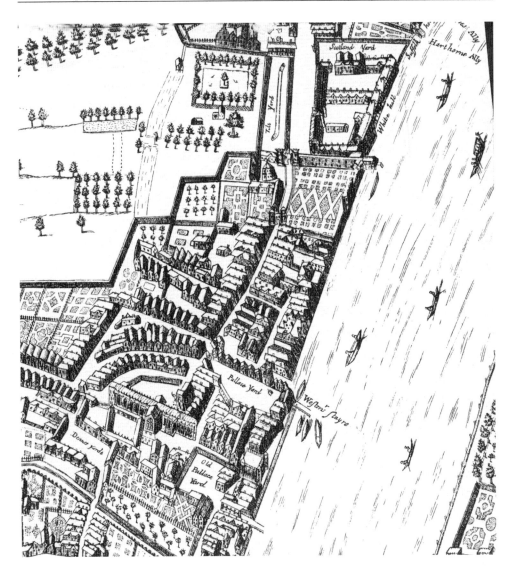

46 *View of Palaces of Westminster, lower left, and Whitehall, right centre. St James' Park top left.* Map by Faithorne and Newcourt 1658

Edward III at Windsor to serve St George's chapel and at Westminster to serve St Stephen's. Accommodation for the canons and their vicars (to continue the daily round of services in place of the canons when they were absent) was found immediately in the vicinity of the chapels. Houses, in the case of Windsor, two-storey and timber-framed, were grouped round a cloister. Eating was in common in a refectory. The arrangement was very similar to that provided in the fourteenth century by colleges in Oxford. The vicars and canons found it difficult to get on with one another so they were separated in 1409 and the horseshoe-shaped cloister was added with 21 small houses to the west of St George's chapel for the vic-ars (St John Hope, 1913, 501-2, 517-18). These timber-framed houses with brick nogging (called 'brike fillying') still survive. At Westminster accommodation for the dean and 12 canons, helped out by 13 vicars to service the chapel of St Stephen, was provided as an afterthought. The chapel was well under construc-tion when in 1348 the king established a college. He gifted an area to the north of the chapel on which the cloister was built and the chapter house planned. To house the vicars a row of little houses was constructed between the cloister and the river and extending northwards. The canons, who were expected to build their own houses were accommodated along a street known as Canon Row to the north of the palace precincts (Allen Brown, Colvin, Taylor, 1963, 525). (**46**)

Chapels comprised an important architectural element in castles and palaces reflecting the profound religiosity of society. The powerful regulated their lives by following the ritual of the church. Henry II may have fidgeted in church and John is said to have told the preacher to cut short his sermon, but the point is that both these powerful monarchs attended church frequently. The next chapter looks at power from the point of view of the clerical practitioners. First the papacy which accumulated an astonishing conglomeration of powers in this period. Then the artefacts which symbolised the supreme power of the papacy and the other princes of the church are described. We consider how secularism in the form of dynastic and family monuments invaded the sacred space and describe the seating arrange-ments within churches. Finally the chapter ends by analysing how the church fought back to maintain its sacred aura towards the end of the Middle Ages.

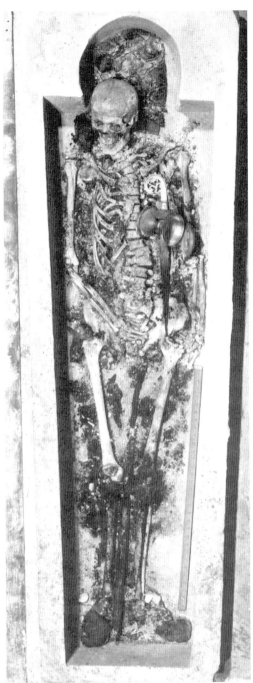

Left: *York Minster. Painted lid of coffin of Archbishop Walter de Gray.*
Right: *York Minster. Vertical view of de Gray coffin after opening. Note pastoral staff,*
chalice and paten in situ.
Photographs courtesy of Society of Antiquaries, London

4 Power and the Church: popes, prelates and priests

Decline, recovery and degradation: the papacy 800-1500

The Papacy, during the two centuries after Charlemagne's coronation in 800 by Pope Leo III, declined in power and influence in Western Europe. Too often the Vicars of Christ were short-lived nonentities, chosen from warring Roman families, with little claim to holiness or even respect who frequently spent their resources on petty bickering on the Roman stage. They thus lost what spiritual authority they had in Italy and their claims to lead the church universal sank into insignificance. Other religious forces took over in guiding Europe during this difficult time when its cultural, economic and social life had been severely damaged by the Viking, Moslem and Magyar raids of the ninth and tenth centuries.

The monastery of Cluny in Burgundy led the way of reformation; it was founded in 910 and eventually became the head of an order of several hundred monasteries following a reformed Benedictine rule. In sustained missionary activity the lead was taken by German and Anglo-Saxon bishops and monks co-operating with Christian lay rulers. Such was Otto I's project of converting the Slavs, whose lands were newly conquered by German warrior farmers between Elbe and Oder, by setting up the archbishopric of Magdeburg. Other missionaries founded the Bohemian diocese of Prague which was subjected to Mainz: Hungary and Poland both managed to organise Christian churches which were outside the Empire and largely independent of Germany.

In the middle of the eleventh century all this changed. The Emperor Henry III took the degraded Papacy firmly in hand, appointed reforming popes such as the remarkable Leo IX (1049-54) and they instituted annual councils at Rome and elsewhere which passed reforming decrees. These, in turn, were backed by imperial muscle power. The Papacy in 1059 shook itself free of imperial control by becoming elective, but the election was in the hands of the College of Cardinals, vital if the head of the church was to be free from subservience to the Roman mob, or, for that matter, to the German emperor. Decrees against the sale of ecclesiastical offices (simony) and clerical marriage (non-celibacy) were repeated. The Papacy now bid fair to take up again the leadership of the church in Western Europe. The Eastern church (Greek Orthodox) in the meantime broke away and became a tool of the Byzantine Emperors for the next 400 years.

47 *Papal* bulla *of Clement VI (1342-52). All papal documents were authenticated by the* bulla *or leaden seal, attached by a string of silk or hemp. The seal contained the Pope's name, in this case CLEMENS VI. Of the apostles' heads, those of SS Peter and Paul are surrounded by a fixed number of dots, increased or diminished in different pontificates; to count them was a test of genuineness.* Ashmolean Museum, Oxford; photo by Vernon Brooke

During the 50 years from 1070-1120 the two major powers in Western Europe, Emperors and Popes, were locked in a struggle over who was to control the choice of leaders of the church, the Bishops and the Abbots. This was the 'Investiture' struggle (Brooke, 1947, 171). The king/emperor was accustomed to invest the bishop-elect with the symbols of his office, the episcopal ring and staff with the words 'Receive the Church'. This seemed to reforming popes, like Gregory VII (1073-85), as tantamount to lay control over spiritual offices, a usurpation of his own power as head of the church. It also opened the way to corruption because bishops would look to the secular ruler, the king, their appointee and pay master. A compromise was eventually reached long after Gregory VII was in his grave. The kings of England and France could not afford to lose control over the choice of bishops and abbots and the deal reached guaranteed their continuing control over the church. Papal power probably reached an apogee in the rule of Innocent III (1198-1216). He had an exalted conception of his position 'set midway between God and man, below God but above man', given 'not only the universal church but the whole world to govern'. Innocent played a major part in eliminating the powerful heretical movements of Southern France by unleashing the Albigensian Crusade. The Franciscan and Dominican orders of Friars, the former by inspired preaching, the latter by spearheading the Inquisition, crushed the Cathar heretics with strong Papal support. Thereafter in the period 1250-1500 the Papacy degenerated. It abused its final weapon of excommunication by overuse. It presided over a vast ecclesiastical money-making machine. It attempted to put papal nominees into well-paid church jobs through Europe (Papal Provisions). Its *curia* interfered in legal matters by its claim to hear appeals from the courts of the other powers. It even claimed to be their feudal overlord. It increasingly involved itself in wars in Italy in an attempt to build up and defend the Papal state. Finally the Papacy lost the respect of many in the period 1315-1400 during the so-called Avignonese Captivity (when popes deserted Rome for 70 years in favour of Avignon in South France) and during the Great Schism when there were rival popes for a long period calling one another impostors. As the Papacy was dragged down in the mire, seeds were sown of dissent. Parts of Europe such as England and Bohemia were beginning to break away politically and doctrinally and to look to their lay rulers for spiritual leadership.

Tiaras, mitres, croziers and rings: the archaeology of ecclesiastical artefacts

The papal reform movement of the eleventh century put forward the claim of the popes to hold the supreme position on earth. Popes like Gregory VII were ambitious to control by spiritual coercion temporal powers, to arbitrate in disputes between kings and in effect to claim imperial powers for themselves. Imperial power included the trappings of office. Gregory VII, emphasising the so-called Donation of Constantine (a forgery of the eighth/ninth century, alleging that Constantine had handed dominion over Rome, Italy and the West to the bishops of Rome), interpreted the tall papal tiara as an imperial crown (**colour plate 17**). It was provided with one diadem, a golden circlet, which supposedly represented 'kingship from the hand of God'. By the thirteenth century it became customary to add another to symbolise 'emperorship by the hand of Peter'. Boniface VIII (1294-1303) pushed his luck still further by adding a third diadem, making the tiara a triple crown. He is said to have asserted to the envoys of the German emperor Albrecht: 'I am Caesar, I am Emperor', which, even if this allegation is a smear spread by his political enemies, probably sums up his own perception of his high office (Krautheimer, 1980, 151).(see **colour plate 17**)

The tiara was, in essence, a tall hat, marking out the wearer as exceptionally significant. It had no particular sacral character being derived from the *camelaucum*, a white pointed cap of eastern, probably Syrian origin. The addition of the circlets already mentioned was probably due to a desire to differentiate the papal headdress from the episcopal mitre, by this time the regular liturgical prerogative of bishops, and the more favoured abbots. The circlet was sometimes scalloped like a coronet (very similar in design to the crowns worn by the Plantagenet kings of England), while the shape of the tiara was that of a fools cap, and the colour nearly always white. Sculptured representations of the pope wearing his tiara begin to multiply in the papacy of Boniface VIII: on the five dating from the early part of his reign, he is shown wearing one circlet; the double crowned appears in the latter part (the bust and the recumbent statue in the Grotte Vaticane and the kneeling statue in the Lateran) all show a tiara bound at the edge by a band set with lozenges of pearls from which rises a second band with fleurons and halfway up a third band, also jewelled with fleurons (Galbreath, 1930, 17-20).

No tiara has survived from this early period but mitres have, together with croziers, rings and ecclesiastical vestments, the latter in some numbers. The insignia of high ecclesiastical office, the so-called pontificals, as we have seen, were of utmost significance, especially in an illiterate age when visual images were all important at conveying the idea of authority. When archbishops or bishops died their bodies were dressed in the robes they had worn at their consecration and were buried with their mitres on their heads, their staffs (or croziers) to hand, their pontifical rings on their fingers, and, if archbishops, arrayed in the pallium, the vestment indicating papal approval of their election. Customarily this had involved a trip to Rome to meet the Pope to swear obedience and to receive it from the altar of one of the Roman churches.

Two controlled excavations of archbishop's tombs took place in York Minster, 1967-9, when paving around them was to be renewed. Archbishop Walter de Gray (archbishop of York 1216-55) had been made Chancellor at the extraordinarily young age of 21 (cf William Pitt the Younger, youngest Prime Minister at 24) then regent and ambassador during the minority of Henry III. He organised a fabric fund to rebuild the south transept of York Minster and used it as a gigantic chantry chapel for his own sepulchre. His tomb lid was remarkable in that on excavation the coffin lid was found to have a painted representation of the archbishop, in his mitre, carrying a cross, in full pontificals (see p124). The paint was lapis lazuli blue, gold, black and green, and had evidently still been tacky when the mortar was applied to its upper surface and the effigy, delivered from the Dorset Purbeck marble quarries, was laid upon it. The Archbishop's head rested in a finely woven skull cap and portions of skilfully woven bands found near his neck had fallen from his mitre. The pastoral staff had a head of walrus ivory strengthened by a jewelled metal strip. The design of the scroll of conventional foliage indicates that it was already an antique at the time of the Archbishop's death (1255). He had become bishop of Worcester 41 years before and so it is possible that the staff went back that far, a tangible link with the past. His feet were clad in leather sandals and on his finger was a large and showy ring, gold with a large cabochon sapphire flanked by a minute ruby and an emerald each set separately (Oman in Ramm, 1971, 126).

The ring was also a convenient object to hand on to one's successor; and to give away to one's relations or supporters as a sign of affection or respect (**colour plate 31**). One is reminded of Anglo-Saxon war leaders known as ring givers. The gold ring was a magnificent demonstration of open handedness. Bishops formed large collections of rings. Walter de Stapledon (Bishop of Exeter d.1327) left no less than 91. Bishop John Grandisson willed away seven individual rings in 1368 as well as

1 *Marienburg (Malbork). Tower of palace/fortress of Teutonic knights. Fourteenth century.* Photo by author

2 *Aachen. Rathaus. Carolingian arcade in apsidal end.* Photo by author

3 Avignon. Palace of the Popes.
Fourteenth-century tower.
Photo by author

4 Rome. Arch of Constantine.
Early fourth century.
Photo by author

5   Lincoln Cathedral.
    West front.
    Photo by author

6   Rome. Arch of Titus.
    Set up AD 81-2 to
    commemorate military
    victories of Emperor.
    Photo by author

7   *Rome, Arch of Titus. The Emperor in triumphal procession.* Photo by author

8   *Trier, Porta Nigra. The north gate of the Roman city. Note twelfth-century apsidal end of a medieval church on the right. This front faces into the city.* Photo by author

9 *Westminster Palace. South front of hall. Eleventh-century core, fourteenth-century rebuild.* Photo by author

10 *Lincoln. Bishop's Palace. Kitchen from terrace outside Bishop's palace.* Photo by author

11 *Lincoln. Bishop's palace. Kitchen above vaulted undercroft. Note tiled oven in upper storey.* Photo by author

12 *Hampton Court Palace. Royal kitchen. Mid-sixteenth century. Note hatches at far end.* Photo by author

13 *Windsor Castle. Interior of restored kitchen 1999. Note medieval louvred roof and the generous scale of the kitchen, large enough to cope with the feeding requirements of Edward III's court.* Photo: Royal Palaces

14 *Prague. East face of tower/gate spanning end of Charles IV bridge.* Photo by author

15 *Westminster Palace. St Stephen's chapel. Fourteenth century, destroyed in 1834 fire.* Photo by author

16 *Brightwell Baldwin church, Oxford. Fourteenth-century chest with painting of St George and the dragon. The dragon has disappeared but the princess is still there (top right) kneeling.* Photo by Vernon Brooke

17 *Triple tiara on head of God the Father. Carving of Trinity. Fifteenth century, English. Private collection.* Photo by James Ayres

18 *Magdalen College, Oxford. Buskins, slippers and boots thought to have belonged toBishop William of Waynflete, founder of the college, d. 1486.* Photo by Vernon Brooke

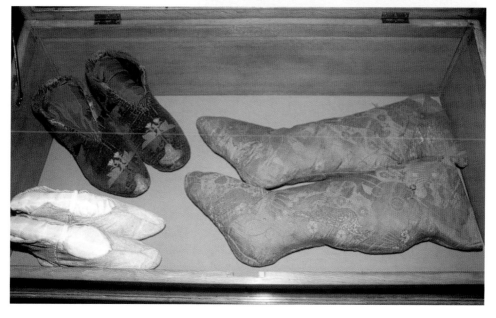

19 Fontevrault, France. Effigies of Plantagenet royal family. Photo by Ian Soden

20 Little Kimble church, Buckinghamshire. Fourteenth-century heraldic glass. Photo by Vernon Brooke

21 *Little Kimble church, Buckinghamshire.*
    Tiles from Chertsey Abbey showing
    king on throne and crusader on horse.
    Thirteenth century.
    Photo by Vernon Brooke

22 *German Imperial*
    crown, called the crown
    of Charlemagne. Made
    in Reichenau Abbey in
    tenth century. Photo
    by Vernon Brooke

23   Crown of Hungary. So-called St Stephen's crown. Parts are tenth-/eleventh-century.
Photo: Budapest museum

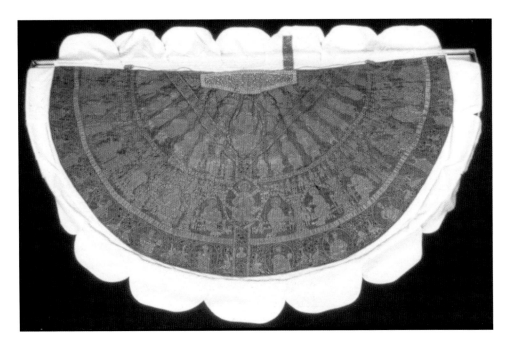

24   Mantle of Hungarian medieval kings. Photo: Budapest Museum

25 *Aachen. Coronation hall of kings/emperors. Heavily restored in nineteenth century.*
Photo by author

26 *Prague Castle. Ladislav hall from north. Early fifteenth century.* Photo by author

27   *Brightwell Baldwin church, Oxfordshire. Brass of John Cottesmore, Chief Justice and his wife.* Photo by Vernon Brooke

28 *Lübeck, Germany. Hostentor, built 1469-78 to defend this Hanseatic city from the west.* Photo by author

29 *Bremen. Renaissance front of town hall 1609-12 with medieval church and market square behind.* Photo by author

30 *Magdalen College, Oxford. Twelfth-century document giving rights to Hospital at Brackley.* Photo by Vernon Brooke

31 *Part of Thame hoard, Oxfordshire. Found in 1940 by the edge of River Thame. The magnificent reliquary ring is set with a double-armed cross of amethyst and the two others are set with stones thought to have magical properties. Ashmolean Museum, Oxford.* Photo by Vernon Brooke

48 Arles. Cathedral
of St Trophime.
Twelfth-century
sculptured figure
of St Trophime
dressed as a
bishop, right hand
held up in
blessing, left hand
clutches crozier.
Note short mitre
and pallium.
Photo by author

the gift of a pontifical ring to any bishop attending his funeral. In 1930 a beautiful iconographic-type ring with an enamelled engraving of the Virgin with the child giving an apple was found near Grandisson's tomb in Exeter cathedral. It is likely that the bishop, who had studied in his youth at Paris under Jean Fornier (later Pope Benedict XII) and had lived in Avignon (as chaplain to Pope John XXII), bought the ring in Paris, the European centre of fine goldsmith's work. We know that he purchased a pastoral staff here, and that he had his predecessor Walter de Stapledon's mitre repaired here at a cost of 200 marks sterling (Cherry, 1991, 207-8).

A second archiepiscopal tomb was opened in York Minster, that of the less distinguished Godfrey de Ludham (archbishop 1258-65). Here, when the tomb was opened, considerable remains of the mitre were seen to have survived. It was 'short and plain of a coarse linen-like material with two straps at the back'. The Y-shaped *pallium*, consisting of a silk band encircling the chest and upper arms, with three maltese crosses, originally black or red, sewn on it and with little lead weights at the ends was found brittle, brown, but intact. Ludham's pastoral staff was of wood with a crooked head designed with two scrolls of elegant thirteenth-century stiff-leaf style. His ring was of gold set with an irregular hexagonal cabochon sapphire and also buried (with both archbishops) were silver parcel gilt sets of chalice and paten.

Another way in which medieval ecclesiastical insignia have come down to us is that they were presented as memorabilia to their collegiate foundations by their users. Two prime examples from the University of Oxford were the gifts of Bishop William of Wykeham to New College and Bishop William of Waynflete to Magdalen College. Wykeham (d. 1404) bequeathed to his college his sandals, dalmatics, crozier and mitre. The mitre with gold filigree and jewels is fragmentary and has been reconstructed, but the crozier, despite many repairs, is still a magnificent object, gilt copper and covered in late gothic niched figures and enamel work. The dalmatics and sandals mentioned in his will have disappeared. A pair of red knitted episcopal gloves, decorated with the sacred monogram once linked with Wykeham, and now thought to have belonged to William Warham, Archbishop of Canterbury, and Warden of the College in the early sixteenth century, has survived. Bishop William of Waynflete 'the only schoolmaster to have become Prime Minister' (or rather Chancellor!) made no mention of bequeathing his episcopal ornaments in his will but a Magdalen College inventory of 1495 lists vestments which must have belonged to their founder (**colour plate 18**). They included his footwear, a remarkable pair of buskins of flowered green silk, and two pairs of shoes, the smaller slippers of soft white leather designed to be worn inside the larger ankle boots of crimson cut velvet, patterned with Waynflete's heraldic lilies and gold thread. His mitre and crozier were stolen by the Puritan vandals in 1646. Such precious objects were not bankable. Their function was to provide tangible manifestations of the founder's personal possessions to accompany the memorial masses sung down the ages in collegiate chapels for the souls of the founder (St John Hope, 1907, 465-92 and Campbell, forthcoming).

The secular invasion of sacred space

The visitor to Westminster Abbey is hard put to appreciate the glories of the Gothic architecture because aisles, transepts and choir are cluttered up with often outsize monuments. Many recall national figures and events but they undoubtedly detract from the sacred aura of the place. It is difficult for anyone going into a church so encumbered to be inspired by a clearer perception of the truths of the Christian religion. This has not always been so. Theophilus, a monk-craftsman of the twelfth century, wrote a treatise on the crafts of stone, glass, metal and paint useful in decorating a church. He referred to the motivation of the Christian artist when he stated:

> By setting off the ceiling panels and walls with a variety of kinds of work and a variety of pigments you have shown the beholders something of the likeness of the Paradise of God . . . thus you have caused them to praise God the Creator in this his creation and to proclaim him marvellous in his works. (Hawthorn and Smith, 1979, 79)

Medieval churches were decorated with scenes from the Old and New Testaments, the lives of the saints and could be compared to vast books explaining visually the major doctrines of the Catholic church. They also from the twelfth century onwards 'became dumps, repositories of memories, associations and, often objects' (Martindale, 1992, 146). It is the way in which they were gradually invaded by monuments of the powerful in church and state that is the subject of the following sections.

Tombs as religious foci

A religious house might well be considered as belonging to God but from the very earliest times it was also thought to have belonged to its saint and to its founder. The planning of many early Christian churches in Western Europe was influenced by the requirement to house and to display saintly relics, whether whole or part bodies, or other objects associated with the saint. The purpose was to provide access for pilgrims, in particular those seeking miraculous cures and this dictated the need to build crypts, alcoves, chapels and tombs all designed to enable the devotee to get as close as was humanly possible to the remains of the saint (Crook, 2000). One of the earliest (seventh-century) and most revered Anglo-Saxon churches in Canterbury, that dedicated to SS Peter and Paul, had a porticus built onto the north-east of the nave which contained the tombs of St Augustine and his immediate successors to the see and another built on to the south-east which acted as a royal burial chapel, containing the tombs of King Ethelbert and his Queen, Bertha (Clapham, 1930, 18-19). In the ninth century a specially contrived tomb shrine, to display the remains of the cult figure of the Bishop and Saint Swithun, was built in the old Minster at Winchester. After the construction of the replacement Norman cathedral the grave was emptied and Swithun's bones were translated in 1093 to a prestigious location in the choir of the new church. His original grave, however, continued to attract pilgrimage and a succession of chapels enclosed a series of monuments (Crook, 2000, 163-4). A similar translocation was carried out when the tomb of Osmund, first Norman bishop of Old Sarum, was removed bodily in the 1220s and reinstated in a place of honour at the east end of the new cathedral risen in the water meadows 1 1/2 miles to the south. The shrine base has three arched niches, convenient for the pilgrim to thrust his afflicted limb near to the body of the bishop.

Another aspect is the commissioning of effigies and tombs of long past and distinguished potentates by churches of somewhat uncertain status which needed a morale booster. Whether these retrospective memorials were meant to deceive the average pilgrim is uncertain. The idea is not unlike the medieval custom of monasteries forging documents to 'prove' their right to age-old privileges. Reprehensible to the eyes of historians, but acceptable even to admirable archbishops like Lanfranc. In 1158 we find Henry of Blois, brother of King Stephen and Bishop of Winchester, industriously collecting all the bones of the pre-Conquest kings and bishops buried in his cathedral, boxing them up and placing the chests round the choir. It was plainly advantageous politically for the Norman rulers to demonstrate their ancestral connections with Cnut and Emma. Bishop Fox, 350 years later, made new chests for these venerable relics some of which are still there, high and lifted up. The abbey of St Germain des Près in Paris also thought it worthwhile to fashion monuments of Merovingian monarchs (Childebert, d. 558 and Chilperic d. 584) thus laying claim to a bit of retrospective veneration. Occasionally an attempt was made to produce a deliberately archaic effect. The canons of Wells placed retrospective effigies of Anglo-Saxon bishops in the south aisle of their new thirteenth-century cathedral. Two, identified as Dudoc and Giso, are shown wearing low mitres appropriate to the Anglo-Saxon period. They would seem to be copies of monuments formerly in the now superseded cathedral. Wells, by no means sure of its cathedral status, was thus emphasising its links to a glorious Anglo-Saxon past (Rodwell, 2001, 147).

Dynastic and family tombs

The most complete example of a conventual interior being enriched with reminders of a secular past is the burial church of the Capetian monarchy at St Denis, Paris. Here a full-scale reorganisation of the Merovingian and Carolingian tombs took place in the 1260s involving the production of numbers of retrospective memorials (Erland-Brandenburg A. 1975). King Louis IX commissioned 16 royal effigies to fill an iconographical gap representing the Carolingian and early Capetian kings (Colvin, 1991, 138). Further rearrangement took place in 1306 when Philip the Fair reordered the tombs putting those of his thirteenth-century predecessors, Philip Augustus, Louis VIII, and Louis IX in the centre, forming a symbolic link, likened to the bar on an H, between the Carolingian group to the north and the Capetian tombs to the south. The result was a veritable genealogy in stone (Crossley, 2000, 161).

Other dynasties did things differently. In Germany in the eleventh and early twelfth centuries the Salian King/Emperors were buried at Speyer cathedral. This great Romanesque building had been founded by Conrad II to be a symbol of royal power and a mausoleum for his dynasty. Conrad II, his wife Gisela, Henry III, Henry IV and his wife Bertha, and Henry V all lay (until 1900 when they were excavated) under plain and unadorned slabs in front of the most prestigious place, the high altar. Conrad's entrails, including the heart, thought to be the seat of the soul and the mind which joined the soul to the body, were buried before the high altar of Utrecht Cathedral while the Emperor Henry III's entrails were buried in the royal chapel at Goslar, his '*patria*' and '*lar domesticus*'. At Bamberg, Paderborn and, it has been recently claimed, at Utrecht, there were crosses of churches where the cathedrals stood at the centre of a cross spanning the city, each of the four arms of which were marked by collegiate churches or cloisters (Mekking, 1996, 101). Here we see the German King/Emperors carrying out the shaping of the townscape to promote the dynasty.

The Angevin dynasty of England and Anjou founded a monastery at Fontevrault in the middle of their French dominions (**colour plate 19**). Here are their effigies. They lie in royal robes, austere in form, but originally brightly painted, as if on their biers awaiting resurrection. Eleanor of Aquitaine rests quietly reading a book, surrounded by the images of her tumultuous husband Henry II and her warring son Richard I (Steane, 1999, 43). King John was hurriedly interred in Worcester Cathedral; his effigy was carved 15 years later. Henry III spent many years, much thought, and treasure in preparing a burial place for himself in Westminster Abbey, his newly reconstructed coronation church. It seems to have been Edward I who conceived the idea (perhaps influenced by the French example) of making Westminster Abbey a regular mausoleum for the Plantagenet dynasty. At any rate he commissioned a goldsmith, William Torel, to prepare gilt bronze effigies of his father and his first wife, Eleanor of Castile. They were placed on table tombs decorated with Cosmati work in the spaces between the columns to the north of St Edward's Chapel, behind the high altar. The place was hallowed because Henry III had already carried out the translation of the remains of the royal saint, the last of the Anglo-Saxon kings, to a glittering feretory, raised up on a splendid tomb, its arcaded sides designed for maximum pilgrim penetration. Here then, in the place of utmost honour and supreme sanctity, are the tombs of the later Plantagenets Edward III, Philippa of Hainault, Richard II and Anne of Bohemia. A Lancastrian, also with a high military reputation, Henry V was interred in the apex of the apse in 1422 (Steane, 1999, 46-63).

This dynastic interest which almost amounted to an obsession with ruling families memorialising themselves spread in the fourteenth century to the rulers of the church, the papacy and the bishops, to the lay nobility and even to the knightly class. It can be traced in a series of papal tombs which became magnificent vehicles for display. Pope John XXII's (d. 1334) tomb in Notre-Dame-des-Doms, Avignon is a particularly interesting one because it shows some of the architectural characteristics seen in the amazing tomb of Edward II (d. 1327) at Gloucester Abbey (not yet a cathedral). The outsize gothic canopy, the extensive use of the ogee arch and the intricate niche work are found in both. English men whether architects, churchmen, diplomats or pilgrims, of course freely came and went between England, Avignon and Rome. Pope John's tomb also contained 'weepers' in its niches, sculptured representations of the funeral cortège (Gardner, 1992, 147). These little figures, usually dressed in the height of fashion and in insouciant poses are usually doing anything but weep. They are found along the sides of the slightly better preserved papal monument of Clement VI (d. 1352) at La Chaisse-Dieu in the Auvergne. Here the pope refounded the church, deliberately rebuilding it to house his own tomb which was ready to receive his body some years before his death. The 'weepers' have been identified as his family and include Alinorda, the pope's sister, and her children. The tomb is also plastered all over with the arms of its patron. The Pope in his tomb has replaced Christ and his

49   King's Langley church, Hertfordshire. Late fourteenth-century tomb of Edmund of Langley, son of Edward III. Plinth of Purbeck marble. The top of the tomb is part of an altar slab. The sides are of alabaster and have shields of arms. On the end (left) arms of St Edward Confessor, Richard II, St Edmund. On side (centre) the Empire (eagle with two heads). Then a series relating to his brothers, Prince of Wales (the Black Prince), Lionel Duke of Clarence, Edmund Duke of York, Thomas duke of Gloucester and ends with Henry of Bolingbroke. Photo by author

saints as the focal point in the building. The takeover of the tomb-patron seems complete (Gardner, 1992, 144-6).

This desire to see the tomb as a kind of family Bible in alabaster and stone is carried a step further in the tomb in Westminster Abbey of Philippa Hainault, Edward III's wife (who pleaded for the lives of the burghers of Calais). It was erected in 1365-7, the brain child of the French court sculptor, Jean de Liège, who made sure that it satisfied the taste of the European aristocratic consumer. Although stripped of its attendant figurines these are known to have consisted of the Queen's continental relations on the south side and her husband's on the north. At her head were images of top people, Edward III (her husband), the Black Prince (her son), William of Holland (her father) and the Emperor Louis of Bavaria (her brother-in-law). At her feet were five kings (Martindale, 1992, 157).

Philippa is surrounded by other members of the Plantagenet dynasty. By her time Westminster Abbey had become the preferred mausoleum of the English kings. The idea of accumulating memorials of members of the same family in the same place, percolated down to the knightly class. The family of Sir John Cobham of Kent is a case in point. The chancel of the church at Cobham is literally paved with 20 brasses, the largest collection in Britain, turning it into 'a village Westminster Abbey'. The essential concomitant of this lavish display was the establishment of a college, a community of five (later increased to 11) priests, charged with praying in perpetuity for the souls of Sir John, and indeed, for the whole family. Their brasses were meant to be an *aide memoire* for the priests to make sure no one was missed out! The doctrine of purgatory, now fully developed with its trials and torments, was a frightening prospect. Perhaps Sir John could thereby shorten the time spent by his soul (and those of his family) in this limbo between heaven and hell (Saul, 2001, 234).

A second well-documented example, but this time involving members of the newly arrived aristocracy, is the very up-market chantry chapel set up by Alice, Duchess of Suffolk (d. 1475) and widow of William de la Pole, first Duke of Suffolk. The Suffolks had already built a palace, reconstructed the church and founded a school with adjoining almshouse in Ewelme, an Oxfordshire village below the Chilterns. The parents of Alice were suitably commemorated in the family church in a tomb standing lengthwise against the parclose screen of the chapel. Two brass effigies depict Thomas Chaucer in full armour (the son of Geoffrey the poet) and his wife Maud in wimple and gown. Both have at their feet the respective heraldic emblems of their families, the Chaucer unicorn and the double-tailed Burghersh lion. Enamelled shields referring to the political affinities of the family were attached later when the tomb was moved to its present position in 1438 (Goodall, 2001, 171-4). More remarkable is the furnishing of Alice's chantry chapel. Wooden angels look down from the carved roof; the walls are powdered with the sacred monogram IHS. A nobly painted alabaster effigy of the Duchess lies in state over and under a canopied two-storeyed tomb. Below her behind a pierced screen is an emaciated cadaver — a reminder that life is short and death certain. The tomb reflects 'the desire to trumpet ancestry and political connections' as well as 'the need to secure salvation' (Goodall, 2001, 197).

In the case of Cobham the focus of attention in the chancel has been diverted away from a place where the miracle of the mass was enacted for all men by the priestly intercessor to a more personal and individualistic ritual stage in which one family, and one family alone, benefits. Ewelme takes this process one stage further. The church by virtue of the complete rebuild has become the possession of the holders of the manor: the Chaucers allied by marriage to the Suffolks have made it their own. The chantry chapel to the north-east by the richness of its decoration in alabaster, paint, glass, carved wood and fretted stone diverts the worshipper from the glory of God to the glorification of the Suffolk/Chaucer connection. The presence of the 13 old men from 'God's House' and the chaplain all praying day in day out, throughout the Christian year, interceding for the souls of their founders and benefactors provided a team of actors repeating the same play for a long run. Within this theatre of memory so far I have pursued the point that tombs, very often of the secular power holders of society, increasingly tended to become the focal points of interest in churches. A similar phenomenon has been noticed in the subject matter of stained glass. In the early Middle Ages churches were often windowed in stained and painted glass, the subject matter of which comprised scenes representing Old and New Testament figures, prophets and saints, as well as scenes from Christ's life and prefigurations of it found in the Old Testament. These were paid for by invariably well-heeled and sometimes devout donors. After the thirteenth century the newly ennobled and knightly families, aspiring to social emulation, commissioned glass incorporating heraldry of their own, their neighbours' or their allies' coats of arms (**colour plate 20**). This heraldic glass has often survived when the figured representations offensive to Puritans were smashed.

Let us take a couple of examples from Northamptonshire churches, whose glass has been meticulously studied (Marks, 1998). The east window of Stanford-on-Avon is 'a visual manifestation of feudal overlordship and reads like a Roll of Arms'. Marks considers that the earlier of two heraldic groups at Ashby St Ledgers and a series at Lowick underline the value of heraldry as establishing a newly arrived seigneurial family in the community. The churches in his striking phrase became 'theatres of memory' whereby the royal, knightly and newly ennobled solicited prayers for the souls of the donors (Marks, 1998, 10-11, 177-271).

What is true of glass can be extended to the whole fabric of the church. The patron of the living, the lord of the manor, used periodic rebuildings or additions to the church as opportunities to remind peasant congregations as to who was in charge. Many churches were subject to continuous or overlapping building campaigns throughout the Middle Ages. The building would be under scaffolding, a constant reminder of lordly involvement. Local pride in their parish church would burgeon. To add an aisle here or a west tower there was a useful way of bridging the gap in men's minds between the death of one leading member of a local family and the succession of another, perhaps a minor. A tower or a set of bells was an especially telling image; it had no particular liturgical function but it could be seen from afar. 'Build me a tower a few feet higher than that provided by the Jones' in the next parish'! All this was a way of fostering local pride, of harnessing local enthusiasm, much of which must have rubbed off to benefit the reputation of the local lordly family (Graves, 1989).

Seating the powerful

The symbolic role of the seat as a sign of authority and power has long been recognised in Western Europe. It still survives in the special seats of privilege accorded to the English sovereign at ceremonies such as the coronation or the opening of parliament. Judges preside over courts from seats constructed on a generous scale (these need to be comfortable, their users have to endure many hours of listening, and in bulky robes!). The authority of bishops is signalled by the provision of splendidly decorated seats (known in Greek as the '*cathedra*') from the siting of which derives the

50 Norwich Cathedral. High altar with apsidal end of Presbytery. Between clustered columns and above steps is the bishop's throne in a central and lofty position. Photo by author

name of the church at the centre of the diocese, the cathedral. Committees were still (before the age of political correctness) controlled by 'chairmen'.

In early Christian churches in England very little is known about seating arrangements. Several stone chairs of bishops and abbots, reputed to be of Anglo-Saxon date, have survived at Canterbury ('St Augustine's Chair'), Hexham and Beverley. Some weathered fragments of a chair, heavily burned but still bearing recognisable Anglo-Saxon carving, have been preserved in Norwich Cathedral. All these chairs, bulky and heavy though they are, have been moved around as the liturgical fashions of the day dictated. At Reculver, Kent in the seventh-century church there was a stone bench to seat the clergy running round the interior curve of the apsidal east end, but in other churches the seats of honour were at the west end. At Barnack (now Cambridgeshire) there is a gabled recess in the west wall of the tower which formed 'the abbots' or presidents' chair', doubtless used by the celebrant at the western altar (Taylor, 1984, 1066). The archbishops'

51 Salisbury Cathedral. Medieval stalls, north side. The seat of the Treasurer which is half as wide again as that of the neighbouring canon. A seat of power!
Photo by author

throne in the pre-Conquest cathedral at Canterbury was sited in the western apse (Blockley *et alia*, 1997, 105). At Norwich the shattered fragments were incorporated in a chair sited at the top of steps behind the high altar in the eastern apsidal end of the Norman cathedral, and physically attached by a stone-lined pipe to a relic chamber underneath. This positioning, which had been favoured in Early Christian churches in Europe during the first millennium, was deliberately anachronistic in England after the twelfth century. It was perhaps thought to be an appropriately reverential gesture to place it in the same position as it had probably held in the church of St Felix, the first bishop of the East Angles. So, once again we find that the holders of ecclesiastical power are conscious of the advantages of referring to the past.

The new position chosen for the bishop's throne in churches of cathedral rank by the early thirteenth century was on the south side, just east of the stalls of the choir, next to that of the chancellor. Craftsmen lavished their art of carving and sculpture on these very large seats of power; wooden ones are still to be found at

52 Magdalen College, Oxford. Interior of chapel looking west. A very 'medieval' interior, created by Cottingham 1829-34. The screen dividing the chapel proper from the ante chapel, the stalls, for president and Dean facing east and for fellows, in rear with backs to wall; and in front the more junior members of the foundation.
Photo by Vernon Brooke

Exeter, Hereford and St Davids dating from the fourteenth and fifteenth centuries. That, at Exeter, is the highest and largest bishop's throne ever known. Bishop Stapledon (1261-1326) who commissioned the throne was a grandee of enormous power and ambition; he was Lord High Treasurer to Edward II, was well in with the Pope (he had been appointed papal chaplain by Clement V) and had scholarly pretensions being Professor of Canon Law and founder of Exeter College at Oxford. His throne in Exeter cathedral was carved by Robert de Galmeton in 1316-17 and images made for it 1317-20. It was also painted and inscribed with 250 letters in 1323-4 so it was meant to serve a didactic purpose. Its siting meant that it was visible even from the nave (Sekules, 1991, 175). All this glory did not save Stapeldon in the long run from a sticky end. He was associated with the unpopularity of the government. His head was hewn from his shoulders by a London mob in the general breakdown of law and order towards the end of Edward II's reign. His throne at Exeter lasted however and was soon being used by John Grandisson (bishop 1327-1369). Such an impressive seat, accommodating a series of episcopal bottoms for nigh on 700 years, must have been a great source of comfort and satisfaction to the successive incumbents of the testing job of ruling the south western diocese.

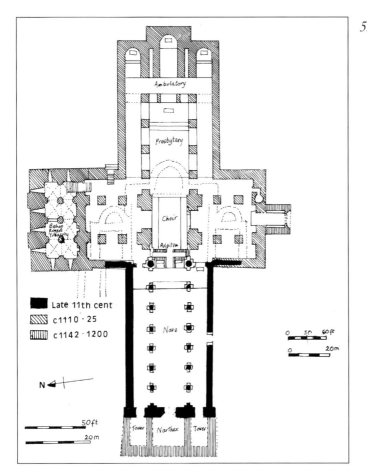

Late 11th cent
c1110 · 25
c1142 · 1200

N

Ambulatory

Presbytery

Bishop Roger's Treasury

Choir

Pulpitum

Nave

Tower   Narthex   Tower

50ft
20m

0 30 60ft
0 20m

53   *Old Sarum and
      Salisbury
      Cathedrals.*
      Left-hand plan
      after John Hope,
      1917; opposite
      plan after
      RCHM (E) 1993

We know a great deal about the seating plans ordered within the choirs of secular cathedrals. In the main they follow the instructions of the *Sarum Consuetudinary*, a liturgical book, the brain child of Bishop Osmund and revised by Bishop Poore of Salisbury Cathedral. *Sarum use* was the main source for liturgical practice in the churches of much of England during the later Middle Ages. The four chief canons who held the critically important offices within the community had the end stalls. Their seats were half as wide again as those allotted to the other canons. By referring to the plan (**53** opposite) it can be seen that the Dean, the president of the chapter had the place of honour in the choir entry at the west end where he sat in the right-hand stall. The Precentor took his seat opposite on the left. At the east end the chancellor was on the first on the right on the south side: opposite him the Treasurer on the north. Next to the Dean and Chancellor were ranged the archdeacons and along the back row were the rest of the canons. The lesser dignitaries, the vicars and finally the choir boys sat in front of the canons along the so-called *secunda forma* and *prima forma*. The use of the term is interesting: it means a bench (as distinct from a chair which of course has a back) and has been carried into the terminology of schools, a form being a group of students of like age and status sharing a bench. The other

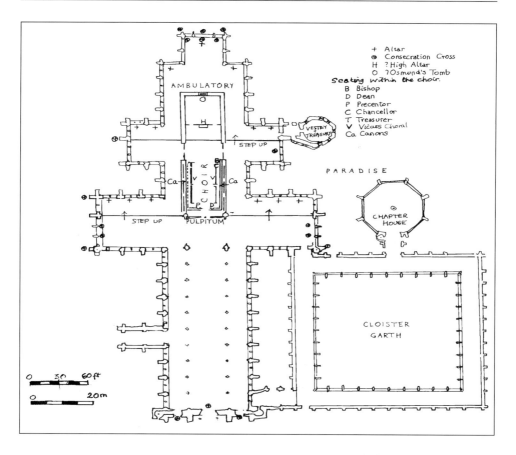

cathedrals of secular canons, Lincoln, Chichester, Wells, York, St Paul's and Hereford all showed roughly the same hierarchical pattern of seating (Bradshaw and Wordsworth 1892 with diagrams).

Similar tendencies towards hierarchical groupings are found, less uniformly because they arose from tradition rather than prescription, in parish churches. Seat reservation in churches can be traced back to the thirteenth century. A Durham synod of 1287 is quoted as saying:

> Also we have heard that, on account of seats in churches, the parishioners are often vexed; two or more persons claiming one seat. By reason that grave scandal is generated in church and the divine office is often impeded we enact that no one from henceforth may claim a seat in church as his own, noble persons and patrons of churches only excepted.

Notwithstanding such episcopal decrees by the late Middle Ages it had become general practice throughout the country for the lord of the manor and his family to be seated (if the church was pewed) towards the front of the nave, for women to occupy space to the north, and for servants and the poor to be relegated to the back of the church. Sinners and excommunicate were forbidden entry and stood outside.

Two interesting developments relating to the seating of the powerful took place in this period. There are signs of what might be called a privatising tendency, whereby a growing number of the aristocracy and the higher gentry constructed for themselves private chapels or chantries within the parish churches and staffed them with chantry priests. Alternatively they are found building private oratories and mini chapels within their houses and employing private chaplains to officiate. Such were the fourteenth-century chapel of the Stonor family in Oxfordshire or that attached to the sprawling fourteenth-/fifteenth-century manorial complex at Haddon Hall Derbyshire. In the latter the box pews for the lord of the manor and his guests were in the chancel and the long oak benches for the servants were in the south aisle. The second development was the invasion of the chancel by laymen, hitherto the preserve of ordained priests, which the clerical antiquary J.C. Cox referred to as 'the offensive and irreverent custom of the squire claiming a large family seat within the chancel' (Cox, 1923, 115-16). Cox reckons that manor pews multiplied soon after the Reformation and that they had their origins in parcloses which surrounded the endowed chantries of local lords. When the Chantries act did away with the chapels and the priests, the lay lords held onto the space they had occupied and this became the family pew.

The Church fights back

To combat these increasing laicising tendencies the church adopted a series of strategies to protect its interests. Over three centuries from *c.*1200-1500 barriers were put up to enclose choirs and presbyteries in conventual churches (called the *pulpitum* or screen) and therefore to keep out laymen, and to separate off chancels from naves in parish churches (the rood screen). Note that these were barriers not walls; aimed at excluding lay folk from penetrating into the more sacred spaces, monopolised by monks, priests and clerics, but not at totally depriving them of some communal participation in services. The sound of singing, intoning or reading aloud going on in the eastern parts of the church could drift over the screens and be heard by the worshipping laiety. Similarly screens can be made both restricting and transparent by being constructed of solid walls or planks in the lower stages but pierced (tracery or holes) in the upper. Some of these screens in cathedral churches (Canterbury, York, Durham for instance), in addition to serving as barriers were exercises in royal propaganda; within the rows of niches lining their western faces were sculptured images of kings — an impressive display of royal and sacerdotal power. Kings, as it were, seen in co-operation with higher ecclesiastics, populated the choir behind. The *pulpitum*, as the major screens were called, had other functions; along the top, and accessed by staircases, were stations where the epistle and the gospel were read to the congregation beneath. Also on the top of rood screens in parish churches the rood (a wooden crucifix) with figures of St Mary and St John were built.

54 *Christchurch Gateway, Canterbury Cathedral. Built 1517 by Prior Goldwell in commemoration of Prince Arthur, oldest son of Henry VII who predeceased his father. Heraldic shields of the great and the good.* Photo by author

The church, secondly, fought back by making its services more mysterious, more magical, more esoteric. Steps were introduced into chancels ensuring a graduated ascent to the high altar. Special stone seats also hierarchically disposed in groups of five or three (for the priest, deacon, sub-deacon) were erected for the clergy on the south side of chancels (the *sedilia*). Special washing places both for the priests hands and for the sacred vessels used in the mass were built into the east end of south chancel walls (*piscinae*). Lockable cupboards or *aumbries* with shelves for the secure storage of the sacred vessels were inserted into the north or more rarely the east side of chancel walls. The host, or communion wafer, had to be made of pure wheat or flour; sometimes an oven for its baking was to be found within the church. All these features became universal with episcopal direction and visitation and can be seen in most of the 9000 or so medieval churches to be found in England. They provided a sophisticated physical framework for the mass — the central sacrament of the church. Here detailed instructions were laid down by the *Sarum Use*, involving a series of highly theatrical movements on the part of the officiating priest, culminating in the elevation of the host. Archaeology provides us with plenty of evidence that this episode in the service was meant to be seen, if only dimly and with difficulty. Screens were frameworks, holes were bored in them at kneeling level, squints were punched through piers, all to enable the devout to witness the display of Christ's body at the supreme moment in the liturgical drama.

At rare times the laiety were allowed to penetrate the screen and enter the chancel, when taking part in processions like the Candlemas and the watching ceremonies associated with the Easter Sepulchre (Duffy, 1992, 112). This was a two-way process. When procession took place the clergy moved out of the sacred space, through the door in the centre of the screen and so into the nave. Processions can be enormously exciting. I remember being in the great Romanesque pilgrimage church of Vezelay in Burgundy on Easter Sunday 1998. First there was the tension of waiting; the church was packed, a subdued murmur arose. Then far-off singing: the procession itself entered the south aisle from the sacristy, crossbearer first, then censing acolytes, then robed choir and in ascending dignity the ministers in their robes and the bishop with tall white mitre and crozier, leading parishioners and pilgrims. The quiet, purposeful and steady marching of this great body of people though clouds of incense, from the darkness of the western end of the great church towards the brightness of the eastern choir. It was very moving to the onlooker.

Elaborate processions were structured according to rank: crossbearer, those carrying the holy water, incense and candles, the clergy, all in ascending order of dignity, followed by the participants. In the great urban Corpus Christ processions of the later Middle Ages the processions were politicised. The clergy lost their central place which was taken over by laymen. The guilds vied with one another to be next to the sacrament, the body of Christ borne along in a jewelled and gold monstrance, as it was carried along the processional path. Their position in the procession fluctuated according to their economic status; if their trade was in decline the magistrates allocated others to the superior position. The procession was a vivid expression of the current realities of power (Rubin, 1991, 251).

This chapter began with Popes; it ends with priests. It has attempted to trace the theme of this book, the phenomenon of power, within the church over 800 years. It suggests that much can be learned from the material manifestations of power, from a close study of the tombs and the tiaras, the mitres and the monuments. The next two are concerned with the ways in which kings and emperors used coronations and crown wearings to buttress their claims to earthly power and how they created a class of lawyers to uphold it.

It should by now be apparent that medieval rulers had a symbiotic relationship with the church. Each needed the other. Marx would have seen this as part of a conspiracy of the feudal establishment to keep the peasants and the bourgeoisie in a state of submission. Resonating throughout was a reliance on ritual. The coronation ritual was the most exciting and emotionally demanding event in a king's life. It was likely to be witnessed by hundreds of the most important of his subjects. It was impressive because of its length and the numbers of people involved, because of the solemn and age-old liturgy used, because of the magnificence of the regalia. The next chapter considers the coronations of the kings of England, France, Germany and Bohemia. The architectural setting of the coronations was clearly an important part, the theatre in which these solemn enactments took place. The crowns, sceptres, swords and mantles were the essential 'props'. Fortified by these events the medieval rulers issued out of the cathedrals to start their reigns.

5 The crowning glory

Anglo-Saxon coronations

The coronation ceremony went back deep into the Anglo-Saxon past. Christian kingship was conferred, confirmed and publicised in new ceremonies of anointing and consecration which were thought up in the tenth century. But the ideas which crystallised in the coronation of King Edgar in 973 were much older. Already kings of Britain are thought to have sat on thrones from the sixth century. Offa, King of Mercia 757-96, was anxious that his son Egfrith should succeed him on the throne and persuaded Papal legates who happened to be visiting to anoint him. Again Aethelwulf King of Wessex returned from Rome in 856 and married Judith, princess of Francia at Rheims. He agreed that the archbishop might consecrate her as queen and it seems likely that he, too, had been consecrated king. The coronation *ordo* was characterised by extreme conservatism. Its unchanging liturgy lasted from the tenth to the twelfth century. A number of coronations of West Saxon kings took place at the royal township of Kingston-upon-Thames. This was on the border between the old kingdoms of Mercia and Wessex, a significant location for a king anxious to be recognised in as wide an area as possible. Other crownings took place at Bath (Edgar) and Winchester (Edward the Confessor). Edgar's coronation at Bath was a particularly interesting choice of location. Again Bath is near the boundary between Mercia and Wessex, and moreover has resonances of Roman rule; the ruins of former buildings were constant reminders of former imperial greatness. Edgar significantly waited until he was 31 before being consecrated king: this was the age at which priesting took place and also when Christ began his ministry and his decision was a 'solemn expression of Christocentric kingship' (Cannon and Griffiths, 1988, 30). The desire to associate kingship with '*Romanitas*' is born out by the images which Anglo-Saxon kings caused to be engraved into the dies of their coinage. King's heads are shown in profile, like Roman emperors with diadems (Alfred penny, struck in London after 886) and open crowns (Aethelstan penny struck in Winchester in mid-930s and Edgar penny struck at Hertford before *c*.973). A third design involving a helmeted head is found in the coinage of Aethelred III 978-1016 when a penny was issued which was a close copy of an Antonianus of the Emperor Maximian. A contemporary pointed helmet is shown on the penny struck at Hereford for Edward the Confessor (Oman 1931. 74, plate XII, 8).

Westminster Abbey: a building designed for coronations

After Edward the Confessor all English kings for the next 200 years, except Stephen, were crowned in his new abbey church at Westminster. The sense of inevitability which arises after centuries of carrying out coronations in the same place was by no means assured in the eleventh century. William I was crowned at Westminster, thus, as Schramm puts it, forging a link with the last Anglo-Saxon king whom he recognised as legitimate and whose heir it was his ambition to be recognised (Schramm, 1937, 76). Rufus was crowned at Westminster in a great hurry to anticipate his brother. The church was very convenient and Lanfranc archbishop of Canterbury was on the spot. To do the same thing twice was, to the medieval mind, well on the way to becoming a precedent. It is noteworthy that Henry I thought it worthwhile to waste time going from Winchester to Westminster to be crowned there. This principle hardened into tradition in the twelfth century. By 1216, because London was in the hands of the French, a makeshift first coronation for Henry III took place at Gloucester. Significantly a second coronation at Westminster was thought proper in 1220 (Carpenter, 1990, 13-14, 187-8). The abbey combined for the English the traditions and rights of Rheims cathedral and the abbey of St Denis as the place of coronation and the guardian of the French regalia. It was very much with the French example of Rheims in mind that Henry III began to rebuild the Confessor's church. His reverence for Edward the Confessor was expressed by his donning of St Edward's regalia at his coronation; it was confirmed in the naming of his eldest son, Edward. The planning of his church at Westminster created a great central space with maximum room for large numbers of witnesses. The choir, located in the nave as at Rheims, helped to keep the central crossing space clear for coronations. The layout also resulted in an eastern end of comparatively small size with the bays of the chevet contracting eastwards to make space before the high altar for the performance of coronations (Binski, 1995, 76, 93). Further the wall passages and the galleries above in the transepts were accessed by newel staircases allowing their use by crowds. Finally Westminster Abbey's proximity to the palace made it a coronation church *par excellence*. (see fig **44**)

The English coronation ceremony

There is a fairly detailed account of Richard I's coronation but little is known about Henry III's or Edward I's. The so-called Fourth Recension, first used in 1308 for the coronation of Edward II, gives a much fuller description (Wickham Legg, 1901, 112 *et seq*). First there was to be prepared a stage somewhat raised between the high altar and the choir of the church near the four high pillars in the crossing. At the ascent of the stage were to be steps ascending to it from the choir through which the prince approaches. A further set of steps leads to the altar. On it is prepared a lofty throne 'that the prince may sit on it and be clearly seen by all the people'.

55 *Impression of seal of Edward I. Note*
    the elaborate throne supported by lions
    with the king seated, crowned. In his
    right hand he holds a long straight
    sceptre with a dove; in his left, an orb
    with a long cross. The castles refer to
    his first marriage with Eleanor of
    Castile, the fleur de lys to his second
    with Margaret of France. Public
    Record Office, London. Photo by
    Vernon Brooke

Procession

On the eve of the coronation the king elect was to ride from the Tower of London to the Palace at Westminster in royal robes to be seen by as many people as possible. This care to make him visible and unforgettable occurs again and again through the arrangements. The night before the king was to perform a vigil of prayer, meditating on his high office. This was followed by a gathering of clergy and nobles in the palace. A ceremonial bath (followed by the creation of knights of the Bath) was succeeded by installation on a throne in the Palace. The king elect issued out of the palace, crossed the street and entered the abbey through the portals in the spectacular north transept. The nave was out since it was under construction for most of the Middle Ages. A procession of clergy led the king to the high altar in Westminster Abbey. With the king installed on the stage the archbishop presented him to the four cardinal points of the church to be acclaimed by the people. It was at this point in William I's coronation that the Norman soldiers mistook the shouts for revolt and set fire to neighbouring houses.

Oath

It is not clear what oath William I swore — something along the lines 'that he would govern the people as well as any previous king had done'. The oath was sworn by William upon the gospels, by Stephen and Henry II upon the gospels and relics, and by Edward I in 1273 on the consecrated host. By 1308 we get a clearer idea of its full terms; it had now three main clauses. The oath promised protection to the church, justice to the people, and the suppression of evil laws and customs. A further clause vowed to protect the rights of the crown

(Richardson, 1960, 161). Whereas to constitutional historians the oath was of fundamental significance, to contemporaries it was the next part, the anointing, which was the culminating stage in the ceremony.

Anointing

Anointing was significant because it set the king apart from his subjects. It conferred quasi-priestly powers upon him, although this was denied by Bishop Grosseteste in a letter answering Henry III who wished to enquire into its exact nature. It was usually performed by the archbishops of Canterbury and involved rending the king's vest down to the girdle before administering the anointing on head, chest and hands (Richardson, 1960, 140). The French kings claimed to be anointed with holy oil which had come down from heaven. The English kings, in rivalry, used holy chrism which had been allegedly given to Thomas Becket by the Virgin Mary. This was rediscovered by Richard II in the Tower of London. He wished to have a second coronation using this holy oil to enhance the mystical aura of kingship but was disallowed by the archbishop. It was used at the coronation of Henry IV who needed anything that could buttress his uncertain claim to the throne. Each of the Lancastrian and Yorkist successors used the ampulla of oil and a golden eagle (Cannon and Griffiths, 1988, 202). Shakespeare recognised the importance of anointing:

> Not all the water in the rough rude sea
> Can wash the balm off from an anointed king
> (Richard II, III, ii, 54-5)

Investiture

The next stage of the ceremony was the investiture. The king was given a tunic, buskins and spurs, and then the sword; these objects represented secular power and were full of chivalric symbolism. The sword implied protection of his kingdom and people; the ring was the 'seal of holy faith', the crown, sceptre and rod represented the glory, virtue, equity and justice. Despite the wholesale destruction of the coronation regalia at the Commonwealth various lists of regalia have come down to us. Richard I at his second coronation, according to Gervase of Canterbury, used sandals, tunic, mantle, *armillae* (bracelets), sword, spurs, virge (rod or wand), sceptre and crown. The next list is that of John, 1207, when sandals, tunic, mantle, sword, spurs, virge, sceptre, crown and gloves are mentioned. There were at least two sets of regalia, one jealously kept by the monks of Westminster which was the hereditary regalia and actually used in the ceremony itself. The king kept a personal set which was added to and taken away from time to time (Lightbown, 1998, 257-60). When vested, the king was then crowned and given the ring of St Edward. He presented the sword to the high altar and then put on the gloves and took up the sceptres, one in his right hand and the bird-headed virge in his left. Having kissed the clergy the crowned king, magnificent in his vestments, returned to the stage under the crossing in the abbey. Here he

56 *Impression of Henry IV's Second Great Seal, in use c.1408-13. The king is enthroned and crowned, holding a sceptre and orb. He is surrounded by no fewer than 21 figures and animals, including shields and figures of St Edward and St Edmund, indicating an attempt by the Lancastrian usurper to claim a genealogical connection with Henry III. He also cites the support of the Virgin and Child, a king crowned and a martyr holding a palm. Public Record Office, London.* Photo by Vernon Brooke

was seated and listened to the hymn *Te Deum Laudamus*. There followed a ritual of homage whereby the magnates of the kingdom touched the crown and the royal person by way of fealty. The final stages of the coronation ceremony involved a sung mass, an offertory, whereby the king and queen made oblations at the altar and the taking of communion of both kinds. Then they deposited the crowns and regalia on the altar of St Edward and equipped with substitute crowns they returned to the palace to take part in the banquet.

Coronation banquets

The arrangements for the coronation banquet give a useful insight into the hierarchy of powers within the kingdom. At the end of Westminster Hall opposite the door was a dais on which was placed the table at which the king was to sit (Wickham-Legg, 1909, lxiii). The body of the hall was filled with two sets of tables arranged lengthways. Down one side, the king's right, sat the archbishops, bishops, barons of the Cinque Ports, judges, the solicitor and Attorney General. Below them on the same side sat the Lord Mayor of London, with the Aldermen and Sergeants at Law and masters at Chancery. The third table on this side was occupied by the heralds. On the opposite side of the hall sat 'the Dukes of Normandy and Aquitaine', the king's officers, the Dukes and Duchesses, the Marquesses and Marchionesses. Below them, sitting at the second and third tables, were the rest of the peerage and their ladies. There was a great expenditure on food and drink at

57 Westminster Hall, London. Statues of kings of England. Reigate stone with Totternhoe stone crowns. By Thomas Canon, 1385. Orbs, sceptres, swords are Victorian.
Photo by author

Edward II's coronation banquet. Forty ovens were constructed to cook the food which included £100 spent on corn, £40 on beer, £100 on large cattle and boars, 100 marks on sheep, pigs and more large cattle, £400 on poultry, £150 on fish, £20 on small pike and 10 marks on lampreys. Coronation feasts were used to glorify the royal line, by the preparation of elaborate dishes known as 'subtilties' which had a heraldic or symbolic message. In a banquet given to Henry V's wife, Queen Katherine of France on 24 February 1420-1 a 'leeke lombard' (a kind of jelly) was decorated with SS livery collars (a badge of the house of Lancaster) and a device of Charles VI of France, the whole symbolising the union of France and England. Similar delicacies were prepared at Henry VI's coronation feast; here a boar's head was set in a 'castell royall' and there was a jelly with a 'whyght lyon crowned there-inne' and a 'custardys ryale' with a royal leopard of gold 'set ther-in holdynge a fleur de lyce' clearly pointing towards a union between the two countries (Lightbown 1998, 138, 187). Doubtless such fare generated huge thirsts among the participants.

Among a number of temporary timber halls was set up a fountain flowing day and night with red and white wine and the spiced drink known as pimento (Allen Brown, Colvin and Taylor, 1963, 507). It appears that earls and barons did services at table and the citizens of the two royal cities of London and Winchester were involved in the cellar and kitchen, lending a hand and thus demonstrating their close connection with the king (Schramm, 1937, 68).

The regalia

Crowns

Since they have not survived physically the form of the crowns of medieval English kings has to be reconstructed from coins, sculptures and manuscript illuminations. The sources which inspired their makers went back into the Roman period. The Roman emperors were reluctant to adopt the crown; republican tradition regarded it as a symbol of detested oriental tyranny. They were content to use the wreath and the garland. This may well have been in the minds of certain Anglo-Saxon diadem makers. The crowns of Byzantine emperors were composed of linked plates of precious metal decorated with enamelled portraits of emperors and, at the end of the Iconoclastic movement (AD 842) with the figures of saints. Such is the famous Hungarian crown of St Stephen (**colour plate 23**). Imperial German crowns from the ninth century developed a closed form of crown with arches. There is some evidence from coins and seals that Edward the Confessor had adopted the imperial form. From the eleventh to the fifteenth century the design of English crowns was open topped with a golden circlet elaborately worked and decorated with precious stones or enamels (Steane, 1999, 33). The ornaments along its upper edge were shown as fleurons (as on the seals of Henry I, Stephen, Richard I, Edward I, Edward II and Edward III and Richard II) or more rarely, crosses, as on the seals of William I, William II, Henry V and Henry VI. At the beginning of the fifteenth century a decisive change took place in the form of the English crown. That used in Henry IV's coronation was described by Froissant as '*archée en croix*'. This sounds like a 'closed' crown which has bands of metal crossing from one side to another, and from back to front so they meet in the middle. Sculptured representations of the coronation of Henry V in Westminster Abbey show the king sitting in state with an 'imperial' crown with four arches meeting and crossing, topped by a mound and a cross (RCHM (E), 1924, plate 135). Various manuscript illuminations of the fifteenth century confirm this and pilgrim badges of Henry VI of Windsor show him in majesty with the arched crown (Spencer, 1998, 190-1).

Sceptres (**colour plate 21**)

A second piece of regalia inseparable from kingship was the sceptre. This as a symbol of monarchical power has a long ancestry going back to the time of Sutton Hoo ship burial (Filmer-Sankey, 1996, 1-9). The seal of Edward the Confessor shows the king holding in his right hand a sceptre ending in a trefoil and in his left hand an orb. Harold in the Bayeux tapestry sits on a throne with his right hand holding a long sceptre, seemingly sprouting leaves. The sceptre was to the king what the crozier was to the bishop; the shepherd's staff or guiding wand of the flock. Sometimes it is shown ending in the form of a dove — or at least a large bird, and this has been plausibly suggested as being inspired by the eleventh-century, German imperial eagle-headed sceptre. Such a sceptre is to be found in the cathedral treasury at Aachen, it was placed there by Richard, Earl of Cornwall, brother to Henry III and King of the Romans. It consists of two hollow rods of silver gilt held together with plain knops in the middle and either end and an eagle on the top (Alexander and Binski, 1988, 203). Another was found when the coffin of Edward I in Westminster Abbey was opened in 1744. This was a 'scepter (sic) with cross made of copper gilt. This scepter is 2ft 6in long and of the most elegant workmanship. Its upper part extends unto and rests on the King's right shoulder' (Ayloffe, 1786, 385-6).

Sceptres continued to be essential attributes of English kings until the end of the Middle Ages and beyond. The royal effigies of Edward III and Henry V in Westminster Abbey had pairs of sceptres placed in their hands, subsequently stolen by souvenir hunters. Again the statues of kings of England built into niches on the interior south wall of Westminster Hall originally had sceptres, swords and orbs (Cherry and Stratford, 1995, 69-71) (**57**). Sporley, a monk of Westminster, drew up a list of 'relics of holy confessors, preserved at the shrine of Edward the Confessor and used at coronations: they included a golden sceptre, a wooden rod plated with gold, an iron rod and two other rods'. It has been suggested that these had been taken from St Edward's grave when he was transferred by Henry III to his present shrine in the mid-thirteenth century (Holmes, 1959, 214).

Swords

A third vital artefact used in English coronations was the sword or rather swords in the plural. Duke William, before being made king, is shown holding a sword in the Bayeux Tapestry. It was widely employed as a symbol of authority, whether ducal, royal or imperial, throughout the Middle Ages. The sword of the Lord is mentioned in the Old Testament Psalm 44: 'Gird thy sword upon thy thigh, O most mighty, with thy glory and thy majesty'. The sword had two functions, the defence of the church and the defence of the people. Peter Damian reminded the Emperor Henry IV 'the king is girded with a sword so that he may go armed against the enemies of the church'. Abbot Suger describing the coronation of Louis VI of France in 1108 says that he put off the sword of secular knighthood and girded himself with an ecclesiastical sword to do justice to malefactors. In the coronation liturgy, girding 'with the sword the king shall know that the whole kingdom is committed to him'. The privilege of bearing the sword at coronations was hotly contested by the English magnates. This was partly solved by increasing the number of swords involved. At Richard I's coronation in 1189 three swords were carried by the brother of the king of the Scots, the Earl of Leicester and by John the king's brother. Three were borne in fourteenth-century coronations and four in those of the fifteenth century.

The symbolic functions of the swords used in coronations became steadily more complex in the Middle Ages. The 'curtana' so called was 'naked and without point in token that justice is to be done without rancour'. On the other hand the lack of point was regarded as justice tempered by mercy. Another weapon, the so-called Lancaster sword, was sheathed and carried in token of the augmentation of military honour. A third sword held by the constable was reckoned to be 'the sword of his office for the establishment of justice' (Lightbown, 1998, 179-81).

French coronations

European kings and emperors from the early Middle Ages until the twentieth century had their power inaugurated and confirmed at the beginning of their reigns by rituals which went back to the Carolingian period (Nelson, 1987, 137). The main elements of this were anointing, enthronement and coronation. The anointing was of particular importance. Legend connects it with the baptism of Clovis, King of the Franks at Reims by the local bishop, Remigius, in AD 496. A sculpture in the centre of the west front of the cathedral recalls the story that a dove descended from heaven bearing an ampulla of holy oil with which Clovis was baptised. By the ninth century the coronation rituals were being performed by ecclesiastics within a church. The church in fact attempted to assert its ideological dominance. Most coronations in France were held in the cathedral at Reims from the tenth century with the archbishop of Reims officiating.

A disastrous fire swept through the town in 1210 destroying the old cathedral. This led to the rebuilding, planned on an impressive scale, and deliberately designed to be a coronation church. The plan was in many respects similar to that of Chartres but the nave was three bays longer to take greater numbers of people. The nave and aisles of the western arm were broadened out in the eastern arm into a nave and double aisles. The projecting transepts were thus enveloped and the space used for the accommodation of coronation ceremonies. The eastern end had a semi-circular ambulatory ringed round with five chapels in the form of a chevet (Banister-Fletcher, 1946, 183-5). In sum *'la cathédrale fut conçue pour recevoir des foules lors des cérémonies du sacre'* (Vitry, 1958, 16).

The preparations for a French coronation were complex. The throne was placed on a platform in the church between the nave and choir. This was raised up on high so that the king might be visible to all; it was important to impress as many witnesses as possible in this crucially important ceremony. The king elect came the day before and was met by a procession; he went to the cathedral for a nightly vigil and returned to the archbishop's palace, situated immediately to the south of the cathedral. Coronations required a number of sacred artifacts. At dawn a procession left for S. Remi, the great church in the south of the city to collect the Holy Ampoule of oil. This was brought to the cathedral by the abbé of S. Remi. He carried it under a canopy of silk supported by four poles held by four acolytes. In the meantime the abbé of St Denis, Suger's church near Paris, the repository of the coronation regalia, brought to the altar the objects of which he was the guardian. The spurs, the sword and its scabbard, the sceptre, the *main de justice*, the vestments and the crown. Two bishops now went in procession to find the king in the archiepiscopal palace. He processed to the cathedral along a wooden gallery hung with tapestries and took his place in the choir. Around him were the cardinals, the six ecclesiastical peers (the archbishop-dukes of Reims and of Laon), the bishop-counts of Langres, Beauvai, Châlons and Noyon, the ten lay peers and the three marshals of France. The first phase of the ceremony was oath taking. The king took two, an ecclesiastical and a royal one, his hand on the gospels. He then climbed to the altar. On the eve of the coronation he had worn a simple brown robe, a sign of penitence. He now removed it and put on some of the royal panoply; he was helped to array himself in the symbols of chivalry, the fleur-de-lys powdered shoes, the spurs and the sword. The fleur-de-lys is said to be a solar symbol, which began to appear on the seal of the kings of France in the twelfth century; it acquired new layers of religious meaning in the thirteenth century when it was associated with both Christ and the Virgin Mary. From this time it was used on royal banners and became a heraldic symbol inseparable from the French monarchy. When Edward III claimed the French throne in 1340 he took care to quarter his royal leopards of England with the fleur-de-lys of France.

The next stage in the coronation ceremony was the anointing. The archbishop anointed the king with a little of the holy oil mixed in the golden paten of the chalice of S. Remi. The tunic of the kneeling king was opened and the holy oil applied to his chest, back, head, between the shoulders, on the back of the shoulders, and on the inside of the elbow. Then the tunic was closed and the Grand Chamberlain helped the king to put on the fleur-de-lys powdered dalmatic (an ecclesiastical robe with wide sleeves). At this point he received the other insignia of high office, the ring, the sceptre (which he took in his right hand) and the rod (the *main de justice*) which he took in his left. The final part of the ceremony involved the ecclesiastical and lay peers who approached the altar for the crowning. The archbishop took the great crown brought from St Denis and put it onto the head of the king. They then conducted him to the throne raised on the high platform between nave and choir. The archbishop kissed the king, followed by the other peers and shouted the acclamation, 'May the king live for ever'. After the acclamation there was a release of doves, and (later in the early Modern period) a salvo of musketry and at length the king returned to the archbishop's palace. The ceremony concluded with a banquet (Gaborit-Chopin, 1987, 20-1).

German and imperial coronations

The imperial idea

The history and the archaeology associated with the English and the French coronations is complicated enough but it is straightforward when compared with the complexities of the German and Imperial. The notion was current in the early Middle Ages that any ruler who reigned over more than one kingdom was an emperor. Athelstan (924-40) after conquering the kingdom of Northumbria in 927, and thus becoming ruler of all England's petty kingdoms, used the title of '*imperator*'. Sancho the Great, king of Navarre (1004-35), conquered León and Astorga and is called an 'Emperor'. This notion of multiple ruling was overlaid by an appeal to the classical and to the Roman past. The last Roman emperor to be crowned in the west had been Romulus Augustulus (475-6). Thereafter the western Empire had disintegrated into barbaric kingdoms. The most successful of these in the eighth century was the kingdom of the Franks ruled over by

Charlemagne. Charlemagne's conquests made him effectively king over parts of Germany, much of Italy, as well as most of what had been Roman Gaul. He was crowned emperor in Rome in 800 by Pope Leo III, not apparently because he wanted to be honoured in this way but as the result of 'a curious chain of events of intrigues and dissidence in Rome itself' (Barraclough, 1955, 109). This event, while it did not renovate the Roman Empire, was to prove to successive German rulers a political chimera which drew them away from German affairs and involved them in the morass of Italian politics for some 800 years. Henceforward the coronations of German rulers are not deemed complete until they have been crowned at Aachen (Charlemagne's palace/chapel, subsequently cathedral) and at Rome in some way involving the citizens of Rome and the Papacy.

Charlemagne's 'empire' fell apart in the ninth century but the memory of the hugely dominating figure of the Frankish king remained overshadowing and at the same time inspiring his successors. For a while the rulers of the western part aspired to the imperial title (e.g. Louis the Pious, Charles the Bald) but in the tenth century it was the Ottonian dynasty, the rulers and heirs of the eastern part of Charlemagne's empire, that took on the imperial role, to be followed by the Salian and the Hohenstaufen dynasties.

Imperial coronations in the eleventh and twelfth centuries can be fruitfully considered under three headings. First the ceremony itself, second the artifacts involved and the methods used to store and protect them. Thirdly the changing procedures of election over the period 800-1600.

Coronations of German kings/emperors

Otto I was crowned king of Germany at Aachen in 936. A detailed description was made by a Saxon chronicler called Widukind (Leyser 1994, 27). At every point the ceremony resonates with memories of Charlemagne. Otto had been designated by his father Henry the Fowler as his successor but a form of election had to be gone through so it was in the hall of the imperial palace of Charlemagne at Aachen that the dukes, officials and warriors of his kingdom gathered together to elect him. This emphatic element of election runs all the way through German and imperial history. A number of dynasties emerged (Ottonian, Salian, Hohenstaufen) which tried to establish hereditary succession and thus freedom from the conditions likely to be imposed by the electors, but ultimately the elective principle triumphed. Otto was set on his throne and his electors, giving him their hand, swore fidelity to them. The Carolingian hall is still there, battered but recognisable (**colour plate 2**). A short processional walk brought the newly elected monarch to the adjacent palace-chapel of Charlemagne where the ecclesiastical part of the ceremony took place. The archbishop of Mainz, the senior German churchman, the clergy and the people waited. The archbishop brought the king-elect into the middle of the church where he could be seen by all. As we have noticed with the English and French coronations visibility of the main actors was a vital part. Here he asked the people if they agreed to Otto's election as king and there followed general acclamation.

Next the investiture. The objects involved represented a fascinating mixture of ancient classical, eastern and Mediterranean symbols of imperial power (such as the crown and the sceptre) mingled with other insignia (swords, bracelets, spurs) derived from northern and barbaric sources (Blair, 1998, 28). The archbishop first invested the king with the sword (representing power over the Franks, with the aim of expelling the enemies of Christ and ultimately establishing peace). Next he was clad in the mantle and the bracelets (the ensigns of perseverance in faith) and then the staff and sceptre were handed over (the power to correct and chastise but also to show mercy to churchmen, widows and orphans). At this point a golden crown was put on Otto's head by the archbishops of Cologne and Mainz and the crowned monarch was enthroned on high for all to see. This is likely to have involved the so-called throne of Charlemagne which, as we have already noticed, was made of second-hand Roman *spolia* and probably dates from this occasion, not from the time of Charlemagne. Solemn *lauds* were sung and the king descended, processed to the palace hall, and clad in his royal robes, held a feast. Here the greatest nobles of the land, as in the English ceremonies of the twelfth and thirteenth centuries, served as butler, steward, marshal and so on. Most of the elements of this ritual were used again and again throughout the Middle Ages. Some of them were repeated in the crownwearings which took place from time to time as focus points throughout the realm to impress followers with the mystical and magnificent aspects of monarchy and to summon possible would-be conspirators to renew bonds of fealty. The once-in-a-lifetime ritual event was thus buttressed at intervals by repeat ceremonies.

Otto I was said to have been acclaimed emperor by his warriors after the famous victory over the Magyars at the battle of the Lech in 955; this, however, was only the acclamation given to a victorious military leader. It was necessary to endure the long, dangerous, and disease-ridden journey to Rome to take part in a coronation involving the pope that was the crowning glory.

Coronation regalia of the German kings

In the secular treasury of the Hofburg, Vienna is a majestic and magnificent object, the German imperial crown (Reichskrone) (**colour plate 22**), sometimes known as the crown of Charlemagne. It consists of eight gold plates, semi-circular at the summit, fastened by gold pins which fit into beaded slots. This enabled it to be taken to pieces and laid flat, for ease of transportation. The plates at the front, back and sides are encrusted with pearls and precious stones set alternately with four lesser plates, each enamelled, with figures of our Lord enthroned in Majesty, Kings Solomon, David and Hezekiah and the prophet Isaiah. A single arch and a cross were added by the Salian Emperor Conrad II: this consists of eight small arcades and an inscription in tiny pearls (Twining, 1960, 329-31). The origin of this outstanding piece of regalia is dubious. Twining thinks it was made in the monastery of Reichenau for the emperor Otto I in preparation for his coronation in Rome in 962 and there seems no doubt that he was properly equipped with regalia for this occasion. However, the pope himself usually preferred to provide the crown and

58   Reichskrone, Vienna. Kunsthistorisches museum. Schatzkammer der Hofburg. Drawn by author from photograph in Catalogue Das Reich der Salien 1992

through the Middle Ages is found giving crowns away to deserving monarchs. Its style owes a considerable debt to Byzantium, that other power centre of Roman political continuum, but appears to postdate Charlemagne by about a century and a half. Its importance did not derive from its use in coronations. From 936, when Otto I was crowned at Aachen, until 1530, 29 coronations of kings and anti-kings took place there (**colour plate 25**). At ten of these the German imperial crown was not used. Further in 18 imperial coronations held at Rome between 962-1452 the pope was known to have provided the crown on five occasions. The significance of the *Reichskrone* lay in its symbolic status. Its possession was necessary if the emperor was to be widely recognised as legitimate.

The survival of such a notable piece of regalia is remarkable enough. Our knowledge of the form taken by more workaday crowns has been expanded by the recovery of a number of funerary furnishings of German imperial tombs in 'excavations', which sound more like licit tomb robbings taking place at Speyer cathedral in 1900. The grave of the Emperor Conrad II (d. 1039) produced a crown which was a circlet of copper gilt, its rim decorated with three riveted trefoil ornaments and the band inscribed *PACIS URBIS AMATOR*. The grave of the Empress Gisela yielded a circlet of copper with a cross and three fleurons on the upper edge and the inscription *GISELA IMPERATRIX*. The crown found in the grave of the Emperor Henry III (d. 1056) was similar in form with that of Conrad II but had two projecting pieces of copper round the ears. An orb made of leather and wood also accompanied the burial. The staff in coronations appears to have been replaced by orbs by the end of the eleventh century. Finally the funeral crown of the Emperor Henry IV (d. 1106) was of copper gilt surmounted by four fleurons and with a single arch from front to back. Inside was a bonnet or mitre

157

of silk with a broad brow band and two bands of gold embroidery; at the rear hand two pendant ribbons (Twining, 1967, 42).

Charlemagne, so his secretary Einhard records, was happy to go around dressed in the rough and ready traditional Frankish costume but on festivals he arrayed himself in garments interwoven with gold, a mantle fastened by a gold brooch, a diadem adorned with gold and gems and jewelled sword and shoes. A number of additional pieces of imperial regalia have survived. Most were fashioned in the imperial workshops of Palermo, Sicily and were made for the Norman kings Roger II, William II and the Emperor Frederick II. They include a sword with a pommel ornamented with the imperial eagle and the Bohemian lion (added by Charles IV), a tunic or dalmatic, an ecclesiastical type of garment made of dark purple serge-like material bordered on the hem with gold; an alb of heavy white silk with an embroidered inscription in Latin and Arabic, and a fantastically lengthy stole (19ft) worn crossed over the breast and looped up by a girdle. These latter three items all emphasized the priestly role of emperors, an aspect supported by the Bible (Melchisedek, the priest-king, Genesis 14-18, Psalms 109, Letter to Hebrews 7:17) but denigrated by successive popes, anxious to retain the spiritual upper hand in their struggle for supremacy in medieval Europe.

Imperial treasuries

It seems likely that the regalia was moved around the country in the baggage train of the itinerant ruler but gradually as a regular succession of emperors appeared in the tenth century and as dynasties established themselves, more permanent and stable treasuries were established. These included fortresses and cathedrals. The castle at Trifels in the Rhenish Palatinate, perched 1000ft up above the valley floor near the little town of Annwater in Wasgau Forest was one such imperial bank deposit box. It was in imperial hands in the last years of Henry IV's reign and Henry V ordered the imperial insignia to be kept there. Trifels was a prison as well as a treasury, sharing this characteristic with the Tower of London. Richard I was briefly incarcerated there by Leopold of Austria when he was captured on his way home from Palestine. The imperial regalia was inventoried in 1246 and many of the items which eventually were to be found in Vienna were already listed including a crown, an orb, imperial cross and ceremonial robes. It was said 'whoever possesses Trifels possesses the Empire' (Barber, 1986, 250-2).

A second treasury was established at Aachen cathedral. We know that Richard Earl of Cornwall, the only Englishman ever to be elected king of the Romans (he was crowned in Aachen in 1257), gave a set of regalia to be used by his successors and to be kept in Aachen cathedral (Alexander and Binski, 1987, 203). Aachen thus became, to some degree, the German equivalent of the French St Denis, and the English Westminster Abbey. Later rulers had other ideas. The Emperor Rudolf of Habsburg moved the treasure from Trifels in the late thirteenth century to Habsburg castle at Kyburg in the canton of Zurich whence it was taken in 1350 to Prague by the Emperor Charles IV of Luxembourg, King of Bohemia. As we shall see he removed it to the specially built Castle of Karlstein where it remained for two generations, being annually displayed in Prague. Charles' son Sigismund removed it to Hungary, hearing that it might fall into the hands of the Hussite rebels. In 1424 he handed it over to the city of Nuremburg where it stayed until the Reformation. It was the prize exhibit in a solemn annual religious procession, only leaving the city to be used in imperial coronations.

The election process

Germany only achieved political unification in 1871; England had emerged as a nation state in the thirteenth century, France in the fifteenth century. One of the reasons adduced is that the medieval German monarchy never became hereditary but remained elective. This meant that the electors, the princes, were able to wring concessions out of successive imperial claimants — whose powers were accordingly diminished as the Middle Ages wore on. This process was to some extent forced on kings who wished to avoid dependence on an increasingly aggressive and power seeking papacy. In the fourteenth century there were two main stages in this attempt to win freedom from the holy see. Lewis the Bavarian ensured in 1338 that imperial coronations in Rome from now on would be by majority vote of the people of Rome — the papal confirmation or approval was ignored. More significantly the Golden Bull of Eger, 1358, confirmed the right of election to the seven princes, three ecclesiastical, four secular, who formed an electoral college like the college of cardinals at Rome. They made their decision by majority vote. Three cities were involved in the process: Frankfurt-on-Main, the seat of elections; Aachen the place of coronation; Nuremburg the venue of the imperial diet. Germany as a consequence at the end of the Middle Ages lacked a centralised state, an unfettered monarchy, a capital city and a sense of national identity (Jones, 2000, 22-3, 554).

The Bohemian experience

The English and the French coronation ceremonies were compilations which absorbed traditional elements over periods of hundreds of years. It is not possible to attribute these disparate components to the inventive mind of any one individual, ecclesiastic or monarch. When we turn to Bohemia the situation is different. Here one fourteenth-century king, Charles IV, played a key part in reconstructing the coronation ceremony. He reordered the topography of Prague to provide a backdrop for the ceremonies of his coronation city; he rebuilt St Vitus' cathedral, his coronation church, he transformed the Bohemian coronation liturgy; he instituted a cult of the crown jewels with a special building to house them. All this has been worked out recently in convincing detail by art historians combining archaeological, architectural and historical evidence (Crossley, 2000, 99-172).

Charles IV was a typical product of the international aristocracy of the Gothic Middle Ages. He was born in 1316, his father was John of Luxemburg, half French and half Brabantine; his mother was Queen Elizabeth of the ancient stock

59 Prague, Czech republic. Rider's staircase in Prague castle, built by master Benedict Rejt of Pístor (1487-1500), by which knights came on horseback to the tournaments held in the hall in the sixteenth century. Photo: Courtauld

of the Premyslid dynasty of Bohemia. Whereas his education was French (he was brought up in the court of his uncle, Charles IV of France, from whom he took his name), he was baptised Wenceslas in honour of the tenth-century martyr-duke recognised as the patron saint of the Bohemian kingdom. He was thus exposed at an early and impressionable age to the age-old traditions of the Czech monarchy on the one hand and the Valois kingdom, with its powerful aura of Charlemagne, strengthened with added charisma from Louis IX of France, on the other. In his time at the French court he got to know the celebrated treasures of St Denis, experienced the polychromatic brilliance of the Sainte Chapelle in Paris which had been built by Louis IX (St Louis) to house relics of the Passion, and he absorbed theocratic concepts of kingship from the French example.

Charles ascended the throne of Bohemia in 1346 after the death, on the field of Crécy, of his father, the blind King John of Bohemia. He was elected Holy Roman Emperor in the same year and was crowned in Aachen. He decided to move the capital of the Empire to Prague and re-shaped the city as a second Rome. He laid out the New Town on the right bank of the Ultava river. His urban cre-

60 Prague. Powder tower (left) as it was before radical restoration in the nineteenth century. Old Bridge tower, east façade. Both from nineteenth-century engravings in Courtauld Institute of Art. Drawing by author

ation, with a 3.5km circuit of walls, monumental gates, and a regular chequer-board street plan, deliberately recalled ideas of classical antiquity. A characteristically medieval element was provided by 40 churches, some proclaiming the cult of Charlemagne, other referring back (through their dedications) to Czech missionary figures of the ancient Moravian past. He linked his new town to the royal palace and fortress on the Hradčany hill by a new Charles bridge rivalling in scale and style the great Roman engineering achievements. At either end was a towered gateway recalling the triumphal arches of the imperial city (**colour plate 14**).

Charles also had in mind the example of Jerusalem as an international centre of pilgrimage when he created what have been called two dominant 'axes of meaning' (Crossley's phrase) running through his New Town at Prague. One route started at the ancient castle hill of Vysehrad, at the southernmost tip of the city; it runs through the vast Charles Square, the biggest urban space in medieval Europe, and entered the Old Town crossing the Charles Bridge to the Little Quarter and thus to the Hradčany (**colour plate 26**). This was the route taken by the royal procession on the vigil of the coronation. The second 'axis of meaning' ran at right angles to the first and again proceeded through the great cattle market of Charles Square. Along this route were a series of churches (St Stephen, St Longinus) wherein relics

161

61 *Prague, Czech republic. St Vitus' Cathedral from south. Triple arched portal ('golden gate') facing castle/palace at foot of south transept. Main body of choir of coronation church with flanking chapels round chevets to right. Much is work of Peter Parler, 1350s-70s.* Photo: Courtauld

were displayed. As in Jerusalem the vista culminated in a dominant circular-planned building, in Prague the church of Corpus Christi, in Jerusalem the so-called Temple of Christ. Charles was catering for columns of pilgrims as well as for future coronation processions.

His second contribution to the revamp of the Bohemian coronation ceremony was the rebuilding of St Vitus' cathedral on the top of the hill, a stone's throw from the royal castle and palace of Hradčany. Close parallels can be traced with Henry III's Westminster Abbey, the royal necropolis of the kings of France at St Denis, the royal national shrine of Sainte Chapelle, Paris, and the coronation church of Rheims cathedral (Crossley, 2000, 99, Stanková, Stursa, Vodera, 1992, 49). Using the skills of an idiosyncratic German architect, Peter Parler, Charles IV created a contrived sequence of spaces designed specifically for use in the Bohemian coronation ceremony. The main entrance to St Vitus, the so-called Golden Gate, faces south and thus is opposite to the Royal Palace. It consists of three pointed arches enriched over with a mosaic of Venetian type representing the Last Judgement. Within Charles reordered the burial places of the principal saints of the Czech past. St Wenceslaus, the ancient protector of the Bohemian state, was removed from his tomb in the pre-existing Romanesque basilica and placed in a chapel immediately to the north and east of the Golden Gate. His ideas for the sacred topography of the cathedral included locating centres of dynastic

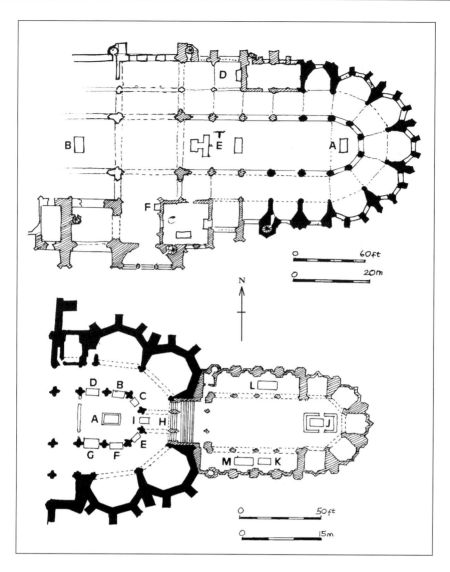

62 (above) Prague Cathedral. Ground plan showing altars and liturgical stations of Bohemian coronation ceremony. A: high altar of St Vitus; B: altar of St Adalbert; C: Wenceslas chapel and tomb of St Wenceslas; D: chapel of St Sigismund; E: Chorus Minor; *T: tomb of Charles IV; F: altar of the Holy Cross.* After Crossley 2000, 101 *(below) Westminster Abbey; east end and Henry VII's chapel (hatched) showing royal tombs. A: shrine of St Edward the Confessor; B: King Henry III (d.1272); C: Queen Eleanor of Castile (d.1290); D: King Edward I (d.1307); E: Queen Philippa of Hainault (d.1369); F: King Edward III (d.1377); G: King Richard II (d.1399); H: Henry V's chapel; I: King Henry V (d.1422); J: King Henry VII (d.1509) and Queen Elizabeth of York (d.1503); K: Lady Margaret Beaufort, Countess of Richmond and Derby (d.1509); L: Queen Elizabeth I (d.1603); M: Mary, Queen of Scots (d.1587).* After Colvin, 1991, 139

and national devotion in its other three extremities; St Vitus was reinterred to the east, St Adalbert to the west and St Sigismund in a separate chapel to the north. In the centre was an altar to the Virgin Mary, the *chorus minor*. Here, the most sacred spot, was to be the royal necropolis. Again Westminster Abbey seems to have been one of the architectural progenitors. The Plantagenets had been disposed and displayed around the translated shrine of St Edward the Confessor, England's equivalent of St Wenceslaus. In this pivotal position was Charles' own tomb and those of his family and successors. Altars were dedicated to St Louis and St Nicholas in memory of his first wife Blanche of Valois (d. 1351), and his second wife, Aune of the Palatinate (d. 1353). It has been suggested that he was here recalling the arrangement of the French royal tombs under the crossing of the abbey of St Denis. Here the centrally placed tombs of Philip Augustus, Louis VIII and Louis IX 'form a symbolic link . . . between the tombs of the Carolingian dynasty to the north and the Capetian to the south' (Crossley, 2000, 161).

Charles and his architect, Peter Parler, having settled the horizontal reordering of St Vitus' cathedral to their satisfaction, turned to the vertical. The upper parts of the east end were a forest of vaults, wide windows and extensive buttressing, mostly the work of Matthias of Arras (d. 1352). A gallery of the Premyslid dynasty was placed at ground level. Above, in the triforium stage, were busts of Charles, his wives and family. The last stage of this vertical hierarchy, the clerestory, had statues of Christ, the Virgin Mary and the Bohemian patron saints. In this way the eye was led up from the murky Premyslid past through the brighter present of the Luxemburg dynasty to the shining eternity of Christ, his mother and the saints.

The rebuilding of St Vitus' cathedral and the restructuring of its sacred layout was motivated by the desire on Charles' part to create a coronation church for himself and his successors. He experienced no less than six coronations in his lifetime: king of the Romans in Bonn in 1346, crowned king of Bohemia in Prague in 1347, officially and for good measure at Aachen in 1349, king of Lombardy in Milan and Roman Emperor in Rome in 1355, and he also picked up a crown of Burgundy in Arles ten years later. All of this accumulated in Charles' mind a strong theocratic theory of kingship; Charles saw himself as priest-king; this was symbolised by his continuing to wear a bishop's mitre beneath the Bohemian crown, an ancient Premyslid privilege. In a remarkable sequence of wall paintings preserved in the royal castle at Karlstein, Charles and his ancestors are portrayed rubbing shoulders with the saints, almost a Christ-like figure (Dvoráková, Krása, Merhautová and Stejskal, 1964). The glorification of the imperial majesty of Charles IV as the uniter of Christendom is the key idea.

Charles derived his ideas for the Bohemian coronation ceremony from the age-old Premyslid ordinals, enriched with elements inspired by the French; he had been present at his brother-in-law's coronation in Rheims cathedral in 1328. As the cathedral grew in Prague so his fresh concepts of the impressive service crystallised. Traditionally the coronation of the Bohemian kings began the day before the crowning in the church of Saints Peter and Paul on Vyshrad. This was to the south of the city and was the legendary stronghold of the Czech monarchy. Here the prince venerated an ancient shoe of one of the early rulers and had his purse placed on his shoulder by the officiating canons. The party then processed via the New Town, the Old Town and across the Charles Bridge as has been already noted. So up to the Hradčany palace. On the next morning the archbishop, accompanied by other bishops, processed from the cathedral to the royal bed chamber in the palace carrying the regalia, a lectionary, the sword of St Wenceslaus, a cross and holy water. The king, roused and robed, surrounded by the princes and nobles awaited their coming. With clouds of incense swirling about him and the bell tolling the king was led through the east gate of the palace, across the yard and through the south transept portal, with its glittering mosaic façade. The king, at this point, knelt at the altar of the chapel of the Holy Cross while the archbishop, carrying the regalia, moved on to the altar of St Vitus. There followed a ceremony involving the elements we have noted in both the English and French coronations, the oath taking, the acclamation, the dedicatory prayers. At this point Charles imported an idea from the French *ordo*. Two mitred abbots sought the holy coronation oil from where it was kept in the Wenceslaus chapel and carried it under a *baldachino* through the cathedral to the high altar. This was a clear echo of the French ceremony involving carrying the holy oil from the abbey of St Remi in Rheims to the cathedral. The archbishop anointed the king with it and they proceeded with the investiture, the homage and, if it was appropriate, the coronation of the queen. All this against a background, as we have seen, of sculptured mementoes of ancient rulers of the Bohemian kingdom, the current royal family, and high up at vault level, the supreme embodiment of royal theocracy, the figure of Christ.

Charles' fourth achievement buttressing his high-flown monarchical ideology was the building of Karlstein Castle. This strange building, unlike any other I have seen, is a short railway journey from Prague, on four ascending terraces of a steep boot-shaped hill, the Knezí Hora. Its design seems to be a deliberate throwback to the earlier Premyslid fortresses. It comprises four separate parts, each rising above the other: the constable's accommodation, the imperial palace (a great hall providing a residence for Charles and his court), the Lesser Tower, occupied by a college of priests (cf Windsor Castle and the canons of St George) and the Great Tower. This contained on its second floor (the height of this and the rising majesty of the staircase approaching it, are significant) the chapel of the Holy Cross. This, Charles, by the end of his reign, used as a repository of the state archive, and the imperial treasure, crown jewels and relics. The nearest parallel to Karlstein is the castle at Trifels in the Rhineland Palatinate built during the reign of the Emperor Frederick II early in the thirteenth century as a repository for the imperial treasure. The published plan (Crossley, 2000, 135) shows pronounced similarities.

As the reign progressed and the king-emperor acquired more relics (including wood from the true cross, the nails, lance and sponge) his ideas for Karlstein developed. It grew from an ordinary fortress, a favoured royal residence, to a reliquary stronghold staffed by a college of clergy. A gift from the Dauphin of two thorns of Christ's crown of thorns from the Sainte-Chapelle led to Charles commissioning from his goldsmiths a grand gold reliquary cross to contain his

63 *Karlstein, Czech republic. Chapel of the Holy Cross in the Great Tower. Before
    1367. Note vaulting and upper part of walls covered with painting, lower part of walls
    studded with glass and precious stones, screen repeating shape of imperial crown.*
    Photo: Courtauld

Bohemian passion relics. By the end of the 1350s, with clergy and chapels
installed, Karlstein had become a sacred nucleus of the kingdom. Small cave-like
oratories glittered with gold reflected in thousands of mirrors and precious stones.
Wall paintings extolling the emperor (Charles is represented no less than six
times) mingle with historiated scenes involving Christ, Mary and the Apocalypse
of St John. I know of no other place in medieval Europe which better embodies
the themes of monarchical sacral power than Karlstein Castle.

The crowned king had to rule within the law which the medievals regarded as
unchanging. He simply was required to reveal it. In fact the law buttressed the
power of kingship. Lawyers were the king's servants first and foremost. Only very
gradually did they begin to assert themselves and used the law to restrain unjust
and spendthrift rulers. The following chapter confines itself to England and
records the special sites and buildings connected with the slowly evolving operation of the law. It points to the fact that the majesty of the law involved the use of
distinctive costume. Towards the end of the period the lawyers begin to organise
themselves so the origins of the Inns of Court are considered.

6 The archaeology of law

The Old English judicial system

It has long been known to scholars that the concept of territorial law, the same rules applying to all men in a given area, and known to the Romans since the time of the Emperor Caracalla in the early third century AD, was foreign to the Anglo-Saxons. For four centuries or so after migrating to England in the fifth century they based their judicial systems on the principle of personal law; that is of different laws applying to different persons or groups of persons. The regulation of the behaviour of persons was a matter for their kin and their neighbours, not the state. During the late Anglo-Saxon period this began to change as kings and their councils issued laws which were subsequently codified applying to all men. It was characteristic that such laws simply supplemented a huge body of custom and unwritten law; they were 'something in the nature of minutes of what was orally decreed rather than statute law in their own right' (Wormald 1978, 48). There may well have been local institutions and complex procedures from the very beginning but as law became more complex it required institutions and regular procedures.

These were articulated in frequent public assemblies in which the religious and lay lordly authorities took part; comprehensive fines were listed for every kind of wrong doing; to ensure the presence of criminals at trials prisons were built. They also played a role in holding convicted felons between conviction and execution. Imprisonment was seldom used as a form of punishment. Capital punishment was ordered for an increasing number of offences ranging from fighting in the king's house and travelling unannounced to absconding by slaves (laws of Ine). Alfred added plotting against the life of the king or one's lord. Athelstan proposed death for thieves who fled; Aethelred for forgers striking false coins, deserting an army under personal command of the king and Cnut used it against corrupt reeves and those violating the protection of the church and the king (Reynolds, 1998, 83-4). There is considerable archaeological evidence for the social control implied in this judicial process.

Prisons and execution sites in the Anglo-Saxon period

In a recent survey of this evidence (Reynolds 1998) only four sites are claimed as Anglo-Saxon prisons. A collection of post-holes to the west of the south end of the period 1 long hall at the royal palace of Cheddar (Somerset) may be traces of such a place of restraint. A similar interpretation has been made for a sunken room found at the monastic site of Wearmouth (Northumberland). Sulgrave (Northamptonshire) had a thegnly hall which may have served as a lock-up. The preconquest tower at Porchester Castle (Hampshire) provides another disputable example.

Less ambiguous are the traces of former execution places. Here a total of 20 have been identified ranging south and east across the county from Somerset to Yorkshire, East Riding. They are recognised by being composed of predominantly male skeletons and having prone burials (where the corpse is placed face down) near the surface in cramped and shallow graves. In addition there are frequent decapitations, and place names in charter bounds suggest that the heads were displayed on stakes (place name element *heafod stocc*). Another mode of execution illustrated in late Anglo-Saxon manuscripts (such as B L MS Cotton Claudius BIV f 59) is hanging. Three pieces of evidence point towards its widespread use. Skeletons are found with their hands tied behind their back. Post-holes for the gallows themselves in groups of two or four are dug into the surface. The terms *gabulos* and *gealga* both meaning gallows, gibbet or cross occur in boundary clauses of Anglo-Saxon land charters. The most interesting characteristic of Anglo-Saxon execution places is their location along boundaries and often in association with mounds. The mounds are sometimes Bronze Age barrows, sometimes pagan cemeteries which are overlain with the graves of execution victims, and sometimes the mounds are freshly built, perhaps to mark the place of assembly.

For those who seriously contravened the social norms Christianity had no place. Wrongdoers condemned to execution were buried in unconsecrated ground, as far away from human habitation as was possible. Decapitation itself served to prevent haunting. Boundaries, particularly major ones such as those demarcating hundreds (administrative sub-divisions of the shires), were chosen. It has even been suggested that execution sites not on Domesday hundred boundaries mark the course of former principal boundaries (Reynolds 1998, 223).

After the Norman Conquest changes take place in the location of execution places. While some continue at sites of pre-Conquest origin like Tyburn where executions were held from before 1002 to 1783, others moved into towns and cemeteries for executed felons are found even in monasteries. This has been attributed to the emergence of a money economy with trade and towns attracting the criminal. A more likely explanation is that it is associated with the emergence of centralised royal criminal justice in the late twelfth and thirteenth centuries. This led to the trial of most criminals in gaols located in towns and their execution close by (P, Brand Personal communication). Guildown (Surrey) execution cemetery 'could be regarded as the type site of representing the convicted deviant population of the adjacent late Anglo-Saxon mint and market town of Guildford' (Reynolds 1998, 251).

The king and justice

Geoffrey of Monmouth, in his largely mythological *History of the Kings of Britain*, struck a contemporary chord by referring to Henry I as the Lion of Justice at whose roar 'the towers of Gaul shall shake and the Island Dragons tremble'. Henry, in his coronation charter, made promises to keep or restore to his people 'the law of King Edward with such emendations as my father made to it with the counsel of his barons'. He emphasised this role in the design of his great seal which shows him sitting on his throne, crowned and sceptre in hand, in an attitude of a judge as seen in Romanesque representations of Christ sitting full-faced in judgement. The Norman and early Plantagenet Kings of England shared a predilection for the doing of justice whether because it meant maintaining royal rights, or because it was a welcome source of royal income, or simply because their subjects expected it of them.

This interest in justice could take the form of personal involvement. Both Henry II and John are well known for the energetic, intelligent and vigorous way in which they intervened in justice. The court before the king himself was in fact the supreme court of justice in twelfth-century England. Henry II took part himself in a famous series of suits involving Battle Abbey, rebuking the parties concerned and calling them to order (Poole, 1964, 7). His second son John showed 'an indefatigable attention to the business of government', as is clear from a scrutiny of the Close Rolls, the Curia Regis Rolls and the records of the Exchequer (Warren 1964, 101). An extreme example of this interest in law is found by his actions at the end of February 1200. He returned from France to England, and stayed there for two months taking stock; he ordered that no less than 119 judicial pleas be put before him; he then crossed the Channel but sent instructions to his justices or asked for them to postpone consideration of pleas until he returned (Warren 1964, 133). Despite this proven interest it is probable that already it was the professional justices who manned the court who played a major part in running it.

While men groaned at the exactions of John they certainly expected a king to involve himself in dispensing justice. Books about kingship recalled the story of the Emperor Trajan, prevailed upon to do justice to an importunate widow as he was setting out for the wars; they enjoyed the picture of King Henry III's contemporary, St Louis listening to petitions under an oak at Vincennes (Powicke 1953, 143 and Joinville, 1938, 17).

Edward I, like his father Henry III, sometimes personally administered justice and a realisation that he was on occasions in court may be at the back of a refusal to plead '*nisi coram corpore domini regis*' ('not unless before the presence of the lord king') (Sayles 1938, lxxii). He intervened brusquely and was not above twisting the law to his own advantage but there are several instances from the first half of the reign where he was determined to see that justice was done. Prestwich concludes that the legal reforms of his reign were not merely a device to draw cases, and with them profits into the king's courts (Prestwich 1988, 296). On the other hand there seems no reason to laud Edward I as 'the English Justinian'. He had no grand idea of romanising English Law. It refers to his legislative activity and in Bishop Stubbs' words 'The dignity of his position in English history'.

The king's personal interest would never have acquired the force and continuity to become a national system of justice if the Norman and Plantagenet rulers had not created a framework within which justices could operate on behalf of the monarch. Green considers that in the reign of Henry I there was a central royal court operating at the exchequer (Green, 1989, 95-117). In addition local magnates and bishops were used by the king to extend royal justice in the counties. Most far reaching, in time and space, was his dispatching itinerant justices to hold courts concerning pleas of the Crown throughout England. In 1124, for instance, a great court was held at 'Hundehoge' in Leicestershire by Ralph Bassett and the king's thanes when, according to the Anglo-Saxon Chronicle, 'there hanged more thieves than ever more known before, that is, in a little while, four and forty men altogether and despoiled six men of their eyes and of their testicles'. This display of zero tolerance to thieves was regarded with horror by the chronicler, but when compared to the breakdown of firm order in Stephen's reign (1135-54) it was seen to be preferable. Stephen was 'a mild man and good, and did no justice'.

By the mid-thirteenth century regular use of royal justices whether they were sitting in what was by this time called the Bench at Westminster, or were itinerant in the shires, had become a permanent feature of government. By then their courts had replaced those presided over by the sheriffs in some ways. The shire and hundredal courts (the latter presided over by the bailiffs appointed by the sheriff) still continued albeit with a reduced burden of cases affecting the pleas of the crown.

Shire and hundred courts

The Norman invaders took over a relatively well governed country in which shire or county courts had been an important feature of national life since the time of King Alfred. From the tenth century kings had asked freemen to attend the shire moots presided over by the ealdormen of the shire, and the shires in their turn were subdivided in Central and Southern England into administrative units known as hundreds. They were 'for the adjustment of taxation, the maintenance of peace and order and the settlement of local pleas' (Stenton 1962, 289). Such shire and hundred moots (there was a similar system of wapentakes in the north) were held in the open air at traditional meeting places often on or around tumuli. The location of these is a challenge to the historically minded rambler. Gelling, a place-name specialist, maintains that 'barrows were often chosen in the pre-Conquest and post-Conquest period as the markers for the open-air assembly places of the hundreds' (Gelling 1978, 132). Support for this is found in Buckinghamshire (Farley 1997, 59-62) and the West Midlands (Hooke 1985, 99-101), but excavation of these mounds has certainly modified this picture. Of 12 meeting places or mounds excavated up and down the country 11 have been shown either to be non-sepulchral, or at least one positively post-Roman in date.

This suggests that the Anglo-Saxons chose the locations for their hundredal centres and dug them for themselves (Adkins and Petchey 1984, 249). There are
admittedly exceptions and anomalies. A well-known landmark such as
Cuckhamsley Hill, on the northern scarp of the Berkshire Downs, was one of the
meeting places of the men of Berkshire. Local tradition links it with the burial
place of Cwichelm, a member of the West Saxon royal family. Excavation in 1934,
however, showed that the mound was erected in the early Iron Age (Gelling 1974,
481-2). The Anglo-Saxon Chronicle records that a Danish army in the year 1006,
having destroyed Wallingford, marched along Ashdown to Cuckhamsley Hill 'and
there awaited better cheer, for it was often said, that if they sought Cuckhamsley
they would never get to the sea'. Clearly a shire meeting place in this case was a
symbolic centre to which an invading force might penetrate out of a sheer sense
of bravado, as well as being a place where decisions were made in peacetime to the
rattling of shields.

It seems apparent that whatever was the situation in the late Anglo-Saxon period the shire moot or county court began to 'come indoors' in the twelfth century. This, however, was not universally true. The Essex county court met in the
thirteenth century in a green place in Chelmsford hundred and at Writtle (Cam,
1963, 107-9). The Kent county court met, among other places, at Penenden Heath
near Maidstone. The process of 'coming indoors' may have been helped by an
order to the sheriffs in 1166 to place the prison in either the king's borough or the
king's castle (Pugh 1968, 59). But there was no necessary connection. Traditional
meeting places died hard. Itinerant justices were not bound to hold their sessions
at the same place as the county court. A place to hold prisoners awaiting judgement either at the hands of the sheriff or the itinerant justice was a convenient
adjunct to the court. By Bracton's time (he died in 1268) the castle was prover-
bially the meeting place of the county court. It might still double as a fortress but
when in the custody of the sheriff it was a public building for county use rather
than a stronghold for royal or baronial power (Morris 1927, 187).

Instances of this triple function of the castle as fortification, administrative and
judicial centre are to be found throughout the country. At Norwich the shire
house (Latin *Domus Vicecomitis*) was within the castle; here it needed repair as early
as 1240 and when a royal official in Suffolk wished to inspect the legal records
pertaining to this county he was told to go to Norwich where the office was and
where the archives were stored (Mills 1957, 254). Evidently Norwich castle was
acting as the administrative centre for both counties. The county court for Suffolk
was nevertheless held in Ipswich. Carlisle Castle was in such bad condition in
Edward I's reign that the sheriff complained he had no house where he could hold
his county court. At Guildford in 1247 the sheriff of Surrey had the use of a hall
and chamber while in Essex the office was at Colchester Castle. A canon of
Barnwell visited the Cambridge castle to copy the sheriff's roll there; he said he
made the copy so that the canons need not in future go to the castle to consult the
roll. At York the shire court met in the precincts of York castle in 1212 and only
on odd occasions in the crypt of York minster.

The situation in Oxfordshire and Berkshire which were linked administratively from 1248 is more complicated. The sheriff of Oxfordshire had begun to build a gaol in Oxford in 1165-6 (Pugh 1968, 60) and this is known to have been in the castle from 1230. In 1275 the sheriff is found holding the county court in the hall of the manor of Beaumont Oxford (Cal Patent Rolls, 1272-81, 127) but it probably moved out when the Carmelites moved in (pers. comm. P. Brand). The shire court is likely to have met in the main hall of the castle throughout the rest of the Middle Ages. A drawing of 1615 in Christchurch archives shows a first-floor hall on an undercroft of (apparently) Romanesque arches (Munby 1996, 6). A building in this area has recently been located by ground seeking radar and is being investigated as I write in advance of a redevelopment scheme for the castle. It was the scene of a notorious outbreak of gaol fever in 1577 which killed the judge and, allegedly, 300 people, and the courts transferred to the Oxford Guildhall (Munby 1966, 7). The old assize hall was succeeded, virtually on the same site by a handsome neo-Norman shire hall in the 1840s with a convenient tunnel connecting the court room to the prison behind for sending prisoners down. In Berkshire, on the other hand, the sheriff made use of prisons at Windsor Castle and built his own at Faringdon which was repaired in 1196-7. Pugh suggested that, rather than maintain this, the sheriff of Berkshire came to an arrangement with the lord of Wallingford Castle whereby the constable received prisoners from the sheriff and justices, involved in gaol delivery, held their courts there (Pugh 1968, 61-2). Other locations for the Berkshire court were Newbury, Ockbridge, and very often at Grandpont on the boundary with the neighbouring Oxfordshire.

It is possible to go some way towards understanding how medieval sheriff's offices were equipped and furnished. When a new sheriff was appointed in the sixteenth year of Richard II at Northampton Castle the hall of pleas contained two *abaci* (simple instruments to aid accounting) with rails round them, as well as benches, 18 chests and tables. The sheriff also needed skippets and hampers for storing records, scales for weighing the silver pennies, supplies of soft white leather for the pouches in which letters were sent to the Exchequer at Westminster, and rods of hazelwood for his tallies (Jenkinson 1911, 367-80). There are 130 of these pouches dating from before 1400 still surviving in the Public Record Office; on them the sheriff's clerk wrote the name of his county, the date, and a note of the contents. The sheriff's messenger then took it to London (Mills 1957, 257).

Special buildings for the administration of justice

So far in this chapter archaeology, the study of surviving material remains of past cultures, has hardly made an appearance. The administration of law leaves somewhat fleeting remains, particularly in the early Middle Ages. The buildings for a permanent administrative and judicial centre of the capital grew up slowly in Westminster around the Great Hall; the Exchequer was the first department of

64 Arles. Twelfth-/thirteenth-century civic building of three main phases. In front is stone bench. Photo by author

state to peel off from the perpetually itinerant court and establish its own building (Steane 1993, 72, 74). The Courts of Justice themselves were accommodated in the Great Hall; no more impressive venue could be found in the whole land. Temporary arrangements of benches, tables and screens were erected and taken down by carpenters when the hall was put to ceremonial use (Allen Brown, Colvin, Taylor 1963, I, 543-4).

The court of King's bench in 1327 is recorded as having three enclosed oak benches, 27ft long, for the use of the justices and the clerks '*in superiori gradu*'; its great and small oak bars with benches of the same length presumably placed under them. Its 'exchequer' table, 20ft long by 6ft wide was placed on three trestles (Sayles 1938, lxxvii). Galleries were erected for the Common Bench (Baker, 1986, 171-5). A 'crib' accommodated 'apprentices' in 1291. Detailed DIY measures were necessary when Westminster-based institutions moved temporarily to Shrewsbury or to York.

Similar *ad hoc* arrangements were made all over the country for the holding of courts, the receipts of fines and rents and the auditing of officials' returns. Special buildings or temporary alterations to buildings were needed to accommodate the accused awaiting trial, debtors, those accused of breaches of the forest law, in fact

65   Arles. Stone bench from which magistrates in the thirteenth century delivered judgement. Behind is the medieval civic building. Photo by author

the multifarious characters caught up in the meshes of the medieval justice system. A recent case has been made to identify a number of these special buildings which are more likely to be recognised from buried foundations or with their surviving walls incorporated in later structures (Saunders 1992, 195-217). Long narrow halls without juxtaposition to kitchens or obvious heating arrangements but fitted with garderobes, usually near principal gateways, which show 'architectural' characteristics as opposed to more workaday stable buildings are the marks of these administrative buildings. Few, apart from that at Oakham (Rutland), survive to roof level but there are considerable remains at Launceston and Lydford Castles in Cornwall and at the Duchy Palace of Lostwithiel in the same county. Lydford is particularly interesting because its well-preserved shell 'demonstrates the operation of a purpose-built medieval prison and judicial centre whose discrete functions are documentarily attested' (Saunders 1992, 205).

Lydford at the time of the Norman Conquest was one of the four boroughs of Devon and the site of a mint (Haslam 1984, 256-9). It came to belong to the earldom of Cornwall and had a further dual function by being the administrative centre for the stannaries (the tin industry of Devon) and the royal forest of Dartmoor. The principal room on the second floor was the hall or courtroom accessed by stairs from a central lobby, heated by a fireplace in the cross wall and with its own garderobe. The resident keeper or gaoler was also accommodated in a smaller room on this floor. Below the rooms were used for prisoners graded according to medieval practice (Pugh 1968, 347-73). The general prison was a large room, 7m x 12m, poorly lit but yet provided with a garderobe. Two smaller rooms did not possess even these conveniences but the worst conditions, presumably reserved for the most dangerous or lowest status felon, was the cellar or pit. Recently fashionable access analysis which generally considers that 'deep' location of space within a complex denotes high status has to be reversed in this instance. The 'visitors' (in this case the felons) are housed in the most secure areas; the 'owners' (in this case the keepers or the gaolers) reside in the more accessible parts of the building (Fairclough 1992, 354). A remarkable survival of a Tudor court room, complete with furnishing and a trap door below the prisoner at the bar leading to a prison, is seen at Knaresborough Castle (West Yorkshire) (**66-7**). Here the bailiff of the Duchy of Lancaster held court.

Lordly jurisdictional controls

Twelfth-century England was a rough place with rudimentary standards of law and order. A primitive self-policing system developed or was externally imposed in large parts of the country whereby persons were made mutually responsible for each other's behaviour (Poole 1954, 394-5). The Anglo-Norman sheriff's duties included holding the view of *frankpledge* whereby all tenants (except barons, knights, freeholders and clergy) were compelled to attend great courts and to be formed into groups of ten or twelve, under the direction of a *tithing* man or chief pledge. His *tourn* was also an important *venue* for enquiries as to what crimes had been conducted in the locality. Henceforward if one of the group was suspected of a crime, it was the duty of the rest to produce him in court. Petty policing powers were delegated widely among lords. The right of *infangthef* was an Anglo-Saxon privilege allowing the lordly holder to bring to justice thieves caught in possession of stolen goods within his own territory. Other lords also enjoyed the right of *utfangthef*, which gave in addition the right to arrest and mete out justice to felons captured anywhere. This latter, however, was in practice fairly rare.

Since policing was so inadequate some sort of order was maintained by the fear of summary capital punishment. The right of lords to set up gallows or the manor was widespread. During the 1270s and 1280s in Lincolnshire lords claimed this privilege in well over 100 towns and villages throughout the county (Platts 1985, 53-5). The distribution of places where gallows might be erected drawn from information collected in the 1274-5 *Hundred Rolls* and the *c*.1284 *Placita de Quo Warranto* conforms to the pattern of settlement. No more than five miles separated any two sets of gallows. The same phenomenon is noticed when we focus down to the single hundred of Bampton in Oxfordshire. Here the lord of Greys Manor in Hardwick, Brighthampton and Yelford had view of frankpledge and other liberties including a gallows. All four lords of Standlake Manor claimed pillory, tumbrell, assize of bread and ale and gallows. In 1579 'for confirmation of the

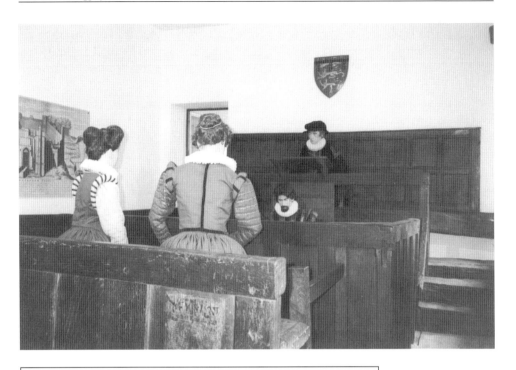

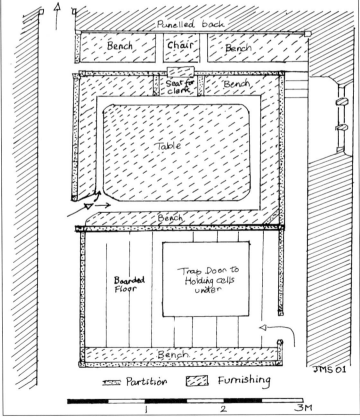

66 *Knaresborough Castle, Yorkshire. Tudor court room of Duchy of Lancaster.* Photo by Harrogate Museums

67 *Knaresborough Castle, Yorkshire. Plan of Tudor Court Room*

liberties and royalty' of the manor, the lord gave an elm for a gallows to be built by the tenants and erected in the 'old place' near Knight Bridge on the Shifford brook where the Aston-Brighthampton road entered the liberty (Victoria County History Oxfordshire XIII, 1996, 3, 139, 195, 214). It sounds as if gallows were an omnipresent and horrendous feature of the medieval landscape. Considerable doubt remains as to how often lords actually inflicted this irreversible punishment on the country's criminals. It may well be that the status conformed by this large-ly symbolic right satisfied them. Most of what hanging was done in medieval soci-ety was authorised by royal justices.

Justice in the fourteenth century

Legislation received a great boost in the reign of Edward I when the king pushed forward the frontiers of royal rights at the expense of baronial 'liberties' with the help of a well trained and committed body of justices (Plucknett 1949). By the middle of his grandson's reign the elaboration of the judicial system of England has been described as 'impressive' (McKisack 1959, 198-9). The central courts of the exchequer, king's bench and common bench were usually to be found at Westminster, although at times all three Edwards moved them to York when the

68 Crypt of St Mary le Bow church, Cheapside, London. This eleventh-century crypt was used as a prison for clerics and others whose trials were held in the Archbishop of Canterbury's Court of the Arches in the church above from the thirteenth century. Artist, F. North 1818. Guildhall Library 391/MAR 1

country was at war with Scotland and it was more convenient for the governmental base to be nearer the centre of operations. The court of exchequer had long dealt with cases arising from audit of revenue. Justices sitting in the court of King's Bench handled cases of special concern to the king and corrected errors in other courts. Cases between subject and subject were heard in the Court of Common Pleas or Common Bench. Obviously it was inconvenient for complainants, or rather their attorneys, to come to Westminster or York in their search for justice. The king had commissioned groups of justices, as we have seen, to make wide searching enquiries and to conduct General Eyres in specially called County Courts. Their place in the fourteenth century was partly taken by more specialised visitations by justices of assize and gaol delivery. In theory no sheriff or bailiff who behaved unjustly or extortionately was safe. In fact the integrity of the justices themselves was frequently called to question. In the 1340s and 1350s they were said to be taking bribes and selling laws 'as if they had been oxen or cows' and the attacks on justices during Wat Tyler's rising of 1381 shows there was widespread suspicion of the highest placed administrators of the law (McKisack 1959, 205, 206).

The legal profession: origins

The origins of the legal profession in England are wrapped in obscurity which has been only partly dissipated by recent research (Ramsay 1985, Brand 1992). In the late thirteenth century, where we can trace the London quarters of individual lawyers, they are found living in Westminster, in Southwark and in the City. In particular there seems to be no obvious reason why lawyers began to congregate in Holborn, an extra mural suburb of London midway between the courts of Westminster and outside the liberties of the city. Why did they not settle at Westminster which in the fourteenth century was a small vill dominated by the Abbey and its near neighbour the royal palace (Rosser 1989)? It has been suggested that the relative emptiness of Holborn may have been one reason; a more plausible case can be made from the proximity of various bishops whose houses were situated close by. Bishops were chosen by the Plantagenet kings to become chancellors and chancery officials found it convenient to live near them. The Knights Templars had moved to a marshy site between Fleet Street and the Thames not later than 1162. Their 'New Temple' became a centre of royal, diplomatic, legal and fiscal activity; they also acted as bankers storing valuables, documents and large sums. Their investment of the profits from these activities involved estate management. Their fall in 1308 resulted in a large part of their property passing to the crown (Roxburgh 1972). The site with its notable round church was convenient for the construction of inns, and in the fourteenth century apprentices of the law moved in to live for the part of the year when the courts were in session.

69 *Back of seal and impression of Martino of Paolo in Terano, expounder of law. A lawyer is shown seated on a high-backed chair at his desk on which is an open book. He wears a fur tippet (cf English lawyers of fifteenth century); on either side are lawyers with the legal close-cap or coif, sitting on benches. The handle has been wrenched off.* Ashmolean Museum, Oxford. Photo by Vernon Brooke

Inns of Court

Whatever the reason it seems that from the early fourteenth century lawyers began to settle in sites off Holborn, Fleet Street and Chancery Lane. There was little incentive for them to buy houses because they only needed to be in London during the law terms. Holborn was particularly convenient because while many lawyers found employment in the courts of the City of London they could move on into the royal courts at Westminster. They clubbed together 'to rent a house, hire a cook and . . . engage a servant or two and be assured of a bed and a reasonable dinner' (Prest 1972, 4). These tenements became known as Inns of Court and Inns of Chancery (from *hospitium*: inn, guest house, court because they were occupied by men of the king's court or by apprentices of the bench). At the beginning of the fourteenth century 'apprentices' were young men learning professional skills. By the end of the century medieval lawyers are found remaining apprentices for up to ten years and sometimes all their lives. They frequented the courts of Westminster acquiring a knowledge of legal rules and picking up practice in legal procedure by listening to pleadings. There is some evidence for formal education (through lectures) from *c.*1275-1300 (Brand, 1992, 57-75). This was, nevertheless, an ill-organised and unsatisfactory way of training for the legal profession and the lack of organised teaching made parents reluctant to set their children at law.

Between 1350-1420 this changed. The Inns of Court and Chancery became educational institutions, places where lawyers lived *and* learned their law. They were, however, fundamentally different institutions at their inception from the colleges of Oxford and Cambridge. They had no founder, no statutes, no endowments, no communal buildings to start with. They differed from modern universities in that they had no fixed annual enrolment, no uniform pattern of attendance during the academic year, and no standard annual turnover of students (Prest 1972, 16). They were more like clubs, offices and lodging houses providing their little bands of members with food, shelter and companionship in a relatively inhospitable urban setting. They resembled Oxford halls rather than Oxford colleges. The students paid their inns for commons; they also paid the barber, the washerwoman, medical expenses, special breakfasts, drinks or dinners. All this cost perhaps 8d a week at a time when students at Oxford were paying 8d to 1s. Salter estimated that an undergraduate's expenses for a year need not have exceeded 50 shillings (Evans 1992, 502). The residence was vital to the creation of a corporate spirit. This is still recognised in the custom of young, would-be lawyers attending so many compulsory dinners in each legal term. Without 'the holding together in commons (of) the companie of this fellowship in their publique hall . . . a companie so voluntarily gathered together to live under government could hardly bee termed a society'.

Halls of Inns of Court and Chancery

Despite these basic differences between Inns of Court and Chancery and Oxbridge colleges, they acquired in the fifteenth and sixteenth centuries communal buildings displaying a number of similarities with collegiate complexes. These have suffered from fire, blitz and radical alterations over the last 400 years but are still worthy of close study for the light they shed on lawyers' presuppositions, their standards of living and their hierarchically ordered societies. There is an early fifteenth-century hall at Barnard's Inn but the oldest hall of an inn of court to survive is that at Lincoln's Inn (**70**). The records of Lincoln's Inn, the so-called Black Books, go as far back as 1422 and contain references to the building of the hall between 1485 and 1492. The capital cost was met from gifts from private members, short-term loans, levies and appropriations. There was a short lived but sharp increase in the usual fine for fornicating with a woman in chambers from 6s 8d to 100s as well as a fine of 20s 'if he shall have her or enjoy her in the garden or Chancery Lane' (Megarry 1997, 5). The fifteenth-century building was built of red brick with dressings of not very durable stone from Merstham or Reigate (Simpson 1928, 63) on an undercroft of brick. The roof, for many years hidden above an eighteenth-century ceiling, has been revealed as of four bays, with principal rafters tied by collars, supported with arch-braces, with two ranges of purlins strengthened by S-shaped windbraces and a cornice topped with quatrefoil pierced squares (Schofield, 1994, 170-1). The original entrance is on the west indicating that access from Westminster came through the walks and gardens of Lincoln's Inn Fields. The hall area was lengthened in 1623 by the addition of

70 *Lincoln's Inn, London. The oriel window of the old hall, built 1485-92, left, the Tudor gateway with brick diapering, centre, and the ashlar masonry of the early seventeenth-century first floor chapel on the right.* Photo by author

two oriel windows; this gave more light to the hall which being hemmed in with other buildings could not be provided with windows in the end walls such as at the London Guildhall or Westminster Hall (Schofield 1984, 137).

The hall was lined at an early date with a 9ft-high wainscot of linen-fold panelling. Portions of this were found reused as a boarded crawling way above the ceiling removed in 1928. It was originally heated by an open central hearth and never provided with a lateral fireplace and chimney unlike many sixteenth-century halls. The smoke escaped through an eight-sided oak 'loover' or 'lanthorn', renewed after 'the great wind' of January 1551. We can recover other features such as the battlemented parapet from the pictures painted in the background of the 1624 window by Van Linge on the south side of the chapel (RCHM London, II, 1925 49 plates 234).

This combination of architectural and archaeological approaches enables us to reconstruct the external appearance of the hall in the sixteenth century; for what went on inside we have to rely on documents. The hierarchical structure of the society using the hall and other buildings was echoed in every aspect of organisation and daily life of an inn of court. There were three ranks or degrees: the benchers, the barristers and the students. The benchers were described in the words of Denton, writing *c*.1540, as 'suche as before time have openly read lectures to whom is chiefly committed the government and ordering of the said houses, as to men meetest, both for their age, discretion and wisdomes'. The barristers were 'for their learning and continuance, called by the said readers to plead and argue . . . doubtful cases and questions, which amongst them are called mates' (Moots). Lastly the residue of learners are 'the younger men that for lack of learning and continuance are not able to reason and argue in these "motes"' (quoted in Prest 1972, 48). The customs for the use of the hall mirror this hierarchy of power within the inn. Members sat down for their meals in the hall at tables arranged according to rank; servants brought meals first to the benches and then to the barristers and the students. Although sitting at separate tables all ate the same food and paid for wine (the benchers received theirs free). The clerks sat separately and waited on the rest of the company (here they are similar to servitors and sizars at Oxford and Cambridge). These ranks were emphasised by costume. Benchers wore knee-length gowns, twisted with silk and velvet, barristers long black grogram robes with two velvet welts in the long hanging sleeves. Students wore plain sleeveless black gowns, with a flap collar (Prest 1972, 48).

Lincoln's Inn Old Hall is the only surviving medieval hall of the four great Inns of Court. Grays Inn Hall (**74**) was rebuilt with a gallery, a hammer beam roof and stepped gables in 1550-60. It was reduced to a smoking shell by the blitz of 1941 and had to be replicated after the war. The great hall at Middle Temple was built between 1562 and 1574 of brick and stone dressings. The louvre and porch are modern additions but the roof, of double hammerbeam construction, has largely survived the bombing and seems to be a deliberate throw-back to a glorious (and mythical) past. Its nearest progenitor is the splendid Henrician roof of Hampton Court Palace, again a building with medieval overtones such as central hearth and louvre. The beams at Middle Temple have Renaissance type mouldings; fully Renaissance too is the decoration of the ornate screen. The hall at the Inner Temple was probably rebuilt after the devastating Wat Tyler's rebellion of 1381. It had a timbered roof of the fourteenth century (Schofield 1994, plate 72b); two medieval vaulted rooms one on top of the other survive at the west end of the now rebuilt nineteenth-century hall.

Legal education

The techniques for improving legal education are intimately connected with the use of the hall. Most of the students in the fifteenth and sixteenth centuries were the sons of country gentlemen, not intended for the legal profession. Hence the inns of court to some degree took over the functions of great noble households; they acted as 'finishing schools' for the young scions of the gentry and offered dancing, singing, fencing and plays among the subjects taught. For the minority who were serious students of the law there was a more rigorous rule (Baker 1991, 6-7). In term-time they attended Westminster Hall to witness the courts in action; throughout the year they were involved in long, intricate moots. For these practical sessions the hall of each inn was arranged to resemble a court, with a bar and bench. Young students sat inside the bar and were named 'inner barristers'. When thought to be sufficiently qualified to argue points of law the student was called to the bar and as an 'utter barrister' stood outside the bar at moots. The next stage of legal learning was that he would be expected to deliver a lecture. Courses of lectures on the old statutes supplemented this vocational training were given during the two learning vacations of Lent and summer each year. When the barrister had lectured (or as the expression was had given a 'reading') he sat on the bench at moots as a bencher. The Christmas vacation was a time of relaxation from this stern programme. A lord of misrule was elected and presided over festivities. Shakespeare's plays were enacted in the halls of Inns of Court.

The legal profession was wholly secular and always had been. During the sixteenth century the balance of forces within society moved from the clerical to the legal. Wolsey was the last ecclesiastical potentate to hold the chancellorship. Henceforward English common lawyers occupied key positions in parliament, the council and other organs of state rule. This process is vividly reflected in the buildings of the Inns of Court. The provision of chapels is minimal compared with the medieval universities dominated by the international Catholic Church and primarily intended for the training of clerics and priests. The colleges of Oxford and Cambridge had elaborate chapels served by the fellows, normally in clerical orders; they also functioned as chantry chapels for their founders and other benefactors. The lawyers in the Inner and Middle Temple made do with the twelfth- and thirteenth-century church built hundreds of years before; they never founded their own chapel (Lewer and Dark 1997, 54-61). Little was spent on the church whereas they contributed manfully to the construction of the splendid Middle Temple Hall. The little chapel at Gray's Inn cowers beside the magnificence of the hall; it barely seats a hundred; it is devoid of quality in either architecture or fittings. The chapel at Lincoln's Inn, admittedly was rebuilt in 1620-3, with its crypt it is remarkable specimen of seventeenth-century Gothic. This conservative reluctance on the part of the lawyers to accept the Renaissance goes with their search for medieval respectability which also finds expression in the decorative imagery of their halls and chapels. It is almost exclusively heraldic recalling not the saints or martyrs but the genealogies of nouveaux riches lawyers (RCHM London West 49 and plates 73-6). In the backgrounds of the few saints portrayed in glass are pictured the buildings of Lincoln's Inn; the lawyers once again betraying their obsessive interest with their professional interests at the expense of the spiritual (RCHM London West 1925 plates 234-5).

Similar hierarchical arrangements to those made for the halls of inns of court were laid down for chapels. At a council of Lincoln's Inn held in 1623 it was declared

> that the middle rowe and double particion of seates ther from the Quire
> downeward, shall be disposed as followeth: The two first double seates next
> the Quire to be set apart and allotted to such Noblemen, Judges, Sergeants
> at Law and other persons of eminent quality, as shall att any tyme resort and

repaire to the chapell. The six next double seates there to be for the Mrs (Masters) of the Bench and the Associates and they to place themselves by three and three in every of them according to their antiquity . . . The associates of the Bench to be last placed, except they be such persons of ranke and quality as Noblemen's Sonnes and Knightes: and they take their places as they doe att the Bench table.

Careful placing was accompanied by exclusion clauses. Women and children were excluded in 1636 'in this time of contagion and infection'. 'Persons of mean quality' were not admitted to the chapel from 1638 (Walker and Baildon 1898, II, 242).

Chambers and courts

Viewers of *Rumpole of the Bailey* or *Kavanagh QC* will be accustomed to the sight of 'chambers'. These are the residences and offices of barristers, solicitors and occasionally simply members of the public. They occupy for the most part four- or five-storey buildings arranged round courts or large blocks. The names displayed at the entrance to each staircase list the occupants; a long list of names denotes a set of barristers' chambers. They came into existence like much else in the Inns of Court in an unplanned and pragmatic way.

To begin with the societies did not gain the freehold of the land they lived on as tenants for hundreds of years. This can be explained by the fact that the landlords of each of their inns were ecclesiastical and this meant that it was difficult, if not impossible, under the rules of both canon law and common law for them to make permanent grants of their property. This seems a more likely reason than to attribute it to the 'nomadic' situation of the individual practitioners of the law. In fact nomadic they may have been, but they still needed to spend an appreciable period of each year near or at Westminster (Brand, pers. comm.). The Inner Temple, for example, were tenants of the Knights Hospitallers until 1540 when the property of the order was vested in the Crown. The society of Lincoln's Inn occupied buildings in the fifteenth century belonging to the Bishops of Chichester. Gray's Inn was originally occupied by the Manor House of the 'Ancient Manor of Purpoole in Holborn' (Cowper 1985, 2-3). In each case as the need arose individuals who had sufficient money, or groups of lawyers clubbing together, built themselves chambers. These were insubstantial half timbered, sometimes rickety structures; gradually they were grouped round squares and courts, rebuilt in brick and accessed by staircases. Examples of both timber framed and brick sometimes can be found in the old square at Lincoln's Inn to the south of the gatehouse and the east of the hall (Numbers 21-25). A second group (numbers 16, 18, 19 and 20) are also of brick and timber framing and here again there is a core of early sixteenth-century work (RCHM London West 1925, 46-8).

The Black Books of the society (general memoranda books which contain some accounts and also admissions and other decisions taken by the benchers

71   *Back of seal and impression. Seal of the Ghibelline (imperial) party in the city of Massa, Tuscany. The imperial eagle, screaming in triumph, is shown perched on the back of a lion passant coward (i.e. his tail between his legs) representing the Papal (or Guelf) party. It may refer to the defeat of the Guelfs at the battle of Monteveglio in 1325. It thus records an event in symbolic and provocative form of a notable military victory.* Ashmolean Museum, Oxford. Photo by Vernon Brooke

which run continuously from 1422) enable us to track the provision of both the communal buildings and the chambers on the site (Walker and Baildon 1898 passim). The earlier accommodation of the fifteenth century was in two storeyed structures and built of timber framing, with walls plastered or daubed. We read of the purchase 'of gloves for the carpenter' and in 1508-9 54s to Walshe 'le dawber' for the 'seelyng librarye' and for 'dawbyng' all partitions of the chambers of the new building and for the 'floryng' of Rowdon's chamber. £4 was paid to Stephen Punchon, carpenter, for 11 doors, 7 windows and 7 'draught plankes' (shutters?) and for 'plankeryng' the said new building.

For the most part the lawyers' chambers were long rooms, inside of which cells called 'studies' were constructed by wainscot. The floor space outside the studies was probably shared in common by the occupants of each chamber and partly occupied by bedding. It was customary as at Oxford for two or more to share such spartan accommodation. The bench insisted that in chambers the junior was to give place to the senior but there does not seem to be any regular supervision of studies by senior over junior such as is built into the statutes of medieval Oxford colleges (Willis and Clark 1886, III, 296-327). There was no heating supplied although panelling covering the inner half chambers would have reduced draughts. The cheer of the central fireplace in the hall must have been appreciated. Inner and outer lockable doors were attached to the inner half chambers (one is reminded of the Oxbridge custom of 'sporting the oak'). The rooms were occa-

72 *Matrix of seal of Giovanni Sciarra, Prefect of Rome early fourteenth century. A female figure representing 'Prefectura' seated on a* cella curulis *decorated with two dogs, symbol of fidelity and vigilance, holding in her right hand the sword of justice. In her left is the golden rose (blessed by the Pope). At her feet kneel two notaries and two hooded judges. Her feet rest on a table with a book and an inkpot. Bottom centre is a heater-shaped shield with the badge of her prefecture.* Ashmolean Museum, Oxford. Photo Vernon Brooke

sionally decorated with painting and in 1885, during demolition of a first-floor room at No 3 Old Square, Lincoln's Inn, a series of decorations was found including arabesque ornaments in black outline, with touches of red and blue and representations of a gardener, a woman with fruit, a cupid, dolphins and floriate ribands (Schofield 1994, 171). The painting was removed to the Victoria and Albert Museum where it deteriorated to a pile of dust!

During the reign of Elizabeth the Privy Council grew concerned at the increase in the number of chambers being built by the Inns of Court and issued orders in 1574 and 1584 against this. Grays Inn seems to have ignored this and carried on building (Fletcher 1907, xxxvii). In 1569 William Butler erected chambers over the pastry house to the west of the hall. In the next year Edward Stanhope added 'Stanhopes Buildings' to the 'back court'. In 1571 Humphrey Purefey was given leave to put up a four-storey house with a double staircase in the north-west corner of the same court. In 1579 Walter Ashton, Edward Stanhope and Edward Ellis added further chambers to the north court. Henceforth Grays Inn consisted of North or Coney Court, Middle or Chapel

Court and South or Holborn Court. A similar process was going on at the same time in Oxford as colleges markedly increased the numbers of the undergraduate body. Here as in London they often built upwards adding 'cock lofts' and fitting young men into attic spaces (Newman 1986, 630).

The societies of lawyers gradually gained possession of their premises. In 1608 King James I conveyed the Temple to the benchers of the Inner and Middle Temple 'to serve for all time to come for the accommodation and education of the students and practitioners of the laws of the realm' (Baker 1991, 16). In this practical and almost casual way the crown furthered the interests of the lawyers. It must have hoped that they would buttress its cause. It is paradoxical that the latter played a major part in bringing down the crown during the reign of Charles I.

The present regular Georgian and Victorianised development has endowed Lincoln's Inn and Gray's Inn with a sense of planning it did not have at the start. Building round courts became of course a regular feature of medieval building; but in Holborn as in Oxford, the development of the court or quadrangle was an architectural accident. Mob Quad, Merton College claimed to be the earliest Oxford quadrangle (Martin and Highfield 1997, 43-4), like Topsy 'just growed'. So it was at Gray's Inn, the Inner and Middle Temple and Lincoln's Inn.

Gatehouses

The prominent part played by the gatehouse in the planning of medieval institutions like monasteries, hospitals and colleges emphasises the desire for security in a volatile and potentially violent society. The Inns of Court were no exception and acquired gatehouses early. That at Lincoln's Inn links the Inn of Court with Chancery Lane and thus with Fleet Street running between the City and Westminster. It is built of brick, a high status material in 1518, the date recorded over the archway. It is H-shaped in plan with massive towers forming first-storey cross wings. A vault was originally planned over the carriageway but never built. The toothing for its springing remains (Schofield 1984, 137 and Schofield 1994, 171). The brick was patterned with diaperwork. It has almost entirely been renewed. Much better preserved are the heavy oaken doors with a small wicket for pedestrian ingress after dark similar to those gateways in Oxford and Cambridge colleges. Defence and exclusivity were not the only motives. An imposing entrance could not fail to impress. Morton's double brick towers at Lambeth Palace provided a magnificent entrance to the London residence of the Archbishops of Canterbury. Wolsey and Henry VIII went in for multi-storeyed gatehouses at Hampton Court. They were vehicles for display. Over the gate at Lincoln's Inn are coats of arms proclaiming antiquity, royal patronage and individual munificence. The lion rampant represents Henry de Lacy, Earl of Lincoln, an historical figure and the institution's alleged (but mythical) founder. The royal arms of Henry VIII are up there next to the squirrels of Sir Thomas Lovell, a distinguished speaker of the House of Commons and a generous contributor to the building (Megarry 1997).

73 *Long Crendon, Buckinghamshire. Court Hall, fifteenth century. The annual meeting of the manor court took place in this big room on the first floor. Roof: queen posts in each of three trusses.* Drawing by author

A complete contrast in materials and scale is the Gateway to Inner Temple. This led from Fleet Street directly south towards the central buildings of the early medieval Temple. It is a timber-framed structure with bay windows at first- and second-floor levels. The building was erected in 1610-11 but was taken down and the ground floor set back 5ft to enable Fleet Street to be widened in 1905. The front room on the first floor is believed to have been the council chamber of Henry Prince of Wales (d. 1612), the eldest son of James I. The plaster ceiling is decorated with the Prince of Wales' feathers and the initials P.H. standing for Prince Henry (RCHM London, 1929, 161 and Baker 1991, 23). Here the gateway is seen as an investment, a piece of early seventeenth-century urban development and a prime site. The house over it (No 17 Fleet Street) was built by John Bennett, sergeant at arms.

The costume of serjeants and judges in the Middle Ages (colour plate 27)

The office of sergeant-at-law goes back into the early Middle Ages. The name used to be thought as deriving from the Latin *servientes ad legem* since the serjeants were originally seen as servants of the Crown. This modern scholarship has exploded.

74 *London, Gray's Inn. Hall of Inn of court 're-edified' between 1556 and 1560 at a cost of £863 10s 8d. Burnt out in May 1941. Rebuilt post-Second World War.* Drawing by author

This Latin phrase is now interpreted as meaning that the serjeants were 'servants' of their clients, and like other servants could have their words and actions disowned by their principals. Anything said or done by the litigant or by the attorney in court was binding (Brand, 1992, 94-5). The king certainly retained the services of one or more serjeants, and in the fourteenth century, acting on advice of the justices of the Common Bench, came to control entry into the profession. In the thirteenth century there were already as many as 30 of them. Chaucer refers to them as meeting their clients at certain allocated pillars in old St Pauls. Appointments to the order were prefaced by writ under the great seal; the actual entrance into the order was through a ceremony in the Court of Common Bench. By the fourteenth century they were seen as the most eminent in the legal profession, with a complete control of the higher courts arising out of their monopoly of advocacy in the Court of Common Pleas. The serjeants at law by the end of the Middle Ages were recognised as a rank of advocates superior to the barristers from whom they were appointed. They provided the judges and it is unsurprising that they were sartorially distinguished as such.

A sense of hierarchy, as we have seen, radiates through medieval society. Ritual was performed when men were admitted to exclusive groups. Costume perpetuated the resulting feeling of exclusivity. Monks were invested, knights dubbed, doctors graduated and tradesmen were admitted to a livery company. They all had distinctive garbs. So it was with sergeants-at-law. 'Those whom God hath made eminent over laymen though inward adornments should also be outwardly distinguished from laymen by their habit' (quoted by Baker 1984, 67).

We can reconstruct the appearance of medieval judges from three main sources: illuminated manuscripts, sculptured effigies and monumental brasses. It seems that judges and serjeants had acquired a distinctive costume by the mid-fourteenth century. Illuminated miniatures show them in long robes of plain or rayed material, hoods and coifs. The *collobium* (a tabard, shirt, sleeveless tunic or cloak) is most often part of their dress. In the abbey church of Dorchester-on-Thames, Oxfordshire, there is a worn effigy attributed to John de Stonore (sergeant and chief Justice of the Common Pleas d. 1354). He is shown in a knee-length *collobium* with wide elbow-length sleeves, worn above the cassock and hood. His head is covered with the coif (Baker 1984, 70). Another mutilated stone effigy found at Gresford church, Denbighshire, shows a man 6ft in length dressed in a *ganache* or tabard with two tongues or labels at the neck and a coif tied round his head. He holds an open book in his hands and has tentatively been identified as Sir David Hanmer, justice of the King's Bench from 1383-7 (Baker 1973, 8-11). In both cases the coif is the distinguishing item of costume of serjeants-at-law and judges.

The medieval coif was a white linen close-fitting skullcap, completely covering (and thus dressing and controlling) the hair. It was worn by judges all the time and was not even removed in the King's presence. In later times (from the reign of Charles II) the coif was replaced by the wig; but a vestigial trace of the coif was pinned onto the crown of the wig in the form of a linen patch.

In the later Middle Ages images of judges multiply. They are found in monumental brasses listed by Herbert Druitt (Druitt 1970, 226-35) and in addition there are a few incised slabs, as at Denton, Leicestershire; Radbourne, Derbyshire; Prestwood, Leicestershire and Egmanton Nottinghamshire (Greenhill 1976). Brasses and incised slabs sometimes lagged behind current fashion and are uncertain guides to costume. They also lack colour.

The most vivid contemporary illustration of late medieval judges and lawyers at work is to be found in the Whaddon Folio in the library of the Inner Temple. This has four illuminated pictures depicting the Courts of Chancery, King's Bench, Common Pleas and Exchequer (*Legal London*, 1971). In the scene showing the Court of Chancery there are two judges in scarlet tabards; at the bar of the court are three sergeants-at-law wearing the white coif. Presiding over the Court of the King's Bench are five judges dressed in scarlet. From these and from images of judges on brasses (**colour plate 27**) it is clear that they had by the late fourteenth century given up wearing the *collobium* and had adopted instead a cloak or mantle (*chiamys*) fastened on the right shoulder. We also know that the mantle was put on over the hood but the tail of the hood was pulled out so that it hung down behind. From the earliest times judges received the material for their robes as royal liveries. There were different robes for winter and summer use. In 1387 they had summer robes of green cloth lined with green taffeta. Dugdale records that in 1442 they had winter robes of violet cloth lined with miniver and summer robes of green cloth lined with green tartarin (Baker 1978, 29-30).

There were practical reasons for distinctive legal attire. The discomfort of sitting in draughty and unheated court rooms for hours on end was mitigated by warm robes. They made clear at a glance which of the bustling multitude of plaintiffs, witnesses and defendants in Westminster Hall or St Paul's were serjeants or judges. Robes were the insignia of those men who had climbed to the top of the legal profession. They have gone on wearing the long gown, hood and mantle ever since (Baker 1978, 27-39).

Serjeants' inns

When a serjeant was appointed he was ceremoniously rung out of his Inn of Court and formally admitted to one of the Serjeants' inns — exclusively organised for the housing of the most eminent in the profession. Again the origins are obscure but by the fifteenth century the serjeants are found in two societies occupying a number of sites. These included for a short time (1459-96) Scrope's Inn which stood on the north side of Holborn. The second inn occupied between 1424-42, known as Serjeants' Inn, was on the south side of Fleet Street, east of its junction with Chancery Lane and was connected by a passage to Inner Temple. A third one was at the south of Chancery Lane (1442-59) where subsequently the offices of the Royal Insurance Company stood (Megarry 1971, 24-5). The great age of the Serjeants was the sixteenth century. They went into rapid decline in Victoria's reign and the inns fell into disuse. Now, after the great fire, the encroachment of insurance companies and the Blitz, there is little to recall the serjeants' halls except their names marked by plaques; the halls in which Elizabethan judges once sat after dinner to discuss knotty points of law have vanished.

When walking along Holborn today, dodging the traffic and deafened by hydraulic drills, Staple Inn comes suddenly into view with its timber-framed gables, jettied storeys and full width attic casements, transporting us back into the Tudor Age. Staple Inn (the name meaning 'pillared hall' from OE *stapel* or post) was associated with a group of lawyers paying rent to a landlord as early as *c.*1420 (Ramsay, 1985, xxxii). It was absorbed for a time in Gray's Inn from 1520. The display front facing Fleet Street was built in 1581-6 by the company of Staple Inn (Schofield, 1994, 189-90). The court behind is one of the unexpectedly tranquil delights of London, cut off as it is from the traffic roar. The hall of brick and stone with its hammer beam roof was badly damaged by a German flying bomb in 1944 but the late Tudor roof now restored is largely intact (Hewett 1980, 230-3).

Staple Inn was only one of a whole series of inns where lawyers and chancery clerks lived in the fifteenth and sixteenth centuries. Their early history has been worked out by Ramsay (1985) and their topographical and architectural remains catalogued by Schofield (1994). Very little remains of archaeological significance except a hall at Barnard's Inn at the south end of a court entered from Holborn. This is reckoned to be the 'only surviving medieval secular timber structure of domestic scale in the city' (Schofield 1994, 190).

In sum there would appear to be more substantial material remaining from the long slow process leading to the rule of law in England *c*.AD 800-1600 than might have been expected. It has been less systematically studied and therefore recorded than the corresponding evidence for the history of the church in this period. Perhaps lawyers have spent their time studying ancient texts rather than the antiquities of their profession. This can be put right in the twenty-first century.

So far in this book the emphasis has been on the possessors of power at the top levels of Western European society. In fact power was exercised at every level of medieval society from the king sitting in state in his palace to the peasant head of household occupying the (only) chair in his cottage. In between were the townsfolk. In the next chapter I have followed three themes: walls, halls and seals. Walls were important as visual images and physical realities emphasising the boundaries between countryside and town, helping too to provide the inmates with security in a violent world. But (I argue) they were also potent symbols of power, showing that the communities within could not be pushed around by kings, feudal nobles, or the great ecclesiastical dignitaries. Halls were likely to be among the largest capital investments (together with churches and hospitals) within a town's fabric. Their style and decoration have much to tell us about the burghers who held power in the teeming medieval towns of Europe. Lastly, seals were not simply vehicles for urban propaganda, but provide a unique window into how these men perceived their towns and their place within them.

7 Town walls and town halls

The rebirth of towns in Western Europe

Roman civilisation had been essentially urban. While urban life decayed during the period of the barbarian invasions dozens of Roman towns survived into the Middle Ages in France, Western Germany and Italy. This was largely because Christian bishops planted the centres of their sees in the fortified enceintes of former Roman towns. Early Christian martyrs were buried in their cemeteries and monasteries grew up in their suburbs, which in turn attracted pilgrims seeking cures from saintly relics. Old urban centres had the additional advantage of being quarries for second-hand building materials and churches and bishops' houses provided a new use for the ruins of Roman buildings. The leaders of the Christian communities thus established gained prestige by being associated, however tenuously, with the past glories of Rome.

This process guaranteed the reincarnation of many Roman town sites. It did not, however, save urban life from decay and virtual extinction. In England, in particular, there was no organised urban existence despite the valorous attempts of three generations of archaeologists to look for continuity. The first glimmerings of urban revival in Mercia and Wessex came about in the eighth-ninth century AD when Offa, and a century later Alfred, encouraged trade and commerce with the Carolingian world and began to found towns. The *emporia*, like Southampton, London and Ipswich, acted as entrepots for incoming and exiting goods from and to Europe. This, in turn, encouraged trade with 'central' places like Winchester, Canterbury and Oxford. The raids of the Northmen in the eighth century, while destructive to begin with, ultimately resulted in stimulating trade. Pirates at first, the Scandinavians turned to commerce when faced with serious resistance and they founded or furthered urban settlements at places like York, Stamford, Nottingham, Leicester and Lincoln. The fortified centres of Anglo-Saxon royal resistance to their raids, the 'burhs' of Wessex and Mercia, in turn attracted markets, as merchants collected at the river crossings, road junctions and estuaries where the burhs were sited. Craftsmen felt safer there and populations grew apace.

This town phenomenon was found in a more extreme form on the continent of Europe. In the tenth and eleventh centuries a notable urban revival took place in Flanders and North Italy, as the search for security in an anarchic world impelled men to live closely together. They made their living practising urban crafts such as weaving, dyeing, tanning, woodworking, manufacturing articles in metal, ceramic, bone, antler and horn and exchanging them for food from peasant producers. The Norman Conquest of England drew it out of the North Sea-Baltic orbit into which it had been impelled by Viking kings like Cnut and substituted direct continental connections with Normandy and Flanders. Cross channel trade flourished. Angevin and Plantagenet kings, ruling lands on both sides of the channel, were keen to make money out of trade, and encouraged town provision. They sold town charters or confirmations, which gave burghers freedom from attendance at the shire and hundred courts. They were allowed to plead in their own borough courts and their commercial careers benefited from exemption from tolls and internal customs duties. They prized the right of collecting the taxation central government imposed on them (Bartlett, 2000, 335-9).

Towns spread rapidly into central and Eastern Europe. The north German plain was opened up to German farmers moving eastwards from the densely settled and over-populated Rhineland in search of land. Fortified posts which developed into towns were planted to defend the frontiers against Northmen and Slavs. This 'drive towards the East' was fuelled by missionary zeal. A network of new bishoprics was established, and the land was studded with well-endowed monasteries which frequently acted as centres of royal residence while the king (or emperor) was on the move. By 1110 there were five times as many towns in the areas which had formerly been in the Roman Empire (all of France and a long sliver of Germany up to the Rhine) as in the area to the east of that line. During the reigns of the Ottonian and Salian emperors *emporia* and markets burgeoned and the roll call of new towns in Central Europe increased tenfold in the twelfth and thirteenth centuries. Each decade from *c.*1240-1300 saw about 300 towns coming into existence, although after 1330 the movement slowed to a trickle (Stoob, 1978, 69). In the late fourteenth and fifteenth centuries, towns were no longer founded and those already in existence contracted in size and population as urban growth faltered for a while.

Town walls: the search for security and control

Mural ideology
Medieval towns proclaimed on their seals towering walls and impressive gates. In most cases these images are symbols of authority and independence unrelated to the topographical actuality. Within the medieval mindset there seems little doubt that towns were seen as defended. City walls also appeared in other art forms on the capitals of Romanesque churches, in medieval Italian frescoes and in illuminated manuscripts all over Christian Europe. Descriptions of cities written at this time are characterised by accounts of walls and gates, but topography was of smaller interest than less tangible attributes such as the power of local saints and relics, and the privileges of the citizen body (Hyde, 1966, 308-40). In Fitzstephen's famous twelfth-century description of London, the walls are only mentioned in passing. A mid-twelfth-century literary portrait of Durham gives the impression of a town fortified by both art and nature (Turner, 1971, 93).

Jerusalem, the holy city and the centre of the world as seen in medieval maps is shown as a cross within a circle, north-south-east-west streets within a circuit of walls. Woodcuts, early engravings and etchings of cities in the early Modern period continued to show walled cities. Fortified cities, using artillery proof ramparts earth revetted with stone bastions, had another 300 years to run.

French experience

The great wall-building period in western Europe lasted from the twelfth through to the end of the fourteenth centuries, as strategies derived from the crusading experience were incorporated into European fortifications. Some towns in France, however, such as Carcasonne, Arles and Nîmes, had walls that dated from the Gallo-Roman era. The line of the inner rampart at Carcasonne had about 30 towers and was of late Roman construction, with its masonry easily distinguishable. Large blockwork foundations, small square blockwork and rubble core and the use of tile bricks as bonding courses are all characteristic of fortifications built throughout Gaul after the later third-century barbarian incursions (Bromwich, 1993, 63-9). At Arles and Nîmes the massive Roman amphitheatres were used in the early Middle Ages as walled enclaves to protect the close packed houses of their inhabitants from Saracen attacks. Towers were added to the amphitheatre which overtop those cities.

Wall building in France experienced two great bursts of activity. The first was in the last half of the thirteenth century after the Albigensian crusade when lords from Northern France, and the Capetian kings themselves, were intent on confiscating lands seized from the Cathar heretics and absorbing them into the kingdom of France. Hence the *Bastide* movement whereby dozens of planned walled towns were built aimed at warding off the land grabbing of rival barons as much as securing strong points against heretic resurgence. The second burst of building started after the beginnings of the Hundred Years War (1340-1450). The north of France, with its proximity to the English coast, was one pressure point; the south-west, with the English foothold in the vineyards of Gascony, was the other. The inhabitants of the towns in these areas were ambiguous in their attitudes, seeking refuge within walled spaces but balking when confronted with paying. Again they took a bit of convincing that it was *their* town which would be in the path of a marauding English *chevauchée*. The Capetian and Valois monarchy is seen as reacting to crises rather than pursuing a consistent walling policy (Tracy 2000, 98-117).

Walls, as well as being extremely expensive to build and maintain, unduly restricted urban growth. In the developing suburbs, dwellers attracted by the availability of land were vulnerable to attack, and to 'scorched earth' demolition by the defenders of the walled town intent on securing a clear field of fire. American studies of French fortified towns like Montpellier are unfortunately largely carried out in libraries. We are told that 'all that remains above ground of the medieval urban fortifications in Montpellier are two towers; la Tour des Pins and la Tour de la Babotte'. However the plan of the boulevards has fossilized the medieval enceinte as in so many French towns; here is a rich field for archaeologists following traces of city walls in the basements of houses and buildings along the boulevardes. It would seem that at Montpellier there were two lines of defence: the inner orthodox method with gates, towers and walls, and in the countryside beyond the city an outer discontinuous defence system with fortress-like gates called the *palissade*.

Clearly the defensive functions of walls were paramount during periods of war or the breakdown of law and order, in some areas of Europe at some times. Walls, however, also played other roles. They aided the running of a well-ordered mercantile community: at their gates taxes were collected on goods entering the town. Watchmen could monitor undesirables and exclude them if they thought necessary. Gates could be closed to keep out the plague or at night to keep out burglars. They were a visual reminder of the bounds of municipal jurisdiction. On their gates were displayed the heads and other body parts of criminals or traitors who had transgressed town rules. In fact, walls 'constituted a town's badge of honor, a sign of its grandeur, wealth and importance' (Tracy, 2000, 17).

Town walls in England and Germany

A considerable proportion of English and Welsh towns were defended in the Middle Ages. Of 249 towns with charters 108 were walled by 1520 (Turner, 1971, 91). By widening the definition of 'walled' to include places defended with ditches and earthworks, 211 can be said to have possessed some sort of communal defences (Bond, 1987, 92). In analysing another category of towns, those defined as planted or planned, Beresford has come to some interesting conclusions. He finds that the proportion of defended plantations in England, Wales and Gascony differed according to time and place. In Wales 86 per cent of the new plantations, foreign colonies of Englishmen in a newly conquered land, were provided with walls or a castle. Bastides in Gascony totalled 36 per cent and planted towns in England 38 per cent. He notes that during the fourteenth century planned towns in England lost interest in walls for defence, whereas bastides in Gascony, exposed to the fury of French counter attack, went on petitioning the English king for help in this matter (Beresford, 1967, 183). A useful comparison is Germany (**colour plate 28**). Here the density of walled towns varies according to geographical region. There are zones in the west and centre where more than 45 per cent were walled. Flanders, the Rhineland, Hesse and Saxony were particularly urbanised and well walled. The contested regions, the Netherlands and the Eastern lands invaded by Teutonic knights were also densely defended. When one adds into the equation the chronological dimension it is seen that 'most walled cities in *Mitteleuropa* were fortified between 1250 and 1450' (Tracy, 2000, 82). This coincided with a breakdown of imperial authority and a period of increasing conflict between German princes, aggressive municipalities, and rival ecclesiastical authorities. Many town walls on borders between principalities or on the Slavonic frontier were seen in the minds of charter-lords as a cheap substitute for castle building. Perhaps more importantly they were 'a material expression of a burgher community's will and capacity to organise its own defence' (Tracy, 2000, 87).

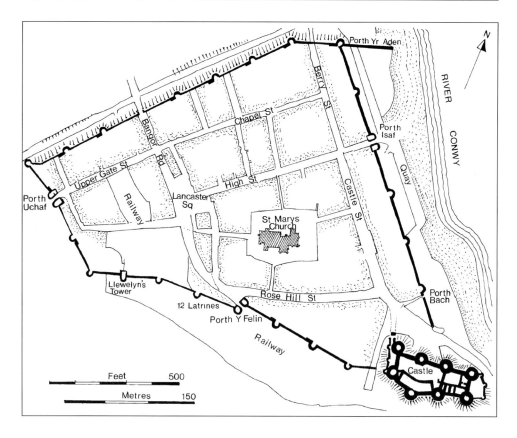

75 *Plan of Edwardian castle and planned, fortified town of Conwy, North Wales. One of the few examples of town and castle being completed in a short time — five building seasons 1283-7 at a cost of at least £14,000. After RCHM, 1956, Caernarvonshire*

Town walls: scale and cost

The sheer scale of medieval urban fortifications impressed observers. This can be assessed from a calculation of the volumes built, space enclosed and estimates of the amount of materials involved. Leiden in the fourteenth century had about 5,000 people when its wall was built; it measured 3700m in length and required 50 million bricks. Florence was much bigger, with a population of 70-90,000: here the outer wall was 8500m long and 11.6m high. Unsurprisingly it took 46 years to complete (1284-1330). The length of the circuit was two and a quarter miles at Norwich. Here, 12 of the original 24 towers remain but not one of the 10 gates. At Yarmouth, the wall was computed as being 2238 yards long, enclosing 133 acres; of the 13 towers, 11 remain, yet again of the 10 gates not one is left. At Chester virtually all the walls, about two miles in circumference, can be seen but the gates have gone. The medieval town of Kingston-upon-Hull, Edward I's foundation as a supply port en route for his Scottish campaigns, was fortified with a wall erected between 1321 and 1400 equipped with 30 interval towers and seven gates or posterns. Here, unusually in England at this date, the major building material was brick. Oddly, in some places gates remain but the walls have virtually disappeared. Examples of this are the Sussex Cinque Ports of Rye and Winchelsea. In others like York, perhaps the most complete and magnificent of the walled and gated towns of medieval England, a very great deal of the original structure remains, efficiently and lavishly published (RCHM (E) York 1972). Here there are over two miles of walls enclosing an area of 263 acres: four of the original gates or bars remain, that at Walmgate even retaining its projecting barbican. Yet even here the Corporation of York made strenuous attempts to destroy its walls in the early nineteenth century. They succeeded in demolishing three barbicans and four posterns and came within a whisker of levelling the lot. At Canterbury the magnificent double drum towers of the West gate, the design of Henry Yevele, Richard II's master mason, were only saved in 1850 from destruction by the casting vote of the mayor. They were reckoned to be obstructing the entry of the elephants and caravans for Wombwells' circus (Cox, 1915, 102). Only from 1855 did the principle of preservation begin to gain credence. The battle is not yet won. Medieval walls one and a half centuries later were still regarded as obsolescent and obstructive to free penetration by motor car in the fearsome redevelopment of the historic towns of Hereford, Gloucester and Worcester in the 1960s (Heighway, 1972). Destruction by excavation and detailed record is a sop to Cerberus: the walls of these places encourage protected pedestrian precincts and should be conserved intact.

The scale of the task involved towns in lengthy and costly expenditure of time and treasure. Newcastle's walls, dating from when the town was under constant threat of Scottish incursion, nevertheless took 50 years to build, between 1265 and 1318. At Norwich, where there are (rare in pragmatic England) signs that the circuit was seen as a planned whole, the work was spread over half a century (1297-1343) and was only completed by an exceptional surge of building paid for by a leading citizen, Richard Spynk.

The desultory and piecemeal approach to the building (demonstrated in the hotch potch of walling noticed in archaeological examination of the fabric) was doubtless connected with the difficulties of financing such time consuming and lengthy projects. Where political strategy dictated immediate action and royal money was available in abundance as in the Welsh castle-towns the job could be completed with speed. Caernarfon was walled within two years (1283-5) and Conwy three years (1284-7)(**75**). These royal foundations were exceptions, brought on by the extreme urgency to hold down the potentially hostile heartland of a newly conquered people. The norm was to accumulate money slowly by applying to the crown for murage grants; license was given to enable the town to levy tax on saleable goods on the understanding that the money be used to construct walls. At first such grants were issued sparingly and on limited terms, such as once a week and only for a year. Gradually the length of time was increased to three, five or seven years. Unfortunately murage grants were frequently diverted from their original purpose, as it is very difficult to tie a murage grant to the building or repair of a particular stretch of wall. The collecting methods were complex at best, chaotic at times. At Shrewsbury so little confidence was lodged in the collectors that they were changed each week! In others the king was asked to provide auditors. Exemptions were rife and included ecclesiastics and foreign merchants, while reciprocal arrangements were made with other towns to be freed from paying murage. Other methods beginning in the fourteenth century involved a direct tax on townsmen according to the value of their tenements, in fact a primitive form of rates. This was supplemented by the diversion of sums arising from the profits of justice, the pardoning by the king of the town's fee farm and the exploitation of customs duties (Turner, 1971).

Town walls and gates: style and decoration

The actual methods of building the walls and gates varied from place to place. In some cases individual masons contracted with the town to build certain specified portions. Robert Hertanger, for instance, undertook to build the South Gate at King's Lynn for £100 in 1416. In others, and London is a good example, the method used was to farm out the collection of murage tolls and give the collectors the responsibility for spending it on the defence of the city. A third method employed at Canterbury, Winchester, Southampton and Sandwich was to recruit workmen by impressing them under royal license. Occasionally town officials like bailiffs took on the job of building parts of the wall or gates.

Although so few remain it is the gates of medieval towns that quicken the imagination and impress the visitor with their strength and power. In a number of places they still stand where the other defences have disappeared, as has happened at Beverley, Canterbury, Hartlepool, King's Lynn, Lincoln, Southampton, Warwick, Winchelsea and Winchester. From early illustrations we know the appearance of now demolished gates at Durham, Hull, Nottingham, London, Bristol, Chester, Newcastle and Norwich. The earliest gates were (as in castles) rectangular structures with a single Romanesque arched passageway flanked by two ground chambers. The stone gate tower might well stand alone or sited in a gap in the earthen walls as at York or Southampton (RCHM York, 1972, 41-2, Lucas 1898-1903, 131-6). During the thirteenth century projecting half-round towers were added on the front face of the rectangle as seen at Conwy and Caernarfon. At York these towers, equipped with portcullises, bartizan turrets and barbicans with sally ports, envelop the earlier Norman work. A variant was at Newcastle (as seen in Brand, 1789 where there were rectangular towers projecting in front of the West and New Gates).

Further developments took place in the fourteenth century. Circular towers linked by short stretches of curtain wall replaced the half round towers and chambers were added projecting backwards at first floor level. The best examples are the Bargate Southampton and the West Gate Canterbury which bears the marks of the king's master mason Henry Yevele (Harvey 1944, 36-7). The square plan's re-emergence at the end of the century may be related to the change of weapons from bows to cannon.

76   *Southampton, Bargate (north gate) of medieval harbour/town. North front. Projecting forebuilding, early fifteenth-century, added to earlier gatehouse (with fourteenth-century drum towers).* Photo by author

77   Southampton, Bargate. South front. Ground stage has three archways. The two light windows at first-floor level emphasise its non-defensive character. The room was used as the fourteenth-century Guildhall. Photo by author

The decoration of gate towers sometimes gives an indication of the preoccupations of the powers-that-be; their broad façades were an ideal display board for civic propaganda. Town seals, as will be seen, frequently paired representations of gates and walls with the image of the town's patron saint (**94, 96**). Although their image niches are now frequently empty the same seems to have been true of town gateways. The theme of protection sought by saintly intercession was pursued in the design of sculptured decoration above the gates at either end of the great bridge across the river Ultava at Prague (completed *c*.1380) (**colour plate 14**). Here, above the gateway leading from the Lower City, are coats of arms of lands possessed by Charles IV and a veiled kingfisher, the heraldic symbol of King Wenceslaus IV. Above is an image of St Vitus, the patron saint of the city standing with figures of Charles IV and Wenceslaus IV: at the top are sculptures of St Adalbert and St Sigismund, patron saints of Bohemia. The display of heavenly protectors is thus backed up by an advertisement of earthly power (Stankova, Stursa et alia, 1992, 65). There is a tendency towards the end of the Middle Ages for the gateway to become a display for heraldic alliances. This is seen in the gates of York; Mickelgate bar, for instance, has the arms of the city of York and the royal arms with a helm above it. The shape of the helmet indicates a date of 1350-75 (RCHM

78 *Winchester City, north gate. Pedestrian gateway to the left. Vehicular gateway to the right. Prison over. Royal and City coats of arms, slits adapted for early guns, fourteenth to fifteenth centuries.* Photo by author

York, 1972, 95). Authority was reinforced by the sight of the heads of rebels and traitors set up on city gates. At York these included the decapitated Sir Henry Perey (1403), Sir William Plumpton (1405), Lord Scrope (1415) and the Duke of York (1460). The Southwark facing gate at London Bridge performed a similar function.

Town defences: functions

It may be doubted whether defence was the most important motive behind the provision of walls for English towns. The reasons which can be adduced for this can be grouped into (1) archaeological — a study of the remaining structures themselves and (2) historical — the circumstances in which they were built, and here continental comparisons are helpful. From a study of the walls (masonry and straight-joints) it seems that the gates, in many places and for long periods, were free-standing, not connected to walls. For whatever reason they were not built to keep people out. The walls were many years in the building and a study of their building materials and the mortars used in them suggests multiple campaigns of work. For instance, at Southampton five different techniques were used, Coventry took 41 years to complete and Norwich, as we have noticed, began its

79   *Salisbury. North gate to
     Cathedral Close.
     Probably built 1327-42.
     It was equipped with a
     portcullis in the fifteenth
     century, a sign of the
     deteriorating relations
     between the city and the
     cathedral. Coat of arms is
     the Stuart royal arms.
     There is a guard room
     above the arch from
     which the portcullis was
     operated.* Photo by
     author

walls in 1253 and was still building in the 1340s. Until the last block was in place the town was vulnerable. Furthermore, the walls themselves were not particularly defensible. Stretches, as at Norwich, had no arrow slits or the slits were well above ground level. Troops would have found it difficult to man them where there was no intramural road, where there were infrequent or no stairways, where the towns were rented out to civilians and where the ditches were used for gardens or lean-to dwellings. Occasionally special steps were taken to protect access to the *pomerium*, as at Merton College Oxford, where the college backed up against the south wall of the city, but this was the exception not the rule. English town walls were seldom planned with the latest military technology in mind. The walling of Conwy planned by Edward I's master mason, the best military mind of the day, showed what could be done to bring defences up-to-date. Here stretches of wall when under attack could be cut off from the rest by gap-backed towers with easily removable planked connections between sections of wall-walks. The technique was not imitated in other towns.

Occasionally things were different. Henry Yevele, the king's master mason, skilfully designed God's Tower, Southampton and brought the West Gate of Canterbury up to date with developments in guns and gunpowder. In general, however, the designs of English town walls and gates remained stuck in the mindsets of the early 1300s. Very few installed handgun ports or were adapted to fire cannon.

Among historical reasons for questioning the ubiquity of defence functions is the fact that England, after a bout of anarchy in Stephen's reign (1135-54) experienced long periods of internal peace. There were brief episodes of baronial rebellion and peasant unrest (as in 1264-6, 1320-7, 1381, 1450) but in general, and in contrast to neighbouring France, Flanders and north-west Germany, England's towns were not often threatened by external foes. The French in the fourteenth century, the Welsh from time to time and the Scots (whenever the English were involved militarily on the continent of Europe) certainly were tempted to play havoc on the coastal and border areas, and these responded by walling and gating to a higher state of military preparedness. A further indicator that defence was not a primary consideration is that England has only one example of concentric urban fortification, whereas at Carcasonne, Paris and dozens of places in the much trampled Netherlands successive circuits of walls were added to enclose suburban growth points. The exception is at Oxford where excavation has proved a thirteenth-century double wall with towers, the inner overlooking the outer, on the north wall of the city (Durham, 1983). The experiment was not completed, nor did the idea catch on. It may have been connected with the tradition that kings avoided entering Oxford city (a would-be royal rapist of St Frideswide had been struck blind trying to do that very thing) and circuited round the outside up Longwall Street. The sight of double tiered walls would have appeared especially imposing at this point.

Consequently we need to seek for other explanations. The answer may be found by asking oneself who was in charge of medieval towns. Where did the power lie? Where there were serious competing factions within a town the provision of walls was an important flash point. Walls of ecclesiastical closes, such as at Salisbury, Abingdon and St Mary's York were designed to protect their inmates, communities of monks and secular clergy from the townspeople, their immediate and often hostile neighbours. The urban wall was often a political statement expressing the town's strength and independence *vis à vis* feudal and ecclesiastical authority. The construction of the walls surrounding the City of York was seen as 'an expression of assertive self confidence on the part of the citizens' and this seems to have been directed particularly at the ecclesiastical authorities within or beside the city (Rees-Jones, 1987). York was far from the Scottish border; the real enemy lay in the rival and nearby clerical neighbours. Rees Jones goes on to maintain that the very development of an autonymous civic government was a response to the growth of a well-organised ecclesiastical fee in the city. Again Coventry, in the centre of Midland England, was unable to plead plausibly any foreign danger from the Scots, French or Welsh. It may be said to have come of age as a municipality when Edward III granted in 1345 to the Mayor, Bailiffs and

Goodmen 'that they might enclose, fortify and embattle the city with a wall of stone and lime'. Pride in their walls and a jealous desire to monopolise their control characterised urban élites.

Foremost in the debate about the functions of medieval urban fortifications is Charles Coulson whose novel and vigorous ideas are put forward in two articles (Coulson 1982 and 1995). He attacks the simplistic notion of the primacy of defence and sees that while towns were outwardly 'castles of communities', inwardly they were 'patrician projects to which the politics of corporate aggrandisement and of oligarchic domination were central' (Coulson, 1994, 195). Furthermore he points out that a town's 'defence' was an apparatus of control, aimed at sustaining the economic and juridical privileges on which its life depended, imposing discipline on the non power-sharing occupants, apprentices, journeymen and beggars. Town defences justified and fortified the power of the top men in the urban bougeoisie. In a word they were buildings of power.

These are plausible arguments but they are couched in disputable terms. Were all towns run by 'oligarchies' — surely 'aristocracies' is a more accurate term for the mercantile families which emerged to the top? Marxist jargon such as 'urban bourgeousie' is a convenient shorthand but oversimplifies a complex reality. Gateways and walls provided for many practical uses and it is unnecessary to put them into an ideological straitjacket. Chester illustrates this point. Here the craft guilds, saddlers, barbers (including surgeons and apothecaries) and painters/stationers rented out the tower from time to time in the sixteenth century. Other towers were occupied by citizen residents. The Northgate at Chester fulfilled a number of functions. The sheriffs of the city kept the gate, received tolls, looked after the pillory and called the citizens to the port moot. The building over the gateway, a horrible hole whose only ventilation was by pipes communicating with the street outside, was used as the City gaol. Condemned prisoners about to die were taken across a Bridge of Death to receive the last consolation of the church in the chapel of St John (Simpson, 1910, 3, 5, 26, 36).

Town halls

Functions

In many medieval towns the principal market place was overlooked by one of the urban churches. Commercial buying and selling frequently generated arguments which led to violence. The church represented order and transactions carried out within its grounds or under its shadow were less likely to be dishonoured. The town hall, also located near the centre of the community, began to challenge the monopoly of the church in this supervisory role in the late Middle Ages and when the Reformation swept away chantries and radically reduced the power of the church, it took its place. The town hall also stood for order, hierarchy and a sense of the past. Its officers regulated the flow of goods, services, people and ideas. Within its walls were stored the equipment for market regulation and it also displayed clocks and housed bells. With their regular chiming of the hours and quarters, these replaced the laxer canonical *horarium*, based on the hours of the mass. In this way the late medieval town was impregnated with the merchants' sense of time and emphasis on work discipline (Gimpel, 1976, 165). On occasions such as fire or attack the bells could be rung to bring the people out into the streets. Proclamations were also read after the alert had been given by the sound of the bell.

The form of the town hall also reflected its close relationship to commercial operations. English and continental town halls were always at least two stories in height. Very many were provided with an arched pillared or arcaded open area on the ground floor. This would provide a cool and sheltered spot which market traders could make use of. Stalls, temporary or permanent might well have had a place within the arches. Some extended the marketing activities outside the building. A corner of the open area was also used as a small gaol, lock-up, or 'blind house'. Here traders suspected of disrupting the market were lodged and awaited trial. All these characteristics are found in the small town hall of Tolsey at Burford, Oxfordshire where the timber-framed first-floor chamber rests on a series of stone pillars within which market traders plied their wares (**80-1**).

The town hall was not only at the commercial centre of the town but was also the focus for political and judicial activity. Here took place the election of the chief citizen, the mayor. At York after the mayor had been elected in the Guildhall he progressed to the council chamber on Ouse Bridge where he, the aldermen and the council of 24 proceeded to elect the city's chief financial officers, the chamberlains, for the following year (Dobson, 1980, xxiii). The mayoral courts also took place in the town hall, and in England were usually found on the first floor. At Norwich for instance the mayor's court was held in the eastern council chamber (Dunn and Sutermeister 3). In Netherlandish town halls the courts of law gathered in a specially defined area called the *Vierschaar*, an area constructed directly outside the council hall. The judges were seated 'untouchable' on a wooden platform or on an area bounded by cords as in a boxing ring (De Bièvre, 1986, 22-3). In later periods the court was sited in the building itself but still in a prominent position so that justice could be seen to be done. Outside the town hall and often seen on sixteenth- or seventeenth-century maps of towns were the pillory and the stocks. Executions sometimes took place on scaffolds erected outside the principal entrance to the town hall.

Administration also emanated from the town hall. Burgesses came to pay their tolls there, a fact recalled from the frequent use of the names 'tolsey', 'tollbooth' or 'chequer house'. Within its walls the council, a group of 24 or 40 men, met daily in their own room to discuss affairs and needs. The mayor, or, in the Netherlands and Germany, the *burgomeister* occupied separate and private rooms. A secure place would be found inside the building to store the minute books, charters, seals and plate, the corporate possessions of the town. While English town halls were not, in general, fortified they were certainly used to keep arms and armour. In the Netherlands they often housed the local militia, controlled by the mayors. In the Netherlands town halls nearly always had towers; some were

80 Tolsey, Burford, Oxfordshire. A small market hall doubling up as a town hall. Ground floor plan by Steane and Harding 2001

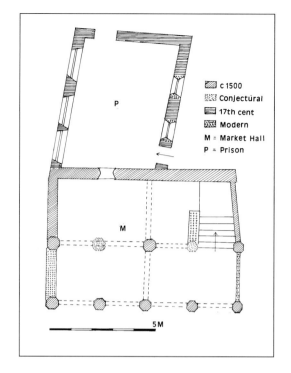

81 Tolsey, Burford, Oxfordshire. Sketch perspective, not to scale. Drawing by author

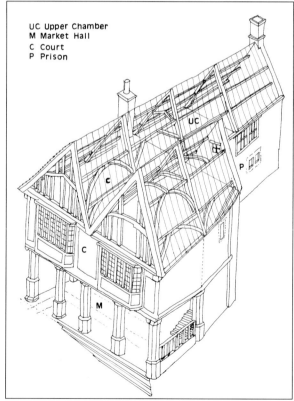

82 *Burford Oxfordshire. The earlier (sixteenth-century) of the two town maces. Of silver, 13 3/16in in length. Plain, slender shaft with iron core to which are attached five wavy flags. The head is globular and surmounted by a coronet of 10 crosses and 10 fleurs de lys. On the flat top within a quatrefoil, the royal arms,* France and England Quarterly. *Lion on base.* Photo by Mr Baines

carefully preserved from the earlier medieval period and incorporated in the later enlarged structure. The poor, sick, and elderly were regulated from the town hall and those accused of crimes were imprisoned there awaiting trial. At times the town's printing press and print were located in the same building (De Bièvre, 1986, 22-3).

Form and structure

Apart from a few exceptions in London and East Anglia English medieval town halls never acquired large or imposing buildings which could rival in magnificence the great continental town halls in Flanders and North Germany. As Rigold says, 'they are a poor lot' (Rigold, 1968, 1). One reason for this is that the population of English towns was insufficient to provide the surplus for municipal building purposes especially as civic pride was channelled into the construction of a multiplicity of parish churches (Brown, 1996, 65). At the Reformation parish church building came to a virtual halt and at this point town hall building took off. Tittler has noticed the construction, conversion or substantial rebuilding of 202 town halls in a total of 178 towns (some towns acquired more than one) between 1500-1640 (Tittler, 1991, 11-15). The structures themselves fall into several groups according to Rigold. Most in the south-east were timber-framed and one favourite form was a mutation of the late medieval dwelling house, with a ground floor hall with a storeyed chamber at either end. Notable examples are the Leicester Guildhall, St Mary's Hall Coventry and Lavenham Suffolk. A second

*83   Goslar, Germany. Rathaus. Built in eleventh century, largely reconstructed in the late
Gothic period with a first floor hall and offices and arcades facing the market place.
The open air staircase was added in 1537. The late Gothic council chamber has wall
paintings c.1500 and there is a tiny frescoed chapel.* Photo by author

type is a derivative of the medieval first floor hall. Some of the oldest examples
were equipped with undercrofts and external staircases (Ipswich and Great
Yarmouth). An intermediate type has an interior space and ground floor divided
into compartments (Fordwich and Milton are examples).

Tittler considers that the types so far mentioned are all related to one another
and differ substantially not within themselves but from a second major tradition,
which he calls 'the town hall carried on pillars'. The ground floors of these
remained open on three sides; they were characteristically sited on islands in the
central marketing area providing, as has been seen, substantial benefits to market
traders (Tittler, 1991, 27-29). The space within the arches or pillars was used for
keeping the town scales, measurements, beams and fire engines; the entertainment of players, the proclaiming of verbal messages and posted notices and ordinary social intercourse occurred within the shelter of the building.

Both Rigold and Tittler admit the presence of a further and very occasional
polygonal plan which may owe something to the covered butter cross. Basic
crosses are often found in the centres of medieval towns; famous examples were
at Coventry, Banbury and Abingdon. Sometimes these evolved canopies such as
developed at Salisbury, Malmesbury, Nether Stowey, Glastonbury and Shepton

Mallet. A canopy might be adapted to serve as the floor of a small polygonal room. Examples are seen at Dunster and Sevenoaks. An interesting variant is an open-sided butter cross over the street from a town hall with an arcade on three sides as seen at Witney Oxfordshire (Rigold, 1968, 1-2, Tittler, 1991, 31).

The plans of the great Netherlandish and North German town halls illustrate the much increased affluence of their builders and patrons in the late medieval and Renaissance periods. Their buildings are also complex interlocking units of many periods. As the business of town government took on more and more functions so new rooms, façades, porches and floors were inserted. They became as complex as many English medieval parish churches, the result of centuries of changing liturgies, architectural fashions and economic vicissitudes. The Rathaus at Luneburg, the largest surviving medieval town hall, is a case in point. It stands in Marktplatz and dates from the twelfth century. Though most was rebuilt in the fourteenth and fifteenth centuries, a Baroque façade was added in 1720. What is notable is that inside there are fifteenth- and sixteenth-century rooms still preserving their original décor. The main council chamber was built in the Renaissance style. The whole has miraculously survived because of the paradox that Luneburg went into a serious economic decline in the eighteenth century and never rebuilt its Rathaus. The Hanseatic city of Lubeck has a fine civic building which reflects the former prosperity of this trading city. With its sandstone columns and arcade it provided a covered market with weights and scales on the ground floor. The oldest part of its brick gothic façade dates from 1230. It has a thirteenth-century Ratskeller and a south wing built from 1298-1398 with long Gothic arcades. The Renaissance loggia was added in 1570 and the outside was further enriched with a Dutch Renaissance open air staircase and bay window in 1594. More sumptuous even than Lubeck's is the Bremen's Rathaus, built in 1405-10. A map by Brown and Mergenburg *c*.1588 shows the gothic façade, higher and more splendid than the neighbouring archbishop's palace. On the broad side facing the market square was an arcade supported by 12 sandstone pillars. The material was brown glazed and unglazed brick. Behind and above were two large halls one on top of the other and below them a wine cellar. The Renaissance front with its façade of glass and sculpture was added 1609-12 by Lüder von Bentheim (**colour plate 29**). The whole is a political statement of the town's freedom and independence (Loest, 1988, 1-47).

When we turn to the Netherlandish town halls of the fifteenth and seventeenth centuries we enter a different league, as far as size and external decoration are concerned. Leiden had been very prosperous in the late Middle Ages as a centre of heavy cloth production. This rapidly declined and by the 1520s the town council diversified encouraging the making of light cloths. The town had resisted the Spanish siege of 1572 successfully and thereafter was showered with gifts and privileges by a grateful Estates General. Its economic fortunes revived and it was allowed to found a university. The decoration of its town hall reflected these developments. The façade 'became more than a mere public notice board of civil morals' (De Bièvre, 1986, 102). Texts on the tablets above the three entrances admonished the citizens to accept God's will in either good or bad times. Others referred to the sufferings of the town at the hands of the Spanish. The citizens' further loyalties were displayed by coats of arms; their own and those of the province of Holland. There were also two large stone statues symbolising Justice and Peace – the latter referring to the city's miraculous deliverance from the Spanish siege.

In several town halls in the Netherlands the portal was of considerable significance. At Delft, for instance, the portal was the place where new laws and other public notices were announced after the ringing of the bells. Above the portal was a balcony with two free-standing Ionic columns supporting a pedimented roof. This was the site of a wooden scaffold temporarily built there for the execution of criminals. In the central pediment were displayed the arms of Holland, the arms of Orange and a figure of Justice. Haarlem's town hall, as it was recast by Lieven de Key, had a prominent set of entrance steps from where the town clerk made his proclamations.

England has very little to show in the design of its late sixteenth- to early seventeenth-century town halls that can compete in architectural impressiveness or decorative flourish. Sir Thomas Tresham's market hall at Rothwell in Northamptonshire is an exception (Summerson, 1991, 171-2). Here is a cruciform building of two storeys, with two orders of pilasters and (originally) open arcades, decorated with 90 coats of arms, the landowners of Rothwell hundred and some other Northamptonshire families (Pevsner and Cherry, 1974, 393). Not only is the building very up to date with its use of the classical orders but it is an advertisement board for its patron's political affinities. There is evidence, however, from illustrations and from the surviving structures themselves that a number were imposing and highly decorated buildings. Norwich and Kings Lynn, for example, had large areas of flint chequer work in their façades, a way of exhibiting municipal conspicuous consumption. The Exeter 'hall' or 'guildhall' was the largest covered space (except for the cathedral) in the city. The Elizabethan additions not only classicized the gothic building, they were an example of prodigal expenditure. Although in the vernacular mode, the Booth hall at Evesham and the Much Wenlock Guildhall evidenced close studding, multiple gables and jettying — all features of display. The town hall at Leominster must have been one of the most spectacular timber framed buildings of its time. Often however, the town halls of this period too obviously show that money was spent slowly, being painfully raised over long periods in times of economic recessions. The reluctant burgesses were perforce content with humbler buildings many of which have not survived to the present day.

Town halls, furnishings, fittings and decoration

Although furniture and fittings have survived in fewer numbers than the structures of town halls themselves they still provide useful insights into the distribution of power within the governing élites of late medieval and Tudor towns. Just as bishops by the end of the Middle Ages had acquired distinctive and, in some cases, splendid seats within cathedral churches, so in the larger and wealthier towns the mayors had come to occupy 'seats of honour'. The most remarkable of these is found in St Mary's Hall Coventry which is reckoned to have stood on the dais in the hall, under the window in front of the tapestry. In its original form it may have been one third of a triple throne to seat the masters of three major guilds in Coventry. Its width may have been necessary to accommodate the mayor in his bulky robes (Cescinsky and Gribble, 1922, 159). Until the provision of a separate chair the traditional place of precedence for the mayor in the council chamber was in the centre of the long bench settle set along one wall. This was likely to have been on a dais. The mayor is said to have 'come down' from the bench to pacify unruly participants at an election in Chichester in 1586. In 1583-4 'the seate for the baylyffs and aldermen in Shrewsberie was waynshotted in more coomlyer aand comme'dabler order then before' (Leighton, 1880, 295). In the city hall at York there was a dais or platform at the west end which when not in use was enclosed by a wooden screen. The Lord Mayor and his brethren took their seats on the dais and behind the Lord Mayor's seat was the Royal Arms (Raine, 1955, 143). A dozen 'semely' cushions were brought for the mayor and his brethren to sit on in the council chamber in 1502-3 which implies that a single bench was still in use but in 1577-8 'a mete and convenient chaire' was made for the mayor, probably for the first time.

Further items of furniture are mentioned in town records. At Exeter the great chest (*magna cista*) in which the rolls were preserved and the city money deposited was kept in the chamber, the room where the council met (Lloyd Parry 1936, 6-8). Other chests were called the *Boffet* and the *Stokke* (1390 and 1415). The capacity of the 'great presse' which is still standing as a room divider in the upper floor of the Guildhall at Boston called for frequent re-organisation. This took the form of feeding out-dated documents to the flames of the kitchen fires below! (Bailey, 1980, xiv).

In general town halls followed the developments noted by William Harrison in his *Description of England* (Edelen, 1994, 197) in that they were made more comfortable. Panelling, tapestries, ceilings and glass all appear:

> This yeare the gyldhall commonly callyd the boothe hall in Salop was enlarged and especially the nether hall next adioyning to the Escheker was newly beutyfieed both with waynsketts and glasse wyndows and a chymney and also sylyd ov hede (ceiling overhead) for the assembly of the alderme' and counsell of the sayd towne. (Leighton, 1880, 280)

Urban oligarchies employed the decoration of town halls to legitimise their authority. Sculpture, paintings and tapestries were all used to create a constant reminder of civic duties and a display of civic virtues. Hence the niches of the south porch on the Guildhall of the City of London were populated with a series of female statues representing Discipline, Temperance, Justice and Fortitude; above these were two male figures of Law and Learning and topping all, in the central panel was Christ in Majesty (Barron, 1974, 27). These were abstract virtues. More complex, but one suspects less intelligible, except to the *cognoscenti*, were the frescoes painted by Ambrogio Lorenzetti, 1338-40 on the wall of the council chamber of Siena town hall. Here in one great scene a group of towns-men is dominated by a figure representing the commune of Siena, watched over by the three theological virtues and attended by the four cardinal virtues with Magnanimity and Peace. On the left is Justice sitting below wisdom dispensing punishments and rewards with one hand and responsibility and charity with the other (Matthew, 1983, 141). The fund of ideas drawn on by the artist were from pre-humanist thinkers such as Brunetto Latini (Skinner 1986). The archaeologist seizes on the material and the tangible, failing to reflect that the commune of Siena spent far more substantial amounts on public ceremonies, costumes and banners which have faded away leaving not a wrack behind.

Whilst the early Renaissance town halls of England were being decorated with images of folk heroes such as Gog and Magog, Bevis of Hampton, Guy of Warwick and Godiva of Coventry or by still and hieratic portraits of past and pre-sent mayors (Tittler, 1991, 151-2), the Dutch town halls were being filled with ambitious historiated paintings. The *Last Judgement* was a subject frequently found in medieval town halls but after the Reformation it made way for the Judgement of Solomon. In Leiden town hall a painting commissioned for the Burgomeister's chamber was the *Journey of the Children of Israel through the Red Sea* by Van Swaenenburg. This appealed to the experience of the Leiden community in the recent siege of the city. It had later to make way for *The prosperity of Commerce and Science under the Government of Peace and Justice*. Again, the mayor's room in the town hall of the Hague had a massive allegorical painting on the ceiling showing Justitia painted blindfold and Astraea, the Goddess of Justice who fled from earth to heaven because the people were so wicked. Carved on the fireplaces in the Haarlem town hall were allegories of civilisation and women representing the five senses, which flourish because of the vigilance and justice of public government (De Bièvre, 1986, passim).

Case studies
Coventry
Coventry had a peculiar medieval topography. At the heart of this sprawling town there was a great churchyard containing two parish churches and the cathedral priory. Flanking it down narrow lanes were the Bishop's Palace and halls for priests. Here also were the main administrative buildings, St Mary's Hall and the gaol. 'It is clear that the whole consecrated area constituted a ritual centre for the city' (Phythian — Adams, 1972, 76).

St Mary's Hall originated in 1340-2 as the hall of the merchant guild of St Mary and was enlarged 1394-1414 for the united guild (the Trinity Guild) of the Holy Trinity, St Mary the Virgin, St John the Baptist and St Catherine. There was a connection between these guilds and the mayor, bailiffs and commonalty after their creation by Edward III's charter in 1345. St Mary's Hall was sited within the enceinte of the obsolescent castle (the castle ditch followed Bayley Lane) and Caesar's tower at its western boundary adjoined the castle bakehouse. It was built round a small rectangular courtyard entered through a vaulted gatehouse. On the west was the hall with undercrofts. The cellars, like the Guildhall in London, are older than the hall above. The main vaulted chamber is of four bays and is 55ft by 28ft. At the north end is a smaller chamber which faces onto Bayley Street and is approached down four steps. Both undercrofts were used for storage, perhaps Guild merchandise in the beginning, then latterly food for the banquets in the great hall above. This is approached by a main staircase in the timber framed cloister on the opposite side of the courtyard. It was built 1394-1414, is 70ft long, 29ft wide and 33ft high. The main features proclaiming that this was the administrative and ritual centre of one of England's great medieval towns are the richly panelled roof with angels making music and heraldic bosses including Richard II's white hart (indicating a date before 1399) and the north window, a late fifteenth-century replacement. Below this and made especially for the space is a fine Tournai tapestry which may well have been worked to commemorate the admission of King Henry VII and his wife to the Trinity Guild of Coventry in 1500. The three vertical divisions echo the three divisions of the window above. In the centre of the lower range is the Assumption of the Blessed Virgin Mary; on either side is a royal personage kneeling, Henry VII on the left, Elizabeth of York on the right, each accompanied by a string of courtiers. Above are apostles and saints each carrying an emblem. The central figure was a Trinity and crucifixion, replaced by a figure of Justice in the seventeenth century. The hall is lit by ranges of windows in the east and west walls and by an oriel which projects over the street in the north-west corner. Behind is a passage which originally led to the Warden's buttery and to a balcony from which proclamations were made (Lancaster, 1981). A reminder that the hall was used for mayoral and guild feasts is provided by the three doorways on the south side originally leading to buttery, pantry and kitchen.

As in the town halls of Exeter and York, there were smaller, richly decorated chambers where the mayor and the councillors did their business, if necessary, in private. The Prince's chamber was traditionally associated with the Black Prince; this graduated from being used as a buttery or pantry to being the room used by the second or common council. The old council chamber was originally a pantry to the former great hall replaced by the 1394-1414 hall. It was used for the mayor's council from 1421 and in 1441 its furnishings were as follows: the table was covered with a green cloth marked out in squares as for an abacus or accounting system and there were two registers of guild benches with coverings of red and green and a pewter inkstand.

While a special room or parlour contributed to the sense of deference due to its mayoral incumbent so did the provision of a large comfortable seat of honour. St Mary's Hall, as we have seen, has the surviving third of a triple throne constructed to seat the masters of the three major guilds of Coventry some time in the eighteenth century. It is possible that this richly carved and ornate piece started life as a stall in the cathedral. It certainly suggests an ecclesiastical context with a figure of the virgin and child on the left arm. There are also carvings of the elephant and castle (the city arms) and a crown supported by two lions — an indication that it may date from the reign of Edward IV (1461-83).

Approached from the old council chamber through a studded door, a small lobby and a massive door of solid oak with three iron bolts moved by separate keys is the treasury, where the city kept its treasure. It reminds one of the fortified muniment rooms at New College Oxford and the Aerary at Windsor Castle and has a tiled floor and a stone tierceron star vault. The chest has three locks and massive hinges.

Delft

The town hall (*Stadhuis*) is located in the centre of the town of Delft, on the west side of the Market Place opposite the great church called the Niewe Kerk. It was largely destroyed by fire in 1536, with only the heavy medieval tower spared and incorporated in the subsequent rebuilding. Brain and Hogenburg's atlas shows the façade of the town hall fronting the market place 1575-1618. Three different structures appear to be attached to the bell tower including a temporary building where justice was dispensed. The Amsterdam architect, Hendrick de Keyser, was invited to design a new town hall. Bleyswijck commented in 1657:

> The town hall has acquired not only a great neat balance of proportions but also a much more striking and more majestic shape — in fact it is like a distinguished palace.

The portal in front of the symmetrical façade was important because here after the ringing of bells, new laws and other public affairs were announced. This also is where a temporary wooden scaffold was erected for the execution of criminals. The tower, early fourteenth century in style, was retained, a symbol of the ancient rights the city of Delft was proud of. The entrance hall (the *Burgerzaal*) was where the Tribunal sat twice a week. Opposite the entrance was a painting of an architectural perspective with a depiction of *Solomon in Judgement*. This subject was popular in German and Netherlandish town halls between 1500-1650, taking the place of scenes of the *Last Judgement*. The rest of the town hall was decorated with paintings and tapestries taken from churches. This was connected with the fact that after the iconoclastic riots of the mid-sixteenth century mayors and town councils controlled former church properties and began to run education and social services formerly the monopoly of the Catholic church. Other pictures in the mayor's room were deemed appropriate as a reminder of his judicial responsibilities. They included the *Ecce Homo* with its reference to the compassion of the ruler Pilate and the *Pieta* of H. von Heemskerk with its inclusion of Joseph of Arimathea — who showed a respect for the law when he went to Pilate to ask for permission to take down the body of Christ. Mayors and other judicial officers would clearly benefit from following both examples. Delft also exemplifies the old custom of displaying statues or painted portraits of ancestors of ruling dynasties. Eight portraits of the Orange family were commissioned by the town council from Michiel van Miereveld in 1620-4, a municipal version paralleling the monumental tomb of the assassinated Prince William in the Nieve Kerk. It strengthened the political stability of the urban oligarchy by linking it with a family whose permanent grasp on power had continued over a long period (De Bièvre, 1986, 164-187).

Exeter

There has been a Guildhall on the present site in High Street, Exeter since the second half of the twelfth century which makes it possible that this is amongst the oldest municipal buildings in England. The Guildhall occupies a narrow strip, a typical burgage tenement, between High Street and Waterbeer Street. The visible building belongs to two periods 1468-70 and 1592-3 (Pevsner, 1952, 155). Of the earlier structures very little is known but it does seem that a large hall was the principal room throughout its history; the Mayor's court was held in the hall and the Provost's court was housed separately. The two courts had cellars underneath and the front of the building had a covered way or arcade, described as a pentice or porch which may have been set on posts. Other rooms include a chamber which may have been on the first floor in front of the hall in the same position as its successors in the 1480s and the 1590s. There were references to a prison which may also have been in the front of the building. Other reminders that the Guildhall was the centre for justice in the city are mentions in the accounts of stocks in the fourteenth century, and the purchase of locks and manacles in 1462-3. Another interesting and significant function of the Guildhall was the storage of records. A chest 'where the Rolls are kept' (1361-2), '15 hides to cover the Rolls' and the construction of a place in which to store the rolls are mentioned in 1428-9. The city's interest in protecting trading standards is demonstrated by the purchase of 'firewood to burn false measures' and the decision to buy a beam for weighing the weights of the Guildhall (Blaylock, 1990, 124-5).

The traditional date for the rebuilding of Exeter's Guildhall is 1466; 'this year order was taken for the buylding of the Guyldhall which was then very ruynose and yn great decay'. The hall is a rectangular structure measuring 19x7.65m internally. Apart from the north window it is substantially a well preserved fifteenth-century building lit by three perpendicular windows in the lateral walls and with a seven bay roof consisting of arch braced principal rafters, collars, purlins and diagonal wind braces in each bay; intermediate trusses enrich the design and the principal trusses rest on stone corbels with carvings of rampant beasts. The main building material was big blocks of red breccia.

The front block was also re-constructed in the 1480s and consisted of a new chamber and a chapel of St George. A map by Hooker surveyed in 1583 shows that there was a third element to the medieval Guildhall, namely an arcaded front to the High Street (Blaylock, 1990, 135-6). Of this a few sculptured fragments have been recovered built into the Elizabethan re-construction of the front. Continuing interest was evident in both the storage of records and the procurement of new weights. Presses were made for the council chamber in 1537-8 and again in 1555-6.

The decision to rebuild the front of Exeter Guildhall came in November 1592. The Chamber Act Book records

> where the foreparte of the Guihald ys ruinous & in decaye and ys to be reedified at the charges of the Cittie.

The result was in Pevsner's words 'as picturesque as it is barbarous' (Pevsner, 1952, 156). It consists of an arcade of granite columns at street level; this floor was open as far as the main door to the hall and was used for mercantile and administrative functions. Above it was a council chamber whose front wall displayed a strange *mélange* of classical features involving arches on top of the columns, an entablature with jutting out corbels and a dado with a series of double columns framing three wide windows; above this, until 1714 when it was taken down, was an even more exotic storey, with further corbels, double columns, obelisks and a central pediment crowning a panel with the Queen's Arms. The whole design may well have been determined by the continuity of purpose in the functions played by the medieval guildhall. The open arcaded ground floor is a common feature in English town halls. There are plenty of examples in Herefordshire (Ledbury and Leominster) and Devon (formerly at Ashburton and King's Bridge). Again the siting of the council chamber in the upper part is common practice and is paralleled at Shrewsbury (1595) and Chipping Camden in Gloucestershire (1627) (Summerson, 1991, 171). The heraldic enrichments, the royal arms in the former pediment and the carvings of the three towers of the city arms in strap-framed panels on the dado show the usual mixture of political loyalty and local patriotism found displayed in town halls as we have seen from the late Middle Ages.

The building in its heyday shone with bright colours. Sampling and analysis of paint traces from the exterior elevations has given a glimpse of the multi-coloured magnificence of the original frontage of the Elizabethan guildhall. A white lead base enabled the costly pigments to be spread further; these included azurite blue, vermilion red, lead-tin yellow and copper green, while the capitals glowed with gold leaf. The Elizabethan urban élite who ruled Exeter projected their refurbished town hall out into the street; with its polychromy it must have dazzled fellow townsmen and contributed to their own sense of *amour propre*.

Norwich

Norwich in 1400 was among the three or four largest provincial towns in the country: its population was about 13,000 (Russell, 1948, 292-3). Up until this date the officials of the town had exercised only a limited authority under the jurisdiction of the king's sheriff of the county of Norfolk. Henry IV's grant of incorporation in 1404 enabled the burgesses to elect their own mayor who was responsible to the king, hold their own courts of law, own property in common, collect their own taxes and, in a word, enjoy the full status of a city. They celebrated their chartered status by building a splendid Guildhall.

84 Norwich. Medieval Guildhall. East front. Prisons were at cellar level. This impressive east gable is decorated with lozenge and triangular chequerwork of flint contrasted with freestone. It may, possibly, be a medieval pun, reminding citizens of the accountant's chequer table inside the building used to collect their taxes. Above is the east window of the mayor's council chamber.
Photo by author

   This replaced a much smaller public building which was so mean that there was room only to erect a seat for the mayor and six more to sit (Howlett, 1903, 163). It was known as the toll-house and was used to collect market tolls. The new Guildhall was large enough to house the multifarious functions of late medieval government in the city. These included the election of the mayor, council meetings which involved 100 members and the provision of rooms within which two courts could sit. These were the sheriff's monthly courts, which heard cases of land, property and debts, and the Mayor's weekly Court of Equity hearing appeals from lower courts and cases involving apprenticeship, trade regulations and bye-laws (Dunn and Sutermeister, 1). In addition there was need to offer accommodation for the Quarter Sessions of Justices of the Peace when they came to the city and the Royal Justices when they held assizes within Norwich. Prisons were sited under the courts to hold suspects until they were tried. In this building there were also provided offices for accounting, tax collection, and the storage of records, money and any regalia. Norwich Guildhall was quite exceptional in the scale of its building: it is possible that this city of traders was inspired more by the example of the great continental city halls of the low countries and the Hanseatic towns of northern Germany with whom they had close economic connections.

   Construction began in 1407. The eighteenth-century historian Frances Blomefield describes how a tax was laid on every inhabitant of the city to raise

85   Norwich. Medieval Guildhall from south. Built of flint rubble faced with knapped flints, carefully laid in mortar and packed with flint chippings. The larger, taller west range housed the assembly chamber (Sheriff's court); the smaller east range, the mayor's court. Like an East Anglian church there is a grand porch to the south. Built 1407-14. Photo by author

money for the work; also the constables had warrants to impress all carpenters, carters and workmen, both citizens and foreigners to work from five o' clock in the morning until eight at night (Dunn and Sutermeister, 2). Much is known about the later stages of construction owing to the fortunate survival of a fabric roll from September 1410 to September 1411 (Howlett, 1903). The basic walling material was local flint, with very limited use of freestone. The upper part of the eastern gable is treated with lozenge and triangular chequer work of flint contrasted with limestone. It has been suggested that it is an architectural pun, referring to the citizens obligation to pay his taxes at the accountants' chequer table within the building. Much of the internal woodwork was made of 'Regall boords' (oak boards brought from Riga in Hanseatic ships) and 'Estrich boords' (boards brought by Easterlings or Hanseatic traders). Some 11,750 tiles were used, partly for paving and walls, but the principal roofing material was lead. The roofs were flat pitched to house the enormous weight of lead. The total value of the lead in question was £53 9s 10½d which provided 18,921lbs or 9 tons. Spread with a thickness of a third of an inch it would have covered a square 41ft by 41ft. Clearly tiles were also necessary.

The Norwich Guildhall stands on the north side of the rectilinear Market Square which stretches for 250m north–south towards the church of St Peter

86 *Norwich. Mayor's seat in Guildhall. Early sixteenth century. The linenfold panelling at the rear is late sixteenth century in date. Note the difference between the honorific seat of the mayor and the bench for the aldermen.*
Photo by author

Mancroft. From its windows the market could be kept under surveillance, an important function for market trading frequently led to uproar and riot. In plan it resembles a medieval church; it originally had two western towers, with the two separate units similar to nave and chancel. At the end of the fifteenth century there was a large ground floor hall known as the 'free prison' where the inmates were allowed to go unchained. There were also separate prisons for men and women. Brick-vaulted rooms still lie under the east end and were probably used for this purpose. Above on the first floor were the two main halls used for council proceedings and court rooms. In the fifteenth century other rooms are mentioned such as a 'medium' and 'upper' solar. A two storeyed porch stood on the south side of the building, another feature resembling a church, and here was sited, on the first floor, a chapel dedicated to St Barbara, the patron saint of prisoners.

The smaller eastern range contained the more important council chamber or mayor's court. The room preserves in its furnishings and fittings an insight into the medieval civic splendour of Norwich and the methods used by the urban oligarchy to demonstrate its power. For one thing the room stands at the top of the building, so any petitioner, plaintiff, or defendant would need to climb the stairs, wait in an anteroom behind a screen and then enter the room. This is square in plan with a dais and stained glass windows at the east end resembling the chancel or a church. Here is the impressive mayoral chair, raised up a little from the bench where aldermen sat. Behind is linenfold panelling of the sixteenth century. The roof dates from 1511 and is low pitched, rich with moulded beams and pendants (Pevsner, 1962, 259). Around the walls are portraits of sixteenth-century mayors: Robert Jannys, mayor in 1517, John Marsham, mayor in 1518 and Augustine Seward (three times mayor 1534-57). As Tittler remarks it is a deliberate attempt to legitimise civic leadership by referring to the historic imagery in the town hall (Tittler, 1991, 154).

York

During the early Middle Ages the hub of the city's government was located in the bridge over the river Ouse. The bridge across the Ouse had collapsed in 1153 under the weight of people wanting to welcome Archbishop William Fitzherbert into the city. When the bridge was reconstructed a council chamber was built on the north side near St William's chapel, accommodating the officers and their records. It is first mentioned in 1376 (RCHM York, 1981, 77a). Within the city there was a hall, already in existence in Henry III's time and on its present site between Coney Lane and the river from the fourteenth century. A lane, surviving under the north aisle of the present Guildhall, gave access to a staithe on the river edge. The mayor could embark here on a barge.

The decision to rebuild the 'common hall' was taken as early as 1433-4 when building materials began to be stockpiled. It was a joint venture between the

87   *York. Guildhall. East Elevation. The great width indicates an aisled hall. Under the hall to the right of the seat a vaulted passage, the Common Hall lane, runs down to the quayside of the river Ouse. The upper part has been largely reconstructed after an air raid (1942) but the rest dates from 1449-59.* RCHM York, V, 77. Photo by author

88 *York. Guildhall. The west elevation facing onto the river Ouse. The medieval hall is the central gable with the large perpendicular window. The arched opening at water level is the river side entry to Common Hall lane. The centre block, with four windows lighting the Inner chamber, and the two storey block to the left are both fifteenth century in date. The right hand block is c.1810. Much magnesian limestone.* Photo by author

mayor and commonalty of York and the Guild of St Christopher which was to have the right to use the hall, buttery and pantry on feast days, as well as to store wine in the cellar and to share the rents of the cellar. Actual construction began in 1449 and the main work was completed in 1453-4.

York's Guildhall was reduced to a shell by German bombing in 1942 and its inner walls show signs of fire reddening. It has been carefully restored. The building, like the town hall of Norwich, is akin to a church in design. It has a nave with two aisles separated by arcades of timber pillars and the walls are largely of glass with much magnesian limestone in the eastern façade. The low pitched roof extends over the nave and aisles in one sweep. As at Norwich it had multiple functions. The city entertained Richard III on his first visit as king in this building. The ceremonies attendant on the assizes began here. The mayor, coroner and bailiff, sheriffs and other officials of York had the right to hold courts in the Guildhall and to exercise jurisdiction over disputes affecting property, criminal offences and trade (Rees Jones, 1997, 115). The king's justices were sent here to listen to cases affecting York citizens. Plays were performed here in 1581 and 1592.

One part of the Guildhall complex escaped destruction in 1942. This was the inner or committee room No 1 on the first floor. It overlooks the river and con-

89   York, Guildhall. Committee room. Fifteenth-century carved bosses with satirical comments on dishonest and lying councillors. Photo by author

tains fifteenth-century masonry visible above the panelling. The doorway leading to the hall is also part of the original structure as is the low pitched roof carved with bosses including foliage, animal and human heads, royal arms, arms of the city of York, merchants' marks, Virgin and Child and cross of St George. The bosses offer an insight into what the carver felt about local politicians — one shows two heads within the same hood in a vivid portrayal of 'two facedness' and another a man with two tongues, clearly a liar!

The Guildhall was surrounded by ancillary buildings, all in some way servicing the hall. They included a kitchen, buttery and pantry. Other premises were used for storage, for keeping prisoners at the assizes in custody and for housing ammunition. Under the hall were cellars accessed from Common Hall Lane.

London
One building has come down to us which gives some impression of the might of medieval mercantile London and this is the Guildhall. This part of London, a lone gravel eminence to the east of St Paul's, has been occupied by a series of public buildings since Roman times. Here was the amphitheatre, the remains of which lie under the square in front of the Guildhall. Six centuries later the burgeoning city built a public hall on part at least of its present site. The earlier Guildhall incorporated several rooms including 'the chamber . . . where meetings of the Mayor, Aldermen and others were held'. Here accounts were rendered and cash stored; here secret and private business was dealt with, legislation was enacted and justice was meted out. The Guildhall, in a nutshell, was the focus of the city's sense of corporate pride, wealth and ambition (Barron, 1974).

90 Guildhall, City of London. A fair is in progress (summer 2001 in front of the medieval guildhall). The fifteenth-century walls, buttresses and corner towers are visible behind the mixed Gothic and classical front added by George Dance, 1788-9. Photo by author

Of this first guildhall only the present western crypt remains; dating from *c*.1270-90 it consists of an aisled space with a quadripartite vault supported on octagonal columns. It is clearly very different in style from the nobler eastern crypt which still underlies the new Guildhall constructed 1411-30. This brought London into the top league of medieval European city halls, in scale, magnificence of construction and beauty of architecture. The building has been badly damaged over the last 550 years, having had at least three major re-roofings. The medieval interior has been obscured by monstrously out-of-scale monuments to warriors such as Wellington and Nelson. Yet careful archaeological observations, meticulous documentation and spirited analysis have combined to clarify its complex story. The design was the brainchild of master mason John Croxtone. The great ingenuity shown in incorporating the western crypt already mentioned allowed the mayor and corporation to continue to govern the city during the 30 years in which the replacement hall was under construction. The scale and richness of decoration was deliberately meant to emulate Richard II's rebuilt Westminster Hall. The fenestration where the windows are confined to the upper part with lower screens of Perpendicular tracery was made necessary by the encumbrance of surrounding buildings. A virtue was made of necessity since the lower wall spaces could be hung with tapestries, paintings and hangings. This surely influ-

91 London, Guildhall. Reconstruction as it might have appeared c.1440. After Barron 1974

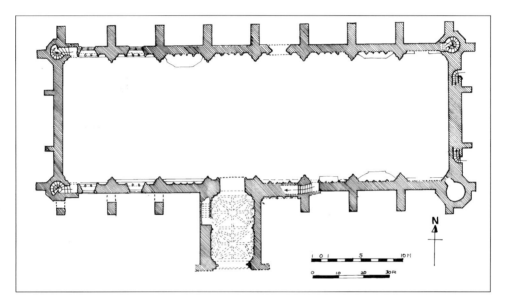

92 London, Guildhall. Plan at hall level. After Barron 1974

enced the future design of the halls of Eltham Palace in the 1470s and '80s and Hampton Court in the 1520s. The south porch was particularly ornate, its surface articulated with arcading and pierced with canopied ruches filled with sculptures. Fortunately the porch was well recorded by Carter in the 1780s before George Dance was employed to attach a highly original Gothick replacement. The gable had been filled with a Christ in Majesty with below two male figures representing law and learning. On either side of the yawning porch were four graceful female figures. Remarkably these have been recovered from the garden of a country house in North Wales; because they had lost their arms, attributes and, for a time, their heads they are difficult to identify with certainty. Discipline, Justice,

Fortitude and Temperance, each trampling on a writhing vice, are certainly plausible civic virtues in the early fifteenth century. A complacent demonstration of civic aspirations sent a powerful political message to those passing through this majestic entrance.

The most controversial aspect, archaeologically speaking, is the original form of the roof of the London Guildhall. One possibility favoured by Barron is hammer beams but this seems ruled out by the presence of huge Perpendicular windows at the ends of the building which could have been obstructed by hammer beams. The clustered piers separating each bay suggest that vaulting, either of stone or (as at York Minster) of wood was proposed. Wilson comes down in favour of a roof supported by stone transverse arches which appear to be visible in Hollar's engraving after the Great Fire of 1666. Other examples of roofs with similar structures are Mayfield Palace (Archbishop of Canterbury) and Conwy Castle (royal). Such an archaic roof form in Wilson's words may well have appealed to a corporation ever anxious to demonstrate that its rights and privileges were rooted in ancient custom (Wilson, 1976, 7).

Town seals

Seals came into use during the twelfth century in Britain, France and the Empire. A seal has been defined as an *intaglio* engraved matrix, an inward oriented symbolic object of personal identity: the impression, made on wax, and attached to a document, was an image outwardly oriented and emblematic of its inner (Bedos - Rezah, 1990, 35). To begin with seals were made for and used by individuals in the upper echelons of society. Inscriptions were engraved around the edges but there were also clearly delineated and instantly recognised icons in the centre of the seal itself. Kings invariably appear enthroned clothed in regalia; lay magnates fully armed on horseback; bishops and abbots garbed in ecclesiastical vestments holding croziers, their staffs of office. Seals did more than associate their use with their owners; they authenticated documents and gave authority to the orders contained in them. Gradually their use extended downwards and outwards despite the remarks of a twelfth-century chief justice, Richard de Lucy, 'it was not usual in former times for any petty knight to have a seal, which is proper only to kings and magnates'. Institutions such as courts, abstract administrative entities and communities also adopted them.

Towns began to use seals in the twelfth century. Seals are a symptom of the beginnings of municipal incorporation in England (Tait 1936, 235). The earliest on record here are at Oxford and York and they coincide with assertions of legal personality. Those first found in the Empire appeared at Cologne (1114-19), Mainz (1118-19), Trier (1171) and Cambrai (1185). They spread to northern France (Arras 1175, Pontoise 1190, Valenciennes 1197 and St Omer 1199), to Italy (Pisa 1160) and to Provence (Arles 1110 and Avignon 1189). Thereafter town seals are found in much of central and southern France and they spread into Germany,

*93   Seal of Dover: first common seal of Barons 1305. On right a single masted vessel with
bowsprit and embattled crows nest, embattled fore and stern castles. Above furled
mainsail a banner flag of England. In forecastle two mariners blow trumpets. In the
ship other sailors, one controlling rudder. Reverse (left) part legend of St Martin of
Tours. On horseback, he passes through gate of triple towered town and divides cloak
with sword while beggar, naked to waist on a crutch stands in a doorway. Round edge
12 lions passant guardant of England*

especially among the Hanseatic ports. Eventually no less than 385 French city
seals came into use indicating that some were from very small places (Bedos —
Rezak, 1990, 42).

The subject matter of town seals, both written and pictorial, is revealing in the
light it sheds on medieval urban preoccupations. One significant aspect of the legends inscribed round their rims is the emphasis on the human group in its plu-
rality rather than on the territorial form, the people rather than the place.
Collective nouns such as *universitas* and *communitas* are frequently found. *Cives* or
civitas are used in referring to episcopal cities. Groups of citizens such as *pares scab-
ini, jurati* and *burgenses* figure on French seals. They are usually placed in front of
the terms *castrum, villa, civitas* and *burgus*, which all refer to the place. The seal of
Avignon (1303), for instance, has the legend *Sigillum consulum castri de avinione*.

This emphasis on the inhabitants rather than the topography is exemplified by
representations or seals of lay people in groups, thus illustrating a correspondence
between the inscription and the image. The seal of Doullens, for instance, shows
the 12 échevins, the urban élite who controlled the fortunes of the city. Burgesses
are seen surrounding their mayor in the city seal at Soissons (1228). An element
of this is seen in the extraordinary design of the thirteenth-century seal of London
(Pedrick, 1904, 84-5). Here a group of the citizens are shown as suppliants at the

94   Seal of London. Obverse (right hand) view of city. Cathedral in centre surrounded by tall spires and towers of churches within an embattled wall with central gateway. Towering behind city is St Paul holding a sword in his right hand and a banner with three lions passant guardant reversed. On left under an arc a view of city including old St Pauls. Seated on a throne supported by a rainbow an archbishop in mitre and pall. Raises right hand in benediction, left supports a staff. Between two groups of suppliants. Those on right are hooded monks; those on left citizens

foot of St Thomas (born in London, martyred in Canterbury) who is seated on a rainbow. Below is a representation of the city itself and on the obverse is a view of walls, towers, church spires and cathedral whilst towering behind on the cathedral stands St Paul, holding in his right hand a sword erect and in his left hand a banner with three lions passant guardant reversed. The inscription on this side refers to the leading Londoners as a group SIGILLUM BARONUM LONDONIARUM.

A number of French and English seals echo this theme of the town as a holy space by delineating patron saints or religious monuments. The city seal of Bergues (1199) has a figure of St Peter with the keys. The commonalty of Castelnaudary (Aude) has a small oval shaped seal with a figure of the Blessed Virgin Mary (Ashmolean Museum No 522). Rochester, Kent, has the martyrdom of St Andrew on one side, the patron of the city and the cathedral (**96**). Religious motifs are mixed with secular in the seal of Lyme Regis: a ship dominates the design but there is a crucifixion scene on one side and the figure of St Michael on the other (Pedrick 1904, plate XVI).

Occasionally city seals went beyond symbolic religious convention and attempted a more realistic representation of actual churches. The seals of Toulouse showed the rocketing tower of St Sernin, that of Agen the semi-circular apse of Saint Caprais and that of Moissac showing the tower of its abbey

95   Seals of Barnstaple (right) and Shrewsbury (left). Shrewsbury 1425 contemporary view of town. Embattled wall with four round towers. Central entrance leads to bridge over Severn. Over central doorway is shield with arms of England. On left another shield with cross and lions. On right three leopards' heads. Barnstaple shows bridge of six arches with a hand rail. Above it a church with spire and on other side a Calvary cross on four steps. In centre an eagle displayed. Fifteenth century

church (Bedos - Rezak, 1990, 44). There is a curious view of the cathedral structure of Worcester which may be the Romanesque building shown with a central spire, surmounted by an orb and a cross, two spires with large crosses and two with small, and three stories of arcaded work. The centre motif is an enormous Romanesque door with decorative hinges. Here the COMMUNE CIVIUM WIGORNIE are allying themselves with their cathedral church.

Towns which doubled up as ports frequently adopted images of ships as the main components of seal design. This is the case of the Hanseatic cities such as Elbing (1242) and Stralsund (1329) where it may have referred to the importance of maritime trade in their economy. The fact that the ships in English seals are often warships, equipped with embattled castles fore and aft, carrying trumpeters and soldiers and defiantly flying royal flags, shows an element of naval aggression suitable for the Cinque Ports which provided a portion of the royal navy. Such are the seals of Winchelsea and New Shoreham (Unger 1980, 145). Melcombe Regis, Dorset has a seal with a ship floating between two shields each blazoning quarterly first and fourth a lion rampant, and second and third a triple-towered castle referring to Queen Eleanor of Castile (Pedrick 1904, plate XVI). Poole, another Dorset port, has a one masted ship with a shield showing a sword in pale hilt downwards, honouring the memory of William Longspée. A less happy design which tries to do too much by combining nautical, ecclesiastical and heraldic themes is the seal of Lydd

96   Rochester seal. Obverse (left) displays water of Medway below. A view of keep of castle as seen from city. Gateway between two embattled towers. Over entrance to keep a banner flag of England with three lions passant guardant. On reverse (right) Martyrdom of St Andrew, patron saint of city and cathedral. Stretched on a saltire cross

Kent, a Cinque Port under the rule of bailiff, jurats and commonalty which was not incorporated until the reign of Henry VI (Cox, 1903, 190-1).

Among the most numerous urban sigillographic images are walls and castles. These to begin with are abstract and symbolic. They incorporate ideas of security, urban independence and self identity and emphasize a clear division between the community within and a possible hostile world without. An early and simple twelfth-century design is the seal of the community of the lordship of Striguil, Chepstow (Ashmolean 797). This shows a keep with two hatched flanking towers. York's seal has the emblem of a crenellated tower enclosed by a wall with three embattled turrets on one side and on the counter seal St Peter between two angels, neatly suggesting earthly and heavenly guardians (RCHM York, 1981, 99 and plate 92). Colchester's seal has a castle surmounted on an arcade with water and fish inside and similarly depicts saintly protection (of St Helena and the true cross) on the reverse. Exeter's seal has an elaborate edifice of two stories with a pent roof and flags between two circular towers, embattled and enriched with arcades (de Gray Birch 1907, 147).

These simple castellated designs of two or three turrets are found in German city seals such as Freiburg (1225), Ravensburg (1267) and Torburg (1360) (Oexle and Scheider, 1992, 96, 151, 152). Such elaborate designs representing whole towns derived from city seals in which Carolingian and Germanic rulers wished to recall to lively remembrance *renovatio*, the recrudescence of the Roman Empire. Cambrai's twelfth-century seal is based on such an imperial seal and shows a king of heavenly Jerusalem, with towers, gates and domes. English seal engravers took

97   Bristol seal. Obverse (right) representation of a castle masoned and embattled, semi-circular headed windows and doorway and great gate. Lofty tower on right. Watchman with horn on left side. Reverse (left) on right a galley with a single sail and mast, steered over waves by a sailor towards a semi-circular headed archway. On a crenellated battlement a watchman indicates entrance

this up and produced a series of birds' eye views of towns from that of London already mentioned with its ranks of spires and towers to the battlemented wall gates and castellated form seen in the fifteenth-century seals of Colchester (Pedrick, 1904, 36-7) and Shrewsbury (Pedrick 37-8).

So far we have considered the seals which illumine ways in which urban élites thought of their towns, subjects of pious protection or projections of economic or military power. Just occasionally remarkable events were recorded. The city of Massa in Tuscany shows the imperial (i.e. Ghibelline) eagle displayed, screaming in triumph and perched on the back of a lion passant (with its tail between its legs) representing the papal (guelph) party. This is thought to refer to the notable defeat of the Guelphs by the Ghibellines at the battle of Monteneglio in 1325 (Ashmolean 794) (**71**). Another event of great significance, the martyrdom of St Thomas, is recorded on the reverse of the seal of Canterbury, with a representation of Canterbury cathedral and the slaughter of the archbishop engraved between figures of kings with crowns and sceptre. The obverse of the city seal is a standard three-turreted castle within a cusped Gothic rosette of eight parts (Pedrick 1904, 52-3).

Just as there is an occasional ecclesiastical building recognisably displayed so at Rochester (**96**) the engraver has produced a realistic image of the castle keep as seen from the city, with a gateway with two towers overlapping the inscription on the ruin. Below is water, a reminder of the town's position on the Medway (Pedrick 1904, 106-7). At Shrewsbury, a seal of 1425 is a contemporary view of the town showing a crenellated wall with four round embattled towers and a central entrance with an arch leading to a bridge across the Severn (**95**). Bridges were notable civil engineering achievements of which towns were proud. One of six arches dominates the design of Barnstable's fifteenth-century seal (**95**) and water rushes through the gothic arches of the seal of Stirling.

Seals authenticate documents. A vigorous state spawns thousands of documents by which orders are sent, events memorised, transactions recorded and privileges granted. The need for documentation breeds bureaucrats. The next chapter considers the ways in which records began to be made at the beginning of the Middle Ages, how they were preserved and filed for future reference. Institutions within medieval society built special rooms within which they stored their muniments, vital for their economic well-being. The furniture of bureaucracy is described together with the solutions offered during this period to the problems of information retrieval.

8 The archaeology of bureaucracy

Sacred texts

The tangible evidence for ever more effective government in early medieval societies lies in the proliferation of records. Already by the time of the Norman conquest, documents recording the giving of privileges and land were being produced by royal clerks and were stored by their recipients among the precious objects which it was hoped would be passed on to heirs or successors. Archives as we understand them today, that is, buildings specialising in the careful safekeeping of documents, did not exist. Since churches were relatively secure places and since charters were relics of past gifts, made to the patron saint rather than to the clergy themselves, it was appropriate 'to place charters recording gifts as close to the relics as possible' (Clanchy, 1993, 156). Single documents were bound into liturgical books. Eadmer recorded finding in gospel books ancient papal bulls upholding Canterbury's claims over York. Liturgical books, as Clanchy points out, were like family bibles in later generations, the most obvious place to record items of importance. Liturgical books were made of high quality materials, the finest parchments and inks: they were bound in metal and jewels. Their place in treasuries and on altars meant they were protected by the taboos against sacrilege. Documents were mingled with other symbolic objects recalling the memory of past donations including cups, rings, wooden staffs and knives.

Wax tablets

Before describing the first attempts to keep documents together in archives it is worth asking what form these early medieval records took. Ephemeral records such as first drafts and notes were written on wax tablets, ordinarily made of wood and more rarely of bone or ivory overlain with coloured wax. A clear illustration of such a tablet in use is seen in a Brussels manuscript (Baart et alia 1977, 382). Being made of such a perishable material few survive but well-preserved examples from Swinegate York are known (Gaimster Margeson and Hurley, 1990, 221). They have been found too at Battle Abbey and Finsbury Circus, London (Geddes 1985, 149-51). The marks on the wax would have been made by writing with a stylus. Anglo-Saxon styli were made of copper alloy, pointed at one end and with a broad triangular spatula used for erasing at the other. The form of the eraser changed to a T-shape in the twelfth century (Biddle 1990, 730).

Parchment and writing materials

Parchment, known by the Latin *membrana*, was animal skin prepared for writing. It does not usually survive in archaeological contexts, unlike leather, which has been treated with tannins. Untanned skin such as parchment has no resistance to bacterial breakdown but the rare find of parchment fragments in a garderobe pit in Winchester Castle shows that in waterlogged deposits under anaerobic conditions it can survive (Biddle, 1990, 733). The skin, whether it be calfskin (creating *vellum*) or sheep or goat, has to be stretched and allowed to dry under tension. The finest medieval manuscripts such as the Winchester Bible were made of choice calf skins; 250 skins would have been used to create this one book, an indication of the high cost in materials even before the scribe set pen to parchment. Royal records, on the other hand, used sheepskin; it was cheaper and had the additional advantage (in a forgery ridden culture!) of being difficult to make an erasure without it showing obviously. During the 1220s and '30s, when records were increasing exponentially, the cost to the Exchequer of parchment for its records was, at the most, about 80 shillings annually.

Far more costly was the scribe's time. In 1222 Robert of Bassingbourn was paid 3s 2d for ten days work and the customary payment for a scribe was 5 pence a day (Clanchy, 1993, 121). The writing equipment quite frequently turns up in excavations. Parchment prickers (for perforating folded parchment pages to act as guides for ruling lines), lead *styli* (for ruling lines), ink pots and the pens themselves (goose quills) have been dug up in urban contexts at Winchester (Biddle, 1990, 729-59), Oxford (Lambrick 1976 and 1985, Hassall 1989) and in at least 15 religious houses. This care in writing documents reached an apogee in the twelfth and thirteenth centuries. Fitzneal, the author of the *Dialogus de Scaccario*, for instance, describes the correct layout of an Exchequer roll in all its bureaucratic detail, complete with instructions on how to rule the lines and space the headings (Johnson, 1950, 29). Scribes even went in for a form of what we would call 'highlighting'. They picked out the key points by underlining or by ruling through the middle of a word with red ink (known as a rubric). Ink was an expensive item. It was made of oak gall or soot and gum arabic. The distinctive Oxford ink was dark brown with a pale yellow/green metallic reflection (Steane, 1996, 205). In Fitzneal's time 2 shillings a year had been allowed for ink; by the 1230s this had increased to 40 pence for the half year. All this writing must have resulted in eyestrain. Spectacles showing a high degree of refinement in design dating to *c.*1440 have been found in London (Rhodes, 1982, 57-73). The similarity of their design to those in many contemporary continental paintings suggests that they may have been imported from the Low Countries where there was a flourishing spectacle-making industry.

The writing of rolls

Domesday Book is an excellent example of a beautifully laid out text with rubrics, red lines drawn through the midst of headings. Domesday Book, however, is

98   *New College, Oxford. Shelving in muniment tower with rolls and bundles of documents shelved in a cupboard.* Photo by author

uncharacteristic in its book form. Unlike continental governments from the Papacy downwards, the royal government of England from the twelfth century onwards kept their most important documents in rolls not books. The system seems to have been going at full steam in the 1170s when Fitzneal wrote his *Dialogus*: there were 'rolls of the treasury', 'rolls of the chancery', 'rolls of receipts', 'the lesser rolls of itinerant justices' and others (Clanchy 1993, 136). It is difficult to understand why this method was adopted and went on being used, with bureaucratic conservatism, for centuries. Certainly the roll had ancient origins, being the usual format for writing in the Greco-Roman world. The idea may have originated in the reign of Henry I from the Jews or from cosmopolitan arithmeticians who knew about Arabic practice. Rolls are distinctly inconvenient to consult. It is true that they could be conveniently stored simply by rolling up the membrane parchment, but finding one's place or referring to an item was fraught with difficulties and delays. They were also of different lengths. It was customary in the Exchequer to stitch together two membranes only, forming a length of less than 2m. Chancery rolls, on the other hand, would be made of a continuous series of membranes of parchment, up to 4m in length, while the law courts from about 1190 adopted the custom of using one membrane *per rotulus*.

Major advances in bureaucratic practice occurred at the end of the twelfth century. The regular dating of royal documents began with the accession of Richard I. Henceforward such royal acts record day, year and place of issue. It is possible from that time to reconstruct the itinerant programme of kings, but more important is the recording of outgoing documents which began in John's reign. Systematic copies were kept of solemn grants (*Charter rolls* from 1199), *Letters Close*, initially called *Liberate rolls* (where the order is sent sealed and folded) from 1200, and *Letters Patent* (sent sealed and open) from 1201 (Bartlett 2000, 199-200).

Although the keeping of accounts or records of government on rolls seems cumbrous this did not stop other authorities from adopting the same system. The pipe rolls of the bishops of Winchester were begun during the episcopacy of bishop Peter des Roches, a former royal clerk and baron of the king's exchequer, where he had doubtless become familiar with the rolls system (Vincent 1994, 30). The towns of Leicester (1196), Shrewsbury (1209) and Exeter (1230s) followed suit and colleges such as Merton College Oxford adopted the same system (Highfield 1964).

Royal archives

It is one thing to create a class of documents, quite another to store it securely and for future reference. This ability to recall was clearly an advantage once government began to make use of writing to issue hundreds of commands, to record the myriad of transactions and to set down information in an orderly way. The king and his entourage were still itinerant so one method was to pack documents up in chests and cart them about the country. This was a recipe for disaster since they would get mixed up and lost; thus Fitzneal's statement that Domesday Book was kept in the treasury along with the Pipe Rolls, many charters and units seems to indicate that the exchequer needed to consult it frequently and implies the beginnings of a royal archive. Winchester, where the castle was the seat of the treasury of the Norman kings, was the first home of Domesday Book (Keene, 1985, 101). But the treasury was not located in any one place in the twelfth century. We know that King John dispersed his treasure (and the documents that went with it) among a number of royal castles and abbeys. He dispersed and provincialised the standing reserves (Joliffe 1948, 117-140). The Chancery Rolls were transported from place to place and some Cistercian abbeys were required in rotation to find a strong horse to transport the rolls and books (Clanchy, 1993, 164).

By the reign of Henry III the royal household had hived off separate departments of state and the courts of law were now settled at Westminster. It is unsurprising that more permanent repositories were sought for the royal archives now piling up after 50 years or so. To begin with ecclesiastical houses were sought. These included the *Domus Conversorum*, the New Temple and Westminster Abbey. The first was in the area between Holborn and the New Temple. Here Chancery clerks tended to congregate and take up residence. Their documents were stored in the *Domus Conversorum*, a well-endowed foundation by Henry III for the housing of Jews converted to Christianity. It was near the New Temple, another major repository for books and documents until the dissolution of the order in 1312 (Hallam and Roper, 1978, 74-94). Westminster Abbey, a recipient of generous royal patronage and located next door to the royal palace was another record repository. Here the vaulted crypt below the chapter house was adapted for the purpose (Allen Brown, Colvin, Taylor 1963, 143). It was subject to a burglary, probably carried out with the connivance of the monks (Tout 1914-15, 348-69) which undermined the king's trust and resulted in pressure to seek for other, more secure arrangements.

Already the Exchequer, the first department of the itinerant household to be detached, had found a permanent home at Westminster. Henry III built a new Exchequer which, from 1244, came to occupy the site at the north end of Westminster Hall. Although the building has gone, swallowed up in Barry's great rebuilding of the Palace of Westminster after the fire of 1834, we can reconstruct it with a fair degree of confidence. This is thanks to the drawings by Carter and Buckler and the plans and sketches preserved in Sir John Soane's museum (Allen Brown, Colvin, Taylor, 1963, 540). It was evidently a long, low building constructed at right angles to Westminster Hall; its roof line was kept deliberately low pitched to avoid it obstructing the light of the windows of the hall. It was lit by two-light Gothic windows with quatrefoil tracery. In the lower Exchequer or Receipt the king's officers received, weighed and put away the money in sealed chests. In the Upper or Great Exchequer they made up the accounts using a chequered tablecloth on which financial calculations were made and which gave the department its name. We can even get a picture of the layout of the office. Round the table the treasurer and his colleagues occupied four benches. They were able to withdraw for private discussion into an inner room, the so-called *thalamus secretorum*.

In Edward I's time the New Temple in London is likely to have been the largest repository of royal records. The Templars had developed into an international organisation, acting as bankers to the kings and leading lords of Christendom, and with much experience of administering estates (Barber 1994, 9). Whether they kept royal records in good order is to be doubted. When Edward I required historical evidence to support his claims to the overlordship of Scotland he ordered a chest of chancery rolls at the New Temple to be broken open and searched: in vain. The documents unearthed did not materially support his case. Another attempt was made to use the records in 1300 to justify the English case to Boniface VIII; again their sheer number and lack of organisation seems to have defeated the searchers. It may, however, have led to a greater realisation that the crown was sitting on a formidably large archive, which if indexed and better ordered, could be made to serve royal policies. The dissolution of the order of the Templars which came in 1312 meant that the crown had to find alternative places to store its records.

The Tower of London had provided a secure location for royal treasure since Henry II's reign. After the burglary at Westminster and the end of Templars it emerges as a major record repository. New cupboards were bought for storing the older records. A reorganisation of the records was undertaken at the Tower by

Bishop Stapledon, Bishop of Exeter and Treasurer of England in the years 1320-2 (Hallam and Roper 1978). The chancery records were stored in the White Tower until 1360 when they were removed to the Wakefield Tower to make way for the captive king of France. While the names of various keepers of the records are known, it does not seem until the reign of Elizabeth I that a serious attempt was made to order them. William Bowyer, keeper until 1581, produced a six-volume summary but the enthusiastic and learned historian of Kent, William Lambarde, who was both keeper of the Rolls and of the Tower made good progress in producing order out of chaos. He donated a calendar of the records to the queen (Rowse, 1951, 37). Up until then the royal records were

> in many offices, unarranged, undescribed and unascertained, many of them
> . . . exposed to erasure, alteration and embezzlement . . . and lodged in
> buildings incommodious and insecure. (Hallam and Roper 1978)

Tallies

The archiving of the royal records may have left much to be desired but the medieval civil service in many ways showed ingenuity and adaptability in thinking out effective techniques of governing. One of these was the tally system. The word comes from the Latin *talea* which means a slip inserted into a stock for purposes of grafting. Already by the time the *Dialogus de Scaccario* was written in the 1180s there was a well organised and well understood system of tally cutting (Jenkinson 1911, 367-380). Tallies were sticks mostly of hazel but sometimes willow or box, squared or flattened with a knife and cut or notched for purposes of calculation. They were then split through the notches in such a way that if the two were put together each notch upon one tallied with the corresponding notch on the other. The writer of the *Dialogus* describes in detail how tallies were to be cut. When recording the receipt of thousands of pounds the cut measured the thickness of the palm of the hand. A hundred pounds was distinguished by a cut the breadth of a thumb, twenty pounds that of the little finger. The cut for a single pound was of the thickness of a grain of ripe barley and a shilling was indicated by two converging cuts when a small notch is made. Finally a penny was marked by a single cut, nothing being taken away. The stick was usually flat rather than square; the cuts for the notches were made on the narrower surfaces; on the two broader surfaces that nature of the transaction was recorded in ink. One of the two parts of the tally was larger than the other, having a handle, and was called the stock; this went to the payer, the accountant. The smaller was known as the foil and was kept by the Exchequer. When the account was finally made up the stock was returned to the Exchequer. This simple but effective way of keeping accounts and giving receipts was significant in an age when writing was a skill limited to the minority; even the illiterate could check that the number of notches coincided. The system went on being used into the middle of the nineteenth century (Jenkinson, 1925, 289). A great number of tallies were destroyed in a fire which led to a general conflagration of the palace of Westminster in 1834. A hoard of several hundred dating from the thirteenth century was found during repairs to the Chapel of the Pyx at Westminster. They can be studied in the Public Record Office. The British Museum also has a few (*Guide to Medieval Antiquities*, 1924, 233-4).

It was characteristic of the Middle Ages that while the crown usually set the pace with constructing new methods of government, it was generally closely followed by ecclesiastical and secular lords. Seignorial administration bears many of the marks of imitation of royal models. The greater the landed estate the more essential it was for the lord to develop centralised bureaucratic methods to maintain control over his financial affairs. Since they received years of administrative experience in royal government, civil servants who became bishops applied these methods to the administration of their own lands. The Bishops of Winchester, for instance, had vast estates spilling over into half a dozen countries in southern England; their 60 knights' fees and 30 or so manors were so extensive that it was necessary to use the latest techniques in financial practice if these estates were to be fully exploited. This accounts for the adoption of royal exchequer methods at Winchester early on in the episcopacy of Bishop Peter des Roches (1205-38). There was an exchequer court furnished by a table with chequered cloth and counters, probably meeting at Wolvesey. The bishops' accounts were kept on pipe rolls, and tally sticks and memoranda were also used to help the bishops' clerks assess the level of arrears owed from individual accounts (Vincent, 1994, 25-42).

The experience so gained in the administration of their own sees led bishops, ambitious to found educational institutions, to make ample provision for secure record keeping. Oxford from the thirteenth to the fifteenth centuries benefited from no less than eight bishops and one archbishop who founded colleges, from Merton (in 1264) founded by Walter de Merton, Bishop of Rochester to Corpus Christi (in 1517) by Bishop Richard Fox of Winchester. Thus here are prime examples of medieval muniment rooms, complete with furniture and fittings.

Muniment rooms at Oxford

During the first century of the University's existence most of the scholars and teachers had lived in halls which were indistinguishable from the houses of the citizens. In the middle of the thirteenth century colleges began to be founded for the most part by bishops. These were more permanent than the academic halls, with impressive buildings designed as communal living halls, libraries and gate towers. Their activities were regulated by statute and they were held accountable to visitors, important lords who could be called upon in crisis for support. They were richly endowed with dozens of manors and these agglomerations of land needed to be effectively controlled if the wealth that flowed from them was to be channelled back to the colleges. The proof of legal possession of lands lay in title deeds (**colour plate 30**)and it was to protect and secure these that the first muniment rooms were built in Oxford.

99   Salisbury Cathedral, Hampshire. Octagonal treasury and muniment room to south-east of cathedral. Note narrow barred windows of this security-conscious detached building. Photo by author

The first purpose-built muniment room at Oxford was the so-called treasury building at Merton College, constructed between 1288-91 (Aston 1986, 311). This was built to a well thought out design which was to be imitated in some respects by later colleges. In the first place it was to be free-standing and therefore like many medieval kitchens less likely to suffer from fire damage. Only later was it physically joined to the other buildings in Mob quad. This fear of fire also determined the unique form of the roof: a steep pitched gabled roof of stone which internally sprang from three two-centred and chamfered arches lying on the side walls (RCHM Oxford, 1939, 81). Additional security was gained by siting the room on the first floor approached by only one narrow stone built newel staircase barred by solid doors. Moreover it was paved with glazed tiles resting on a stone vault of the room below. This latter was a place where rents were paid and accounts made up. Of the furnishings and fittings nothing has survived earlier than the eighteenth-century cupboards but we know that the books and muniments were kept in chests, each with three locks for which each bursar had a key and no document was to be sealed except in the presence of the warden and the vice-warden.

Muniments were often the targets of local insurrections of which the Peasants' Revolt of 1381 is the most notable. Protection from arson for charters on which

100 New College, Oxford. Muniment Tower. Fireproof floor of Penn tiles. Date 1380s.
  Photo by author

proof of title rested, together with secure lodging for plate, jewels and ready cash, prompted the founders of colleges to make special provision in the last quarter of the fourteenth century. William of Wykeham's foundations at Winchester and at New College Oxford have excellently preserved medieval muniment towers.

As a civil servant of long standing, Wykeham would doubtless have been aware of Bishop Stapledon's re-organisation of the royal records in the Tower of London back in Edward II's reign. At any rate he decided to lodge the muniments of both foundations in towers. Both had strong approaches. The muniment tower at Winchester was sited next to the chapel in one corner of the second quadrangle. It could only be approached by way of the chapel and up a stone built newel staircase. At New College access was even more convoluted. The ground floor room at the lowest stage of the tower was reached directly from the quadrangle. A second room immediately above was entered from a door at the head of the stairs leading to the cross passage of the first floor hall. A third door led from the passage to a stone newel staircase connecting the second and third floor rooms. These were immensely strong and fireproof, with doors sheathed in iron, floors paved in Penn tiles (**100**) and stone vaulted ceilings: iron bars formed a grid over the shuttered windows. There was no heating. The documents were stored in chests to which we shall return (Steer, 1974, xi-xii).

The only other college to create a separate muniment tower was Magdalen, the foundation of Bishop William of Waynflete who was deeply influenced by Wykeham's ideas (Davis, 1993). Waynflete built his tower next to the chapel; as at New College entrance was through the chapel and up a stone newel staircase.

101 *Magdalen College, Oxford. Muniment tower. Early sixteenth-century Pyx or document storage box, with sliding lid. Inside are title deeds to the college lands.* Photo by Vernon Brooke

102 *Magdalen College, Oxford. Newel staircase to Muniment Tower. Steel plated door at head of stairs, date 1480s. Photo by Vernon Brooke*

There was however an alternative approach, up the nearby Founder's Tower and through the president's lodgings. This, in effect, made the president the guardian of the college's muniments and it was influential, being adopted by other colleges as we shall see. In his statutes Waynflete prescribed that the room on the lower floor was to contain valuables such as the plate, not often required for use, and the money saved out of daily expenditure. This he had the foresight to put aside for litigation expenses and for a future estate purchase fund. The room on the upper floor was to contain other sums devoted to similar purposes and to offset sudden disasters such as fire damage — a kind of insurance fund. This room has a tiled floor and windows heavily barred and shuttered. It was not stone vaulted however, nor were the doors originally sheathed in iron; thus it was not so strongly fortified as at New College. All the muniments were distributed in various chests, the originals and copies being kept in different chests. The keys of the chests and of the doors were all to be different and entrusted to various members of the college (Willis and Clark, 1886, 477).

The idea of siting the muniment room through or above the lodgings of the head of house had earlier been adopted at All Souls, the foundation in 1440 of Archbishop Henry Chichele. He employed Wykeham's own words when he directed that the common seal and the common chests were to be placed over the gate of entrance, in a building 'after the manner and form of a tower'. Entrance was through the medieval warden's lodgings (personal communication Professor Salway). The room on the lower floor was to contain all registers and moneys set aside for weekly expenditure; copies of documents were to be kept separately from originals which were to be stored, together with plate and all money left in hand after the payment of yearly expenses. While these rooms retain their ancient doors and shutters they went out of use in 1766-75 when the muniments were removed to the upper rooms in the south wing of the Codrington library (VCH Oxon 1954, III, 187).

The gatehouse tower accessed through the warden's lodging became the norm for muniment rooms of Oxford colleges in the fifteenth and sixteenth centuries. At Lincoln the tower was the first building to be erected (Green, 1979, 22). Here the Rector lived until *c.*1468 when the rooms became the college's treasury where the chests were kept. At Exeter similarly the muniment room was on the top floor of a gatehouse tower known as Palmer's Tower which was the original entrance and faced on to Exeter Lane running along the city wall at this period. Similar arrangements were made at St Bernard's college, Balliol, Brasenose, Corpus Christi and later still Oriel and University Colleges also placed their muniment rooms in the upper parts of their gatehouse tower (Trevor Aston's lecture notes)

Furniture and fittings

All great households, from the king's to the bishops' and the nobles' were originally itinerant. As Walter Map commented on Henry II ' . . . he was ever on his

103 *Hereford Cathedral library. Chest. Poplar wood. Planks strengthened with iron strapping with fleur de lys matching terminals. It bears one long articulated handle at each end for pole suspension. The concave-sided, centrally-placed lock plate is original. c.1350-1400. It may be of Flemish rather than English workmanship.* Photo Hereford Cathedral Library

104 *Magdalen College, Oxford. Muniment Room. Iron bound chest. Note carrying handle, domed lid, triple locking. Probably a travelling chest. Fifteenth-century.* Photo by Vernon Brooke

travels, moving by intolerable stages like a courier, and in this respect he showed little mercy to his household which accompanied him.' (Douglas and Greenaway 1961, 389). This meant that all possessions from the chapel furniture to the pipe rolls had to be packed into chests to accompany the king. Despite the fact that institutions like monasteries, colleges and guilds were no longer on the move, muniments and valuables continued to be kept in chests. These were of two main kinds: round-topped coffers were in general smaller and thus more portable. Their lids were designed to throw off rain and they were not in general footed and thus were more suitable for travelling purposes (**104**). They have iron handles at each end, or iron hoops through which one or two carrying poles could be placed as with two of the chests at Salisbury and one at Hereford (Eames 1977, 163) (**103**). The other type, rectangular, flat and sometimes provided with feet, were hardly portable but provided a secure, dry and rat free environment for documents (Eames 1977, 108). Most were made of oak planks but there are some using soft wood. Both types are likely to have been imported from the Baltic. One of the Magdalen chests is made of pine encased in iron bands. Chests can be very large indeed. The late twelfth-century ones in Westminster Abbey are 3.8m (12ft 7in) long, 61cm (2ft) wide and 43cm (17in) high excluding the legs; another is even more colossal, being 4.1m (13ft 6in) long, 1.12m (3ft 9in) wide and 68cm (27in) high excluding legs. Clearly chests of these dimensions were not meant to be moved; some, in fact, appear to have been built *in situ* since they are so large that they could not have been taken up or down the narrow spiral staircases.

The Magdalen College chests

The chests housed in the chapel and the muniment tower at Magdalen college have been investigated using the latest dendrochronological techniques. The college was founded in 1458 on the site of the Hospital of St John the Baptist whose own history goes back to a refoundation by Henry III in 1231. For the first 16 years the hospital buildings were used by the nascent college. Building began in earnest in 1474 and the muniment tower itself was under construction in 1478-9. Of the three chests sampled the largest and most elaborately decorated is in the north-east end of the choir of the chapel. It proved to date from 1326-58, predating the foundation of the college by over a century and suggesting that it might be a survivor from the days of the hospital. A large iron bound chest, reputed to have been William of Waynflete's treasure chest, was allotted a construction date of 1375-1400 (**104**). A third chest with a round headed lid, originally covered in leather, proved to be made of boards with a felling date of between 1426-42, making it possible that it was one of the founder's travelling trunks. Both the latter were constructed of timber from the eastern Baltic region (Miles and Worthington, 2000).

105 Norwich Cathedral. Chest with rows of dowels for suspending small bags with title deeds within. Note labels indicating subject matter. Photo by author

Information retrieval

Among the disadvantages of chests for storing documents is the difficulty of retrieving a particular item. One way round this was to separate out the documents into different categories. To keep royal documents like charters separate from papal bulls, for instance, subdivisions within chests were possible. One of the Westminster Abbey chests is divided internally. Long chests could be packed with smaller boxes or divided as in the cathedral muniments at Ely and Norwich into compartments. There are references to such divisions coming from different parts of the inventory of documents. An example is that a particular charter of King John had been triplicated and two of the versions were to be found in the next compartment (*scrinio*). The chests used for dividing many of the title deeds at Norwich cathedral priory were divided by a series of short wooden pegs protruding from the inner sides of the chest. I have seen two such chests now stored in the triforium between the south transept and the east end. They are 2.1m (7ft) long with internal widths of 25cm (10in) and depths of about 22cm (9in). The pegs which protrude some 7.5cm (3in) are often notched 12mm ($\frac{1}{2}$in) from the free end. In one chest there are 14 pegs along each side and in the other 12: in both there was one peg in each of the short ends (Dodwell 1965/6 xviii). Manuscript evidence provides a clue as to how they were used. The rotulet listing the char-

106 Windsor Castle, Berkshire. The Aerary (treasure house and muniment room of the Canons of St George). Note fireproof tiled floor and stone vaulting. At rear is multi-drawer armoire. The building dates from 1353-5. The furniture, if 1422/3, is the earliest identifiable multi-drawer armoire. Photo by author

ters of Sedgford and Thornham bears on its face a little note: *'prima virga'*. The *virgae* were clearly the pegs of the chests. Presumably the documents were placed in bags which were then suspended from the notched sticks. The advantages of this system are that air circulated round the bags and the subject matter could be indicated by little parchment tags attached near each peg and cross referenced to the inventory. It was an effective filing system!

This system of dividing the documents by subject and storing them in separate bags could be extended out of the chests and onto the walls. In the first floor room of the muniment tower at New College a recent clear out of furniture revealed that attached to the walls was a light timber framework consisting of uprights holding a series of planks at head-height. These bore the marks of pegs which had been driven through and by the side of each were little parchment tags indicating the names of manors. The pegs at some point had been cut off flat and replaced with L-shaped iron hooks. It would seem that documents stored in bags in this way would have been for immediate reference, perhaps by clerks sitting in the room dealing with accounts.

107 Windsor Castle, Berkshire. The treasury or Aerary (1353-5). The Muniment Room. Note rib-vault fire proofing from above, and iron grid over window, providing security below. Photo by author

Two other methods of storage incorporating information retrieval were developed in the fifteenth century. The first is the multi-drawer armoire. The one in the Vicars Choral Wells probably belongs to the initial furnishing of the suite of rooms begun *c.*1457. The unit is divided horizontally into two parts; the upper part is fitted with six rows of small drawers lying in pairs with uprights set between pairs of drawers, many of which are now lost. The centre of the bottom board of each drawer is elongated to form a tab which serves as a handle (Steane 1984, 204). A second armoire is in the Aerary — the name given to the muniment room and Treasury of the Dean and Canons of Windsor. The large nest of drawers were added to the Aerary in 1422-23 (Bond 1950, 2-6). It is 2.1m (7ft) tall and 3.4m (11ft) broad. It is built of massive oak framing which houses recesses for 63 drawers in 9 vertical and 7 horizontal rows. They were pulled out by means of tinned iron rings hanging from iron plates on each drawer. Each drawer is labelled with the names of manors in large free brush strokes (Eames 1977, 41). While it is a roughly carpentered piece of furniture, it is still intact and until very recently was used for its original purpose in storing rolls.

108 Magdalen College, Oxford. Muniment Room. Early sixteenth-century cupboards for documents. Note fireproofed tile floor. Photo by Vernon Brooke

The chest system of document storage was supplemented but not superseded in the sixteenth century at both Winchester and New Colleges by nests of drawers similar in design to those already described at Wells and Windsor. At Winchester there are eight bay and four bay multi-drawer armoires. The drawers are unusual in that their fronts are carefully carved with linenfold out of the solid wood. A more workaday version with knob handles and the names of manors painted on the front of the drawers was made for New College.

A second method which is transitional between the cupboard system and chests of drawers was to create a series of cupboards within which were stored small boxes for documents. This was the system adopted at Magdalen in the early years of the sixteenth century. Along two sides of the second floor muniment room are banks of cupboards made of solid oak framework and planking: one has 15 (3 x 5) and the other 12 (3 x 4) (**108**). Each cupboard is numbered with small copper alloy plaques stamped with Roman numerals and each has an iron ring for opening. The cupboards are protected from roof leaks by a lead capping. Within are over 100 little boxes with sliding lids (called by Aston *pixides*) (**101**). Each is labelled with a little rectangle of parchment and contains title deeds, seals and other documents relating to separate manors.

109 Magdalen College, Oxford. Seal box, with college seals. Note triple locks and massive construction. Late fifteenth century. Photo by Vernon Brooke

Again dendrochronological analysis has securely dated the Magdalen muniment fittings. Three of the little deed boxes were examined. The so-called Winchester deed box contains 63 deeds dated 1221-1556 concerning lands owned in Winchester by Selbourne Priory. This was closed in 1484-5 and the property transferred by Waynflete to his college. The felling date range of the boards making up the box was of a date range 1467-79. The Guton Hall box contains 54 deeds dating from the twelfth to the sixteenth century relating to this Norfolk manor which Waynflete contrived to be acquired by his college in 1483. As there was no sapwood, only a *terminus post quem* date of after 1464 could be given for this box. A third box called St Mary's deed box contained sapwood which produced a felling date range of 1495-1511. This last suggests that it was constructed during a re-organisation of the college records at least half a century after the foundation. As with two of the chests the timber used had the same Baltic source (Miles and Worthington, 2000).

9 The archaeology of the high life

The emergence of an aristocracy: the English experience

The top people in the Middle Ages were not a static élite. Over the centuries from AD 1000-1600, they varied in ranks, numbers, obligations, prestige, economic and political power. In England they were nearly all descended from the military commanders who had supported William, Duke of Normandy, in the Hastings campaign and who had been rewarded with the spoils of his victory over the Anglo-Saxon monarchy. A revolution in landholding followed that subverted the late Anglo-Saxon political order. England was divided up among its new rulers. For a century and a half from 1066-1216 they had estates on both sides of the Channel but with John's loss of Normandy they had to make up their minds as to where their future lay, England or up-and-coming France. The continental lands of the Angevin empire of Henry II were completely lost by the middle of the thirteenth century. The Anglo-Norman aristocracy responded by becoming an exclusive class, almost caste, grouping (Crouch 1992). The number of ennobled families began to diminish during the first quarter of the fourteenth century to 119 at the opening of Edward III's rule in 1327. Despite lavish creations the number continued to diminish to 81 holders by 1399. McFarlane demonstrated that the reason was not death in war or plague, but failure to reproduce male heirs (McFarlane, 1973, 145-152).

The upper ranks of English medieval society, whether secular or ecclesiastical, derived the bulk of their revenues from land. Noble estates tended to be distributed across two or three regions with minor holdings scattered across the land. Kings were sufficiently conscious of the dangers of overmighty subjects on the French model not to aid the build-up of power bases. The nobility slowly accumulated estates in return for providing society with military and administrative services. Earlier on in the twelfth and thirteenth centuries they held land directly from the crown as tenants-in-chief in return for obligations to provide knight service and thus contribute to the feudal army. As knight service became an obsolescent way of raising royal-led armies, they continued to provide the leadership and man power on a more commercial basis, with indentured retinues succeeding feudal levies.

The incomes the emerging aristocracy could command varied tremendously. The king, of course was the greatest spender, with a peace-time income of some £30,000 in 1300. In the fourteenth century a younger brother of Edward III, John of Gaunt, Duke of Lancaster (who also later claimed to be king of Castile in

Spain) received some £12,000 per annum. Around 1300 there were six earls with incomes over £300 per annum. There were about 100 baronies with incomes ranging from £200 to £500 per annum. Eleven hundred knights each had a minimum income of £40 per annum. In addition the 17 archbishops and bishops commanded incomes ranging from £400 (the poorest see, St Asaph's) to £3000 (as we have seen, Winchester). Altogether this exclusive élite of medieval England commanded annually a total spending money of about £100,000 in 1300: this had increased to about half a million pounds by the fifteenth century (Dyer, 1989, 49).

These incomes were accumulated by means of more or less effective estate management, dynastic conglomeration and war. The aristocracy were tenacious in maintaining their landed and manorial rights: 'the commonest impulse detectable was to exploit every imagined right, to push every promising advantage to its limit' (McFarlane 1973, 49). Agricultural incomes might be stationary or falling but they were able to offset losses by marrying into more money. Families fortunate enough to produce male heirs went on accumulating estates by marrying heiresses. Again they profited by war: directly from plunder or ransoms and indirectly from pay attached to military commands or from revenues derived from the capture of French estates. Henry V was enthusiastically supported in his 1415 campaign by his fellow nobles who wished to recoup their falling fortunes in this way. Enough cash could accumulate from such sources to enable *condottieri* like Sir John Fastolf or Sir John Talbot to buy land in England and to build castles and palatial homes.

The getting and spending of these sums accounted for a sizeable portion of the total economic life of the country (Dyer, 1989, 49). How was this spent? Archaeology supplements the written record to a vivid degree and much study into the complex undercurrents which influenced consumer behaviour has resulted. Social emulation is seen as a key theme.

Changing fashions in table vessels

Take table vessels. Wooden vessels seem to have been in common use among all classes of society in the early Middle Ages (Morris, 2000). There was a gradual changeover to ceramic forms. As ceramic bowls and jugs came into customary use by the artisan and peasant classes so the upper classes maintained class distinctions by using more expensive materials such as metal. The fact that metal objects when worn out or broken could be returned to the foundry to be recast means that only a fraction have survived but the archaeological and documentary records agree that there was increased use of metal vessels during the period *c*.1150-1450. Inventories of aristocratic households which itemise metal vessels show how precious they were, well worth handing down to heirs.

The aquamanile is a good example of these prestigious vessels. They are found in pottery and metal from the twelfth century onwards (**111**). These were decorative water containers brought to the table as part of the documented social ritu-

110 Bronze Aquamanile.
  Thirteenth century. Probably
  of Rhenish manufacture.
  British Museum. Drawing
  by author

al of welcoming guests by providing them with the means of washing hands before, during and after a meal. This was particularly necessary since forks did not come into use before the fifteenth century and it was customary to eat with a knife and one's hands. Their iconography links them securely to the knightly class, with many modelled to represent knights or riders with saddled and bridled horses. Other favourite subjects were animals: lions (**110**), dogs, rams, roosters and fabulous creatures. Of 130 ceramic examples found in Europe, 45 came from urban contexts, 25 from castles, 10 from other settlements and 4 from churches. They occur not only in Germany, Central Europe and England, with ceramic examples from kilns as wide apart as York, Lincoln, Nottingham and Tyler's Hill (McCarthy and Brooks, 1988) but are also found in Normandy and Paris (Verhaeghe, 1991).

Gradually metal versions appear from the twelfth century and reach an apogee in the later Middle Ages. They were often donated to church treasuries since washing of the hands was a part of the ceremony of the mass. Again the subject matter of these metal aquamaniles reflects the ideology of the governing class with its emphasis on the lion, a Christian symbol of courage and strength. It also symbolised opposition to the German emperor who favoured the (Roman) eagle as his zoomorphic symbol. Verhaeghe remarks that with less than 1000 surviving in Europe they were not part of the normal equipment of the household; instead they were the means 'to conform to one of the more elevated social customs and rituals and offered a way to engage in social emulation'. The centres of production for these metal vessels were Lorraine, the Meuse valley and lower Saxony (Haedeke, 1970, 55).

Bronze jugs and ewers also made their appearance on the tables of the great in the thirteenth and fourteenth centuries (Ward-Perkins, 1967, 199-200). The most famous of these is the great bronze jug with inscriptions and badges in relief dating from the reign of Richard II which was found, extraordinarily enough, in the capital of the kingdom of Ashanti when the British expedition made its way there

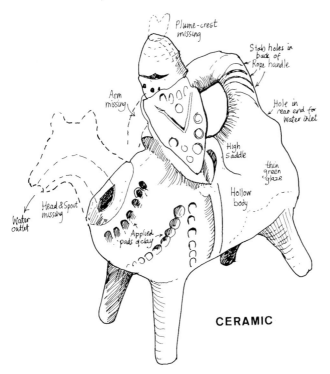

Plume-crest
missing

Stab holes in
back of
Rope handle

Arm
missing

Hole in
rear end for
Water inlet

High
saddle

thin
green
glaze

Hollow
body

Water
outlet

Head & Spout
missing

Applied
pads of clay

CERAMIC

*111 Aquamaniles. Upper
one of ceramic,
thirteenth century.
Lower one bronze,
thirteenth century.
British Museum.
Drawing by author*

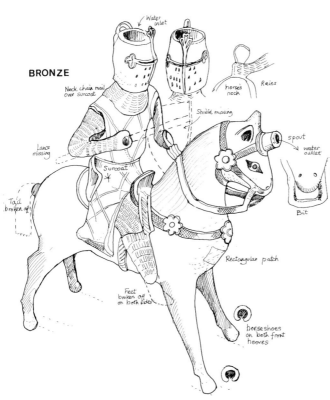

Water
inlet

BRONZE

Neck chain mail
over surcoat

Shield missing

horse's
neck

Reins

spout

water
outlet

Lance
missing

Surcoat

Bit

Tail
broken off

Rectangular patch

Feet
broken off
on both sides

horseshoes
on both front
hooves

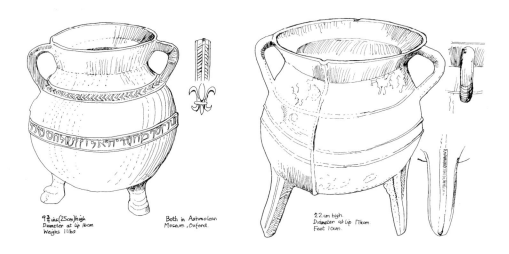

112 Bronze bowl and cauldron. Ashmolean Museum, Oxford

on a punitive expedition in 1896 (Alexander and Binski, 1987, 524-5). Other vessels were three-legged ewers with tubular spouts and claw-shaped feet (**113**). Accompanying these water (and possibly wine) holding jugs were basins and bowls. Bronze basins (referred to as a *bacinum*, a *pelvis* or a *pelvicula*) with their chased and engraved designs were made in North Germany from the lower Rhine to the Baltic. They had a didactic purpose; as the user plunged his hands into the basin he would see engraved on the bottom scenes from classical mythology, biblical scenes from the Old or New Testaments and various allegorical figures, the vices and virtues (Haedeke, 1970, 60).

While metal containers such as these were used at lord's tables pottery was preferred when it came to serving and presenting food. Contemporary culinary commentators thought food tasted better when served off pottery than off pewter or silver because it did not pick up bad odours (Gutierrez, 1997). Consequently there was heavy demand from the richest and most powerful social groups for pottery from such exotic sources as Malaga and Valencia. While in the earlier Middle Ages the custom involved eating with the fingers communally from centrally placed bowls, changes in the later Middle Ages led to the introduction of individual sets of bowls and plates. This, in part, reflected changes in the ways food was cooked and served. In the earlier period the emphasis was on meat that was cut up roughly in big hunks and cooked in stews. Butchery techniques improved, saws were used and meat cut into smaller, personal portions. Deetz noted the same phenomenon operating in colonial America in the seventeenth and eighteenth centuries (Deetz, 1996, 76-80). A greater variety of food could be served using a multiplicity of platters. Status was reinforced through the refinement of the palate; as knowledge of wines and foods grew, they could become a device for social exclusion (Gutierrez, 1997, 73-81).

Much has been made of the presence of imported ceramics at high status sites. It has been claimed that the higher the social group, the greater the access to distant markets is likely to be either through travel or social and economic contacts (Courtney 1999, 99). Earlier distribution maps of Saintonge ware including the highly decorated parrot beaked jugs tended to link them with castles and monasteries. They probably came into the country as what Courtney calls 'an integral part of a wine-drinking cultural package'. What archaeology fails to tell us is who actually used the jugs. Did they grace the constable's table or were they a normal adjunct to the merchants' kitchen? They could even have been relegated to piss-pots.

A second and recently very well-documented example is the wide use of Rhenish stonewares across northern Europe in the late fifteenth and early sixteenth centuries (Gaimster, 1997). Cheaper than metalware or glass, stoneware enabled middle class consumers to imitate the dining habits of their social betters. Stoneware pitchers and larger jugs are shown in late medieval Burgundian pictures of courts being used for transporting wine or water from cellar to dining room and then decanting to glass and metal containers at the table. Drinking cups and drinking mugs form pottery assemblages which dominate castle sites in Scandinavia and the Netherlands. They were made more attractive to higher social groups by the addition of roundels and reliefs moulded with figures, heraldry and coin and seal motifs (Gaimster, 1997, 129).

At Acton Court, Avon, excavations of a moated site revealed several ranges of masonry buildings including a large building decorated in Renaissance style dated to 1534-5. This seems to have been constructed by Nicholas Poynts for the visit of Henry VIII to Acton Court in August 1535. What is significant in the context of this chapter is that 43 per cent of the whole pottery assemblage consisted of imported wares. The main sources were the Rhineland and Iberian Peninsula with smaller quantities from Low Countries, France and Italy. It seems that for this royal visit the household of Nicholas Poynts was supplied with these prestigious wares. The high rate of breakage may well be connected with the high spirits generated by the presence of the royal court (Vince and Bell, 1992, 101-9).

In such ways metal table vessels and highly decorated imported ceramic wares graced the tables of the great in the later Middle Ages. As they became increasingly available to the urban middle classes, there was a tendency for aristocratic consumers to invest in the yet more fashionable and expensive material, glass. In England vessel glass shows decisively a distribution limited to high-status sites (Tyson, 2000). It has been excavated from 19 castles, 10 manors, 2 royal palaces and 2 Bishop's palaces. Among the more luxurious assemblages were at Restormel Castle (Cornwall) where an Islamic gilded and enamelled flask, an eastern Mediterranean decorated manganese purple base and a Venetian enamelled beaker were found. Again at Ludgershall castle (Wiltshire) there were quantities of most types of glass including European finned glass goblets and an opaque red high-lead glass beaker. They were usually decorative, expensive, fragile and liable to frequent changes of fashion, forcing high-status consumers frequently to buy 'to keep up with the Joneses'.

There are a number of characteristic features of vessel glass which elevate it above utilitarian wares. One of the most distinctive is the knop round the centre of the stem of goblets. This is a direct copy of the knops fashioned on precious metal chalices used in the eucharist. Tyson has interestingly suggested that such glass goblets were designed to emulate the Christian chalice and to acquire thereby some ecclesiastical charisma. She draws parallels between the medieval feast and the mass; wine was drunk from the secular goblet and from the chalice; both were shared by a number of drinkers but the ritual was limited to certain guests and members. All are traits shared (Tyson, 2000, 24-5). The lidded cup, in particular, was a vessel of special distinction: only the most important guests were entitled to drink with the cup cover held underneath. Sir Geoffrey Luttrell is shown at the head of his table, presiding over a feast, holding a large cup. Such customs still go on in Oxford college feasts.

Glass vessels were also decorated in ways that imitated high quality metal work. The designs on enamelled beakers of late thirteenth to mid-fourteenth century are similar to those on contemporary enamelled metal work (Wenzel, 1984, 1-21). Heraldry was a common theme in both art forms. A glass beaker found at Foster Lane London has a heraldic shield depicting a wolf over a lobed object, arms used by the Von Wolfsberg family of Germany (Clark, 1983, 152-5). Glass with bright enamel colours, reds, blues and gold was an ideal medium for heraldic illustration. Some items may have been individually commissioned but others used heraldic themes such as pelicans plucking breasts and robed figures between columns which were more generalised decoration. As Tyson says, 'it draws upon the symbolic code of the nobility and heightens the status of all glass vessels with heraldic themes' (Tyson, 2000, 25).

When we turn from the high table to the lordly kitchen we find a similar changeover from ceramic to metal cooking vessels. At the top end of the social hierarchy John Earl of Huntingdon (d.1400) had in his kitchen

> 4 great 'standard' pots, 5 lesser 'standard' pots, 6 small pots (*porre olle*) and 5 smaller pots, all of brass: 2 great cooking vessels, 2 small cooking vessels, 4 great copper '*patel*', 4 small brass ladles, 4 frying pans (*frixoria*), 3 great iron griddles (*gradal ferri*), 6 iron 'rakkes', 19 iron windlasses (*verna*) 5 great mortars, 13 dozen tin dishes. (Calendar of Inqs. Misc. VII 1399-1422, 78)

Clearly this battery of cooking utensils could serve all the members of a great household including ravenous retainers.

The standard design of the medieval metal cauldron, found throughout northern Europe, is three-legged with angular handles at the rim. A remarkable vessel of this type, known as the Bodleian bowl and now in the Ashmolean Museum, was found in a brook in Suffolk about the year 1698. It has an inscription in Hebrew which records that it was the gift of Joseph, son of the Holy Rabbi Yehiel. It may have been given to the Colchester Jews amongst whom lived Joseph's brother (Katz, 1990, 290-9) (**112**). Fatty deposits on a fragment of a cauldron found at

Height 23cm
Diameter 15cm

17cm diameter

113 Bronze ewer and skillet. Ashmolean Museum, Oxford

Hangleton and an inscription on a cauldron formerly from Warwick Castle, 'I give the meat good savour', indicate that they were used (among other things) for stewing meat (Cherry, 1987, 149). Such tripod pots could be stood over a fire on the ground or the central open hearth of the medieval hall; suspended from a chain over a fireplace, or used on a kitchen range fired by charcoal. They gradually changed in shape while keeping the tripod legs and the handles. The bottom was made as wide as possible while the collar-like lip was also widened. This made it easier to watch the contents while cooking and fish pieces out. Protruding handles tended to replace or be added to the round handles: these got longer and longer and the cauldron took on the shape of a saucepan. Any decoration on these cauldrons was very simple; either a thin line, ridge or furrow running around the sides or vertical lines running up the body on the same line of the legs (Haedeke, 1970).

Power dressing

This phenomenon of using purchasing power to emphasize class differences is also found in the sphere of clothing. In the thirteenth century high-quality garments of the rich were likely to be lined with squirrel fur which was imported from the Baltic in hundreds and thousands of animal skins. As the increased spending power of urban craftsmen brought squirrel skin within their sartorial scope so the aristocracy reacted by following fashions requiring smaller numbers of more expensive furs such as marten and budge (black lamb fur) in the fifteenth century. The court seems to have set the fashion. Richard II, known as a connoisseur of the arts and fashion, bought large quantities of squirrel skins but also spent far more on other furs such as ermine and marten. Henry V indulged himself by buying skins of sable. Henry VI's furs were primarily of marten. Squirrel fell out

258

114 Magdalen College, Oxford. Half length figure of George Lassy BA, Fellow 1488, died after 1496. Figure is dressed in academic robes: in an undertunic, an overtunic with wide fur-lined sleeves, turned back at wrists; a tabard lined and edged with fur and a hood lined and edged with fur. He is tonsured. Photo by Vernon Brooke from a brass rubbing in the Ashmolean Museum, Oxford

of fashionable use both in the English and Burgundian courts. Men of high social standing imitated the practice of the court and invested in the more expensive and therefore more prestigious furs. Thus they distanced themselves from their social inferiors (Veale, 1966, 1-22).

In the same way power dressing dictated that those with the highest social pretensions were no longer content to be clothed in wool. Woollen cloth was in fact an expensive commodity; a single ell (about 0.7m) of the cloth Ghent brought for its town soldiers cost from 1 shilling to 1shilling 4 groats. For a complete outfit of a surcoat, coat, hood and trousers some 15 ells were needed and at this time a master carpenter earned only 6d and a groat a day (Van Uytven, 1983, 151). Wool was expensive but not sufficiently exclusive. Upper garments of velvet, damask, brocaded silk or satin came to be viewed as more desirable than wool in the closing years of the fourteenth century. This is reflected in the increasing numbers of these precious materials found in archaeological excavations in London (Crowfoot, Pritchard and Staniland, 1992, passim). Since England had no silk cloth weaving industry these materials had to be imported or brought in as gifts from abroad. Byzantium had been a source of such royal stuffs in Anglo-Saxon England. Islamic Spain from the twelfth century and Venice, from the thirteenth century, were production centres.

Crusading led to a knowledge and experience of foreign textiles and hence a demand for them. Edward I was on crusade when he succeeded to the throne. His first wife, Queen Eleanor, ordered materials direct from the Near East. The Master of the Hospitallers at Acre purchased £100 worth of cloths and jewels for her.

One particularly luxurious feature in this imported material was the use of gold and silver thread. Gold had deep religious symbolism and was associated with chivalric status: spurs and horse trappings were gilded. Gifts of gold were compared to those offered by the Magi, to a king from a king and the court was seen as the place where gifts of gold flowed. Edward I was fond of donating cloth of gold to churches and to newly dubbed knights (Lachaud, 1992, 280). Hence materials which had previously been used for royal or ecclesiastical ceremonial or for bed hangings now made up splendid suits of upper class costume.

Costume historians have traditionally relied on illuminated manuscripts, sculptured effigies and monumental brasses with which to trace the increasingly exotic vagaries of late medieval fashion. These, however, are generalised sources, often relying on artistic stereotypes and therefore not accurate in the matter of dating changing fashions. They also give little detail about the structure of the costume itself. Archaeology has supplemented such material by providing examples of costumes (or parts of them) themselves. Again London's waterfront excavations have provided new evidence. A difficulty is that there is little indication as to which households the textiles have come from. An exception is that part of a fourteenth-century assemblage is thought to have come from the Great (royal) Wardrobe and thus has high-status materials in it.

Conspicuous consumption in dress

The clothes themselves provide several indications of what Veblen called 'conspicuous consumption' (Veblen, 1899, 75-85). One is that costumes in the fourteenth century were styled to be close fitting. Bodices, skirts, doublets and hose all required much more cutting up of cloth. This meant that instead of consisting entirely, like the previous fashion in the thirteenth century, of rectangular elements which could be cut economically from the length of cloth, there were now curved and cut about elements which left over awkwardly shaped and unusable fragments (Newton, 1980, 3). These are the many waste strips and snippets which form the bulk of the archaeological textile assemblages. The net result may have been costumes with sheer lines and elegance but they contrast with the economy shown in the cutting out and making of a cloth tunic said to have belonged to Louis IX of France (and now in the Treasury of Notre Dame, Paris) which was made out of simple geometrical shapes. This enabled triangular sections cut from the sleeves to be easily fitted into the lower part to add to the fullness. Little was wasted and any scrap left over could be used to make small articles such as purses or seal bags (Crowfoot *et alia*, 1992, 176-7).

Another indicator that style overcame economy in upper class fashions is the popularity of 'Dagges'. This was a process of cutting the edges of cloth into ornamental shapes. It was used for all kinds of garments, cloaks, sleeves as well as head gear and horse trappings. It was extravagant and wasteful and was obviously meant to be recognised as such. Dagges could be further decorated by the attachment of metal ornaments (Egan and Pritchard, 1991, 18-224).

A third indicator of conspicuous consumption is that wardrobes grew steadily bigger. Edward I had the reputation of austerity in his own time and yet in 1275-6 he had 17 new robes made for him. In the following years he had 14, 15 and 16 robes per year. It is likely that his wardrobe totalled 100 garments, requiring several carts to transport. When the queen's wardrobe cart overturned in the water at Burgh in Norfolk in 1290 there were eight mantles and four capes in the cart. The will of the wife of Raoul de Nesle, Constable of France in 1302 had five robes of five garments each all decorated with buttons, three robes of three garments each, all furred, and a cloak lined with cendal. It is unlikely that all these garments were regularly laundered. They faded rapidly and it must have been a blessing limited to the highest in the land to be constantly changing into fresh robes. Old and, inevitably, smelly garments were given away as alms.

Aristocratic consumers were not content with costumes composed of rich and exotic materials, cut in an ostentatiously wasteful way. They also delighted in attaching metal mounts to their clothes, harness and moveable possessions like caskets and book covers. Most of these are made of copper alloy and depended upon repetition for their effect. The majority would have been attached to girdles and other straps. Among the richest examples found in London were three circular, composite armorial mounts, made of copper alloy with silver coating. The design is a shield with a cross engrailed in a bordure engrailed all in a dark material (probably enamel or niello) against a reserved silver field. They are similar to mounts attached to the sword belt on the Black Prince's effigy in Canterbury Cathedral (Egan and Pritchard, 1991, 180-3). Other decorative mounts are geometrical in design, with trefoils, quatrefoils and a rose shape, or figurative, stamped out in the shapes of a crown, a shell, a *fleur de lys* and the letters h, h, h. The latter may conceivably refer to Henry IV but a crowned h would have been more appropriate. Arched pendant mounts were attached to girdles: from them purses swung — this was one of the affectations of the rich, to wear purses conspicuously as a demonstration of wealth and prestige. A particularly rich example complete with heraldic shields, jewelled studs, zoomorphic creatures and an arched pendant mount for a purse was found on the body of the Castilian Infante (dated 1275) in the royal mausoleum at the convent of Las Huelgas near Burgos in Spain. There is some doubt as to whether such a highly decorated assemblage was actually used (Egan and Pritchard, 1991, 222-3).

Sumptuary legislation

There was little point in expending huge sums on costume unless the effect was seen to be exclusive. Both French and English governments passed sumptuary legislation attempting to control costume in the interests of social hierarchy. In 1294 Philip the Fair set out fully the materials forbidden to certain categories of society: vair, grey and ermine were restricted to the nobles, as were jewellery and costume accessories in gold, silver and gems (Lachaud, 1992, 132). Legislation was passed in England from the 1330s to the early sixteenth century to reinforce the ideas of status embodied in cloth. The motives behind the sumptuary laws of 1357, 1363, 1463, 1483 and 1509-10 were threefold. Firstly, to preserve class distinctions so that any stranger could tell at a glance by looking at a man's dress to what rank of society he belonged. Secondly there was (ostensibly) a desire to check luxury and extravagance — the moral argument. Thirdly, to encourage home industries by discouraging the import of foreign goods (Baldwin, 1926, 10). The act of 1337 limited people except the king, queen, their children, prelates, earls, barons, knights and ladies, in fact anyone who could not spend £100 a year from wearing fur. In 1363 an act was passed for correcting 'the outrageous and excessive apparel against their estate and degree'. Grooms, servants of lords, and artificers were forbidden to clothe themselves in costume worth more than two marks. They were to wear no budge but only lamb, cony, cat and fox. Gold, silver ornaments, embroidery and silk were all forbidden. Esquires and gentlemen were limited to garments valued at $4\frac{1}{2}$ marks. Knights, on the other hand, who had a rent of over the value of 400 marks a year were allowed to wear at their pleasure except ermine and lituses and apparel of pearls and stones except for beads (Statutes of the Realm vol i, 1810, 380-1). The Act was repealed in the next year and is more interesting in the light it throws on social attitudes than a realistic attempt to control sartorial excesses. Other acts followed in the fifteenth century. In 1420 gold and silver ornaments were limited to knights' spurs and 'all the apparel that pertaineth to a baron and above that estate' (Statutes of the Realm, ii, 1816, 263). Again an act of 1463 limited the wearing of cloth and sable furs to those above the estate of a knight and forbade esquires and gentlemen from wearing velvet or satin. This act was also concerned with morality: it forbade jackets or coats unless they be of such length that the same may cover his privy members and buttocks! All this shows that costume was a signifier of power; it also indicates that wealthy townsmen and ambitious gentlemen were continually vying to transgress these costume barriers.

Lords and livery

Lords emphasized their control over their own households by using livery of robes to provide a group identity to the members of their affinity. Costumes thus donated defined status and gave what has been called a 'visible expression to the bond between lord and man' (Saul, 1990, 302-15). The king led the way. From the early thirteenth century, liveries of clothing are regularly recorded in the Exchequer accounts. Robes were part of what household members could expect to receive from their lords and were valued because of their expense. The quality, quantity and cut of the garments would have given a strong clue as to the rank of the member of the household. A robe for a knight banneret in Edward I's reign cost between £4 and £8. This was about 10 per cent of the qualifying income for the rank of a knight (Lachaud, 1996, 285-7). The value of the robes for a banneret was £10 13s 4d: for knights £5 6s 8d; for squires £2; for sergeants £1 6s8d and so down to a palfrey man who was only given 5s worth (Lachaud, 1992).

From the point of view of the lord, livery was a form of largesse. Just as the Anglo-Saxon kings handed out rings to their followers so medieval kings distributed robes. The appearance of the members of the court directly reflected the image of the king. As Robert Grosseteste advised the countess of Lincoln

> Order your knights and your gentlemen who wear your livery that they ought to put on the same livery every day, and especially at your table, and in your presence to uphold your honour, and not old surcoats and soiled cloaks and cut off coats. (Lamond, 1890, 135).

It has been suggested that status was indicated by colour coding. There was certainly a great range of colours available as we know from the scraps of cloth recovered from the London excavations. The king customarily wore scarlet, at least at Christmas. In 1219 at Christmas robes of green cloth were given to knights and to some of the sergeants of the king; robes of russet were distributed to other sergeants and robes of blue cloth to the *garciones*. There is evidence that blue cloth was becoming a mark of high status towards the end of the thirteenth century: evident improvements in dyeing (increased use of woad) had something to do with this. At any rate some uniformity was coming in. Giles of Rome, writing to the prince later to become Philip IV of France advised that 'all those who can be seen as belonging to the same grade . . . ought to be dressed in the same way, so that by the conformity of their dress it is known they are serving the same prince.' (Lachaud, 1996, 291). Costume thus reinforced the hierarchy of the princely household.

Transport for top people

The itinerant nature of royal and aristocratic households made heavy demands on those whose responsibility it was to transport personnel and possessions. The crucial element in the process was the horse. Horses had to be acquired by breeding, exchange, purchase or capture in war. They needed to be provisioned, harnessed, cared for when sick and replaced when old age, incessant labour or injury meant they could no longer serve. As one would expect there were numerous types or grades of horses, each bred or trained up for different purposes. William Fitzstephen in 1171 described the Friday horsemarket at Smithfield. Among horses for sale were the most expensive, war horses known as destriers *staturae honestae* ('of noble size'); these carried knights into battle or into tournaments. Then there were the *graduarii* ('amblers') which moved both their legs forward together on the left, then both to the right. Amblers were favoured by women and by inexperienced riders seeking comfort for long journeys. There were mares suitable for drawing ploughs, sledges or carts; increasingly horses took over from oxen for these duties (Langdon, 1986). The so-called *summarii* were pack horses, recognisable according to Fitzstephen by their stout and nimble legs. In addition there were horses 'more suitable for squires with rougher but fast gait' and well-bred younger colts (Dent and Goodall, 1988, 97).

Horses, like cars nowadays, were expensive to run. The best military horse, the destrier (*dextrarius*) would cost £50-£100 or even more. The horse ridden by the non knightly man-at-arms, the rouncey (*runcinus*) cost £5-10. A carthorse or a peasant workhorse (*stottus* or *affer*) cost about 2s 6d. Thus as Davis remarks, 'a cheapish riding horse would cost 24 times as much as a peasant workhorse, a good palfrey 400 times as much and a good warhorse 800 times as much' (Davis, 1989, 67). With the initial outlay, say, at between £3-10 for a riding horse this was the equivalent to six months or a year's wages for a skilled craftsman (Clark, 1995, 8). Horses, in addition, were costly to keep, requiring more expensive food to fuel them than did oxen. Horsebread, baked of 'pure beans and peas without a mixture of other grain or bran' cost $\frac{1}{2}$d a day, and hay for one day 2d. In addition the better quality horses had to be fed on oats. In 1314-15 the cost of housing and feeding a horse for a day might have been as much as $6\frac{1}{4}$d to $7\frac{1}{2}$d (Davis, 1989, 44).

Equine imports

English medieval kings acquired valuable horses from abroad. They might come as diplomatic gifts as when Henry II acquired horses from the Moorish king of Valencia and Murcia in 1162. When Raymond V did homage for Toulouse in 1173 an annual tribute of 40 very valuable horses was demanded (Hyland, 1999, 14). King John imported 100 heavy stallions from Flanders, Holland and the area round the river Elbe. Spain was perhaps the greatest reservoir of valuable horses at this time. King John sent Thomas Briton to Spain with 200 marks to buy horses. Both Henry III of England and Louis IX of France acquired Castilian chargers for the war of 1242 in Aquitaine. Edward I provided for his war needs by importing steeds from Castille and Navarre and this trade increased in Edward II's reign. Edward III had agents stationed in Gascony with instructions to buy horses from Spain.

Most of this lively trade was in war horses. In the sixteenth century Henry VIII laid the foundations of the royal racing stable as a result of gifts of horses from the Marquis of Mantua. The Marquis had a particularly fine stud and Henry regularly exchanged horses with him. In 1525 he bought 300 horses in Holland and in 1544 acquired 200 Flanders mares. By 1542 Marillac reported to Francis I that the king had two stables of 100 horses and obtained 150 animals annually from his stud in Wales and the North (Edwards, 1988, 41).

The size of horses

It might be thought that archaeology could usefully contribute to the debate on the relative size of medieval horses. The truth is that no large quantities of horse bones appear in the reports of excavations. The reason is that there was a strong taboo in England against eating horseflesh. It was generally only in the last stages of a siege when starvation threatened that the horses were consumed. An occasional worn out horse might be fed to hounds but they were usually fed on bread; meat and blood only when the kill took place in hunting. Horses then were buried where they fell; occasionally in ditches outside towns although this was frowned at. Medieval illustrations do not suggest that horses were particularly large. Horse armour shows that with padding it would sit comfortably on a modern horse of between 15-16 hands. Horse shoes should theoretically give a reliable indication of size — though only that of the foot 'and the size of a horse's foot, like that of its jaw, gives no more than a general indication of its overall dimensions' (Clark, 1995, 29). Only the largest of medieval horseshoes would fit an average modern horse and so it seems that the great majority of medieval horses did not reach the 15 hands height of the modern riding horse. The conclusion is that most were decidedly small. Small size could have a tactical advantage as King Robert Bruce found before the battle of Bannockburn when, riding a pony, he vanquished Sir Henry de Bonne mounted on a war horse (Dent and Goodall, 1962, 109-10).

Breeding medieval mounts

The Plantagenets were not content with importing horses from abroad; they were also interested in breeding horses on a large scale. There was a bureaucratic framework to underpin this big business. Under John the most important official was known as the Chief Keeper and in Henry III's day as King's Farrier, Sergeant or Keeper of the King's Horses. Stud locations in the thirteenth century included London, Berkshire, Kent, Yorkshire, Northamptonshire, Worcester and Wiltshire. The administration grew so that in Edward II's reign the studs were divided north and south of the river Trent and by Edward III's reign there were studs in 25 English counties, mostly in East Anglia, the Midlands and the south east (Hyland, 1999, 15). This interest in horse breeding continued in Henry VIII's reign. After the Dissolution of the monasteries surveyors were sent to monastic lands to find suitable places for royal studs. Two principal studs were set up at Tutbury (Staffordshire) and Malmesbury (Wiltshire). Henry also passed legislation aimed at the owners of parks throughout the country. He expected them to keep a certain number of brood mares at least 13 hands high. In 1542 dukes and archbishops were expected to maintain a stable of seven and clergy with an income of £100 and gentry whose wives wore silk gowns, French hoods or velvet bonnets were asked to maintain at least one brood mare (Edwards, 1988, 42).

115 Mappa Mundi, *Hereford Cathedral. Mounted figure with decorative horse harness. Pendants and bells are shown suspended from the breast band and rear strap.* Photo: Hereford Cathedral library

Horse harness

In any attempt to recreate the appearance of the horse belonging to the upper echelons of medieval society the remains of harness are significant. These include pendants, spurs, bits and saddles. Among the most frequently found small items are pendants which were attached to horse harness from the twelfth century and became frequent in the thirteenth. They were suspended from the peytrel, the breast band, from the crupper and from horses' head ornaments. Sometimes they were placed in the centre of the frontal. A drawing of a horseman on the Hereford Cathedral Mappa Mundi shows a peytrel decorated with quatrefoils from which hang alternately shield-shaped and circular pendants (Harvey, 1996, 2). The rear strap, for good measure, has a row of little bells. The pendants can be of many shapes and sizes including shields (33 per cent of all known examples), lozenges, circular, rectangular with the shield set in the rectangle, quatrefoil, kite-shaped, octofoil and cruciform. Some are found in the shape of a miniature banner. All are made of copper alloy or copper and many are enamelled. This was done by the *champlevé* process, chiselling out the groundwork, filling it with enamel and firing over a charcoal or coal fire at a temperature of 900 to 1000 degrees. The exposed parts of the metal were frequently gilded (de Prideaux, 1911, 226-38). Among the most spectacular were those attached to a horse's head-stall. A number of examples in the British Museum, in Salisbury and a remarkable one in the treasury of the cathedral at Termoli all have a vertical metal shank attached to the horse's head harness; above is a sphere from which project arms, each carrying dangling heraldic pendants. The whole may be capped with the figure of a stylised bird (Ward Perkins, 1949, 1-5). They are usually found by chance in fields and roads where doubtless they dropped. Occasionally the coat of arms directs us to an individual in a place at a particular time. Such is the pendant with the arms of Sir Robert Fitzpayn, lord of Launver; he was a knight who held a number of official positions under Edward I and II and was very likely to have visited Clarendon Palace where the pendant was found (Saunders, 1991, 18). They went on being used in diminishing numbers into the fifteenth century; a head mount formerly belonging to Alice, Countess of Salisbury, mother of the Earl of Warwick 'the kingmaker', has distinguishing heraldic pendants. They were only one way of displaying the insignia of their owners, which could also be painted on cloth horse covers (known as trappers), on surcoats (the linen garments worn over armour), and banners.

Spurs

Most of the fine collection of medieval spurs found in London were picked up in or near the river Thames. Horses were watered and exercised near the river. They are also found in the stable sweepings which made up some of the dumps of refuse built into the area behind the successive river embankments (Ellis in Clark, 1995, 124). A number have similarly been dredged from the river at Salisbury — the so-called drainage collection (Ellis in Saunders, 1991, 54-79). They were very much a status symbol of the horseman. Gilded spurs were buckled onto a man's heels, as part of the formal ceremony of making him a knight. The golden spurs were also part of the coronation regalia of a king and those used in France have survived (Gaborit-Chopin, 1987, 61-2). Spurs went through a number of developments, starting with single pointed goads where the broad end of the spike was meant to give resistance preventing too much damage to the side of the horse. These were succeeded by the earliest rowel spurs; they usually had ring terminals worn on the outside of the foot which held an attachment to a long strip of leather running under the rider's foot and passing through a slot terminal to a buckle. Occasionally high-status spurs were spectacularly decorated, as one found in London (from the neighbourhood of the King's Great Wardrobe) which was decorated with roses and a tiny swan (Ellis in Clark, 1995, 132-3). By 1400 rowels were becoming larger and the necks of spurs were becoming longer. The fifteenth century saw a fashionable trend towards lengthening and pointing everything and so it was with spurs. They grew fantastically long necks which must have made them easy to trip over.

Stabling

The housing of horses is a subject presenting some difficulties. Stables are plentifully mentioned in the documentary record; they occur infrequently and ambiguously in the archaeological records. There are a mere eight references in 36 volumes of *Medieval Archaeology* and, in fact, many years go by with none — all the more surprising given the supreme importance of the horse in medieval society. This means, I take it, that excavators are wary about attributing 'stable' to the exiguous remains of their 'farm buildings'. This doesn't exclude the possibility that medieval stables were substantial timber-framed buildings, well jointed and sitting on top of the ground, ie with no postholes or beam slots, only a slight pressure pad.

Perhaps it will help if we list what we are looking for. Horses, ridden hard, need a thorough rubbing down before being led into a draught-free, well ventilated, and lit building. So, look for bits of curry combs and shed horseshoes! Secondly, the building needs to be large and long enough to accommodate multiple standings (horses are not encouraged to lie down except when foaling or dying). Since they are mettlesome and sometimes aggressive they kick the floor and one another, to obviate the damage of which hard standings of pitched stone were *de rigueur*. To keep them from bumping into one another partitions were made which leave no trace in the archaeological record. Wattle walls however figure in the painted scenes of the Nativity found in late medieval manuscripts. Next, the walls which the horses face are likely to be windowless; the floors, in addition, will be crossed by drains.

An instance of much of this at ground level is found in the semi-fortified mansion of the Lovels at Minster Lovel, Oxfordshire, probably a fourteenth-/fifteenth-century stone rebuild of earlier equine accommodation (**116**). The siting is interesting, immediately to the left of the gateway which penetrates the exterior wall of the outer court. One can imagine (with the help of the account in *Sir Gawain and the Green Knight* Harrison, 1998, 31) the rider, being admitted by the porter, getting off his horse at this point. It is then led away by the groom into the stable building to be groomed, fed and watered and bedded down. A stable is likely to have been two storeyed — with a loft above for hay which was pushed down through a slot in the floor to reach the mangers from which the horse feeds. Such a building survives *in toto* at New College, Oxford where the statutes allowed the Warden (alone) to have a horse (Munby, personal communication).

I know of only one large example which is impressively complete, that at the archbishop of Canterbury's palace in Maidstone, Kent. It is now incorrectly known as the Tythe Barn, but in fact was built by archbishop Courtenay in the 1390s to house his horses, baggage and servants as they travelled the interminable road between Canterbury and London. The archbishop's horses were stabled on the ground floor; on the first floor, reached by an external staircase, was stored hay, straw, and feed for the animals below. A simple piece of medieval technology, a wooden crane, would swing out between the double doors above the porch (Maidstone Borough Council, no date, no pagination!).

116 Minster Lovell Hall, Oxfordshire. Fortified manor house of Lovell family. Across centre, main path leads from gatehouse left to outer court. Behind are foundations of stables with pitched stone floor and drains. In background domestic fishponds. Fifteenth-century. Photo by author

Horses were more fragile in health than oxen, so their stabling and their food (hay enriched with buckets of oats) had to be of a higher standard. A stable could be magnificent in aristocratic households in the sixteenth and seventeenth centuries. The case of Bolsover, with its riding school attached, comes to mind although it is a bit late in date for this book (*c*.1640). Such stables were infinitely preferable as living places to contemporary peasant housing. Englishmen from the Iron Age to the present have looked after their horses better than their children or servants.

If archaeology is not very informative, what do the documents tell us? One thing is that the stables could be very large. The great stable at Chester Castle required 21,000 welsh slates to roof it. At Wallingford Castle, £20, a substantial sum, was spent on the construction of the stable. At Corfe Castle there was a stable for 20 horses (Pounds, 1990, 195-6). The *Kings Works* mentions stables at the royal house at Clipstone, Nottinghamshire (1282-3) for 200 horses at a huge cost of £104 8s 5d. Presumably this was to shelter the entire entourage of the itinerant monarchy or possibly a royal stud. At Freemantle, Hants, a stable for 80 horses is mentioned while at Sheen, Surrey, a new stable, 105ft long and 30ft high was built in 1369 (Colvin *et alia*, 1963, 919, 940-1, 996-7).

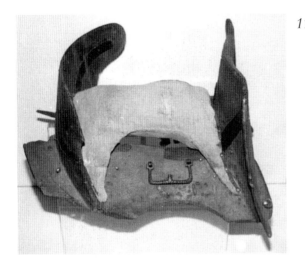

117 Henry V's saddle, Westminster Abbey. Now displayed in the museum. Formerly on beam above tomb which carried his accoutrements of war: helmet, sword, saddle, together with an arrow (possibly from Agincourt). Note the seat raised off the bars, the retaining cantle and the high pommel which gives protection to the lower abdomen. Photo by author

Manorial stables required frequent re-roofing and it is clear that the lord's horses were kept separate from the bailiff's and the cart horses were divided from the riding horses (Currie 1992, 137-42). Salzman, that exceptionally rich quarry of information about all aspects of medieval building, cites several contracts for building stables. They were usually timber framed and could be substantial, involving the services of carpenter contractors (Salzman, 1992, 446-7, 480, 518).

The artifactual evidence for stabling is threefold. Firstly, there are curry combs, made of sheet iron of circular or angular section with serrated edges to which a tanged handle was riveted (Goodall in Biddle 1990, 1053). London has yielded several, lost in the straw and refuse, carried out of town stables and dumped behind foreshore revetments (Clark, 1995). Secondly, there are horse shoes, a baffling subject, being seldom dateable although a recent typology is attempted for London (Clark, 1995, 75-123) which supersedes that of Ward Perkins 60 years ago (Ward Perkins 1967, 112-7). Also, as already noted they are an unsure indicator of the size of the animals to which they were attached.

Thirdly, and finally, there are remains of saddles. The only complete saddle which has been claimed as surviving from medieval England is that associated with Henry V, hanging formerly over his chantry and tomb in Westminster Abbey. It was made of wood, leather, and cloth with a bag of straw between the rider's crotch and the horse's back. All this would have given the would-be jouster or knight in battle considerable protection. The horse wouldn't have been so comfortable however since such a contraption would cause callouses on the back (Laking, 1920-2, 3). Saddles were usually hung on pegs jammed into stable walls.

Aristocratic pastimes

Life in tenth- and eleventh-century northern Europe for the nascent aristocracies, as for everyone else, was nasty, brutish and short, though perhaps not particularly

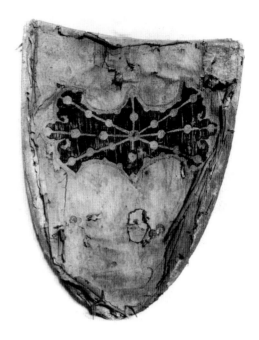

118 Westminster Abbey. Henry V's shield. This is one of two surviving medieval shields (the other is the Black Prince's in Canterbury Cathedral). Originally hung, with the other royal accoutrements, on a beam above Henry V's tomb. Now in the Westminster Abbey Museum. Photo: Dean and Chapter

solitary. It was a society dominated by the male and the mailed. Everyone who was anyone was a soldier of some kind — even monks and bishops on occasions bore arms. Living was dangerous. There were threats from Vikings, Magyars, Moslems and marauders. Generally men helped themselves to one another's property, especially land, in this comparatively lawless environment. Hence the main pastime was soldiering to hold onto one own property and to grab other peoples'. The eleventh- to thirteenth-century garrisons at Hen Domen (Montgomeryshire), for example, on the marches of Wales were not noted for their material possessions. The impression of the finds is that they are 'not numerous, that they are generally functional pieces like tool fragments, arrowheads, locks and horseshoe parts'. If these men were rich their wealth was not displayed (Higham and Barker, 1992, 334-47); maybe like the Masai in Tanzania it lay in livestock, in heads of cattle. During the intervals between battles and sieges warriors passed the time dicing and gaming.

Dicing and gaming

Several sets of bone or ivory counters and chessmen have been dug up in north European castle settings. The most notable to my mind are those from Gloucester, England, now in the British Museum and, more recently, from Mayenne in France. The Oxford Archaeological Unit undertook a major series of excavations at this urban castle and discovered a multi-phased occupation from a late Carolingian tower with early Romanesque features through to a twelfth-/thirteenth-century heightening of the tower and filling in of the basement rooms for defensive reasons. Within this fill was a total of 201 artefacts including coins, pottery, metal, bone and stone objects. The *chef d'oeuvre* was part of a backgammon board *in situ* and many gaming pieces, chessmen and dice. Several of the gaming

119 Gaming pieces from castle at Mayenne, France. Courtesy of Oxford Archaeological Unit; drawing by author

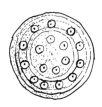

pieces are decorated with exquisite carvings of animals and birds, including Pegasus the flying horse. The male-dominated environment was demonstrated by the predominance amongst the metal objects of arms, arrowheads, blades, stirrups, spurs and horseshoes. Women might as well not have existed, judging by the archaeology (Diez in Miles, 1998). Doubtless the lowest room would have served as a prison — reminding one of Dickens' *Little Dorrit*.

Dice are undatable because gaming was prevalent in northern European societies from the Roman period to the Renaissance and beyond. They figure in manuscript representations of the soldiers dicing for Christ's possessions at the foot of the cross. They were made of bone and, more rarely and later, of ivory. They were subject to fraud; holes were bored and mercury poured in to weight them (Egan, 1999, data sheet 23).

All this emphasis on machismo begins to change in the thirteenth century. Although war is still a pastime it is waged with intervals of peace and punctuated by truces. Opportunities burgeon for other sports. The main ones are hunting and hawking in which women now join men.

Hunting and hawking

Hunting and hawking in the early Middle Ages were pursued in the open countryside and in forests, many of which were royal game reserves (Steane, 1984, 163-9). The Norman and Plantagenet monarchs, in particular, led the way in the hunt. It was a handy method for training one's troops in warlike skills, charging about on a horse, loosing off arrows at moving targets and generally surviving the rough and tumble of a day out on horseback in the early medieval countryside. It required energy and staying power. William I, Rufus (who died of it), Henry I, Henry II and John had plenty of this. They were all ardent in the chase (Steane, 1993 and 1999, 146-52).

In the later Middle Ages as the country became steadily more cultivated hunting was done more in parks and various lordly protocols were followed making it a more decorous and not so dangerous a pursuit. Books were written on rules to be followed including those by Gaston de Foix translated into English by Edward Duke of York. Hunting, from being a chivalric, became a gentlemanly pursuit. Animals such as the red and fallow deer were lured into parks which acted as reservoirs for royal and aristocratic fun. Venison was prized on the tables of notables (Dyer 1989, 60) and deer bones are often found in castle and manor house excavations. Wild boar were hunted to extinction in England by *c.*1290 according to Rackham. Foxes were chased by but were not eaten except by hounds. Wolves' heads were paid for at five shillings a time!

Parks have engaged and caught the interest of a number of landscape historians including the redoubtable scholars L. Cantor and C. Taylor, now joined by S. Mileson. The latter is at present compiling a data base of all known fourteenth- and fifteenth-century English parks and is relating them to governmental policy, analysing the social origins of their makers and constructing a chronology. Some interesting observations are emerging. Licenses to impark are a very inadequate index of imparking. They were sometimes granted before the park was made or, like many modern planning applications, were retrospective. Given the laxer medieval administrative machinery in the later Middle Ages lots of parks escaped being licensed at all. In the twelfth and thirteenth centuries they were the preserve of the king and magnates, lay and ecclesiastical. By the fourteenth century, knights made parks and eventually the king's judges ruled that anyone could make a park provided it didn't upset the landed right of anyone else! They were all shapes and sizes but an oval, circular or broad-bean shape with internal ditches tended to be the most economic way of enclosing a tract of land; such enclosures were expensive to maintain. They involved much ditching, paling and policing. Parkers were appointed living in lodges.

Peasants tended to regard the king's deer as fair game. A vivid illustration of this can be found at Lyveden, a forest edge industrial settlement, in Rockingham Forest, Northamptonshire. Here a well had been stuffed full of the complete skeleton of an unfleshed red deer. It is likely that it had just been poached when the king's forester was seen wending his path down the Harley way and the evidence was hidden (Steane and Bryant, 1975, 156-7). This book is not about peasant potter/poachers but this incident shows that venison was appreciated right down the social ladder from top to bottom: protected for the king, poached by the peasant.

The late medieval landscape was exploited for the royal courts and the aristocratic élites. The aristocratic hunt was a favourite subject figuring in rich tapestries, made in the Low Countries in the fifteenth century and hung in great halls and chambers of noble residences (McKendrick in Barron and Saul, 1995). The Devonshire tapestries (Victoria and Albert Museum) made at Arras or Tournai in the 1420s and '30s show an idealised wooded Flemish landscape interspersed with meadows sprinkled with flowers. Across it ride groups of splendidly dressed aris-

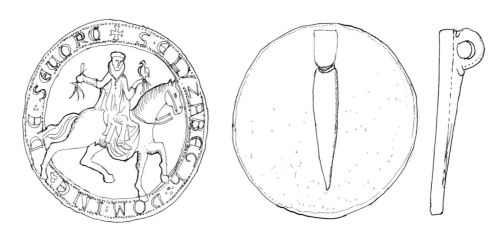

S·Є·LYZABЄGh·DOMITNЄ·DЄ·SЄUORQ✠

120 Seal matrix of Elizabeth of Sevorc, a noble lady of northern France, shown riding side-saddle with her hawk. Late thirteenth or early fourteenth century. British Museum. Drawing by author

tocratic folk, chatting together and then energetically chasing an assortment of beasts including stags, hares, rabbits and bears. It probably never was quite like this, except in poetry, but the illuminator of the *Très Riches Heures du Duc de Berry* made the same point.

Hunting has left various traces in the artifactual record as well as in the linear, mounded and ditched deer parks. Hunting arrow heads, often referred to as 'broad heads' are picked up in areas formerly hunted over (Steane, 1973, 13). They were designed to become firmly embedded in the prey after having cut through tendons and muscles (Jessop, 1997, Data Sheet 22). A stag, wounded in this way, would slowly bleed to death as it fled pursued by a revolting and motley mixture of hounds. Bones of dogs and canine representations in books on hunting resurrect for us the medieval hound. Their bone crunching habits are displayed in the analysis of middens and monumental brasses depict them fondled by feet. Intelligent breeding produced greyhounds, mastiffs, bloodhounds, ferriers and lurchers, all of which breeds were used at different times and in different places in the late medieval hunt. They were cunningly kept in reserve on leash until the appropriate time came for them to intervene.

Lodges
The last feature connected with hunting which archaeology has enlightened is lodges. Lodges were necessary to rest in after a hard day's hunting. They were consequently sited in the middle of areas of royal parks, chases or parks. King John held Tollard Royal, on the Dorset Hampshire border within Cranbourne Chase,

in right of Isabella his wife. Here are substantial remains of a two storeyed hunting lodge dated to the first years of the thirteenth century. Tollard Royal was immaculately published by General Pitt Rivers in one of his sumptuous purple and gold volumes in 1890. The report is remarkable for its day; not only did he measure up the building and phase it, but he also studied the ancillary structures and illustrated the report with 22 pages of beautifully drawn finds in the first substantial account of excavated medieval objects (Pitt Rivers, 1890).

The hunting lodge of Richard, Earl of Cornwall, brother of Henry III, was situated on the top of the hill at Beckley, Oxfordshire overlooking a large stretch of hunting country enclosed and named Beckley Park. Traces of foundations and a moat were observed by White Kennet, a keen antiquarian-minded clergyman from Ambrosden. The lodge was burned down in 1233 in a raid by a neighbouring baron. It was rebuilt in the fourteenth century in a more defensive site in the middle of Otmoor, about a mile to the north. This time it acquired triple moats. Beckley Park, as it was re-named, now has a mid-sixteenth-century brick house with three garderobe towers, the work of Lord Williams of Thame (VCH Oxon, V, 57). The royal hunting lodge at Clipston, Nottinghamshire, was well placed for chasing the deer in Sherwood. Rahtz's excavations recovered the plan of an undercroft with a central row of pillars for holding a vault, likely to be the lower part of a principal building paid for by Edward I. There were, however, traces of timber buildings beneath. The same feature, a timber phase, was found by the Rahtz at Writtle, Essex. Here the full complement of hall, solar, kitchen, chapel and gatehouse surrounded by a palisaded moat (to keep animals and interlopers out during the long periods when the lodge was not being used) and vouched for in the documentation, was recovered. Writtle retained royal favour and was frequently rebuilt and its facilities brought up to date (Rahtz 1957 and 1969). Perhaps the greatest royal hunting lodge in Medieval England was at Clarendon, Wiltshire, surrounded by a park, the subject of an impressively detailed study by Tom James' students at King Alfred's College, Winchester (King Alfred's College 1996, 1998).

There were, of course, dozens of these hunting lodges, places where kings and nobles could retire to and wash, feast or sleep in securely. They have not so far been studied systematically and the subject cries out for attention. To appreciate what was sought by their patrons it is helpful to study the siting, planning and facilities of modern forest lodges. There are two on the northern and southern edges of the Serengeti, the vast area of grassland grazed by myriads of wild beasts in Tanzania. Each has the elements of medieval English hunting lodges, a hall for communal eating, kitchens, a parking area (in place of stables) and individual huts for the modern punters (not hunters!). Each has wide views from which to watch and track game. Each is near a bountiful water supply. Such hunting lodges are as vital to the economy of a modern African state, as they were vital to the smooth running of the life style of a medieval king or noble.

Epilogue

We began with the Romans and we end with the Renaissance. The continuing influence of 'Romanitas' runs like a bright thread through the rich tapestry of the period AD 800-1600. It inspired Charlemagne in his palace building and in his enthronement at Aachen and in Rome. It empowered the medieval Popes and Emperors. The former, presiding over the ruins of greatness of the eternal city, ordered a Christian empire which grew in the lands in the west of Europe formerly ruled by Rome. The latter, attracted as moths are to an incandescent candle, spent their lives and treasure in trying to control parts of Italy and the Papacy itself, in fact acting out the part of Neo-Roman emperors. Culturally Rome was of supreme importance. It inspired medieval architects to produce the Romanesque style. Its literature was the mental pabulum of monks. Monasticism, peculiarly medieval in many ways, relied on regulation and the life of an ordered community, a very Roman concept. Roman law profoundly influenced the medieval legal minds: its power to reinvent itself was obvious in the last two centuries of our period. The Renaissance began, as one would have expected, in Italy, and was given a great spurt by the sack of Byzantium and the arrival of Greek scholars exiled from Eastern Europe. It spread rapidly as we have seen into Central Europe, where Hungary and Bohemia were among the first states to be deeply affected. France was the chief medium through which classicizing influence reached England and Scotland. For these reasons alone Latin should not be abandoned in the schools of twenty-first-century Europe!

Bibliography

Adkins R.A. and Petchey M.R. 1984, 'Secklow Hundred mound and other meeting place mounds of England', *Arch Journal* 141, 243-51

Alexander J. and Binski P. 1987, *Age of Chivalry, Art in Plantagenet England 1200-1400*, London

Allen Brown R. 1988, *Castle Rising Norfolk*, London

Allen Brown R., Colvin H.M. and Taylor A.J. 1963, *The History of the King's Works*, London

Allen T. and Durham B. Forthcoming, *Excavations at Mount House, Witney*, Oxford

Allmand C. 1997, *Henry V*, New Haven and London

Aston T.H. 1986, 'The External Administration and Resources of Merton College to *c.*1348' in Catto J.I. (Ed) *The History of the University of Oxford, I, The Early Oxford Schools*, Oxford

Atherton I., Fernie E., Harper-Bill C. and Smith H. 1996, *Norwich Cathedral, Church, City and Diocese 1096-1996*, London and Rio Grande

Ayloffe J. 1786, 'An Account of the body of Edward the First as it appeared in opening his tomb in the year 1774', *Archaeologia*, 3, 376-413

Baart J. et alia 1977, *Opgravingen in Amsterdam*, Amsterdam

Bailey J.F. 1980, *Transcription of Minutes of Corporation of Boston, vol 1, 1545-1607*, Boston

Baker J.H. 1973, 'Effigy of a Judge in Gresford Church', *Denbighshire Historical Society Transactions*, 22, 8-11

Baker J.H. 1978, 'History of English Judges Robes', *Costume*, 12, 27-39

Baker J.H. 1984, *The Order of Sergeants at Law*, Selden Society, London

Baker J.H. 1991, *The Inner Temple. A brief historical description*, London

Baldwin F.E. 1926, *Sumptuary Legislation and Personal Regulation in England*, Baltimore

Banister-Fletcher, 1946, *A History of Architecture on the Comparative Method*, London

Barber M. 1994, *The Trial of the Templars*, Cambridge

Barber R. 1986, *The Penguin Guide to Medieval Europe*, Harmondsworth

Barlow F. 1989, *Edward the Confessor*, London

Barraclough G. 1955, *History in a Changing World*, London

Barron C.M. and Saul N. 1995, *England and the Low Countries*, Stroud

Barron C.M. 1974, *The Medieval Guildhall of London*, London

Barron C.M. 1995, 'Centres of Conspicuous Consumption. The Aristocratic Town House in London, 1200-1550', *The London Journal*, 20, 1, 1995, 1-15

Bartlett R. 2000, *England under the Norman and Angevin Kings*, Oxford

Beaume C. 1985, *The Birth of an Ideology. Myths and Symbols of Nation in late Medieval France*, Berkeley, California

Bede, 1944, *The Ecclesiastical History of the English Nation*, London

Bedos-Rezak B. 1990, 'Towns and seals. Representation and signification in Medieval France' *Journal of John Rylands Library*, 72, No 3, 35-48

Beresford M.W. 1967, *New Towns of the Middle Ages*, London

Bernage G. (ed.), 1978, *Encyclopedic Medievale d'apres Viollet le Duc*, Bayeux

Bernhardt J.W. 1993, *Itinerant Kingship and Royal Monasteries in Early Medieval Germany c.936-1075*, Cambridge

Biddle M. 1986, *Wolvesey. The Old Bishop's Palace, Winchester*, London

Biddle M. 1990, *Object and Economy in Medieval Winchester*, Oxford

Biddle M. and Clayre B. 1983, *Winchester Castle and the Great Hall*, Winchester

Binding G. 1996, *Deutsche Königspfalzen*, Darmstadt

Binski P. 1986, *The Painted Chamber at Westminster*, London

Binski P. 1995, *Westminster Abbey and the Plantagenets*, New Haven and London

Blair C. (Ed), 1998, *The Crown Jewels, the history of the Coronation Regalia*, London

Blair W.J. 1996, 'Palaces or Minsters? Northampton and Cheddar reconsidered', *Anglo-Saxon England*, 25, 97-121

Blair W.J. Forthcoming *The Church in Anglo-Saxon England*, Oxford

Blanc J. 1992, *The Palace of the Popes*, Paris

Blanc J.P. 1992, 'The Builder Popes' in *The Palace of the Popes*, Paris, 22-46

Blaylock S.R. 1990, 'Exeter Guildhall', *Devon Archaeological Society Proceedings*, 48

Bloch M. 1973, *The Royal Touch*, London

Bond J. 1987, 'Anglo Saxon and Medieval Defences' in Schofield J. and Leech R. *Urban Archaeology in Britain*, Council for British Archaeology research report 61, 92-116

Bond M.F. 1950, 'The Windsor Aerary' *Archives* 4, 2-6

Bott A.J. and Highfield J.R.L. 1994, 'The Sculpture over the Gatehouse at Merton College, Oxford, *Oxoniensia*, LVIII, 233-40

Bradshaw H. and Wordsworth C. 1892, *Statutes of Lincoln Cathedral Part 1*, Cambridge

Brand J. 1789, *History and Antiquities of the Town and County of Newcastle-upon-Tyne*, London

Brand P. 1992, *The Making of the Common Law*, London

Brindle S. and Kerr B. 1997, *Windsor Revealed: New Light on the History of the Castle*, London

British Museum, 1924, *Guide to Medieval Antiquities*, London

Bromwich J. 1993, *The Roman remains of Southern France*, London and New York

Brooke Z.N. 1947, *A History of Europe 911-1198*, London

Brown A. 1996, 'The late medieval English church: parish devotion in buildings and the landscape', Blair J. and Pyrah C. (Eds) *Church Archaeology. Research directions for the future*, CBA Research Report 104, 63-8

Brown S. 1999, *Sumptuous and Richly Adorned: The Decoration of Salisbury Cathedral*, London

Cam H.M. 1963, *The Hundred and the Hundred Rolls*, An Outline of Local Government in Medieval England, London

Cambridge Medieval History IV part 1, 559 et seq

Cameron A. 1987, 'The construction of court ritual = the Byzantine Book of Ceremonies' in Cannadine D. and Price S. *Rituals of Royalty*, Cambridge

Campbell M. forthcoming, 'Medieval Founder's relics: Royal and Episcopal Patronage at Oxford and Cambridge colleges', in Copps P. and Keen M. 'Patronage, Heraldry and Social Display in Medieval England', Woodbridge Colvin H.M. 1991, *Architecture and the After Life*, New Haven and London

Cannon J. and Griffiths R. 1988 *Oxford Illustrated History of British Monarchy*, Oxford

Carlin M. 1985, 'The Reconstruction of Winchester House Southwark, *London Topographical Record*, XXV, 33-57

Carlin M. 1996, *Medieval Southwark*, London and Rio Grande

Carpenter D.A. 1990, *The Minority of Henry III*, Berkeley and Los Angeles

Carpenter E. 1988, *Cantuar, the Archbishops in their Office*, London

Cescinsky H. and Gribble E.R. 1922, *Early English Furniture and Woodwork*, London

Cherry J. 1987, 'Cauldrons and Skillets. Metal and Pottery in Cooking' in Vyner B. and Wrothmell S. *Studies in Medieval and Later Pottery in Wales presented to J.M.Lewis*, Cardiff

Cherry J. 1991, 'The Ring of Bishop Grandison', in Kelly F. (Ed), *Medieval Art and Architecture at Exeter Cathedral*, British Archaeological Association Reports, London

Cherry J. and Stratford N. 1995, *Westminster Kings and the Medieval Palace of Westminster*, London

Christie H. 1966, 'Old Oslo', *Medieval Archaeology* X, 45-58

Clanchy M. 1993, *From Memory to Written Record*, Oxford

Clapham A.W. 1930, *English Romanesque Architecture: Before the Conquest*, Oxford

Claridge A. 1998, *Rome. An Oxford Archaeological Guide*, Oxford

Clark J. 1983, 'Medieval enamelled glasses from London', *Medieval Archaeology*, 27, 152-6

Clark J. (Ed) 1995, *The Medieval Horse and its Equipment c1150-c1450*, London

Coghill N. 1977, *The Canterbury Tales*, Harmondsworth

Collinson P., Ramsay N. and Sparks M. 1995, *A History of Canterbury Cathedral*, Oxford

Conant K.J. 1978, *Carolingian and Romanesque Architecture 800-1200*, New Haven and London

Conloch C. 1995, 'Battlements and the Bourgeoisie Municipal Status and the Apparatus of Urban Defence in later Medieval England', in Church S. and Harvey R. *Medieval Knighthood* V, Woodbridge, 119-95

Conseil General des Pyrenees Orientales, 1985, *Le Palais des Rois de Majorque*, Amelie-les-Bains

Contamine P. 1988, 'Peasant Hearth to Papal Palace: The Fourteenth and Fifteenth Centuries' in Ariès P. and Duby G. *A History of Private Life*, Cambridge and London, 425-505

Cooper N. 1999, *Houses of the Gentry 1480-1680*, Newhaven and London

Coulson C. 1982, 'Hierarchism in Conventual Crenellation: an Essay in the Sociology and Metaphysics of Medieval Fortification', *Medieval Archaeology* XXVI, 69-100

Courtney P. 1999, 'Ceramics and the history of consumption. Pitfalls and Prospects.' *Medieval Ceramics*, 21, 95-108

Cowper F. 1985, *A Prospect of Grays Inn*, London

Cox J.C. 1903, *Kent*, London

Cox J.C. 1923, *English Church Fittings, Furniture and Accessories*, London

Crook J. 2000, *The Architectural Setting of the Cult of the Saints in the Early Christian West, c300-c.1200*, Oxford

Crossley P. 2000, 'The Politics of Presentation: The architecture of Charles IV of Bohemia' in Jones S.R. Marks R. Minnis A.J. *Courts and Regions in Medieval Europe*, York, 99-172

Crouch D. 1992, *The Image of Aristocracy in Britain 1000-1300*, London

Crowfoot E., Pritchard F. and Staniland R. 1992, *Textiles and Clothing c1150-1450, Medieval Finds from Excavations in London*, 4, London

Currie C.R.J. 1992, 'Larger Medieval Houses in the Vale of the White Horse', *Oxoniensia* LVII, 81-244

Darwall-Smith R. 1996, *Emperors and Architecture. A Study of Flavian Rome*, Brussels

Das Reich der Salier, 1992, Exhibition Catalogue, Sigmaringen

Davis R.H.C. 1989, *The Medieval Warhorse*, London

Davis V. 1993, *William Waynflete, Bishop and Educationalist*, Woodbridge

De Bièvre E. 1986, *The Decoration of Netherlandish Town Halls*, Unpublished Ph D thesis, Courtauld Institute of London University

De Gray Birch W. 1887-1900, *Catalogue of Seals in the Department of Manuscripts in the British Museum* 6 vols, London

Deetz J. 1996, in *Small Things Forgotten*, New York

De Joinville, 1938, *The History of St Louis*, Oxford

Dent A.A. and Goodall D.M. 1962, *The Foals of Epona*, London

Diez V. 1998, 'The Finds from the Chateau' in Miles D. (ed.), *Chateau de Mayenne, Investigating a Thousand Year Old Building*, Oxford

Dillange M. 1985, *The Sainte Chapelle*, Paris

Dixon-Smith S. 1999, 'The Image and Reality of Alms-giving in the Great Halls of Henry III', *J.B.A.A.*, CLII, 79-97

Dobson R.B. 1978/9, York City Chamberlain's Account Rolls, 1396-1500, *Surtees Society*, 192, Gatehead

Dodwell B. 1965-6, *The Charters of Norwich Cathedral Priory* part 1 Pipe Roll Society, New Series, 40

Douglas D.C. and Greenaway G.W. 1961, *English Historical Documents, 1042-1189*, London

Druitt H. 1970, *A Manual of Costume as illustrated by Monumental Brasses*, London

Duffy E. 1992, *The Stripping of the Altars. Traditional Religion in England c1400-c1580*, New Haven and London

Dunn T. and Sutermeister H., no date, *The Norwich Guildhall*, Norwich
Durham B. 1983, 'Oxford's Northern Defences; Archaeological Studies 1971-82', *Oxoniensia*, XLVIII, 13-40
Durham B. *et al.* 1991, 'The Infirmary and Hall of the Medieval Hospital of St John the Baptist at Oxford', *Oxoniensia*, LVI, pp17-77
Dvoøáková V. Krása J. Merhautová A. and Stejskal K. 1964, *Gothic Mural Painting in Bohemia and Moravia, 1300-78*, London
Dyer C. 1989, *Standards of Living in the Later Middle Ages*, Cambridge
Eames E. 1985, *English Medieval Tiles*, London
Eames P. 1971, 'Documentary Evidence concerning the character and use of domestic furnishings in England in the 14th/15th century', *Furniture History*, 41-60
Eames P. 1977, 'Furniture in England, France and the Netherlands from the twelfth to the fifteenth century', *Furniture History* xiii
Edelen G. (ed.) 1994, *The Description of England by William Harrison*, New York
Edwards P. 1988, *The Horse Trade of Tudor and Stuart England*, Cambridge
Egan G. 1997, 'Dice', *Finds Research Group 700-1700*, Lincoln
Egan G. 1998, *The Medieval Household. Daily Living c1150-c1450*, London
Egan G. and Pritchard F. 1991, *Dress Accessories c1150-c1450*, London
Ellis P. (ed.), 2000, *Ludgershall Castle, Wiltshire*, Wiltshire Archaeological and Natural History Society Monograph Series 2
Emery A. 1996, *Greater Medieval Houses of England and Wales*, vol I, Northern England, Cambridge
Emery A. 2000, *Greater Medieval Houses of England and Wales*, vol II, East Anglia, Central England and Wales, Cambridge
Erlande-Brandenburg A. 1975, *Gisants et Tombeaux de la Basilique de Saint Denis*, Paris
Evans T.A.R. 1992, 'The Number, Origins and Careers of Scholars' in Catto J.I. and Evans R. *The History of the University of Oxford*, II, Late Medieval Oxford, Oxford
Fairclough G. 1992, 'Meaningful constructions — spatial and functional analysis of medieval buildings', *Antiquity* LXVI, 348-366
Farley M. 1997, 'Buckslow at Swanbourne and other Saxon Mound names in Buckinghamshire', *Records of Bucks*, 39, 1997
Farmer D.H. 1985, *Saint Hugh of Lincoln*, London
Fawcett R. 1995, *Stirling Castle*, London
Fehring G.P. 1991, *The Archaeology of Medieval Germany*, London and New York
Fenn R.W.D. and Sinclair J.B. 1990, *The Bishops of Hereford and their Palace*, Hereford
Filmer-Sankey W. 1996, 'The "Roman Emperor" in the Sutton Hoo Ship Burial', *Journal of British Archaeological Association*, CXLIX, 1-9
Fletcher R.J. (Ed), 1907, *The Pension Book of Gray's Inn*, London
Gaborit-Chopin D. 1987, *Regalia. Les Instruments du Sacre des Rois de France*, Paris
Gaimster D. 1997, *German Stonewares 1200-1900*, London
Gaimster D., Margeson S. and Hurley M. 1990, *Medieval Archaeology* xxxiv
Gallbreath D.L. 1930, *Papal Heraldry*, Cambridge
Gardner J. 1992, *The Tomb and the Tiara*, Oxford
Geddes J. 1985, 'The Small Finds' in Hare J. *Battle Abbey*, London, 149-151
Geddes J. 1999, *Medieval Decorative Ironwork in England*, London
Gelling M. 1974, *The Place Names of Berkshire* part 2, English Place Name Society vol L, Cambridge
Gelling M. 1978, *Signposts to the Past*, Chichester
Gerevich L. 1971, *The Art of Buda and Pest in the Middle Ages*, Budapest
Gilyard Beer R. 1959, *Abbeys*, London
Gimpel J. 1976, *The Medieval Machine*, London
Girouard M. 1989, *Cities and People*, New Haven and London
Goodall J.A. 2001, *God's House at Ewelme*, Aldershot
Gooder E. 1963-4
Gooder E. 1971, *Coventry's Town Wall*, Coventry
Goodridge J.F. (ed.) 1959, *Piers the Ploughman*, Harmondsworth
Graves C.P. 1989, 'Social Space in the English Medieval parish church', *Economy and Society*, 18, No3, 297-321
Green J.A. 1989, *The Government of England under Henry I*, Cambridge
Green V.H.H. 1979, *The Commonwealth of Lincoln College 1427-1977*, Oxford
Greenhalgh M. 1989, *The Survival of Roman Antiquities in the Middle Ages*, London
Greenhill F.A. 1976, *Incised Effigial Slabs*, London
Grimm P. 1976, 'Die untere Vorburg der Pfalz Tilleda, Voberichɬ', in *Zeitschrift für Archäologie*, 261ff
Gutierrez A. 1997, '"Cheapish and Spanish' Meaning and Design on Imported Spanish pottery', *Medieval Ceramics*, 21, 73-81
Haedeke, Hanns-Ulrich, 1970, *Metalwork*, London
Hafta M. and Mierzwiński, 1992, *Malbork, Castle of the Teutonic Order*, Munich
Hallam E.M. and Roper M. 1978, 'The Capital and the Records of the Nation. Seven Centuries of housing the Public Records in London' *The London Journal*, 4, 1, 74-94
Halliwell-Phillips J.O. 1841, *The Book of Curtasye, an English poem of the fourteenth century*, London
Harrison K. 1998, *Sir Gawain and the Green Knight*, Oxford
Harvey J.H. 1944, *Henry Yevele c1320-1400 The life of an English Architect*, London
Harvey P.D.A. 1996, *Mappa Mundi, The Hereford World Map*, London
Harvey P.D.A. and McGuiness 1996, *A Guide to British Medieval Seals*, London
Haslam J, 1984, *Anglo-Saxon Towns in Southern England*, Chichester
Hassall T.G. *et al.* 1989, 'Excavations in St Ebbes Oxford 1967-76', *Oxoniensia*, LIV, 71-277, style p227
Hawthorn J.G. and Smith C.S. (Eds), 1979, *Theophilus on Divers Arts*, New York
Heaney S. 1999, *Beowulf*, London
Heighway C.M. 1972, *The Erosion of History, Archaeology and Planning in Towns*, Council for British Archaeology, London
Heslop T.A. 1994, *Norwich Castle Keep. Romanesque architecture and social context*, Norwich

Hewett C.A. 1980, *English Historic Carpentry*, Chichester

Higham R. and Barker P. 1992, *Timber Castles*, London

Highfield J.R.L. (Ed) 1964, *The Early Rolls of Merton College*, Oxford, Oxford

Hill D. 1988, 'Unity and diversity — a framework for the study of European towns', in Hodges R. and Hobley B. *The Rebirth of Towns in the West AD 700-1050*, CBA Research Report No 68, London

Hillier B. and Hanson J. 1997, *The Social Logic of Space*, Cambridge

Hindle B.P. 1978, 'Seasonal Variations in travel in Medieval England', *Journal of Transport History*, second series, 4, 170-8

Holmes M.R. 1959, 'New Light on St Edward's Crown', *Archaeologia*, 97, 213-23

Hooke D, 1985, *The Anglo-Saxon Landscape: the Kingdom of the Hwicce*, Manchester

Hope-Taylor B. 1977, *Yeavering. An Anglo-British centre of early Northumbria*, London

Horn W. and Born E. 1965, *The Barns of the abbey of Beaulieu at its granges of Great Coxwell and Beaulieu St Leonards*, 1965, Berkeley and Los Angeles

Howard F.E. and Crossley F.H. 1919, *English Church Woodwork*, London

Howell M. 2001, *Eleanor of Provence*, Oxford

Howlett R. 1903, 'A Fabric roll of the Norwich Guildhall' *Norfolk and Norwich Archaeological Society* XV, part 1, pp 164-80

Hurst J.G. 1961, 'The Kitchen Area of Northolt Manor', *Medieval Archaeology* V, 211-99

Hyde J.K. 1966, 'Medieval Descriptions of Cities', *Bulletin of John Rylands Library*, 48, 308-40

Hyland A. 1999, *The Horse in the Middle Ages*, Stroud

James T.B. and Robinson A.M. 1988, *Clarendon Palace*, Report No XLV of Research Committee of Society of Antiquaries of London, London

Jenkinson H, 1911, 'Exchequer tallies', *Archaeologia* LXII, 367-80

Jenkinson H. 1925, 'Medieval Tallies. Public and Private.' *Archaeologia* xxiv, 289-351

Jessop O. 1997, *Medieval Arrowheads*, Data Sheet of Finds Research Group 700-1700, Lincoln

Johnson C. 1950, *Dialogus de Scaccario*, London

Joinville Jean Sire De, 1938, *The History of St Louis*, Oxford

Joliffe J.E.A. 1948, 'The Chamber and the Castle Treasures under King John', in Hunt R.W., Pantin W.A., Southern R.W. *Studies in Medieval History presented to F.M. Powicke*, Oxford, 117-140

Jones M. (Ed) 2000, *New Cambridge Medieval History* VI, c1300-c1415, Cambridge

Jones T.L. 2001, *Ashby de la Zouche Castle*, London

Katz D.S. 1990, 'The Conundrum of the Bodleian Bowl. An Anglo-Jewish mystery story' *Bodleian Library Record* XIII, No 4, 290-9

Keene D. 1985, *Survey of Medieval Winchester*, i, Oxford

Keevil G. 2000, *Medieval Palaces. An Archaeology*, Stroud

King Alfred's College, Archaeological Consultancy, 1996, *Clarendon Park, Salisbury, Wiltshire, Archaeology History and Ecology*, Unpublished English Heritage Survey 2 vols, Winchester

King Alfred's College, Archaeological Consultancy, 1998, *Clarendon Park, Salisbury, Wiltshire, Historic Landscape Management Plan*, Winchester

Krautheimer R. 1980, *Rome, Profile of a City*, 312-1308, Princeton

Lachaud F. 1992, 'Textiles, Furs and Liveries: a study of material culture of the court of Edward I (unpublished University of Oxford Ph D thesis)

Lachaud F. 1996, 'Liveries of Robes in England 1200-1300', *English Historical Review* III, 278-98

Laking Sir G.F. 1920-2, *A Record of European Armour and Arms through Seven Centuries*, London

Lambrick G. and Woods H. 1976, 'Excavations on the second site of the Dominican Priory, Oxford', *Oxoniensia*, XLI, 168-231, page 217 object of lead pencil 29, 30

Lambrick G. 1985, 'Further Excavations on the Second Site of the Dominican Priory, Oxford', *Oxoniensia*, L, 131-208 lead pencils p164, objects 6-7

Lamond E. (ed.) 1890, *Walter of Henley's Husbandry together with an anonymous husbandry, Seneschaucie and Robert Grosseteste's Rules*, London

Lancaster J.C. 1981, *St Mary's Hall, Coventry*, Coventry Papers 3, Coventry

Langdon J. 1986, *Horses, oxen and technological innovation*, Cambridge

Laszlovszky J. (ed.) 1995, *Medieval Visegrád*, Budapest

Legal London, 1971, *Exhibition Catalogue*, London

Leighton W.A. 1880, Early Chronicles of Shrewsbury. *Trans of Shropshire Archaeological and Natural History Society* III Shrewsbury

Lepper F. and Frere S. 1988, *Trajan's Column*, Gloucester

Lewer D. and Dark R. 1997, *The Temple Church in London*, London

Leyser K. 1994, *Communications and Power in Medieval Europe*, London and Rio Grande

Lightbown R. 1998, 'The English Coronation Regalia before the Commonwealth' in Blair C. (Ed) *The Crown Jewels*, vol 1, London

Lloyd Parry H. 1936, *The History of the Exeter Guildhall*, Exeter

Loest H. 1988, *Bremen Town Hall*, Bremen

Long C.D. 1975, 'Excavations in the Medieval City of Trondheim, Norway', *Medieval Archaeology* XIX, 1-33

Lucas R.M.D. 1898-1903, 'The Heraldry and exterior decorations of the Bargate, Southampton', *Hampshire Field Club IV*, part 1, 131-6

Macdonald W.L. 1982, *The Architecture of the Roman Empire*, New Haven and London

Maidstone Borough Council, *The Archbishop of Canterbury's Palace at Maidstone, Kent*, Maidstone

Marder T.A. 1997, *Bernini's Scala Regia at the Vatican Palace*, Cambridge

Marks R. 1998, *The Medieval Stained Glass of Northamptonshire*, British Academy, London

Martin G.H. and Highfield J.R.L. 1997, *A History of Merton College*, Oxford

Martindale A. 1992, 'Patrons and minders: the intrusion of the secular into sacred spaces in the late Middle Ages', *Studies in Church History*, 28, 143-79

Matthew D. 1983, *Atlas of Medieval Europe*, London
Mayr-Harting H. 1999, *Ottonian Book Illumination*, London
McCarthy M.R. and Brooks C.M. 1988, *Medieval Pottery in Britain AD 900-1600*, Leicester
McFarlane K.B. 1973, *The Nobility of later Medieval England*, Oxford
McKendrick S. 'Tapestries from the Low Countries in England during the Fifteenth Century' in Barron C. and Saul N. *England and the Low Countries during the Late Middle Ages*, Stroud
McKisack M. 1959, *The Fourteenth Century*, Oxford
Megarry, Sir R. 1972, *Inns Ancient and Modern*, London
Megarry, Sir R. 1997, *An Introduction to Lincoln's Inn*, London
Mekking A.J.J. 1996, 'A Cross of Churches around Conrad's Heart' in De Bièvre E. *Utrecht. Britain and the Continent*, British Archaeological Association Conference Trans XVIII, Leeds, 99-111
Mertes K. 1988, *The English Noble Household 1250-1600*, Oxford
Mesqui J. 1993, *Chateaux et Enceintes de la France Médiévale*, Paris
Miles D.H. and Worthington M.J. 2000, *Tree Ring Dates from Oxford Dendrochronology Laboratory*, Mapledurham
Millar F. 1992, *The Emperor in the Roman World*, London
Miller E. 1951, *The Abbey and Bishopric of Ely*, Cambridge
Mills M.H. 1957, 'The Medieval Shire House', in Conway-Davies V. *Studies presented to Sir Hilary Jenkinson*, Oxford, 254-71
Mollat G. 1963, *The Popes at Avignon 1305-78*, London
Moorman J.R.H. 1945, *Church Life in England in the Thirteenth Century*, Cambridge
Morant R.W. 1995, *The Monastic Gatehouse*, Lewes
Morris C.A. 2000, *Wood and Woodworking in Anglo Scandinavian and Medieval York*, York
Morris W.A. 1927, *The Medieval English Sheriff*, Manchester
Munby J. 1996, *Oxford Castle Heritage Survey*, Oxford Archaeological Unit
Myres J.N.L. 1933, 'Butley Priory, Suffolk', *Archaeological Journal*, XC, 177-281
Nelson J.L. 1987, 'Carolingian Royal Ritual', in Cannadine D. and Price S. (Eds) *Rituals of Royalty: Power and Ceremonial in Traditional Societies*, Cambridge, 137-80
Nelson J.L. 1999, 'Rulers and Government' in Reuter T. 1999, *The New Cambridge Medieval History*, III, c900-c1024, Cambridge
Newman J. 1986, 'The Physical Setting. New Building and Adaptation' in McConica J. (Ed) *The History of the University of Oxford, vol III, The Collegiate University*, Oxford
Newton S.M. 1980, *Fashion in the Age of the Black Prince*, 1340-65, Woodbridge
Nicholson A. 1997, *Restoration: The Rebuilding of Windsor Castle*, London
Nordeide S.W. 1997, 'The Palace as a reflection of the changing role of an archbishop', Papers of *Medieval Europe*, a conference vol II, 209-16, Bruges
Oexle J. and Schneider J.E. 1992, *Stadtluft, Hirsebrei und Bettelmönch*, Zurich, Stuttgart
Oman C. 1931, *The Coinage of England*, Oxford
Orde-Powlett H. No date, *Bolton Castle*, Leyburn
Oswald A. 1962-3, 'Excavation of a thirteenth-century wooden building at Weoley Castle, Birmingham 1960-61', *Medieval Archaeology*, VI-VII, 109-34
Parnell G. 1993, *The Tower of London*, London
Parsons D. 1986, 'Sacrarium: ablution drains in early medieval churches' in Butler L.A.S. and Morris R.K. *The Anglo-Saxon Church*, CBA Research Report No 60, York
Pedrick G. 1904, *Borough Seals of the Gothic Period*, London
Peers C. 1946, *Kirkham Priory*, Yorkshire, London
Pevsner N. 1952, *The Buildings of England. South Devon*, Harmondsworth
Pevsner N. 1962, *The Buildings of England. North-East Norfolk and Norwich*, Harmondsworth
Pevsner N. 1970, *The Buildings of England. Cambridgeshire*, Harmondsworth
Pevsner N. and Cherry B. 1973, *The Buildings of England. Northamptonshire*, Harmondsworth
Phythian Adams C. 1972, 'Ceremony and the Citizen. The communal year at Coventry 1450-1550' from Clark P. and Slack P. *Crisis and Order in English Towns 1500-1700*, Toronto 1972
Pitt Rivers, Lieut General, 1890, *King John's House Tollard Royal, Wilts*, Privately printed
Platts G. 1985, *Land and People in Medieval Lincolnshire*, Lincoln
Plucknett T.F.T. 1949, *Legislation of Edward I*, Oxford
Pognon E. (ed.) 1983, *Les Très Riches Heures du Duc de Berry*, Chantilly
Poole A.L. 1954, *From Domesday Book to Magna Carta*, Oxford
Poore D. and Wilkinson D. 2001, *Beaumont Palace and the White Friars. Excavations at the Sackler Library Beaumont St. Oxford*, Oxford Archaeological Unit
Pounds N.J.G. 1990, *The Medieval Castle in England and Wales*, Cambridge
Powicke Sir M. 1953, *The Thirteenth Century*, Oxford
Prest W.R. 1972, *The Inns of Court under Elizabeth I and the Early Stuarts 1590-1640*, London
Prestwich M. 1988, *Edward I*, London
Prestwich M. 1996, *Armies and Warfare in the Middle Ages*, New Haven and London
Price M.J. and Trell B.L. 1977, *Coins and their Cities. Architecture on the ancient coins of Greece, Rome and Palestine*, London
Prideaux W. de C. 1911, 'Notes on medieval armorial horse trappings', *Proc. Dorset Natural History and Antiquarian Field Club* 32, 226-38
Pugh R.B. 1968, *Imprisonment in Medieval England*, Cambridge
Rady J., Tatton Brown T. and Bowen J.A. 'The Archbishops' Palace Canterbury', *Journal of British Archaeological Association*, CXLIV, 1-60
Rahtz P.A. 1979, *The Saxon and Medieval Palaces at Cheddar*, Oxford
Rahtz P.A. 1957, 'Clipstone, Nottinghamshire', *Medieval Archaeology* 1, 162-3

Rahtz P.A. 1969, *Excavations at King John's Hunting Lodge, Writtle, Essex 1955-7*, Society for Medieval Archaeology Monograph series 3, London

Raine A. 1939, York Civic Records *Yorkshire Archaeological Society Record Society*, XCVIII, York

Raine A. 1955, *Medieval York*, London

Ramm H.G. 1971, 'The Tombs of Archbishops Walter de Gray 1216-55 and Godfrey de Ludham 1258-65 in York Minster and their contents', *Archaeologia*, CIII, 101-47

Ramsay N. 1985, *The English Legal Profession c1340-c1450*, Unpublished PhD University of Cambridge

Rees-Jones S. 1987, *Property, Tenure and Rents. Some Aspects of the Topography and Economy of Medieval York* University of York unpublished History D Phil thesis

Reynolds A.J. 1998, *Anglo-Saxon Law in the landscape* Unpublished PhD thesis, University College London

Rhodes M. 1982, 'A pair of fifteenth-century spectacle frames from the City of London', *Antiquaries Journal* LXII, part 1, 57-73

Richardson H G and Sayles G.O. 1955, *Fleta vol II*, Selden Society, 129, London

Richardson H.G. 1960, 'The Coronation in Medieval England', *Traditio*, xvi, 111-203

Richardson M. 1998, *A New Approach to the Study of Queen's Apartments in Medieval Palaces*, unpublished dissertation for BA degree in History/Archaeology, King Alfred's College, Winchester, University of Southampton

Richmond I.A. 1930, *The City Walls of Imperial Rome*, Oxford

Rigold S. 1968, 'Two Types of Court Hall', *Archaeologia Cantiana*, LXXXIII, 1-23

Rodwell W.J. 2001, *Wells Cathedral, Excavations and Structural Studies 1978-93*, London

Rosser G. 1989, *Medieval Westminster*, Oxford

Rowse A.L. 1951, *The England of Elizabeth*, London

Roxburgh, Sir R. 1972, 'Lawyers in the New Temple', *Law Quarterly Review*

Royal Commission on Historical Monuments, England, 1924, *Westminster Abbey*, London

Royal Commission on Historical Monuments, England, 1925, *West London*, London

Royal Commission on Historical Monuments, England, 1929, *London The City*, London

Royal Commission on Historical Monuments, England, 1939, *City of Oxford*, London

Royal Commission on Historical Monuments, England, 1972, *City of York, vol ii, The Defences*, London

Royal Commission on Historical Monuments, England, 1981 *City of York, V The Central Area*, London

Royal Commission on Historical Monuments, England, 1988 *City of Cambridge*, London

Royal Commission on Historical Monuments, Wales and Monmouthshire, 1956, *Caernarvonshire*, I, East, London

Royal Palace and Gothic Statues of Medieval Buda, 1990, Exhibition catalogue at the Budapest Historical Museum

Rubin M. 1991, *Corpus Christi; the Eucharist in late Medieval Culture*, Cambridge

Russell J.C. 1948, *British Medieval Population*, Albuquerque

Salzman L.F. 1992, *Building in England down to 1540*, Oxford

Samson R. 1994, 'Carolingian Palaces and the Poverty of Ideology' in Locock M. (ed.), *Meaningful Architecture: Social Interpretations of Buildings*, Avebury

Saul N. 1990, 'The Commons and the Abolition of Badges', *Parliamentary History*, IX, 302-15

Saul N. 2001, *Death, Art and Memory in Medieval England*, Oxford

Saunders A.D. 1992, 'Administrative Buildings and Prisons in the Earldom of Cornwall' in Reuter T. (ed.) *Warriors and churchmen in the High Middle Ages*, London, 195-217

Saunders P. and E. 1991, *Medieval Catalogue of Salisbury and South Wiltshire Museum*, Salisbury, part 1

Schofield J. 1984, *The Building of London from the Conquest to the Great Fire*, London

Schofield J. 1994, *Medieval London Houses*, New Haven and London

Schramm P.E. 1937, *A History of the English Coronation*, Oxford

Schulze H.K. 1991, *Hegemoniales Kaisertum Ottonen und Salier*, Berlin

Sedlar J.W. 1994, *East Central Europe in the Middle Ages 1000-1500*, University of Washington

Sekules V. 1991, 'The Liturgical Furnishings of the Choir in Exeter Cathedral' in Kelly F. (Ed), *Medieval Art and Architecture at Exeter Cathedral*, British Archaeological Association, London

Shoesmith R. 2000, 'The Close and its Buildings' in Aylmer G. and Tiller J. *Hereford Cathedral, A History*, London and Rio Grande, 293-310

Simpson F. 1910, *The Walls of Chester*, Chester

Simpson J.W. 1928, *Some Account of the Old Hall at Lincoln's Inn*, Brighton

Sinor D. 1959, *History of Hungary*, London

Skinner O. 1986, 'Ambrogio Lorenzetti. The Artist as Political Philosopher' *Proceedings of British Academy*, LXXII, 1-57

Smirke S. 1836, Westminster Hall, *Archaeologia* XXVI, 406 et seq

Smith E.B. 1956, *Architectural Symbolism of Imperial Rome and the Middle Ages*, Princeton

Smith J.T. 1965, 'The Structure of the timber kitchen at Weoley Castle, Birmingham', *Medieval Archaeology* IX, 82-93

Solier Y. 1986, *Narbonne, Aude. Les monuments antiques et médiévaux*, Paris

Solier Y. 1986, *Narbonne (Aude)* Guides Archéologues de la France. No place

Spencer B. 1998, *Pilgrim Souvenirs and Secular Badges*, London

St John Hope W.H. 1907, 'The Episcopal Ornaments of William of Wykeham and William of Waynflete', *Archaeologia*, L, 465-92

St John Hope W.H. 1913, *Windsor Castle*, London

Staňková J., Stursa J., Voděra S. 1992, *Prague. Eleven centuries of architecture: historical guide*, Prague

Statutes of the Realm, vol i, 1810, vol ii 1816, London

Steane J.M. 1973, 'The Forests of Northamptonshire in the Early Middle Ages' *Northamptonshire Past and Present*, V, No 1, 7-19

Steane J.M. 1984, *The Archaeology of Medieval England and Wales*, London

Steane J.M. 1993, *The Archaeology of the Medieval English Monarchy*, London

Steane J.M. 1996, *Oxfordshire*, London

Steane J.M. 1999, *The Archaeology of the Medieval English Monarchy*, revised edition, London

Steane J.M. and Bryant G.F. 1975, Excavations at the Deserted Medieval Settlement of Lyveden, Northamptonshire, *Journal 12*, Northampton, 3-160

Steer F.W. 1974, *The Archives of New College Oxford*, London and Chichester

Stenton F.M. 1962, *Anglo-Saxon England*, Oxford

Stoob H. 1978, 'The Role of the Civic Community in Central European Urban Develop-ment during the 12th-15th Centuries', *Tr of Ancient Monuments Society*, N.S., 23, 67-93

Sugar P.F. 1992, *South Eastern Europe under Ottoman Rule 1354-1804*, University of Washington

Summerson J. 1991, *Architecture in Britain, 1530-1830*, New Haven and London

Tait J. 1999, *The Medieval English Borough*, Manchester

Tatton Brown T. 1991, 'The History of the Archbishops' Palace in Canterbury', *Journal of British Archaeological Association*, CXLIV, 1-60

Taylor C.C. 1974, *Fieldwork in Medieval Archaeology*, London

Taylor H.M. 1984, *Anglo-Saxon Architecture*, 3 vols, Cambridge

Thompson M.W. 1995, *The Medieval Hall*, Aldershot

Thompson M.W. 1998, *Medieval Bishops' Houses in England and Wales*, Aldershot

Thurley S. 1995, 'Royal Lodgings at the Tower of London 1216-1327', *Journal of Society of Architectural Historians of Great Britain*, 38, 36-57

Tittler R. 1991, *Architecture and Power. The Town Hall and the English Urban Community c1500-1840*, Oxford

Tout T.F. 1914-15, 'A Medieval Burglary', *Bulletin of John Ryland's Library*, 2, 348-69

Tracy J. 2000, *City Walls*, Cambridge

Turner H. 1971, *Town Defences in England and Wales*, London

Turner T.H. 1851, *Some Account of Domestic Architecture in England*, Oxford

Twining Lord, 1960, *The Crown Jewels of Europe*, London

Twining Lord, 1967, *European Regalia*, London

Tyler R. 1998, *Mayenne, La Chateau, vol. 3, Etude Architecturale*, Nantes

Tyson R. 2000, *Medieval Glass Vessels found in England AD 1200-1500*, Council for British Archaeology Research Report 121, York

Unger R.W. 1980, *The Ship in the Medieval Economy*, London, Montreal

Van Uytven, 1983, 'Cloth in Medieval literature of Western Europe' in Harte N.B. and Ponting K.G. *Cloth and Clothing in Medieval Europe*, London

Veale E.M. 1966, *The English Fur Trade in the later Middle Ages*, Oxford

Veblen T. 1899, *The Theory of the Leisure Class*, New York

Verhaeghe F. 1991, 'An aquamanile and some thoughts on ceramic competition with metal quality goods in the Middle Ages', in Lewis E. (ed.) *Custom and Ceramics*, Portsmouth

Victoria County History Oxfordshire 1954, III *The University of Oxford*, London

Victoria County History, 1957, V, *Oxfordshire*, London

Victoria County History, 1996, XIII, *Oxfordshire*, London

Vince A. and Bell R. 1992, 'Sixteenth century pottery from Acton Court, Avon' in Gaimster D. and Redknap M. *Everyday and Exotic Pottery from Europe c650-1900*, Oxford

Vincent N. 1994, 'The Origins of the Winchester Pipe Rolls, *Archives*, xxi, nos 91-2, 5-42

Viollet le Duc, (1978 edn) *Encyclopedie Medievale*, Bayeux

Vitry B. 1958, *Notre-Dame de Reims*, Paris

Walker J.D. and Baildon W.P. (Eds) 1898, *The Records of the Honorable Society of Lincoln's Inn (The Black Books)*, London

Ward-Perkins J.B. 1949, 'A medieval harness mount at Termoli', *Antiquaries Journal* 29, 1-5

Ward-Perkins J.B. 1967, *London Museum Medieval Catalogue*, London

Ward-Perkins J.B. 1984, *From Classical Antiquity to the Middle Ages Urban Public Building in Northern and Central Italy AD 300-850*, Oxford

Warren W.L. 1964, *King John*, London

Weaver J. 2000, *Middleham Castle*, London

Wenzel M. 1984, 'Thirteenth-century Islamic enamelled glass found in medieval Abingdon', in *Oxford Journal of Archaeology* 3, no. 3 1-21

Whiteley M. 1989, 'Deux Escaliers Royaux du XIVe siècle. Les Grands degrez du Palais de la Cité et la Grand viz du Louvre', *Bulletin Monumentale*, 133-54

Whiteley M. 1996, 'Public and Private Space in Royal and Princely Chateaux in late Medieval France' in Renoux A. *Palais Royaux et Princiers au Moyen Age*, Le Mans, 71-5

Wickham-Legg L.G. 1901, *English Coronation Records*, London

Wightman E.M. 1970, *Roman Trier and the Treveri*, London

Willis R. and Clark J.W. 1885, *The Architectural History of the University of Cambridge with the colleges of Cambridge and Eton*, vol III, Cambridge

Willis R. and Clark J.W. 1886, *The Architectural History of the University of Cambridge*, Cambridge

Wilson C. 1976, 'The original Design of the City of London Guildhall', *J.B.A.A.*, CXXIX, 1976, 1-14

Wilson J. 1995, *The Archaeology of Shakespeare*, Strand

Wood M. 1968, *The English Medieval House*, London

Wormald P. 1999, *The Making of English law, King Alfred to the Twelfth Century*, Oxford

Yule B. 1989, 'Excavations at Winchester Palace, Southwark', *London Archaeologist*, 6, No 2, 31-9

Zarnecki G. 1988, *Romanesque Lincoln, the sculpture of the Cathedral*, Lincoln

Zotz T. 1993, 'Carolingian Tradition and Ottonian Salian Innovation. Comparative observations on Palatine policy in the Empire' in Duggan A.J. (Ed) *Kings and Kingship in Medieval Europe*, London, 69-100

Zsuzsa I.L. 1986, *The Hungarian Royal Crown*, Budapest

Index

284